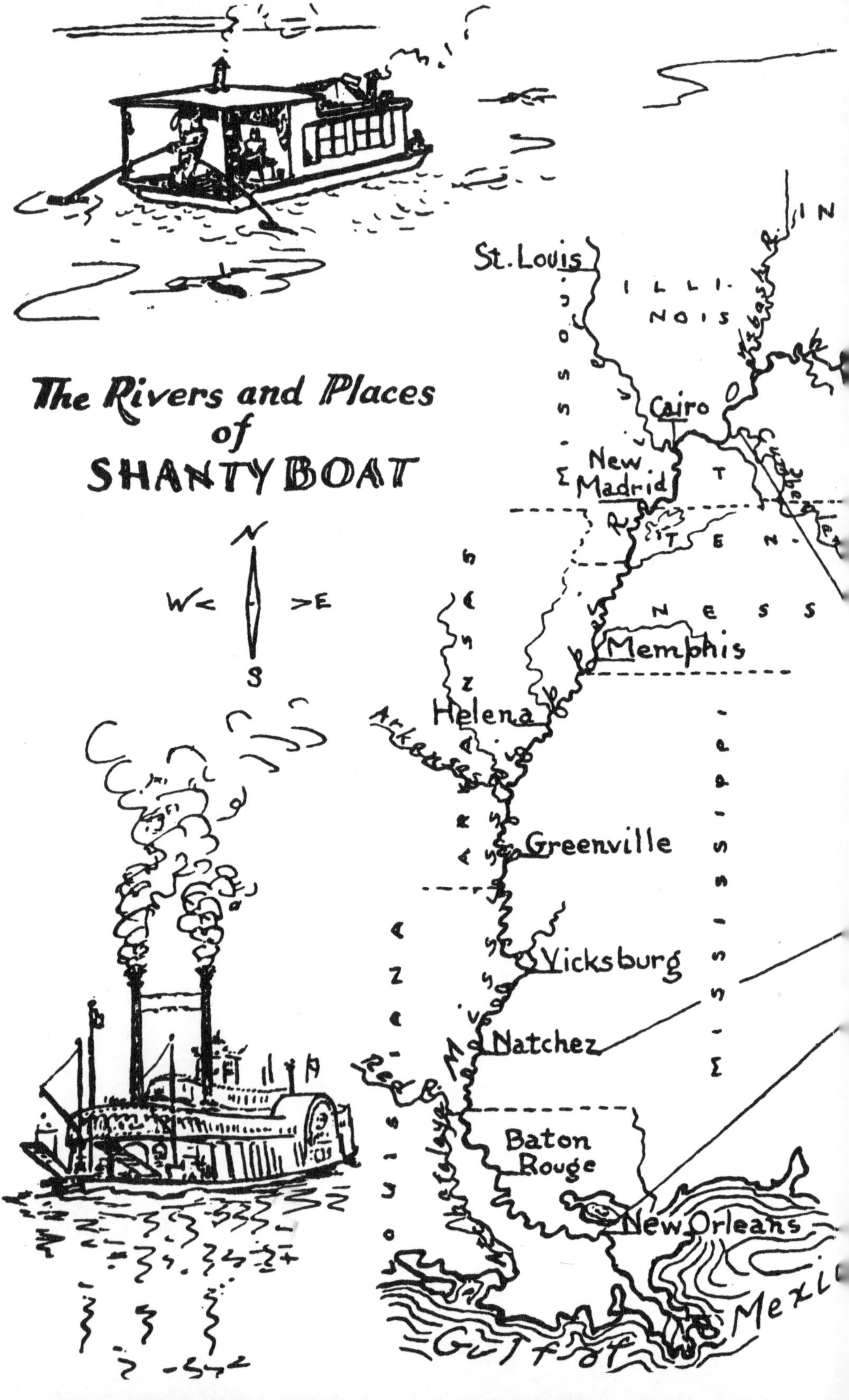

The Rivers and Places
of
SHANTY BOAT

N
W← | →E
S

St. Louis

ILLINOIS

IND.

Cairo

New
Madrid

TENNESSEE

Memphis

Helena

Arkansas

Greenville

Vicksburg

Natchez

Red

Baton
Rouge

New Orleans

Gulf of Mexico

P E N N

Pittsburgh

O H I O

Cincinnati

W.

VIR-

GINIA

Louisville

K E N -

K Y

Brent—Here we built the shantyboat in the fall of 1944 and lived for two years. Then we began the drifting voyage

Payne Hollow—the first long stop, an entire summer

Owensboro—Near this place our boat was caught in the ice

Bizzle's Bluff on the Cumberland River where we spent another summer

The third winter of drifting, on the swift Mississippi, took us to

Natchez, where we lay over for ten months

New Orleans was reached in March 1950

Distance from Brent 1385 miles

Shantyboat

Shantyboat

A River Way of Life

HARLAN HUBBARD

with illustrations by the author

and a Foreword by Wendell Berry

The University Press of Kentucky

Scholarly publisher for the Commonwealth,
serving Bellarmine University, Berea College, Centre College
of Kentucky, Eastern Kentucky University, The Filson Historical Society,
Georgetown College, Kentucky Historical Society, Kentucky State University,
Morehead State University, Murray State University,
Northern Kentucky University, Transylvania University,
University of Kentucky, University of Louisville,
and Western Kentucky University.
All rights reserved.

Editorial and Sales Offices: The University Press of Kentucky
663 South Limestone Street, Lexington, Kentucky 40508-4008
www.kentuckypress.com

09 10 11 12 13   6 5 4 3 2

The Library of Congress has cataloged the first printing of this title as follows:

Hubbard, Harlan.
Shantyboat : a river way of life / Harland Hubbard ; with ill. by the author ;
and a foreword by Wendell Berry.
—Lexington : University Press of Kentucky, c1977.
is, 352 p. : ill. ; 22 cm.
Autobiographical.
ISBN-10: 0-8131-1359-8
1. Shantyboats and shantyboaters—Ohio River. 2. Shantyboats and
shantyboaters—Mississippi River. 3. Ohio River—Description and travel.
4. Mississippi River—Description and travel. I. Title.
GV836.H8   1977   797.1'2   77-73701
MARC
Library of Congress   77[8111r81] rev
ISBN-13: 978-0-8131-1359-3 (pbk. : alk. paper)

Manufactured in the United States of America.

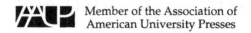 Member of the Association of
American University Presses

FOREWORD

Beginning in the fall of 1944 with the building of a shantyboat on the shore of the Ohio River at Brent, Kentucky, Harlan and Anna Hubbard have fashioned together a life that is one of the finest accomplishments of our time. For seven years they lived on their shantyboat, making their way from Brent to New Orleans and then into the bayou country of Louisiana. There followed a period of wandering by road, which eventually led them back near their starting place. They bought "seven acres more or less" in Payne Hollow on the Kentucky shore of the Ohio, not far from Madison, Indiana. And they built a house there "out of rocks and trees."

They have lived at Payne Hollow ever since—now almost a quarter of a century—largely without benefit of the roads, machines, utilities, communications, comforts, and "labor-savers" that pass with us for modern civilization. Using fundamental tools and skills, they have done without nearly everything that the salesmen tell us we must have. Their life is comely, orderly, ceremonious, full of health. Though their days are necessarily strenuous, they are also leisurely, allowing time for music and painting, reading and writing, taking pleasure, entertaining visitors. Their life, in short, is exquisitely and deeply civilized, for reasons and by means that our industrial ideology holds in contempt. This is their claim on our attention and our imagination. It is a claim we can ignore only at our peril.

Out of, and about, this homeseeking adventure, which a fellow-riverman once appropriately called "a real odyssey," Harlan has written two books: *Shantyboat*, first published in 1953, and *Payne Hollow*, which came out in 1974. Together, the two books are one work, remarkably fulfilled—never mind the twenty years that divide them. *Shantyboat* is a leisurely book by a drifter who knows what is interesting, who says out of his experience of fortune and flow: "One never knows, and must be always alert." *Payne Hollow* is an exacting, brief, swift book by a settler who has determined finally, and with enough passion, what is important.

These books belong to an ancient impulse or necessity that, since the beginning, has carried people back to the wilderness, imposing again and again upon civilization the simplifying rigors of wildness and solitude. This experience gives to the civilized mind an austerity, purity, and sweetness that civilization alone cannot produce. Harlan Hubbard, having passed through the wilderness of the Ohio and Mississippi rivers in winter flood, has earned a kinship with ancient forebears who spoke from mountain hermitages, the deserts of exile, the wine-dark sea. His is another of those essential voices that remind us of the elemental facts of our existence in nature as well as of the fundamental human necessities.

More specifically, his books are the culmination of an American literary tradition, and they resolve the oldest and deepest American conflict. Harlan Hubbard has written, as he has lived, in the rift between wilderness and civilization. A highly cultivated man, of urban upbringing, living at a time when the wild has survived only on the fringes of industrial enterprise, Harlan nevertheless made himself answerable to the oldtime American conviction that freedom and independence were to be found in the wilderness. He thus became a man of the margins, who spent his young manhood rambling and painting along the banks of his native Ohio River and in the woods, fields, and isolated hill and river towns of northern Kentucky. Given his predilections and his circumstances, he might have become a sort of dilettante, fatally divided against himself—an artist dabbling in nature, a nature-lover dabbling in art. Or, of course, he might have given over the "eccentric" side of his character altogether, and joined the "practical" men of business and industry who, supposedly having chosen civilization over nature, are rapidly destroying both.

That the Hubbards' life has tolerated no such simple divisions and resorted to no such simple choices, testifies to its integrity. Civilization and nature are reconciled in skill and in discipline, resulting in a life "in harmony with the landscape," an enlightened and forbearing domesticity that preserves its sources and its place.

vi

Harlan's most obvious literary ancestors are Mark Twain and Henry David Thoreau. But I think it has not been fully appreciated how their work is brought to maturity and fulfilled in his. My point and my difficulty are equally embedded in the realization that this is not purely a literary judgment. I do not mean to argue that Harlan Hubbard surpasses these two predecessors as a writer. But he does surpass them, I think, in the practical force of his wisdom that, among other things, makes it impossible to judge him in purely literary terms. When we speak of the work of Mark Twain and Henry Thoreau we are speaking of their writing; they lived, in varying degrees, apart from their work. Aside from their writing, we can take only a biographical interest in what they did. But when we speak of Harlan's work we obviously cannot be speaking just of his writing. We are speaking of his life—or, more exactly and complexly, of his and Anna's life. Or we are speaking of the lifework of an adventurer, husband, shantyboater, subsistence farmer, carpenter, fisherman, student, musician, painter, who at times has had to make use of writing—to complete himself, to speak to others, to attach himself more exactly to things and meanings. And this difference is involved in others.

Harlan and Anna Hubbard "lit out for the territory" in a sense, and for some of the same reasons as Huckleberry Finn. But Huck's contemplated flight was simple-minded and aimless: civilization, as it had showed itself to him, was narrow and corrupt, and he wanted to escape from it. The "territory" has only a negative value for him, representing a vague possibility of "freedom"; he has no notion of how to live there. In relation to the whole of Twain's work, Huck's impulse to escape is the result of a desperate misanthropy. It was also doomed; for any boy's fate, as Twain saw it, was to grow up and become a liar.

The Hubbards' intentions have never been so vague or so desperate. They wished "to live close to the earth and free from entanglement with this modern urban world. . . ." From the beginning, apparently, they have desired to "get all our living by as direct means as possible, that we may be self-sufficient and avoid contributing to the ruthless mechanical system that is destroying the earth." The negative judgment, in Harlan's work, is thus invariably accompanied by an articulation of desire; he knows as well as Mark Twain what he would like to escape from, but he knows much better what he wants to escape *to*. He states his purpose plainly in the second chapter of *Shantyboat:*

> I had no theories to prove. I merely wanted to try living by my own hands, independent as far as possible from a system of division of labor in which the participant loses most of the pleasure of making and growing things for himself. I wanted to bring in my own fuel and smell its sweet smoke as it burned on the hearth I had made. I wanted to grow my own food, catch it in the river, or forage after it. In short, I wanted to do as much as I could for myself, because I had already realized from partial experience the inexpressible joy of so doing.

And so the Hubbards undertook their freedom with a full, lively sense of what they wanted from it. They also understood the required endurance, resourcefulness, and skill. The shantyboater's life is conceived as a discipline, calling for alertness and mastery, a peculiar combination of "roughness and refinement"—the result, as *Payne Hollow* makes clear, of tension and then of harmony between Harlan's and Anna's contrasting natures. Their successful escape is the result equally of hardihood and of artistry, qualities developed during their years afloat and carried over into their land life at Payne Hollow. Living well in "the territory" is a great and difficult advance over the mere boyish wish to go there.

And if the Hubbards went, like Thoreau, to the wilderness, their life there has been no simple moral experiment. They are, after all, a married couple, who have become permanent settlers in their woods. For those reasons, their life has raised and resolved issues at once more practical and more complex than Thoreau's life at Walden Pond. They have made a more demanding journey, and got farther from Concord, than Thoreau ever did. The Mississippi River in winter flood is a more difficult wilderness than Thoreau encountered at Walden or on his summer canoe trips in the Maine woods. The difference is that whereas Thoreau's stay at Walden resulted in a change of moral viewpoint, a new sense of "economy," the Hubbards' long journey downriver and their much longer stay at Payne Hollow have resulted in a livable life.

Because it was so long and difficult, requiring them to be so thoroughly practical, the Hubbards' river voyage was not just an encounter with a formidable kind of wilderness; it was, paradoxically, an encounter with domesticity. *Shantyboat* is an account of life amid the elements: the backlands and backwaters, weathers and currents that require human skill to be great because human control is so small. But it is, by the same token, and even more, an account of domestic life. There is no way to distinguish this book's concern with the great, intricate, mysterious life of the rivers from its concern with the human household of the shantyboat. The boat conveys its household into the wilderness. From its windows carried down the wild currents "by the inexorable law that governs drifters," the world is newly seen and understood. But also newly understood are the meanings of being married, of living together, of having neighbors, of the skills and arts by which people house, feed, and please themselves, and care for one another.

And this journey also involves a rediscovery of the arts—of music, painting, books, the meaning of these to people living elementally. It turns out that they are among the necessities of life, more poignantly needed by people living by their hands and wits in solitude than by the people of cities. In *Payne Hollow*, having spoken of his few simple tools as "noble" and "beloved," Harlan speaks of music as "this ephemeral pleasure which yet has the power to transfigure existence."

In ending, I want to say what I think is the finest quality of Harlan's writing: that is his modesty, the *justness* of his speech, his care to write of each thing as no more or less than it is. He will let nothing stand either for its price or for some alien "meaning." He would not say, like Thoreau, that "The sun is but a morning star." Harlan is neither lecturing nor prophesying; he makes no such presumption upon our attention or our understanding. He is speaking to us simply because we happen to be listening, which is both discriminating and polite. And the sun is the sun to him; aside from seeing well by it, he shows no wish to improve it. He speaks, instead, of the peewee's "timid whistle expanding and rising into ecstasy, a burst of joy in the face of approaching darkness." That is a proper human hope and recompense. We know that it is, because that is what Harlan has quietly given us.

WENDELL BERRY

ix

Shantyboat

1

A river tugs at whatever is within reach, trying to set it afloat and carry it downstream. Living trees are undermined and washed away. No piece of driftwood is safe, though stranded high up the bank; the river will rise to it, and away it will go.

The river extends this power of drawing all things with it even to the imagination of those who live on its banks. Who can long watch the ceaseless lapsing of a river's current without conceiving a desire to set himself adrift, and, like the driftwood which glides past, float with the stream clear to the final ocean?

With me, the attraction of flowing water goes back as far as I can remember. My river is the Ohio, whose channel from the first has borne the dreams of men from the old and known to the new and strange. The early voyages were made in quest of a Golden Fleece which to some meant a new, free land in the west, to others a better market in the south for their homemade and home-grown products. To these men the river was first of all a means of transportation. Some of them must have loved the river for its own sake, or learned to love it, for they

made repeated voyages downstream, selling boats and cargoes in the south, and toiling overland back to their starting places, like boys dragging their sleds uphill to coast down again.

These drifting argosies came to an end with the perfecting of the steamboat, which, overcoming the laws of nature, was able to go upstream as well as down. The tradition of drifting was carried into our day by an amphibious race usually called shantyboaters. A shantyboat is a scow with a small house on it. Nearly always a homemade job, it is put together of odd scraps of material and pieces of driftwood and wreckage. The shantyboat may be embellished by any of the appurtenances of living. Yet it is more than a floating homestead: it is an ark which the river bears toward a warmer climate, better fishing grounds, and more plentiful and easier work on shore. The voyage often begins near headwaters, or on one of the river's tributaries. At one place after another the hopeful boatman lays over for a spell, until disillusioned, he lets his craft be caught up again by the river's current, to be carried like the driftwood, farther downstream. At last he beaches out for good somewhere in the south, where his children pass for natives.

A shantyboat on its way, drifting slowly along in the swirling current, is a sight to see—colorful and gay, yet, too, of a somewhat pathetic drabness: women and children peek out of windows; dogs bark from the decks, which are draped with lines and other gear; the roof is piled with plunder, a crate of chickens or pigs, fish boxes, and piles of nets; wood smoke from the cookstove in the cabin rises through a crooked chimney; the master guides his clumsy craft with long sweeps, or oars; a collection of johnboats and perhaps a small scow trail along.

Some boats are so neatly constructed, fitted, and kept up, being painted handsomely, with railings to the decks and curtains to the windows, that shantyboat is not a suitable name. Nor will houseboat do: it is too prosaic a term for the unfixed dwelling of water gypsies and nonconformists.

The true shantyboater has a purer love for the river than had his drifting flatboat predecessors. These were concerned with trade or new land. To him the river is more than a means of livelihood. It is a way of life, the only one he knows which answers his innate longing to be untrammeled and independent, to live on the fringe of society, almost beyond the law, beyond taxes and ownership of property. His drifting downstream is as natural to him as his growing old in the stream of time. Away from the river he languishes, as if taken from his natural element.

It is to be regretted that the race of shantyboaters is dying out. Today you are likely to find even an active fisherman living in a house on land, or in a trailer. Those who still live on the water have motorboats to shove their fleet upstream—and down, too—so that the art of drifting is forgotten. The younger generation seem to have interests away from the river. They will never be able to tell the tales their granddads can.

I cultivated the acquaintance of old-time river people whenever possible, and listened to their yarns almost with reverence. The simplicity and naturalness of their way of living fascinated me, and gave a definite shape to the vague longing which the flowing river had inspired.

To build my own boat on the river shore, and drift down the Ohio to the unknown Mississippi, and on southward to the river's end—I cherished this project for so many years, even after reaching an age when the dreams of youth have been usually abandoned, that it became more like a dreamed-of or imagined adventure than a definite plan of action; so I did not recognize the opportunity when at last chance formed the right combination of circumstances; not until Anna said, "Now we can build the boat we have so often talked of, and drift down the river."

It was I who had done most of the talking about a shantyboat. The idea had never occurred to Anna until she married me. In fact, she had

3

never really seen the Ohio River until we went down to it together, boating on reaches long familiar to me, and visiting the river people I knew. Then the river showed itself in its most favorable aspects; life on its waters seemed innocent and serene. Anna began to share my enthusiasm, and now the realization of the adventure meant almost as much to her as to me.

Our eagerness to begin was increased by the lateness of the season, now at the end of September. Perhaps it would have been wiser to wait until spring to undertake such outdoor work as this would be. We were afraid, however, that our opportunity might slip away, and determined to make a start at once.

At the outset we were faced with the difficulty of obtaining boat-building material. It was a time of shortages, and all available lumber was being allotted to construction more essential than ours could claim to be. After some scouting about, I was lucky enough to find suitable timbers in an old building which was being wrecked in Covington. These timbers were three inches thick, fifteen inches wide, and twenty feet in length, of longleaf yellow pine. We were delighted. The wood was of higher quality than any new stuff, and did not Captain Slocum use southern pine in planking the *Spray?*

It was fitting that the building from which our timbers came should have stood near the river. It had watched the packets come and go, and its lower floors were washed by successive floods. Yet we could not build the boat there, within the city. The best place we could think of was Brent, on the Kentucky shore six or eight miles upriver from Covington. Here we could work in familiar surroundings, and Brent was just under the hill from our present quarters. I hired George's truck, for George lived at Brent, to haul the timbers out from town.

The difficulty was that the wrecking of the building had been stopped. After some discussion the wreckers said I might get the timbers out myself, and sent along an old man to help me. The building was a shambles. The roof had been removed, the topmost joints dropped in confusion on the floor below. Taking my time, I examined them all, enjoying meanwhile the view of the Cincinnati waterfront across the river, seen through the mizzling rain. Then the old man and

I slid our twenty hand-picked timbers down to the ground by means of a chute the wreckers had made. We also got out some smooth oak boards and a sufficient quantity of flooring, almost new.

All this loaded the truck flat. In addition, it was a temperamental affair, which only George really understood; so the return was slow. When I reached Brent at evening, George drove the truck to the river-bank, and I watched apprehensively while he hoisted the truck bed and pulled out from underneath the load.

There it lay, a pile of lumber. Yet I could already see a boat in it. I did not like to leave it for even one night.

At that time Anna and I were living in what was called, rightly enough, my studio. It was located in Fort Thomas, Kentucky, a town close to the river but of such an elevated position that in no way is it a river town. I had built the studio myself. It shared the grounds of a house which was also of my construction, though a score of years earlier. This house we had rented; a clever stroke, we thought, since it relieved us of the burden of maintaining it in the style it required, and at the same time gave us an income which covered our modest running expenses. To live in the studio suited us better, anyway. It was a place of character, with walls of old brick, whitewashed within. Almost one whole end was of glass. There was a fireplace in the corner, a hearth with a circular, tapering hood of brick over it. Anna cooked on this fireplace, or on another one in the garden. It was an idyllic, Arcadian existence, though our neighbors looked upon it as primitive. Its simplicity and informal character made the transition to the riverbank easy.

The studio was located far back from the street, so that there was convenient access to the open fields. These paths, however, did not lead to the river. To reach its banks we had to traverse the streets of Fort Thomas to River Road, then descend a long, winding hill, a walk altogether of three quarters of an hour. The hill was called Three Mile Hill, which seemed no exaggeration if you were climbing it, a little weary, after an outing on the river. It was really only one mile from top to bottom. The name came from Three Mile Creek, which the road crossed at the bottom of the hill.

A mile up the river from Three Mile was Four Mile Creek. Between the two ran a small branch called Pleasant Run. A little settlement there was once called Pleasant Run. Nowadays it is Brent. It lies on the outside of a river bend, at the foot of a steep hill which rises from the river so abruptly that the road, the railroad, and the few houses of Brent live on intimate terms.

The site we chose for our boatbuilding was downstream from Brent, almost around the bend, where the river begins a straight reach to the north. Even at low water, the open shore there is only a narrow strip, rather steep, and covered with flat rocks. Though almost too rough for working handily, the spot appealed to us: under the hill, and beyond the houses of Brent, we could be to ourselves there, with the least possible interference from curious onlookers. We would feel at home, too, having often frequented that clean, deep-watered shore.

We were down at the riverbank early next morning; very early, in fact, for I had mistaken the late-rising moon for dawn, as often happens on great days. Our timbers lay where they had been unloaded, on a level space beside the railroad. Now they must be carried across the tracks and down the steep slope to the river. The timbers being too heavy for us to manage by ourselves, one of the Brent bystanders was persuaded to lend a hand, though he protested that he was busier than he appeared to be. We toted the heavy planks across the tracks, shoved them over the bank. Then one man could fasten a short line to an end of a plank and, sometimes pulling and sometimes keeping out of the way, guide it down to the shore near the water. By the time the last plank made the trip, the path was clear and wide and well metaled with cinders and gravel dragged down from the railroad ballast.

That night Anna and I camped in a pup tent on the stony beach. Next day we set about building a shack which would give us more protection from the cold fall rains which were to come. Using boards, flooring and roofing which would later go into the cabin of the boat, and piecing out with canvas and driftwood, we set up a little hut at the bankline, where the open, stony shore abruptly changed to the steep, brush-covered slope of the hill. It was a rather curious tenement, with not enough headroom for standing up straight, yet unexpectedly long, for of course we would not cut our flooring boards. It was narrow because of the sloping ground. The entire front, which faced the river, was covered with a canvas which could be raised to the roof. Inside the hut were our air-mattress beds, lard cans containing food, a duffel bag full of clothes, a small shelf of books, a box of tools, nails, paint, oakum, and such stuff. There was plenty of room for all.

Though our married life had so recently begun, Anna had already had several experiences in setting up housekeeping under extraordinary conditions; so this new abode did not faze her in the least. Compared with the limitations of a canoe trip, for instance, it was elaborate and commodious. She soon made the place homelike. Together we contrived low chairs and a table, a higher wash bench, a hearth of current-scoured stones, all conveniently arranged about our shack. It was pleasant to sit there, watching the river and the passing boats, as we ate our meals or rested, our work in progress spread out before us.

For some time we had only the timbers to look at. Even though we were established on the riverbank, it was not yet possible to begin actual construction. For one thing, there was delay in obtaining large enough spikes for our three-inch timbers. In the meantime we pulled out all the old nails. These were square and of wrought iron, testifying to the age of the building from which the planks had come. Then the nail holes must be plugged with wooden pegs dipped in paint. At this time I looked over my tools and sharpened them. I bought a new cross-cut saw and a wide chisel. Few tools are needed to build a flatboat; in the old days it was done mostly with an axe.

Though we were eager to get ahead with our work, these days of almost marking time gave us a chance to adjust ourselves to this new life on the riverbank. Also, we could become acquainted with the neighborhood into which we had moved.

Our nearest neighbors were the Detisches, who lived in a large shantyboat a short distance up the river. Their boat was not afloat, but beached out higher up on the bank, under the trees. Andy and Sadie Detisch were of long river experience and knew all the ins and outs, and ups and downs, of river life. Some people, less tolerant and good-natured than they, might have resented our moving into their territory. On the contrary, Andy and Sadie helped us all they could with their advice and encouragement. They loaned us tools, and watched over our camp when we were away. Their boy, Donald, was grown to

7

be capable and experienced about the river. He became almost our junior partner.

Above the Detisches, along the railroad, were a few little houses and shacks, the lower fringe of Brent. These houses always seemed much farther from the boat than they were, such was our isolation on the riverbank, down under the shaggy overhang of trees and brush. Some of the people who lived up there were retired shantyboaters, like Aunt Mary, who told us doleful yarns about the windy reaches of the lower Ohio. Aunt Mary, Sadie, and Dellie were pals. Dellie lived in a house so close to the tracks that the engineer of the eastbound George Washington sometimes dropped off a chunk of ice at her doorstep. She had a cistern from which Sadie got drinking water. When we asked Dellie about water, she was very generous, saying that water was God's gift and that she wouldn't refuse it to anybody. Later we learned that the town on the hill assisted Providence in this matter. Since the limits of Fort Thomas extended into this unprofitable section, Dellie as a taxpayer was entitled to water. It was cheaper for the town to haul it down as needed than to build a pipeline.

Walking along the railroad toward Brent, one had a splendid view as he crossed the fill over Three Mile Creek. Inland was the narrow valley of the creek, up which was no road, only a lane to Andy Fueglein's farm. Downstream the river ran along a range of wooded hills on the Kentucky side, so wild one would not suspect that Cincinnati lay around the next bend. Upriver was Lock and Dam Number 36, and two miles away, on the right bank, the smoking C & O yards at Silver Grove. Beyond were far blue hills which had a suggestion of mountain country about them.

It was but a short walk along the track to what might be called the center of Brent. Here was Witte's store, George's gas station, Grimm's lumber and coal yard, the railroad station, and half a dozen houses backed up the hill. On some days the place would be as desolate as an abandoned mining camp, with only an old man or two in sight, members of the Edwards clan, by all odds, since they formed the basic population of Brent. Another time it might be humming with activity —people coming and going to the store or waiting for a bus, trucks

8

arriving and leaving, a switch engine banging freight cars about, cars already on the siding being unloaded. We took our place on the Brent scene, often coming up along the track, followed by a dog or two. Sometimes our errand took us to the lumber yard. We never knew what kind of greeting Mr. Grimm would shout at us as he scurried about with a handful of orders, but he served us well in spite of his abrupt, outspoken manner, rough as sandpaper. Our business was more often with the store, which we found to be a more important institution in the community than we had realized.

In fact, everything about Brent took on a new significance now that we were living there. It had long been familiar ground to us. We had kept a canoe there, and spent many days on the river. Most of the inhabitants were known to us. Yet when we came to live on the river ourselves, a change took place in our relation to Brent and the people who lived there. Though not a word was said and nothing intimated, the few Brent families, the store people, the solitary men and women who lived in little houses, squatters' shacks, and shantyboats accepted us as one of them. Brent itself became as a new place to us. At the time we did not grasp the meaning of all this, but it was the beginning of a deep and permanent alteration in us. The river would leave its mark.

Among our friends and former neighbors on the hill, a few looked on us as if we had fallen from grace. None were much surprised, for we had never been orthodox townspeople. Our best friends were much

9

interested in our venture; some congratulated us, and even envied us our good fortune.

Though our tools were idle in these days of preparation and groundwork, we went over in our minds the procedure to be followed in building our boat. It was to be a square-sided, flat-bottomed scow, with slanting ends and a boxlike cabin, like so many Ohio River houseboats we had seen. I had a fairly good idea of how to go about its construction, having watched and asked questions whenever I came upon any riverbank boatbuilding. Much of my information came from a onetime shantyboater on whose disused boat I had spent my first night afloat, a solitary, thrilling vigil among a lot of nets and fishing gear. Here at Brent were several experts ready to advise us. We relied most on Andy Detisch who had built many boats. Sometimes when the authorities disagreed, we followed our own hunches, working out original ideas. It was a great satisfaction to have these turn out well, in spite of the head-shaking of the more experienced. It should be thus, for is not independence the keynote of shantyboat life?

Now came a long succession of sunny days as often happens in October. Nights were cool, and there was usually a heavy river fog in the morning. This meant a fair day, but it was often so wet and dark at the beginning that we could not imagine the sun would ever shine. Soon, however, its pale disk appeared, light broke through the shreds of fog overhead. By a lucky chance our camp was exposed to the warmth of the rising sun, and in the late afternoon when it might have been too hot, the high hill to the west cast its shadow over us. Just to live on the riverbank at this season would have been pleasant enough, but to be building a boat and preparing for a voyage long cherished—these were days of near ecstasy.

Our work was really under way now. We were building the hull of our boat right side up, after listening to many arguments to the contrary. Old Bill Edwards had encouraged us to start it upside down, saying that the planking and caulking of the bottom would be much easier in that position. Admitting this claim, we hesitated to try it, fearing that with our lack of equipment and experience we might damage or strain the hull in turning it over.

We found that even the building of a boat requires a foundation in the earth. For this, a flat ledge or rock on the open shore was made use of. Two timbers were laid from this ledge to a cribbing of rock and discarded railroad ties cut in half, which was built up on the sloping shore below the ledge. On these timbers, properly spaced and leveled, we set up the two shoe gunwales. These are the lowest planks on the boat's sides, those to which the bottom is nailed. The shoe gunwales had a slanting rake cut at each end. Our twenty-foot pieces did not give quite the length of hull we wanted, but not liking to splice the shoe gunwales, we gained as much overall length as possible by making both rakes long and sharp. In this very beginning we found that the boat's design, as well as that of everything we made, was affected by the material at hand, and we took this into account in our future planning.

The twenty-foot timbers, when cut in two for the bottom, gave us a ten-foot width, which was just what we wanted. Before nailing the bottom planks onto the shoe gunwales, the edges of the planks were outgauged to receive the caulking later; the edges and bottom were painted. We got Donald Detisch to help us with the bottom planks, and borrowed two light jacks from Andy to hold them in place. We drilled holes to avoid splitting the ends, and drove the spikes up. After receiving advice for and against it, we spaced the planks the thickness of an eight-penny nail, to allow for expansion under water. This still seems a good idea, though we have seen boats on which the bottom planks were drawn up tight without any caulking in the seams.

The bottom need not have been of three-inch stuff—nearly twice as thick as would ordinarily be put on—yet we could not then find any thinner material of good quality. Many times since, when there has been unusual strain on the hull, the shock of heavy floating snags or ice floes, or the weight of a steel barge against it when we were side-swiped, then we have been thankful for the heavy bottom.

The next step was to put the lower planks on each rake. The angle between bottom and sloping rake is usually rounded off, but we left ours a sharp angle to avoid ripping the wide planks. It made a strong job with few seams, but I like a curved, bargelike rake better: it makes a more graceful, easier-running hull. We stopped further construction to caulk, or "cork," as Andy called it, the seams, and paint this much of the hull, to have it ready if the river should rise. There was now something on our ways that had the appearance of a boat, though it was very flat and shallow. Yet in our minds we could already see it floating on the muddy water of a rise, and rolling in the waves.

One might think that the work accomplished so far would take only a few days. Ours was a hull in its simplest form, but any kind of boatbuilding is slow work, and this was our first attempt. It is well to be painstaking and thorough in the construction of the hull in particular, for the hull, after all, is the boat.

Also, there was so much to see and attend to on the riverbank, that our work was often interrupted. We were never too busy to watch a passing boat, particularly the majestic progress of a stern-wheel steam towboat. The pillars of coal smoke which rose from its twin stacks made a fantastic cloud as they joined and floated into the changing currents of the air, reflecting the sunlight like dark masses of rock. With a great blast of steam the boat whistled for the lock above, each note chiming in separately, and forming a glorious chord which echoed among the hills. Often we could see the deck hands wheeling great barrow-loads of coal from the fuel flat lashed alongside into the boiler room. We observed the curious details of construction and ornament, the long pitman slowly turning the red paddle wheel from which poured a cascade of white water.

Our work was interrupted by visitors, too, for everyone along the river is interested in a new boat. We were always glad to stop work and talk with old Bill Edwards, who often came along in his johnboat on his way to some driftpile to hunt for likely boards for a little hull he was building. I went to see Bill's boat one day. It was small and light. The gunwales were salvaged from an old wreck, the rotten parts hacked off casually with a hatchet. The rakes had been cut the same way. The bottom was of driftwood, the pieces all different. When I visited him, he was straightening out old nails, and said he hoped to find a few more boards somewhere, so that he could finish his boat. Bill was living with his daughter in a house, at the time, and this boat was to be an escape back to the river.

The river went deep in old Bill. With him and his like, we still feel our own greenness. They are true river people, and love the river in their own way, even more deeply perhaps than we do, more simply and directly. The river takes them to her and reveals her secrets.

Sometimes Sadie Detisch stopped to talk and inspect our work as she walked down the beach picking up driftwood and piling it into the boat which Donald rowed. Sadie was a ship's carpenter in her own right, and told us how much she had liked to help Andy in the old days when he was building boats. The young boys in the family would wash the dishes by choice to be excused from the hard work. This had left Sadie free to do the sawing and hammering.

Donald was often in our camp with his puppy, Ring, whether we needed him to help us or not. He was a rather shy boy, but keenly observant, thinking and expressing himself after his own fashion. His delight was to have a meal with us, for our food was usually new to him. On such occasions he would set up a little table of his own, a driftwood board balanced on stones, and gravely discourse with us as he ate.

13

One day Donald brought us a pumpkin from a volunteer vine that had grown up near their boat. Along with this, he delivered a special invitation from Sadie to visit them that evening. We were glad to go. After supper, we mounted the sloping gangplank to the deck of their boat, shouted a greeting, and entered the kitchen. It was softly lighted by an ungainly oil lamp, placed on a table off to the side. The table was covered with a bright-colored oilcloth. Donald was seated there; Andy was in his favorite armchair by the range, on the other side of the room. Sadie entered from the middle room, saying she had not been asleep, but just resting—weary, no doubt, of carrying her weight about through the long day. We looked at the jigsaw puzzle at which Donald was working. This is their pastime on winter evenings. When completed, the puzzles are pasted on heavy paper, hung on the walls along with the picture calendars.

The conversation began on general topics, the state of river and weather, local gossip. Encouraged by our interest, Andy and Sadie told us about their earlier life on the river, of the many boats they had owned. Some were of their own building. They showed us a picture of the *Sadie D,* a little stern-wheeler which had towed their fleet on the upper Ohio and its tributaries. They related tales of ice and flood, and of runaway barges in collision with their boat. All this was fascinating; even ordinary events of river life sounded like adventures to us on the threshold. We lingered a long time enjoying their talk and unpretentious hospitality. When at last we made ready to leave, Sadie said, "Needn't be in no hurry!" but we lit our lantern and walked down the shore to our dark hut.

The nights were becoming cold now, the mornings often frosty. The cardinal and song sparrow had ceased to sing, and bathing in the river was not entirely pleasant. The warmth of fire would be welcome in our little hut; so I looked about for some kind of stove. On Three Mile Hill was the town dump, often a source of supply for me. I went there to look for a discarded ash can to use as a salamander, but my eye was taken by an oblong tank more than two feet in length, the ends about sixteen inches square. This, for no reason at all, suggested a fireplace to me; so I started home with it and a few sections of rusty smokepipe. Putting it down to rest on the way, I noticed that the tank was soldered together. Thinking that the first fire would melt the lead and that the tank would fall apart, I was about to abandon it. Hoping, however, that it might be fastened also with rivets, I packed it the rest of the way to the boat. We have since been glad that I did, for the tank made a fireplace that has been our delight and comfort all this time. I turned it over with the closed side up, and cut out one of the long sides, rolling back some of the sheet iron at the top into a suggestion of a hood. The tank had a small, square compartment on the bottom, and this, being on top now, relieved the plainness of the design and made a smoke chamber in which I cut a hole for the pipe. Now in front of our shack I built up a platform of stones to the height of the floor, and here mounted our fireplace. Most gratifying it was to sit inside on cool nights and mornings with a blaze on our hearth. We still raised the canvas to have a full view of the river. Before going to bed, we had to put out the fire and drop the canvas between us and the fireplace. Later, to be more comfortable as the nights became still cooler, we rearranged this, placing the canvas outside the fireplace. Then we missed the view of river and sky as we sat by the fire, but it was a cozy apartment, lacking only a window or two.

We did well to make our shack comfortable, for a change of weather followed, bringing rainy days and nights. It must have rained upriver, too. The clear water became muddy and the current increased. Both bear traps were opened at the dam, then the dam was lowered—a rise was on its way. We heard Andy out corking his boat, making it ready to float if the river should rise that high. Our own hull, unfinished as it was, must be put in the best shape possible. We gave all our time to caulking seams and painting, urged on by the river which slowly crept up toward the boat.

Drift began to run close to shore, as it does on a rising river. One night we were awakened by a towboat, and looking out from our bed we could see, as the searchlight of the boat swept the surface of the river, so much driftwood floating by, that it seemed to our sleepy eyes that the water was covered with it.

"This," we said, "is life on the river. We will spend many sleepless nights on watch during a rise."

We were fortunate this time. The river came close to the bottom of

15

the hull, and then stopped. For a day or two it neither rose nor fell; it was like a cup brimful. Then late one afternoon Sadie yelled down, "The river's a-fallin'!" She always watched it that closely.

We now undertook to complete the hull. First the sides were built up by placing another fifteen-inch plank on top of the shoe gunwale. On account of the flaring rake at each end, these upper sections of the sides were longer and must be spliced. To be tight and strong, the splicing must be carefully done. Such work made us feel that sometime we would like to build a boat that was not just a scow, but one of finer lines and more exacting workmanship.

To stiffen the sides, short heavy pieces were bolted across the two sections. Four of these pieces, one at each corner, were allowed to extend above the side about eight inches, to make timberheads for the fastening of lines. These timberheads and cleats were made of short pieces of oak timber that we had found in a driftwrack, following Bill's example. In this he did not regard us as competitors but rather as brothers, telling us the best places to look.

After the remaining planks had been spiked on each rake, two streamers were put in, the entire length of the boat, to stiffen the bottom. For these, I ripped the last of our twenty-foot timbers in two. After more caulking and painting, the hull was finished. It was a pleasure to look at it, perched there on the stony shore, an object of symmetry and proportion, smooth and clean, in contrast to the irregularity and roughness which surrounded it. It seemed a high-sided craft now, but later when afloat in rough water we found there was no freeboard to spare.

While we were working on the hull, Anna's mother had spent a bright, chilly autumn day on the riverbank with us. She was much interested in our boatbuilding, helping me with the splicing of the side timbers by holding one end while I fitted the other. The smell of oakum and shavings brought back to her a memory of childhood, some of her family having been shipbuilders along a canal in Holland. Later she sat in a sunny, sheltered spot, knitting, near to where Anna was preparing dinner.

The presence of her mother in camp reminded me how different Anna's life and environment had been before she followed me to the riverbank. There had been no indication in her previous living that she might depart from the conventional way. She was a librarian when I first met her, in the Cincinnati Public Library, a fascinating place also because of its steamboat-age building, originally intended to be an opera house. I was known to Anna then only as an obscure local artist and borrower of Art Room books and music. We had much in common. She was an excellent pianist and a sympathetic accompanist, as I found when we began playing violin and piano sonatas together. I recalled the prim apartment in which Anna then lived with her sister. We naturally went to concerts and art galleries together, then into the country, along the river. Anna must have been puzzled by the enthusiasm I displayed for the muddy waters of the Ohio and the somber shores, for it was winter; and by my suddenly dashing through a field to a break in the willows where I could get a good view of a passing boat. I soon discovered that she had a real love of country and water. She told me of her vacations on the inland lakes of Michigan, which was her home. Accustomed to sparkling water and brilliant northern skies, she was imaginative and unprejudiced enough to see that the Ohio River, swiftly carrying to the sea the silt and debris of so vast a section of the United States, was beautiful in its own way.

As I recalled all this, I ceased my hammering to watch Anna as she moved about the stony beach, tending the fire and cooking, setting the rude table with camp tinware as carefully as if it were fine china and silver upon a linen cloth. She was tall and slender, fair-haired. I marveled that she could keep her clothes so neat and clean; even her camp slacks were smart and trim. Then I thought, momentarily, that the approaching months of shantyboating and riverbank might be a trying ordeal to one so constituted, but I was confident that she would evolve a pattern of living which, while still giving scope to my wild longings, would satisfy her innate delicacy, her femininity and self-respect. She would make something of our shantyboat life that her family and friends would respect and admire and enjoy, even though some of them might look askance in the beginning.

As our plan must be kept at least one step ahead of construction, we had to decide now the basic design of the cabin. The traditional shantyboat has a deck at each end, of equal size, over which the cabin roof extends to make a sort of porch. On a boat as short as ours, such decks would have to be small to allow room for the cabin. Still, when we thought how pleasant it would be to eat our meals out on deck, and possibly sleep there, and seeing no particular use for two decks, we decided to have one deck large enough to meet all our demands. On the other end of the boat would be a small open deck just large enough for the handling of lines and spars. We have never regretted this departure from the customary design. Our large deck proved to have even more advantages than we could foresee.

Another matter over which we puzzled at the time, and whose solution we now see could not have been otherwise, was the cabin floor: whether to make it flush with the decks which were even with the top of the hull or set it down at a lower level. Old Bill argued that decks and floor should be on one line, his main point being the difficulty of sweeping out the "cab" if its floor were lower than the deck. But when we considered how tall this would make our boat in proportion to its length, and how much more seaworthy it would be with the weight at a lower level, we decided to place the cabin floor two steps down from the decks.

Our windows were a further departure from tradition. A small shantyboat usually has windows hardly large enough for a man to put his head through, and like as not with a piece of cardboard in them replacing a broken glass. Some small boats are even windowless and the inhabitant must keep his door open to see what he is about in the dark interior. Contrary to this, we wanted all the light and air that could be had, and large windows to look out of. So we planned a window in each side which would be eight feet wide, made up of two sash four feet square. Since the cabin was sixteen feet long, a space of four feet was left between windows and ends of cabin. The sash would slide back into this place, leaving the whole opening unobstructed.

As for doors, it seemed inevitable that we should make one at either end of the cabin. The door onto the main deck, as we called the large deck, would be full height, with a sloping hood over it. One must stoop to go through the other door, which led to the afterdeck, that is, the smaller one. We hesitated about this, but found the low door not inconvenient when we became used to it.

Since all our seasoned lumber was used up, the cabin must be built of new material. It was promptly delivered by Mr. Grimm, a lot of unseasoned, knotty stuff, yet the best to be had at the time. I packed it over the bank to the boat and stacked it up ready to use. The work with the lighter boards went faster than the heavy-timbered hull. It was a joy to see it growing, almost like the unfolding of a flower, into the shape we had planned. Yet the proportions were a surprise to us, no careful drawings having been made beforehand. At the corners we put in long braces at an angle, to strengthen the cabin against the strain of wind and waves. The roof joists, which Andy termed "carlins," were curved on top to give a crown to the roof. To match this line we curved the bottom of the carlings as well. Before putting up the carlings and roof sheathing, Anna stained the wood a light blue-gray. It made an attractive yet unobtrusive ceiling.

It was well into November now, and there was often a skim of ice on our water bucket. One morning, upon opening the canvas flap of our tent, we discovered that snow had fallen in the night, transforming the familiar landscape, and making us conscious anew of the miracle of winter. On other nights we awoke to hear rain pattering on the roof overhead. We were warm and dry, and outside all was shipshape; so we enjoyed the rain. One feels more snug and cozy, and secure, too, in a slight and flimsy shelter, provided it serves its purpose, than when insulated within thick walls and roofs which do not allow even a consciousness of the weather to penetrate.

The storms made us realize it was time to close in our boat cabin. We worked steadily, taking advantage of all the daylight. Soon there was a roof overhead, and the sides were sheathed. The roll roofing was used as a deck covering, too. Considered temporary when applied, it wore so well that we left it. With a coat of roof paint now and then, its life seems to have no limit.

The large window openings must be closed before we could have much protection from weather. On the river side I installed the glazed sash which I made from stock bought at the mill. On the other side, where there was not so much to see, I made the wooden shutters and nailed them in place, since that went quicker than the sash, and time was precious. Then I contrived two doors which would answer present needs, and the cabin was closed in.

We now began spending our days on board, or so we called it, even though there was no water under the boat. In the evening, when our day's work was done, we would go to the shack and build a fire in the fireplace, which would warm us, cook our supper, and light us to bed.

In one corner of the boat we had set up a little cookstove. The first meal that Anna cooked on it, the first of many to come, was our Thanksgiving dinner. I had bought this stove in a junk shop a long time ago, recognizing it at first sight as a perfect shantyboat stove. It had four small lids, a small oven with a door on each side, and it stood on long spidery legs. My inspiration must have been a good one: the little stove has fulfilled all expectations. Anna has learned its whims and weaknesses, and developed all its possibilities, so that between the two of them, marvelous cooking is achieved.

20

There was one curious condition to these first days: before the floor was laid, we walked on the bottom planking, and every time we crossed the cabin we must step over the streamers which were like hurdles. This became familiar to us in a few days, so that later when the floor was laid on top of the streamers, it took us some time to become accustomed to the new level.

Although we had never seen a shantyboat with a fireplace, we decided to have one. The open fire in our shack was such a joy that we felt that an ordinary heating stove would never satisfy us. The same sheet-iron fireplace that I had made for the shack seemed just right for the boat. Before we could move it over, the cabin floor must be laid. This meant dismantling our shack where the flooring boards were already in use. The little hut had been an adventure in itself and was abandoned with regret. Our compensation was that we could soon begin living on the boat.

During the interval required for this change, it seemed best to sleep at the studio. We went down to the boat each morning, and in the evening climbed back up the hill. Some days I went down alone on the bicycle. Every down trip was loaded to capacity. There was always something needed for the boat, either for construction or for our living there. If we walked we carried the inevitable sack. One day, when I had gone down ahead, I was surprised to see Anna appear with my Norwegian pack on her shoulders. I often rode the bicycle with the pack on my back and a loaded sack lashed to the handle bars. Once at this time I rode down with a long pole intended for a spike pole under my arm, like a knight on horseback. Sometimes I would vary my route and come down by way of Dodsworth Lane, picking up pears and walnuts on the way.

One morning when I went down alone a little black and white dog, hardly more than a puppy, crawled out from underneath the boat. She was not one of the neighborhood dogs. No one knew where she came from, and by now she herself has no doubt forgotten. I fed her a little, and she was underfoot all day. Next morning the little dog was there to greet me, and again kept me company through the day. It began to look serious. We wanted a dog; no shantyboat is without at least one. Here was a suitable candidate offering herself in the nick of time. We hesitated only because we had never had a lady dog before. However, as she had made up her mind, we let it go at that, and named her Skipper. Perhaps had she known that the rest of her life would be spent afloat, she would have hesitated about casting her lot with us, for she does not like water. To this day, she will balance herself on the stageboard and reach down a foot to drink, rather than get her feet wet at the water's edge. Yet at times she is a muddy tramp, and on the whole has enjoyed shantyboat life, plunging with enthusiasm into each new scene. On our part, we are glad she came to us. We have found her always a lady, quite different from the roughnecks we have been accustomed to. The nine litters of pups she has had on board have been exciting business for everyone.

The fireplace required further work before it could be installed in

the boat. I fashioned a metal bottom on it of several layers, the heaviest of which was a square highway SLOW sign. This I had found in a driftpile, fastened to its post, which I later put to another use. Four legs of light angle iron raised the bottom of the stove about eight inches off the floor. With this space under it, and several thicknesses to bottom and back, there should be no danger of fire. The bottom extended forward allowing just space enough for three bricks in a row, which made a tiny hearth. We set up the fireplace in the corner opposite the cookstove, turned so that it faced the middle of the room. This was a good arrangement, for in cold weather we kept two fires going, and sitting before the fireplace, our backs were warmed by the stove. Our fireplace is an efficient heater. It burns a big chunk of driftwood, which makes the woodcutting easier. In this I sometimes miscalculate, and after trying in every way to get an awkward snag into the opening, I will at length have to take it on shore and cut off its horns.

The rusty stovepipe which I had carried home from the dump was replaced by a shiny new one. The smoke pipes of both stove and fireplace extended through the roof in true shantyboat style. On the top of each, I made a cone-shaped metal cap to stop down drafts and keep out the rain. The chimneys were guyed with wire, but they never stand quite straight; so that with their flaring caps they have a rakish effect. The chimneys have a hard time of it when our boat is among overhanging trees, as often happens in high water or when making a landing. Many times we have expected our stacks to be carried away, but the only damage so far has been a few dents and a broken guy wire or two.

The floor, though laid in a temporary fashion, was very handsome. Later we would re-lay it, making it into hinged sections which could be raised like hatch covers. We discovered, thanks to the streamers having been put in on edge instead of flatwise, that there was just space enough between floor and bottom of boat for a quart jar to stand. This made a perfect place to store our canned stuff.

Like the laying of the floor, nearly everything we did at this time was only the first draft, and must be revised later. Nothing was completed, but left as soon as usable to carry on or begin another project. This intensive work soon made it possible for us to move completely on board, and spend our nights there as well as days. At first it was much like living in the hut on shore, although we now had plenty of headroom and windows to look out of. The transition from building the boat to living in it was gradual, but now we looked upon ours no longer as a construction project but as our home. The interior details were completed along with the process of adjusting ourselves to the new environment. This insured a perfect fit in the end, but during the period of growth Anna's housekeeping must be kept flexible. It was carried on amid hammering and sawing and the litter of blocks and shavings. She swept the floor time after time, neatly piling up the boards, and burning the smaller pieces in the stove where she was cooking our dinner.

As soon as possible, the inside work was left to be carried on in rainy weather. All fair days were devoted to preparing hull and cabin for the coming season of winter and high water. Our riverbank neighbors had advised us more than once to put water in our hull so that the planks would swell and the seams be tight before the boat floated. Otherwise, they said, we would have a leaky boat, requiring continual pumping for a while; it might even sink before the seams closed. We knew that this warning could not be disregarded, because rain water, caught in the hull before the roof was over it, had leaked through the seams onto some lumber I had carefully piled underneath to keep dry. Still, the idea of pouring water into the hull did not appeal to us: we wanted a dry boat before it was launched as well as after. The solution of this problem was to fill the seams, after the cotton and oakum had been driven in, with caulking compound. This might not be the accepted shantyboat practice, but pumping out the bilge is one experience we have been glad to avoid.

The river was rising again, and we had another race with it. Our work underneath the hull was completed as the edge of the current washed against the cribbing which supported the boat. Yet, as before, the river paused there and fell back. When it rose again we would not be alarmed: the seams were now tight, and the hull had its final coat of paint.

Before the boat should float, we must acquire some rope for mooring lines. Rope was a scarce item in those days; so when old Bill told us of some Manila rope he had made, I went to see it. His source of material was old rope, provided it was sound, or fairly so. He had found many short pieces of barge rope along the riverbank. Often when a tow had been moored to trees, it was difficult or impossible for the deck hands to untie the heavy lines; so they cut them with an axe, leaving a short piece on the tree. Bill unraveled all this stuff, and by means of an apparatus he had bought somewhere, wove it into a long line. Much as I admired his patience and industry, the rope did not seem very trustworthy; some that had been used was loosened up considerably; moreover, I thought his price too high. When I told him so, the old man coiled up his lines in dignified silence, and no deal was made.

We later bought some new rope, not Manila but made of sisal, and satisfactory enough. This, as well as our caulking compound and a valve and plunger for a bilge pump I was to make, we purchased from an establishment in the city which was Cincinnati's nearest approach to a ship chandler's. Its exterior would have delighted Whistler—a gaunt old building on the waterfront, decorated with hanging nets and a steamboat pilot wheel. In its cavernous interior were coils of rope, stacks of oars, bales of oakum. One was greeted by an odd lot of men who seemed to have just drifted in. The affable proprietor had a den off side where there was a coal stove; its walls were decorated with photographs of boats long gone. Our trips to the boat store, as Sadie called it, were among the unexpected pleasures of shantyboat life.

Preparations for rough weather and high water we now considered fairly complete. As the river had fallen back to pool stage, we decided to leave the boat for a few days and spend Christmas with Anna's family in Michigan. Donald would gladly take care of Skipper while we were gone. Knowing that Sadie would keep a watchful eye over all, we went away with no feeling of uneasiness. When we took leave of our boat, so brand-new, the cabin painted white over the dark red hull, not a splash of mud anywhere, I felt a trace of disappointment, and asked Anna, "Do you think it will ever be a real shantyboat?" I need not have been concerned: our boat is the genuine article. In fact, when drifting in muddy weather, with wet lines hanging about, a fish box and other plunder on the roof, a pair of shantyboat dogs barking from the deck, our outfit might even be mistaken, at first glance, for Bill Edwards'.

We enjoy all kinds of travel, and make the most of it, but we have a special fondness for riding on a train. This we do in the good old style, with a box of lunch, a time table, and a book to read, hoping there will be a long wait somewhere. No train is too slow or makes too many stops. The trip north was one of these excursions. The river was left far behind as we rode through the flat, snowy country, but we were reminded of it by a tiny model of our boat which we were taking along to show the folks. It represented the boat as it would be when completed, with a roof over the deck, and shutters; it had a little johnboat tied to it, gangplank, spars, and lines to shore. On Christmas Eve it was installed under the Christmas tree, an unusual decoration, but gay enough to fit perfectly into the holiday mood.

In all the excitement of seeing our family and friends again, the real boat alone on the riverbank was not forgotten. We thought of all the things that might happen to it; yet we were not really worried since we knew that our good friends were watching it. To get a report on the river, I talked over long-distance telephone to the office of Lock 36, the one upstream from our boat. They said the river was rising, but could not tell how many feet were expected. To check again, I called on Christmas night, and learned that the river had risen sharply and would continue to rise several days, with the crest still uncertain. We took the night train back.

As we traveled southward, the snow gave way to sleet, and we arrived in a land coated with ice. Naturally we were in a hurry, but speed was impossible. One could hardly walk on the icy pavements, buses could not make the grades. At last we reached the studio, where I left Anna without even starting a fire. I got into my bad-weather clothes and heavy boots, took a short cut through yards and fields, and dashed down the steep hillside to the river, following no path, since it was less slippery in the woods and grass.

I looked anxiously for the boat. It lay where we had left it, but the yellow flood swept underneath. The boat's bottom was wet, but it still rested on the rocky ledge and cribbing, as it had from the beginning. I knew it must soon be afloat—if only Anna would arrive in time to see the launching! I noticed that a line had been run from the boat to a tree, and thanked Donald for that. Just then a big diesel towboat, one of the Ashland boats, swung down around the bend from above, running fast with a light tow. When its waves washed against the boat, it was lifted from the cribbing, the pieces of which immediately floated away. The backlash of the waves carried the boat off the rocks into deeper water, and it was afloat.

I was the only person to witness its launching.

2

Our original plan was to begin our voyage down the river that first winter, completing the boat on the way. Now that we were actually living on the water we felt no desire to set ourselves adrift. It was a strange new world we had entered, and, until we should become more used to it, we were glad to be tied to shore, and to a familiar one; that, at least, was unchanged.

We found, too, that there is much to be learned about the care and handling of a boat, even when it is in port. Moreover, we found that we did not know as much about the river as we had thought; we must become better acquainted with that restless companion to which we had attached ourselves. This would take time. To add the complications of drifting, before we were prepared, would be unwise; drifting in itself is an art, one to which an apprenticeship must be served.

Nor was our boat ready for a cruise. It needed more work—the decks must be finished, catwalks or guards constructed along the sides, the other pair of windows put in, and many details worked out. A major hindrance was our lack of a skiff or johnboat to serve as a tender. Without one, the first move is nearly impossible, as we soon discovered.

So our casting off was postponed for an indefinite period, which turned out to be two years. All this time was not needed to complete preparations and make ourselves ready, but life at Brent was to be such a rich experience in itself that it pleased us to remain there for a longer period than we had calculated. Perhaps all this was part of our adjustment to the tempo of the river, where time keeps pace with its slow current, where old things survive long past their day.

It is a common belief that shantyboaters lead a carefree life of uninterrupted leisure, earning their livelihood by such pastimes as fishing and making willow chairs. While it is true enough that river people are free from many of the burdens and cares that go with a conventional life on land, where the demands of society are more exacting, they do have their own peculiar worries, and there are certain rather laborious and insistent chores that go with living on a boat. We soon found this out, and at times the situation has become downright uncomfortable and irksome; so much so that I have wondered, briefly, why people live on boats anyway.

In modern living there is such protection from the elements that those who live in cities pay little regard to the weather unless some extreme condition causes them discomfort or inconvenience. On the river we had lost this sense of communal protection, and were on our own. Our existence tended toward the primitive. Since natural forces affected us directly, we became more alert and watchful, always scanning the face of the sky, noting all changes of wind, weather, and river. We were wary and apprehensive, especially in those beginning days, as if threatened by some unseen, imminent danger.

Special faculties must be developed to live on the water safely and comfortably. Even the cautious and agile are likely to fall overboard. Anything dropped carelessly on deck seems to leap for the water, like the frog which I thought was dead.

On the other hand the river brings as much or more than it takes away. The shantyboater is stimulated to constant alertness by the possibility of seeing some worth-while wreckage floating by. When he looks out in the morning he first scans his stretch of shore to see what may have been stranded there during the night.

Perhaps all this vigilance and care are part of the price the shantyboater pays for his independence. After all, the dangers which beset him are but shadows compared with those confronting the dwellers in cities.

Our senses were sharpened by this continual watchfulness. We noticed the slightest list to the boat, and unless the cause was apparent we looked into the hold to see if it might have water in it; for any boat, even a new one, can spring a leak. In a way, an old boat is safer, as Andy said, because you watch it closer. At night we would wake instantly from a sound sleep at any alarm. It might be a thump against the hull, and I would go out and shove away a huge log which had floated against us. We seldom slept through the night without looking out at least once to check the stage of the river. Often in the darkness the boat must be moved in or out, for the Ohio at this point has been known to rise or fall as much as six feet overnight. This meant changing the whole tie-up, perhaps moving the boat to another position. This work must be done in any weather, perhaps in snow with frozen lines. Sometimes I was outside most of the night, wide awake and ready for action the instant I awoke, returning to sound sleep just as quickly when the task was completed.

Storms seem worse on the river, perhaps because you see so much of the sky, and because winds from certain quarters strike with un-broken force. Heavy rains have a delayed effect. A storm in a creek valley several miles inland sends down a surge of drift-carrying water which may not reach the river until long after the rain has ceased. When an unbroken stream of driftwood flowed past just outside our windows we knew that Four Mile Creek was running out. A tangled mass of trees, boards, hen coops, and the like would collect at the head of the boat. This had to be poled away to ease the lines. One morning when I happened to be working away at this task, an old man who usually had not a word to say came by in his johnboat and made a remark that could be a river proverb—"You're payin' your rent now, Son."

On the long reach to the north from Brent, a strong upstream wind, and very likely a cold one, whipped up the whitecaps over the river, and tossed us about with an irregular, pitching motion. The boat jolted against the spars which held it offshore, until it seemed to be pounding the bottom. These rough days were hard on us at first. Even now if the wind waves are long continued, we find something to do on shore at intervals. Aside from its unpleasantness, a high wind sweeping down a long stretch of river can be very dangerous, as we found out when we drifted into unfamiliar sections of the river.

30

Not only wind waves but swells from passing boats often rocked us. The heavy, slow-moving tows made no disturbance as they went by, but there were some fast diesels that often came down with a few empty oil barges, tearing up the river. Also at that time the upriver shipyards were building various craft for the Navy. The LST's, larger and heavier than any river boat, made a tremendous suction along the shore. More than once they pulled our spars out of position, and the following waves drove us on the rocks. Our worst encounter, however, was with a big, screw-driven steam towboat of a class which rivermen call DPC's. It passed after dark, and must have been running light. I went on deck, and heard its waves rushing toward us, breaking like ocean combers. When they hit us, the boat heeled way over, and the waves washed over the decks. With each succeeding wave the boat was thrown heavily against the spars, but they held and kept us offshore. The worst was soon over, but when I went into the cabin I saw a shocking spectacle. It looked as if everything we had was on the floor, where rolled back and forth a confusion of broken glass, kettles, books, and water. At first I thought the waves had broken through the window, but Anna, rather amused by the accident, explained that a large pan of water and a kettle of soup had slid off the stove. The shelves along the walls had spilled dishes and pans; the books and every loose object had fallen down. No serious damage was done, and we learned some valuable lessons. In future construction, everything was made firm and secure to withstand even the most violent rocking. Our permanent cupboards have doors, and there is nothing loose overhead where the motion of the boat is more strongly felt. We soon learned that waves were not serious if our boat was lined up correctly; then it did not get in the trough of the waves, but took them quartering, or end-on, with an easy, loping gait. It is not difficult to understand, though, the feud between shantyboaters and boat pilots, which has existed since the days when flatboats and packets were on the river together.

All this was in the beginning. Now these alarms and apprehensions, this feeling of instability, are not so distinctly felt, but have been woven into the fabric of our river existence. Yet even from the first, in contrast to the roughness and asperity of our environment, we

found our shantyboat such a cheerful and snug place, and our enjoyment of living there so keen, that we felt we were celebrating a continual holiday, one about which the rest of the world did not know.

Returning home in the winter twilight after some errand or excursion on land, I was each time reminded of how far down we lived. One would expect the lowest stratum of human habitation to be along the railroad; yet I crossed the track and went down over the bank, down past Detisches' boat, and there at the lowest possible level was our lonely craft. It looked small on the dark river and showed no light from the land side, since that first winter the glass was not in all the windows and doors. At my whistle the door opened, light streamed forth, I heard a sweet voice and the fierce barking of a little dog. Within all was comfort and good cheer. A fire blazed on the hearth, and in the lamp's mellow light Anna was preparing supper. The cookstove was busy, too; its crackling fire gleamed through the slits of the grate. We ate our evening meal on a low table before the fireplace, with a candle burning to give more light. Skipper slept under the fireplace until she became too hot and had to crawl out. There was always some reading in the evening, one reading aloud while the other worked at some fireside chore.

To light our reading, the two kerosene lamps were taken from their wall brackets and placed on the low table between us. The lamps stood on a wooden block which supported a wire frame. This held two pieces of white cardboard at such an angle that they reflected the light and shaded our eyes. It was an efficient reading light in spite of its somewhat flimsy and casual nature. When our reading

for the evening was finished, the lamp was quickly dismembered and the parts stowed away.

After our lights were out I lit a lantern and hung it outside for a riding light. We felt proud of our light, there were so few on the water at this season, and the boat pilots, no doubt, noticed it.

Mornings I would take in the lantern, burning pale at daybreak like the fading stars. We were always up early, and often I was out chopping wood in the first light of dawn, before the shore could become muddy in the sun's warmth. I enjoyed all the outside work. Getting in firewood and cutting it up continue to be an adventure. This is partly because driftpiles are such fascinating places. They are the shantyboater's wood lot, and while he is poking around in them for choice pieces which will make a hot fire, and not be too hard to work up, he keeps his eyes and imagination busy and picks up many useful and even valuable items—a good board or box, a broken piece of furniture that might be black walnut or cherry, a stray oar or spike pole. One of our lucky finds was a long plank of white pine which made a first-rate gangplank. This kind of collecting is one of the shantyboater's prime instincts, as the plunder at his landing bears witness.

It was well that woodcutting was pleasurable work. Heat and cold passed through the thin walls of our cabin and the large windows so that both fires must be kept blazing in cold and windy weather. At night when the fires went out, the air inside at once became like out-doors. On some of the zero nights of that cold winter we kept up a fire in the fireplace all night.

Some of our firewood came from a clearing I was making on the shaggy hillside which rose abruptly from the open stony beach. This clearing was to be our harbor in high water, and a swath must be cut up to the railroad, which was nearly sixty feet above the low water level. Our path came down that way, and we hoped to have some patches of garden in the more level places. This ground had been cleared before, many times, perhaps. I remember that a small house-boat was constructed there years ago. The builder had made the gun-wales of a single timber eight inches square; since it was too heavy for him to saw, he bored holes close together the entire length of the timber, so it could be split straight. As I cleared farther up the hillside, I came upon a small rude foundation of brick and stone. This ruin stirred the imagination, but later we learned that it was nothing more than the site of a shack in which Sadie's brother had lived for a while.

The Detisches acquired their fuel in a different manner. Daily, or more than once a day if the demand was great, Sadie and Donald would walk along the railroad track, picking up coal that had spilled from the trains. They would go either separately or together, each with a sack, their eyes downcast, stooping here and there to pick up a piece of coal which might be the size of a walnut, or so large that it required two hands to lift. Sadie knew the track better than the section foreman, and she looked for coal especially where the rails were uneven, for more would be spilled there by the swaying cars.

Aside from keeping us warm, I had other winter chores. The decks and especially the gangplank must be kept clear. If the ice could not be removed, we sprinkled ashes about. There might be several layers of ice and ashes before a thaw came. The path up the hill must be maintained. Near the river was a clay bank too steep for a path. Several flights of stone steps which I built here were carried away before I could get one to survive high water and sliding mud. The riverbank in winter is a mean place to work, nearly always slippery with either mud or ice. I thought seriously of devising removable

cleats for my shoes—like mountain climbers'. One of our neighbors solved the problem by tacking bottle caps on his shoes.

The constant chore of a shantyboater, however, is the taking care of his boat. While it can be aggravating and at times difficult to manage, the handling of lines, tying knots, working the boat, spars and lines into a balance of tension that will withstand any wind, or boat waves from either direction—this from the beginning has been a never-failing pleasure, one of the joys to me of river life. This is so even when done in darkness and foul weather. Then, when your task is completed, you come in by the fire, or back to bed, with double satisfaction.

While I was busy outside, Anna was organizing the interior, developing a system of housekeeping which would fit our small quarters. The arrangement of the cabin was not planned but grew around us as we lived there, a more natural and efficient way, we thought, than to make figures and drawings beforehand and then fit ourselves to them. We had so much fun at all this that we sometimes felt like children playing at keeping house, almost as if we were playing at living. There was not a trace of the dead seriousness and worry that go with planning and building a house. Yet our cheerful cabin became a comfortable and convenient place to live and work in. Its lack of decoration and adornment give it an honesty that few dwellings have.

Since our cabin was so small, about ten by sixteen feet, all space must be put to use. The room must not appear crowded, and we determined from the first to keep the floor an open space with no obstructions. We figured that instead of a house of many rooms, only one of which would be in use at a time, our one room would serve us in succession for our various activities. To make this plan work, there has to be a place for everything, and it must be put there as soon as it is no longer being used. Fortunately Anna has an inherent love of order and neatness. This has been developed in me, too, by her example and the force of necessity. We are by no means fussy about it, though, as a glance at our cabin when we are busy would show. There are no restrictions about what may be done inside, and the wet and muddy dogs are welcome if it is rough weather on deck.

The hitch in this plan is that our different occupations might conflict in that small space if carried on at the same time. We have no serious trouble about this: if I get out my tool box, Anna thoughtfully retires to a corner to write a letter, and when she has ironing on her hands, I do my outside chores. If there is any overlapping, the situation is usually so comical that we see it as an outsider would and laugh at it ourselves. Anna is most patient with me and the dogs in this matter, cheerfully going about her work under such handicaps as wet dogs or a coil of line drying by the stove, or some incumbrance of mine spread out on the floor.

When anyone comes aboard for the first time, and steps down into our cabin, his attention may be attracted by one feature or another, the large windows, perhaps, or the fireplace, or the unexpected feeling of spaciousness. However, one question occurs to all our visitors. Children and forthright people come right out and ask, "Where is your bed?" Some polite guests go home and ponder and discuss the question among themselves until their curiosity overcomes them, and they ask us point-blank on their next visit. It is true that nothing like a bed is visible, but we point to a long, flat wooden box, one side of which can be seen behind the woodbox which forms the step onto the main deck. In the space under this deck the bed is stored during the day; at night it is rolled out like an old-fashioned trundle bed.

No one would believe that so many difficulties would arise or so much experiment and calculation be necessary to carry out this simple idea. We decided to use our air mattresses since they were so comfortable, light in weight, and flat. The bed itself is a shallow wooden box four feet by seven, which rests on the floor when in use. Mornings we make the bed, insert a caster in each corner, and put on the wallboard cover, which is in four hinged sections folding like a screen. After moving the woodbox aside, the bed is rolled back under the deck. A carefully charted course must be followed. The bed must be warped in with precision, cramped hard against the inside stove leg while you turn it sideways. When lined up with the head of the boat, you give a hard shove, for the casters run up the rake a way on an incline. If it goes off the track much heaving is required, and wriggling into small spaces, to recover the casters which drop into the bilge. With long practice we have become so expert that only a minute or two is required to roll it in or out, and a mishap rarely occurs. It is tricky business for the untrained, though. One night when two guests were to sleep in our bed, they insisted that they understood all the steps of the operation. We retired to our beds on deck, and listened to the familiar sounds within: the woodbox was moved aside, the bed rolled out, the cover taken off, the woodbox shoved back in place. Then silence. Anna asked me, "Did you remind them to remove the casters?" Before I could answer, there was a crashing sound. We let our guests find the hammer and nail the bottom of the bed back in place. It was never meant to support the sleepers' weight, but must rest solid on the floor.

There was much to do inside the cabin that winter, and I worked on the outside of the boat in nice weather. The construction of a johnboat was urgent, for it was needed every day. We liked all this tinkering and making things, but found that more important activities which had not the same immediacy were likely to be crowded out. At times a withdrawal from work was necessary. Then, looking about us with detachment, time became as smooth and even as the current outside our windows, and we began to realize our true aims in coming to the river.

One of these was my painting, which I was soon able to take up again. When I had first begun to paint, I turned naturally to the river, which had attracted me from my earliest years. I carried my sketch box along its shores, on canoe trips, and on steamboats. I established camps at various places along the river, which might be called studios; the first one was in an abandoned woodworking shop near Brent; another in a cottage on a river farm, where the yearly round of crops and farm life shared my interest. Later there was another camp high on a hill from which we looked down on an old town across the river, and far up and down the winding Ohio. The structure was without walls, such as might be seen in a Chinese landscape painting, except for its stone fireplace. From these vantage points I painted the river, alone with its sky and reflections; I painted pictures of steamboats, past and contemporary; and of life along the shores. I explored the upriver towns, where I sketched the old waterfront buildings, relics of the days of the packets.

In this way I learned the river fairly well. Desiring to come still closer to it, the answer seemed to be a shantyboat. This would enable me to live with the river, to watch it through the changing seasons, to go with it on its long journey to the sea.

There were other and deeper reasons for my going down to the river. I thought I might be able to engage there in certain harmless and simple activities which town, and even country, interfered with. For where can one find more freedom than on the river? The fields and woods are all owned by someone, and beyond the narrow bounds of the public road the walker is trespassing. I do not say that the river is entirely outside the law, although we have been told of certain sections that are, but it affords a chance for a more unhampered life than any other accessible region.

I had no theories to prove. I merely wanted to try living by my own hands, independent as far as possible from a system of division of labor in which the participant loses most of the pleasure of making and growing things for himself. I wanted to bring in my own fuel and smell its sweet smoke as it burned on the hearth I had made. I wanted to grow my own food, catch it in the river, or forage after it. In short, I wanted to do as much as I could for myself, because I had already realized from partial experience the inexpressible joy of so doing.

The rising river which lifted our boat from the cradle on which it was built carried it to a level some twenty feet higher; first up the steep clay bank, then to a gentler slope where there were convenient trees to tie the boat to. As the river kept on rising our gangplank would not reach to dry ground among the trees. Then it was time to move to the clearing I was making a hundred feet downstream. Thinking it would be easy to drift that short distance, keeping hold of branches as we went, I did not accept the Detisches' offer of their johnboat. Donald was on board our boat at the time, and helped take in the lines. We were off! Almost at once the current swung us out of reach of the overhanging limbs, and as Donald said, we were bound for New Orleans. After several desperate tries, I caught a branch with the spike pole. Although I could not hold it, this caused the other end of the boat to swing around so that Donald, on the other deck, could grasp a tree. By this time we had drifted below our harbor, and had to haul ourselves back there.

People ask us, "What do you do in high water?" A flood is the landsman's problem, not ours. We pull into the backwater where we are safe from wind, current, and floating drift. There, gently swaying between the trees, we enjoy the new outlook and the excitement of the fast-flowing river outside our harbor. A falling river is not so much fun because it leaves a muddy bank, and you are continually sparring off to avoid grounding. Yet it is a thrilling time when you shove out from the trees into the open river again, and have the long vista to the next bend.

This rise floated the Detisches' boat, or I should say fleet, for beside their houseboat they had a hulk of a stern-wheeler called the *Bozo*. It was fitted up with a gasoline engine, pilothouse, and towing knees. The function of the *Bozo* was to shove their houseboat when they were moving upstream. We had never seen it run, and apparently it would need much coaxing and tinkering before it could be made to. This did not matter now—the Detisches were beached out for good. Sadie often spoke longingly of going somewhere, but since Andy "lost his wind" they could not even keep their boats in the water. So the *Bozo* and their shantyboat rested on the gentle slope under some willows and two tall cottonwoods at the top of the steep bank. Posts of unequal length supported the boats in a level position, high enough from the ground that a man could crawl under to work on the bottom. A flight

of perhaps thirty steps, made of pieces of old barge timbers, led up from the river. From their windows they watched the rising water climb these steps one by one. It was an anxious time when it reached their boats, for even though they kept water in the hull the planks contracted, leaving open seams. The *Bozo* floated first, so they did not have both boats to worry about at the same time. They kept caulking cotton on hand ready to stuff into the leaks from the inside when the water seeped through. If the leak was bad they had to brace a board against the cotton to hold it in place. Any pounding was risky, since it might start new leaks in a hull as old as their shantyboat was. Once this crisis was over, they enjoyed being afloat again. At first so much water seeped into the hull that a bilge pump must be set up. This spouted water through a hole in the wall of the kitchen. Sadie did most of the pumping, possibly because her weight collected the water where she stood, and she could pump the hull almost dry.

If the river kept on rising, they had to move closer to the bank. When it fell again, the boat must be gotten back in exactly the same spot where it was before, because the posts or legs which supported it when up in the air were fastened to the sides of the hull by cleats, and so remained in place when the boat floated. If the boat's resting place were changed, these legs would not fit the uneven bank. In order to reach precisely the same spot, they tied pieces of string around the lines before moving the boat from its original position. When moving back, they stopped at the pieces of string, as they payed out the lines, and knew that the boat was in its old location.

When the posts touched bottom again, they prayed for smooth water. If there were waves then, the posts would pound on the bottom, straining and wracking the old boat almost to breaking up. When it was firmly set, the spectacle of the ungainly craft, apparently rising out of the water, was a strange one. Now Sadie must walk lightly for a few days until additional posts can be placed under the middle of the boat. Once when the river was coming up, I saw Donald tying long strings from the deck to these middle posts. I wondered, but found out that the strings kept these unattached posts from drifting away when the hull was lifted off them. I helped Donald replace these posts after the river had fallen, working in the mud under the boat with blocks and jacks. The work required the whole family: Sadie testing the closing of the doors while we jacked underneath, shouting down her orders from the deck above; Andy, not very well these winter days, coming out for a few minutes at a time for advice and inspection. When it was done, Sadie could move around freely.

Winter on the Ohio River is often a season of dark days and muddy banks, but this first winter was a bright, cheerful one. The cold was intense, and our movements out-of-doors were often hampered by icy banks. We were recompensed by a snowy landscape for long periods, and by the starry nights of winter.

The winter season on the river was not so familiar to us as summer when all the equipment one needs for comfortable living can be carried in a canoe. Even in winter, however, there had usually been a johnboat or canoe available, and we had spent some cold days on the water, building huge fires of driftwood to warm ourselves. The river landscape, so gentle and rounded in the confusion of summer, acquires a new strength in its winter barrenness and austerity, and a surpassing richness. Its harmonies are simple and clear: long ranks of russet willows accented by white sycamores; the unadorned symmetry of the enfolding hills; the sweep of the river itself as it curves and recurves into the blue distance.

We had always thought it would be an exciting and rewarding adventure to live close to the river in winter. A shantyboat might be considered as a sort of blind from which one could watch through all weather, day and night. In this our hopes have been realized. It has been occupation enough just to look, all winter long. In the morning you awake to discover an unexpected snowfall; the untrod deck and gangplank are white; the lines to shore have a ridge of snow on them; and where they are twisted around a kevel the snow has made an abstract sculpture. The island of drift that passes silently on the dark water is an irregular pattern of white lace. Then in a winter fog, when all the earth disappears except the immediate shore, and there is little change when day fades into night, you feel your isolation and remoteness and are thankful for shelter and companionship. On such nights of fog, if it is very cold, a rare combination which happens but few times in a winter, a white frost will form, and in the morning the earth is transformed. Every twig and weed and spear of withered grass is white; the willows are white against the dark river. When the sun at last shines through the fog, it is like the caverns of ice. Then at a certain instant the vision is erased completely by the giant hand of the sun.

As we rode out the storms of winter, our cabin was a busy place. There was intermittent work on the interior, and at the completion of each part, our life expanded a little. It was a great day when we put in the other pair of sash, and opened the shutters on a new outlook, even though it was only the familiar winter shore.

Anna's 'cello could not be brought down to the boat until a place for it was ready, nor could we make a suitable housing until the instrument was actually there. Now we could give our attention to this problem. Space was reserved in a corner of the clothes closet, the 'cello was carried down the hill, and an insulated compartment built to fit. In this it was fastened securely, to take the rocking of the boat without damage. It was good to have it with us: now we could play duets, 'cello and violin, or 'cello and viola, the smaller instruments having been with us all the time.

At this time we brought down another bulky item from the studio—the wooden box which serves as woodbox for the cookstove and also as a step onto the main deck. It is broad and flat with battens on the lid, and has a rope handle at each side, very useful on a box that is moved about, as this one is. Its corners are dovetailed and bound with iron. This box was once destined to hold Russian ammunition, but now the Russian letters have worn and faded away, and it has adapted itself to a domestic life.

Bringing this box down to the boat was a winter adventure. I took advantage of the icy roads by nailing two narrow boards on the box to act as sled runners. On the top was piled a lot of stuff awaiting transportation to the boat, one item being a hundred-foot piece of one-inch rope. I easily dragged the heavy sledge through the streets of the town and coasted down Three Mile Hill to the river.

Hardly anyone comes to the riverbank in winter; so we had few visitors then. Contrary to this, the winter birds found the shore much to their liking. In our high water harbor they flitted through the trees just outside our window—chickadees, cardinals, titmice, woodpeckers, the Carolina wren. The song sparrow hopped amid the twigs and grass floating at the water's edge, and with the cardinal sang on the first warm days. The English sparrows came no closer to the river than Sadie's chicken coop, and we saw no starlings. In the winter sunset long lines of crows flew to their roosting place, and their noisy convocation was heard far off. Juncos, goldfinches, and towhees were to be seen in the dry weeds along shore, and the bluebird was heard overhead all winter. There seemed to be more birds than on the hills, perhaps because the water tempered the sharp air. The ducks on the river we found hard to identify. Sea gulls came and went and terns, the wind birds of the river people, who expect high winds after their appearance. We saw an occasional kingfisher, noisy as in summer, and now and then an unexpected bird, like the turnstone.

So much were we alone on the fringe of the world that a trip to Witte's store was a social adventure. Sadie kept us posted as to neighborhood gossip and news of the world as she understood it; also she relayed radio reports of weather and river, one of her interpretations being, "The river will fall in the upper 'potion.'" At the store we gathered additional scraps of news from a piece of yesterday's newspaper lying on the counter, or from the storekeeper's version of a radio broadcast. There too we met all the people Sadie talked about, since everyone came to the store. Old Kits might be encountered, shuffling down from Winter's Lane with her basket and fixed stare, or one of the local hermits in from his lair for coffee and bread. One day in the store a young farmer from a nearby hollow asked me about a painting of his farm which he had seen and recognized at once in the office of a doctor who was our good friend.

The outside appearance of the store did not promise much—a small place with a dingy show window on one side of a recessed door, an ordinary house window on the other. Within was all the charm of a country store. A warm welcome was extended by a big round stove standing just inside the door. To the left was a counter little used except for the sale of notions and penny candy, which was kept in a glass case on top of the counter. On the other side was a confused array of cartons, some already opened, sacks of potatoes and cabbage, a barrel of vinegar, joints of stove pipe. To buy anything, the customer must make his way past the circle of hand-warmers about the stove to a small counter in the rear where all business was done. This arrangement was for the convenience of the Witte family, who lived still farther back and came out as needed to wait on trade. Since they could lay their hands on any desired article, the apparent disorder of the place must have been a kind of order after all. The variety and extent of their merchandise was ever a surprise to us. What other kind of store would have everything that a shantyboater needed? They also kept some long forgotten items which we thought had vanished from the market. Anna's mother found there a favorite old-fashioned peppermint candy.

Moreover, the store was a sort of community center. Besides serving as a clearinghouse for news, gossip, and messages, all mail addressed to Brent was delivered to Witte's store. It was placed on the counter in a box lid, and we rummaged through it with the rest. Everyone used the store telephone, too. Once Donald came running down to the boat— "There's a telegram at the store for you. The operator told Mrs. Witte it wasn't bad news, only somebody coming to see you."

In bad weather we often waited inside the store for the bus, leaving there our riverbank galoshes and rain clothes, to be picked up on our return. The bus trips were often on Saturday night when we went to the symphony concert in Cincinnati. If the evening was fair we might walk up the hill with Donald on his way to a movie, and share his Saturday night excitement. The return trip would be made on the last bus provided we left the concert hall early. If the closing music was a Brahms symphony, say, we heard it all and leisurely took a streetcar, which brought us to the top of Three Mile Hill. We had some wintry walks down to the river, one made memorable by a full moon shining through a cloudy sky, giving the white earth a diffused radiance. When we arrived at the boat, our watch dog, Skipper, barked dutifully, knowing all the time who we were. On frosty nights, late as it was, a fire was kindled in the fireplace and we might have toast and cocoa while warming ourselves, a little tired after the strenuous evening. The music must have been worth it, for at the next chance to hear a good concert we were off again.

The coldest weather came in late January. The river had fallen to a low stage, and after a succession of zero nights we found ourselves threatened with the greatest danger a riverman has to face—ice. In past years we had seen the river frozen over or full of running ice, and understood its power of destruction. We had heard tales of steamboats and barges lost and houseboats crushed like match boxes. Andy had been through many cold winters and told us of the first time he was frozen in. It was 1908, across from Pomeroy. The river had frozen into a solid sheet of ice. The breakup came at night and was announced by continued blasts from all the whistles along the river. The ice broke down the middle with a great noise. Andy abandoned his boat and carried the children ashore, laying their mattresses in the deep snow. Little could be done now but watch and wait. Two circumstances saved his boat: its position on a sandbar, and the planks he had slipped under the hull for skids. When the ice moved, its sideways pressure shoved his boat out on the shore where it was not touched. So his advice was, "Never be frozen in against a steep bank,

45

and always break up the ice between your boat and the shore. Stay out of creek mouths. There might be a runout and your boat will be crushed between the creek ice and the frozen river. Don't worry as long as the ice in the river keeps moving. If it freezes solid, watch out, for the breakup will tear everything loose."

We found the scattered floes of ice bad enough, especially at night. Our bed was even with the water and the sound of crunching ice as it scrapes along the side of the boat a few inches from your head does not put one to sleep. Mornings we would awake to find more ice, until the river was almost full. Boat traffic continued with difficulty. The screw boats fared better than the stern-wheelers whose bucket planks were liable to damage. We kept a clear space between us and shore, and shoved the ice floes away from the headline. Under the pressure of the drifting ice as it hit us this line would become taut, and we would hold our breath until the strain was over. The large sheets we tried to swing away from the boat with a spike pole, or break up. There was an eddy just above us, behind Three Mile Bar, where sheets of ice circled round and round. One made a longer sweep than usual and came directly against the side of our boat. We were eating dinner at the time, and were alarmed to feel the boat heeling over. One heavy ice floe came toward us close to the bank. We saw it in time to trip the spars and pull the boat close in. The ice merely grazed the boat as it passed slowly by. Along the outside of the hull at the waterline I had placed a long pole to take the grinding of the ice.

There was more than a week of this, but with never a long enough succession of intensely cold nights to freeze up the river. Then came milder weather and warm rains. The ice became soft, melted, and sank. One morning we awoke to an unbroken surface of rippling water on the river. It was then we realized what a strain we had been under.

It was one of Sadie's country sayings that half of February should be good weather. After the passing of the ice we thought that perhaps winter had used up the days assigned to it, and made ready to build our johnboat.

A johnboat is a rowboat usually fourteen or sixteen feet long, square at both ends, and flat-bottomed. With this fundamental design, it may

46

be little more than a box or trough. Some of them are just about that. On the other hand, if it is built by a craftsman who has a feeling for good design, a johnboat is a beautiful, easy-running boat. It is to be found the length of the river, and in every tributary and creek big enough to float one. Its name changes, if not its appearance. As we drifted from one section to another our johnboat was called flatboat, joeboat, footboat, dinkyboat, paddleboat, and on the Lower Mississippi, bateau.

Every shantyboater has one johnboat at least. It answers all his needs. It can carry a heavy load; its square ends make it easy to step into from the deck of a shantyboat; its scow bow is good for running up on a bank; and it is better for fishing than a skiff, being more steady and roomier. With the shantyboater the johnboat corresponds to the farmer's wagon or the yachtsman's dinghy. Also it can be used as a temporary fish box. When the river is muddy the shantyboater bails out the rain water from the johnboat for his wife to wash clothes in; "johnboat water" is a common term with us. In addition, we often use ours as a temporary bridge to shore. We take a bath from it, and climbing into it after a swim is easy. The johnboat is often abused and can have little care out in the sun and rain. Ice and snow fill it; it freezes in the ice. I have seen ours a solid cake, inside and out.

In former years I had built two johnboats, but neither had been well designed. This new one I hoped would be more successful. To that end I studied and made measurements of boats which were trim and easy to row, asking questions of their builders. As ours was not to be used with an outboard motor, ease of rowing was a first requirement. To achieve this, we planned its greatest beam well forward, yet with little difference in the width of the bottom: thus there would be no drag from bulging sides or flaring stern. The boat would have a long rake, a high bow to ride the waves, and the sides flaring out sharply at the point of greatest beam would give stability. We were not much concerned about appearance, trusting that a boat which was seaworthy and easy-running must have good lines and proportions.

Suitable lumber to build it of was hard to find. The brash new poplar offered by the Brent lumberyard could not be trusted. The best we could find was redwood, two fourteen-foot planks one inch by twelve, which was not quite wide enough. For the bottom we obtained some cypress but not in long enough pieces to be put on lengthways. Our neighbor, Al Edwards, hauled it all out from town in his little truck, one rainy, springlike day, on his way home from work.

High up in our clearing, where the river would not interfere, we set up some trestles to work on. The first day we fashioned the rakes on bow and stern, set in a stout headlog and stern piece, spread the sides to their proper width. There is no doubt that all our boatbuilding, and our telling about it, too, is the work of amateurs. After all, we are amateurs at shantyboating. Even now when we meet a genuine riverman, one who was "born in a johnboat with the catfish," and who has never in his life been far from the river, we realize that we are still novices. Perhaps it is for this very reason that our river life has continued to hold the same fascination it had in the beginning.

At any rate, the building of the johnboat was a pleasant occupation. We stopped our sawing, planing, and hammering now and then to look across the river, or to sniff the mild air. The sweet smell of the shavings that we made combined with the fragrance of the sun-warmed earth, and the boat with its curving lines harmonized with the natural forms around it as if still related to the trees from which it came. These mild days were not of spring but the weary end of winter; yet they anticipated the coming season. Unseen bluebirds softly whistled as they went by and the faint tinkling of song sparrows was heard now and then. A south wind overtaking the current ruffled the golden water. One day was so warm that Andy ventured over to see how we were getting along. As he talked of the boats he had built in his younger days, we recalled a picture of him seated at the oars—such a vigorous

and aggressive young man that the tales he told could well be believed.

We worked all day in this good weather, knowing that it would not last. Even so, we kept an eye on the river which could be seen through an opening in the trees. Our work stopped whenever a boat went by. In the hazy air, even the color of the white boats and red barges seemed changed. Once we heard a full-toned whistle, familiar yet not to be identified. Then as we watched, the old, almost forgotten towboat *W. C. Mitchell* steamed past, panting and clanking, putting forth clouds of smoke and steam. It was a boat from the past, not like the new white boats, but ancient and gray, in harmony with the sunset reflected in the eastern sky and water.

In the following weeks the *W. C. Mitchell* passed frequently; then after an interval of absence its total loss was reported.

The expected return of winter weather came before the johnboat could be finished. More snow fell. We again had icy banks, frozen lines, and fires of the best-heating wood. Then followed rains and a rising river. It came up fast and surpassed the first predicted crest. A stage of forty-one feet was then forecast, and we moved up into our clearing again, where the outlook was as novel as if we had never been there before. Work was pushed on the incomplete johnboat which was now just outside our windows. Anna and I could be sociable as we worked at our different tasks. Our new boat was well along now. Extra width had been added to the sides to give a good freeboard. A skag was placed on the stern rake. This is a sort of permanent rudder or fin which makes the boat run in a straight line. The boat was turned right side up again, and about all that remained was to put in decks and seat. With a stout ring in each end, and oars and oarlocks, it would be ready for service. It was a handsome boat, at once sturdy and grace-ful, as it rested there on the trestles, dreaming perhaps of rough, swift water, the oars' pull, and the thrust of the wave.

Toward the end of February the weather became warm again. Heavy rains fell for days. There was no sky, only water dripping and pouring from an overhanging mist. Muddy streams cascaded down the bank in unexpected places to be swallowed up by the unheeding river. Its level was unchanged at first, but when Donald came over and said that a stage of from fifty-six to fifty-eight feet was forecast, we were prepared for it. The Detisches were floating now, and Donald wanted me to help him move the *Bozo* closer inshore to be out of the wind's path.

The rising water soon floated our johnboat but it was only an inci-dent in the excitement of the flood. We were tied to the swaying tops of small elms, and more trees above us must be cut to allow for our upward passage. Only a scanty fringe of locusts remained between us and the railroad. We waved at the engineers as the trains roared by almost overhead, and the trainmen looked down at the firelight in our cabin. In this new position the familiar landmarks were all changed. The angle of the railroad and the river's bend seemed different, the distant hills were lower. Being higher up, we saw unfamiliar lights at night—house lights across the river, and headlights of cars on highways which we could never see before. The Four Mile Bar naviga-tion light, once so far above us, now flashed in our windows. The up-bound boats ran close to the willows on the opposite shore, seeking easier water. As the river rose higher their course was behind the outermost willows, of which only the tall tips were above water. On the wide, swift river floated drift of all sorts, islands of matted branches, great trees with all their roots, and many an inviting plank or timber.

Our life went on in its usual way in spite of the different surround-ings, for we had already learned to adapt ourselves to constant change. There was considerable work on the wet shore. One task was to move our loose property farther up the bank. We had already collected some plunder, and even a worthless scrap of driftwood or a worn-out basket, if it is once tossed out on shore, will be cared for and moved ahead of rising water until at last above the crest of the flood—where it is most likely abandoned after all. Firewood was a problem now. The area of the riverbank was restricted, and the bleached piles of driftwood which once lay far back from the river's edge, draped over the uneven bank, were now floating on the high water like rafts. Old railroad ties were our reserve of fuel, and they made good fires in the wettest weather. They were not desirable, though—Anna objected to the smoke and soot which the burning creosote made, almost as bad as coal, and I did not like to saw the ties on account of the gravel imbedded in them.

Most pleasant it was after a bout with some rough work in the cold and wet, to come back to the warmth of our cabin. Each time I marveled again—how neat and clean it was, so insulated from the chaos of the riverbank. What good living there in that small enclosure, floating on the wild river, against the inhospitable shore.

As soon as the planking had swelled enough to make the seams tight we rowed the johnboat for the first time. It promised to fulfill all our hopes, and soon became our mainstay on the river. In it I was a new animal, as a man on horseback is conceived to be. The johnboat was so useful that we wondered how we had ever managed without it. Now I could go out on the river or down the shore, looking for drift. We had a view of our boat and landing from the water for the first time. It made us feel like real shantyboaters to call on our neighbors by water, tying up at their deck and climbing aboard. We were becoming part of the river fraternity now, and as we sat in Sadie's cheery kitchen, with perhaps half a dozen others, we ventured a few words about our own doings and opinions.

There was much to talk about in connection with the high water, for every day brought some change. We knew when the river reached fifty-two feet, or flood stage, for then the Chippy appeared on the railroad. This was a train of one or two antiquated passenger cars and a caboose. It carried the railroad men back and forth between town and the railroad yards at Silver Grove, upriver from us, and went by every two hours. Formerly it was in year-round service, but I suppose it got in the way of the other trains, and it was replaced by buses running on the highway. At flood stage the Three Mile bridge was covered with water. Since the railroad was on a higher level, the Chippy made its trips as of old. We were glad to see it, for it had a little old engine to match the cars. Sadie welcomed it, too—its frequent trips made coal picking better than ever.

The river would soon reach its predicted crest. Now river people respect the forecasts of the Weather Bureau to such an extent that when a certain prediction is made they mark it on their private gauge, which may be a tree, a culvert, or some steps, and expect the river to stop there at the time set. However, they know that it may do unpredictable things. At Brent it has been known to rise sharply and the current slacken. This is caused by a runout of the Little Miami or the Licking, not far downstream, which pours so much water into the Ohio that the big river is dammed up in a slight degree, causing a sudden rise above and holding back the current. Of course everyone knows that all the careful forecasts will have no meaning if the upper river or far distant headwaters have additional heavy rain. Then a new crest to the flood must be set.

Such was the case at this time. It rained and rained in all known manners and over the whole valley. One wet day we heard a call from up on the track. It was Sadie. She stood there, a sodden, dripping figure in a long, yellow-brown overcoat, disconsolate as a wet chicken. "River's goin' to seventy feet," she shouted. "They're movin' out of the store. If you want anything you'd better hurry."

This was news. A major flood to rank with the famous ones of '84 and 1913, and within ten feet of the giant of 1937. The muddy tide would seep into many places where it would cause damage and misery; yet we could think only of Witte's store, empty, the last spool of thread and the barrel of vinegar removed. How could they ever get it all back in place again?

It made little difference to us how high the river went, but some of our neighbors must figure closely. Dellie could not tell for sure, but was prepared to move into the pilothouse of the *Bozo* if the water reached her house. The Detisches must move their row of improvised chicken coops farther up the bank. I don't suppose any one chicken lived through two floods; so it would be a new experience for Crower, Pet, Pidgeon, and the rest. Up near Four Mile, Lou Gander's little boat, which hadn't floated for years, would sink and turn over on its side as usual. We heard that Old Bill had sold his new flat to a flood-threatened household. Now he must begin collecting boards for another hull. There would be good picking during and after the flood, and no doubt he was at work already.

We became so accustomed to clouds and rain that dry, sunny weather was hard to imagine. One wet night we saw strange lights across the river, and heard the grinding of trucks. The town of California was being evacuated. The railroad came next, and it put on a fine show for us. On that last day an N & W passenger train came through from the east, no doubt routed over the C & O when its own tracks were covered by high water. The Silver Grove yards were being flooded, evidently, for some of the rolling stock was taken out. First came a train of bright red cabooses almost like a circus parade; then a stately procession of twelve engines, coupled together, all different types, large and small, each with its crew in the cab, twelve plumes of smoke trailing. Late in the afternoon the Chippy made its last trip. Many of its passengers were women and children. Number Seven came through on time, and that was the end. These last trains had used only the inside track, away from the threatening river.

Now that the railroad was out, the houseboats could tie to the rails, a secure anchor which was most welcome, as other holds were flimsy and scarce. We worked at this by lantern light, and through the darkness heard Sadie's voice as they made their boats fast to the rails. I had already cut a passage through the line of slender locusts, and our boat rose until its roof was level with the tracks. Later, in the summer low water, as we came down our path and looked up at those trees I had cut, it was hard to believe our boat had ever floated so high.

Besides the change of scenery, there were other advantages to our new situation. No bank to climb now, for we were even with the rest of the world, or the lowest part of it. Our yard for drying clothes was the level plot across the railroad where our boat lumber had been unloaded. There was unlimited firewood now in the woods which covered the steep hillside along the railroad to the north.

True, the buses were not running, but we went to the symphony concert as usual, following a new path through the yards of some houses on the hillside to the road. Walking down the hill, it was strange to see the familiar road come to a sudden end in water; and it was almost a shock to see the railroad, which had seemed as powerful as the forces of nature, gradually submerge itself in the passive water. As we looked about from higher elevations we were amazed at the extent of the water, which reached far back in unthought-of places. There was so much water one could not see how it could ever flow away. Our boat was like a mote floating at the edge of a giant basin.

The river asserted itself now, casting a spell over the land, where no wheels moved. Men felt its power and were subdued. The shore was as peaceful and quiet as it must have been before men came, and as it will be when they leave. The river has never changed; now the shores regained some of their primeval simplicity.

The crest was 69.2 feet, about sixty feet higher than the level of low water. This was reached on March 8. It was a somber day, but as darkness fell, the clouds rolled away and we saw the bright evening star on the ridge of the hill. By morning the river had fallen an inch or two.

3

The river is a world in itself, separated from the country through which it flows by invisible walls. Its seasons are not the same as those of the country inland. The river air is softer, a little misty always, except in those times when all the land is scoured by the north wind. Even then, if the shantyboater has chosen his winter harbor well, the wind roars through the trees overhead, and the sun warms his sheltered deck.

When we first came to the river in autumn, the brilliant coloring and stark contrast of the hills were left behind. The green willows changed to gold, faded and scattered their thin leaves as imperceptibly as the course of the sun moved southward. On sunny days the pale yellow shores seemed afloat on the heavy blue water. In the mild air, the migrating birds lingered, softly whistling fragments of their summer songs.

In the nights of summer and autumn, the colder air descended to the river, and we enjoyed a little summer fire when it would be unthought of on the hilltops. In cold weather, however, the water tempers the air. Riverbank gardens often flourish long after the first official frost. Snow melts sooner there, and the river road is bare when the higher roads are coated with ice.

It was a peculiar springtime along the river after the flood. While the hills and fields were becoming green with opening buds and new grass, the receding waters left a dead shore. The stark, muddy trees were draped with trash which floated into them at different levels. The banks were slimy as the primeval shores, and the odor of spring, there, was the odor of decay. Yet the river elms were the first to show a tinge of warmth in their black ranks, and along the creeks the maples flowered before one suspected that spring was astir.

The tips of trees which were above water had sprouted green buds, but the lower branches were lifeless after the river fell. The crest of the flood was marked by a distinct line, spring above and winter below. Slowly the lower part began to show the fresh green of spring, but by then it was early summer above. We found a little redbud tree below the flood line, where none should be, flowering long after the redbuds had faded from the hillsides.

The most natural undertaking at this season is a garden, and it was more by instinct than design that we went up on the hillside above the railroad, since the riverbank would not be dry enough for several weeks, and tentatively cleared a little patch of ground. The owner was unknown to us, but he must have been easygoing and tolerant, for no one ever questioned our gardening there, any more than they had our squatting on the riverbank. We burned the brush and dry weeds, removed some of the stones and bricks which were remnants of an old house that once stood there. The soil was rich and black, for the original forest, which still flourished on the higher slopes, had once extended almost down to the river.

It was pleasant to work up there on the green hillside, away from the desolation which surrounded the boat, looking over the wide river where wind and swirling current made an ever-changing pattern. The warm sun stirred us as it did the growing things, and we responded by

56

extending our garden. We planted lettuce, spinach, peas, beets, and carrots, a little early for some of it, perhaps, with cold rains and frost almost sure to come. Experience has taught us little, for we are still "sooners." Often it pays, the earlier plantings doing as well, or better, than the more cautious later ones.

Our riverbank gardens in succeeding years have been almost as haphazard as this first one. When we are drifting down the river in the wintertime, absorbed in our voyage and the strange shores we pass or linger at, a garden, if thought of at all, is so remote that we even consider drifting on through the summer, or at least until late spring. But when the first warm days come, we begin to pick out possible garden sites, only in fun, of course. At length, however, we give way to the influence of the spring sun, and the desire for some fresh green lettuce, and think seriously about gardening.

It has not been difficult to find a suitable place even in a strange country. There are marginal bits of land everywhere and good-natured, generous owners who are glad to see it put to use. Extra work is usually required to clear the ground and keep down weeds, and there is the risk of an unexpected summer overflow, but the reward is a rich, vigorous soil, needing no fertilizer, and the satisfaction which must always be attendant on making waste land bear fruit.

The river receded by inches at first, but when the fall was well under way, the level dropped four or five feet overnight. Then the boatman must be vigilant, often getting up in the night to spar off. We descended the steep bank shifting our lines from one tree to another, the same ones to which we had tied on the way up, and were soon in accustomed surroundings. The high levels of the flood now belonged to the past, to be talked of and wondered at.

One morning the familiar whistle of Number Eight was heard, and the railroad was soon operating as usual, though the trains ran slow where the embankment had been weakened by the water. There was a soft stretch of track near us, and an extra force of Negroes was brought in to raise the rails to their former level. They sang at their work, and when they lined up the rails, all heaved in unison, kept together by the chant of the leader, the whole gang shouting as chorus with each pull at the crowbars. The words of their song were known only to them.

The railroad was as busy as other flood victims, repairing damages and tidying up its premises. Work trains went back and forth, and many carloads of clean ballast were spread. A crane was moved along the outside track, to pick up runaway ties and timbers that might have lodged within its reach. I had towed in from the swift current several new timbers and a chest which contained cans of oil. The railroad gathered up all this property of theirs, though the timbers were still tied. This was perhaps violating a river law, written or unwritten, that any drift which is tied up belongs to the man who tied it there. We made no claim for salvage, and were glad to be of some small service to the railroad, which we regarded as our benefactor. Even though we did not pick up the coal which it scattered about, we were glad to burn some of the old crossties which it rolled over the bank, seemingly for our use. If we wanted some weights for our fish line, in a short walk along the track we could pick up enough taps and spikes, and no telling what other treasure, fallen from a passing train. And I still keep my saws from rusting with some of the oil which the floating cans contained.

As the river fell, new islands of drift were stranded on shore. The attraction of prospecting was felt as we searched through this wrack of trees, logs, timbers, cornstalks, and the debris of civilization which had been washed into the river, or thrown into it. I found an adze handle, a new one, just after I had acquired the head of an adze and was looking about for a stick from which to fashion a handle. A battered old chest turned out to be white pine, the top being a board twenty inches wide. It made a splendid table top because of its lightness and beautiful surface. In the flat bottomland across the river, collected against a line of trees, was the largest field of drift I ever saw. Some of it had floated out of the amusement park above, and the picking was good. I found some planks and boards which later went into a roof over the deck, and we still have our "Coney Island chair," a broken folding chair which we get out for the third extra guest.

Besides the garden, another rite of spring is the gathering of wild greens. We had long desired to be initiated into this, and were glad to trail along after Sadie and Donald when they went for a mess. Sadie had an old-fashioned, country background, having spent her early years ashore in some upriver hamlet, and was well versed in the art, knowing what could be eaten and what should be avoided, the habitat of each variety, and the best proportions for a tasty mixture. The top authority of the neighborhood was Aunt Mary, to whom Sadie would sometimes take a specimen for positive identification. We walked along the open hillside, picking wild beet, white top, narrow dock, shepherd's sprout or hen pepper, and rock lettuce which looked like chicory. We learned there is a difference in dandelions, the lacy, many-leaved kind being the sweetest and most desirable. "Anything that bleeds milk when you break its stalk is good to eat," said Sadie. Probably few plants cannot be eaten, but some have doubtful value and flavor. One of the best greens was shawny, or milkweed, a slender plant with tender leaves and stem and a delicate flavor. This grew in the woods and we sought our dinner among the yellow violets and trillium. Later we learned that trillium was good to eat. Here also Sadie picked deer-tongue, which was the dog-toothed violet, and a few leaves of bloodroot which she called p'coon. This and "wooly-britches" were added for their medicinal value. Some squaw cabbage was found, but this must be used sparingly on account of its strong, bitey taste.

At dinner we found that our mess of greens was good, and all during the spring it was one of our regular dishes. The gathering of it meant an excursion into the fields and woods, from which we always brought back something in addition to our sack of greens. Later pokeweed was added to the list, and this became our staple spring vegetable.

As we drifted into new regions and became acquainted with greens-gathering natives, usually old ladies whom it was a pleasure to know for other reasons, we learned new kinds of weeds that could be eaten, such as mountain sprout, Indian corn, and sandbar greens.

Without doubt there are many wild plants of high food value and excellent flavor which are neglected or unknown. Our two examples are poke and groundnuts. We consider poke the equal of any garden vegetable, and in taking advantage of this profuse crop we avoid all the toil of cultivation and protection required by garden vegetables. From a hunter who had a part Indian grandmother we learned how

59

delicious poke is when the tender sprouts are split, dipped in cornmeal and fried. The groundnuts are little potatoes the size of walnuts. They grow along the moist sandy river shore, in long strings, each nut separated from the next by an inch or two of root. One spring when we ran out of potatoes, and could not get to a store for a while, we used groundnuts and found that they answered very well.

In that first winter afloat we began to acquire the ability to live at ease and relaxed on the unstable water. Also we learned much about the nature of a river life, how uncertain and everchanging it is, how unpredictable. The oldest and most experienced riverman cannot tell what will come next. The river puts a strain on every shantyboater. Some give way under it and become afraid of the river. We have felt a touch of this at times. But for our enthusiasm, that first winter might have been a trying one. The strangeness of living on the water was accentuated by the almost unknown, almost forbidding river of winter, and by its rising to a high flood. Nor was our boat as comfortable as it was to become when the cabin in all details was completed, a roof constructed over the main deck, and glass put in all the windows and doors. We were roughing it then compared with later winters, yet that is not how we regarded it at the time. The spell of the river was upon us. Our new life was so enthralling that we felt no longing for an end to winter.

To me spring has always been a season of disturbance in which the simple design of winter is shattered and replaced by a complexity which is almost chaos. So much to see and listen for, so much to learn, if one gave all his days to it—and it would be a worth-while dedication of them—he could not keep up with the flowering of spring. Yet being now so much under the open sky, and engaged in activities which did not interfere, I felt less than ever before that the spring was passing unwatched.

With summer, the tension lessened. Even the river seemed to relax and it became the old familiar one that we had known before. As it fell back to normal levels, becoming more clear and gentle, it demanded less of us, and we gave our attention to some projects which were waiting this time for their accomplishment.

The main job of construction which we had in mind, one which would just about complete our boat, was a roof over the main deck. I had gathered up almost enough material for it from driftpiles, or picked it out of the river as it floated by. Old timers have told us of the many boards and timbers they used to catch drifting. It can be well understood, for in those days the banks of many streams were lined with sawmills. Certain high waters were called "timber rises" on account of the quantity of sawed stuff which floated by.

Unacquainted with those good days of the past, we were quite proud of the asserted collection of lumber we had gotten together piece by piece. For joists there were several two-by-sixes from a shipwrecked amusement device. The roof sheathing, of short unmatched pieces, gave a very shantyboat effect to our job. For corner posts we used four-by-fours which some upstate highway department had lost in a runout. Andy advised us merely to tack the bottoms of the corner posts to the deck so that in a collision, with a heavy branch when drifting, perhaps, the corner posts would give way and nothing would be broken. We adopted the opposite principle and made our posts very secure with belaying pins in them to fasten a line to.

Since the deck was higher than the cabin floor, the roof over the deck was, of course, higher than the cabin roof. We had the inspiration to extend the deck roof back over the cabin as far as the edge of the window below. By closing up the open end and sides the space between could be used for storage. This "between decks" has been valuable to us, being dry and easily accessible. That is, the front of

61

it is accessible; to get at anything in the back, you have to take out the front row of stuff. This must be done also to rout out an occasional rat who settles himself between decks and keeps us awake with his gnawing. The overlapping of the roofs improved the appearance of our boat, making the new construction an integral part of the design. Along with the large windows, it gave the boat an individual character quite different from the shantyboat usually seen on the river. However, if I were painting a picture in which there was a shantyboat, the boat would not be ours but one of those familiar craft with a sheer to hull and roof, a porch at each end, and two small windows in the cab.

On rainy days and at odd times we tinkered with our inside fixtures. The white-pine table top which came from the driftwood chest was made to hook into the wall under a window where it is convenient for Anna's work and a delightful place to eat our daylight meals. For our meals before the fireplace, one of the chests is pulled out from under the windows, and the table placed on it. At other times, the table fully set with dishes and food is carried onto the deck or out on the bank. When not in use, the table slips out of sight against a wall.

The interior arrangement followed the initial placing of the little cookstove in one corner, to the left as you step down from the main deck, and the fireplace diagonally opposite. The bookshelf is near the fireplace, where most of our reading is done. Below the bookshelf which is under a window on one side, are two storage chests which can easily be pulled out for benches. Cupboards with solid doors take up all the rest of the space under windows. The tops of the cupboards are wide oak boards which serve Anna as a working space. Beside the door as you come in is a convenient shelf for water buckets, one of river water, one of drinking water. To the other side of the door, above the stove is another cupboard, used for outdoor clothes. It is most handy to one going out or coming in, and damp clothing is dried by the heat of the stove. Across the other end of the cabin are two compartments, on each side of the door to the afterdeck. The one to the left is for clothing and Anna's 'cello; it is covered by a single curtain. To the right of the door is a space for storage and certain conveniences, which is entered from the step to the afterdeck. This step covers a woodbox for fireplace wood; it holds half a johnboat load. Wood for the cookstove is stored in the Russian ammunition box, also a step, to the main deck, and handy to the stove. A little corner across from the fireplace is my "office." It has a cluttered shelf for work in hand, a wooden box underneath containing painting materials, also useful as an extra seat. My easel is usually set up in this corner. It is little more than a flat board wedged between floor and carlings, and stored under the deck roof when not in use.

Every possible bit of space has been put to use, but our cabin does not seem crowded. The center of the floor is entirely open, nothing is standing around. In fact, one sees so few objects on entering that the effect is one of bareness, almost emptiness. One visiting riverman, coming while we were away, looked in the window and decided that we had moved out. The bare windows without a trace of draperies or shades carry out this impression, and make the room seem larger than it is.

The many problems of space arrangement which came up were like puzzles to work out, and often the solution was an ingenious one. Nothing is arbitrary or merely decorative. This shell which we built, or which grew around us, has become as efficient as that of the river mussel, and has almost as little waste space. A visitor does not see how intensively the space is developed. Many innocent objects have unexpected uses, and our guests require some training and instruction in

living with us. We sometimes think of our boat in the hands of a stranger. He would come upon puzzling contraptions and unexpected compartments one after another. The boat would fall apart with some of its secrets undiscovered.

Before the spring was far advanced we acquired more land for gardening. It was down the river perhaps a third of a mile, a level tract of good loamy soil above the flood level. Of late, Dellie had made her garden there, but this year she announced her intention of giving it up. As there were no other claimants, we said that we would take it over. One April morning we dropped down the river in the johnboat to our new garden, the first of many trips. First we cleared a path up from the landing. On a little terrace at the end of the garden we built a fire and had a camp breakfast, surveying meanwhile our new domain and planning how to divide it. We gradually cleared and broke up most of the open ground. Here our main crops were raised, the railroad garden being mostly early stuff. The short voyage down and back from our boat never became in the least monotonous. It was fun to load our produce into the johnboat and row back. Every stone and snag became familiar as we followed the shore closely against the current. Once I saw a wood duck with her brood, but could never find them again.

On our way back and forth we passed a heavy concrete pedestal, weathered and vine-covered like the tower of a ruined castle. Its base was almost in the river, its top level with the railroad. This was "the whirly." No trace remained of the revolving crane which had once operated there. The crane unloaded logs from flatcars on a railroad siding, and, spinning around in a half circle, dropped them into the river, or close to its edge. The logs were then made into rafts and towed to the waterfront sawmills of Cincinnati by some small, almost forgotten steamboats. I remember the *Karlina, J. M. Grubbs, J. R. Ware* —boy-size towboats; as well as the raft towboats *Crown Hill* and *J. O. Cole.*

The log roll was a busy place then, and the chance for work had attracted many shantyboaters. When the mountain timber played out, the enterprise was abandoned. The river people drifted on, or found other work, and our neighbor, Andy, wrecked the machinery of the crane for junk.

In the time of the whirly, a house for workmen had stood nearby. The ruins of its foundation were at the edge of our garden. Perhaps the ground had first been cleared by the log rollers. At any rate, we called our new plot the log-roll garden.

In the earlier days of logging, when timber stood on the mountain tributaries, the rafts had been made up there, and drifted or towed downstream. So many were tied up waiting their turn at the mill that the shores seemed to be lined with an endless log raft. We came upon an early connection which Brent had with logging. The first name of the place was Willison's Landing. Neely Willison, an old-time wood-working craftsman, told us that the rafters often slept in his father's log house on the river shore. Their pistols were placed on the mantle in a long row before the men stretched out on the floor to sleep. They joked with the boy, for Neely was a stripling then, urging him to

65

come up to the mountains and make a trip with them, saying they would save him an oar.

The last bit of logging at Brent was done by a shantyboater named Morton, and his gangling boys. They rigged up a hoist on the end of a small flat, a crude sort of derrick boat, and raised many sunken logs below the whirly. Most of the logs were sound, even after years under water. They were too heavy to raise out of the water, so the Mortons lashed them alongside their flat and decrepit stern-wheel gas boat. In this manner the logs were towed up the river fifty miles to Ripley, the nearest riverbank sawmill. It is not likely that much profit was made, but this is the kind of work that shantyboaters like. In this case, they even thought of it themselves.

Another phase of summer began when a calliope was heard, and the excursion steamer, *Island Queen,* came up around the bend on her first trip to Coney Island from Cincinnati. The dread day was now upon us, for Coney Island lay almost directly across the river. It would be a lively place for the rest of the summer, and the *Island Queen* would make several trips each day. We resented all the disturbance this would bring with it—noise and lights and the gaudiness of carnival. We feared the spell of the river would be broken.

The *Island Queen* was one of the last side-wheelers on the river, and the sound of her enclosed wheels, a peculiar pounding which seemed to rise and fall, brought to mind the old *Greenland* and *Bonanza*. Aside from this and her deep-toned whistle, which had been handed down from an older boat, the *Queen* had no charms for us. As the days went by, her coming and going bothered us not as much as we expected, and before long she was part of the scheme of things.

The rocking of our boat by her "dead swells" was a nuisance in low water. These long smooth waves continued even after the steamer was tied up. Farther offshore they were high rollers, and we sometimes took them in our johnboat or swam in their path.

Coney Island was secluded in a thick grove of huge maples, and we saw little more than was in evidence previous to her opening—the imitation lighthouse at the entrance gate above the boat landing, and behind the trees a green and white striped standpipe. The noise was bad at times. Surely the loud speaker is a contrivance of the devil, an unjust infliction on the innocent and helpless. The lights at night were distracting, too, but we had never enjoyed real darkness. On the thickest nights there was a glow from the floodlights at the railroad yards, or reflected light from the distant city. The unalloyed darkness of night is rare, in this world, perhaps beyond the experience of many.

There were good points to Coney Island. Work in the park in summer accounted for a large part of some river incomes. Andy had been night watchman there for a long time, rowing across to work in the summer sunset. This year Donald had begun early in the spring with the clean-up squad after the flood. Other boys and girls worked there and they made the first crossing of the Brent ferry a lively one. This ferry was a sort of miniature *Island Queen,* operating only during the park season. It bore the intriguing name of *Ferry Queen.*

Like everyone else we enjoyed the Fourth of July fireworks at Coney Island. The rockets rose above the dark line of trees, their slowing curve reflected in the water. Suddenly, with their bursting, sky and river were transformed by flashes of colored light and the hills re-echoed as with the booming of cannon. Some of our friends came down to see the spectacle, which seemed to be for our special entertainment.

The *Island Queen* helped us in an unexpected way. While we never used it as a means of transportation to the city, as we might have, it afforded a novel and pleasant way for some of our guests to come and see us. We would row across to meet them in the johnboat, and later ferry them over again for the return trip. As they waved at us from the upper deck, the *Island Queen* loomed as huge as an ocean liner.

It was well that Skipper's first litter of pups came in the summer, for wintertime puppies on our small boat are something of a nuisance. After repeated experiences we learned to handle the puppies better, but that first batch gave us great concern. Skipper, on the other hand, was so wise and knowing, that one would never have believed it was a new experience for her. A devoted mother, too, keeping her six infants as clean as pins, and fiercely attacking her pal, Ring, when he looked in the door. Yet she lived her own life, leaving her family to go out with us, or to make expeditions of her own. She knew just how long she could stay away: the pups were always quiet until she returned.

They were born behind the cookstove, after some preliminary scouting on Skipper's part for a likely place on the bank. We noticed this on later occasions, but the domestic feeling was always stronger than the instinct to go into the wilderness.

The puppies were a great amusement for us when they got their eyes open and could scoot around the floor. They had a little house and pen on shore in a shady place, but while they were still small we would bring them down to the boat in the evening. Then it was a general roughhouse and we always had to fish one or two out of a bilge hole before they settled down to sleep. They slept on board until almost grown-up. We had to put up side boards to our own bed or they would all be in with us before morning.

There was one a little different, with longer hair, and so large that we at once named her Sadie. She was bold and strong, always up to something, the first one to climb over the fence. Soon they were all over the bank, spending most of their time trying to cross the stage-board. It was funny to see them after they had crawled part way out, frightened at being so high above the water, scrooching down and taking careful steps. When nearly to the deck, they abandoned all caution, and made a leap for it. This often landed them in the water, but a soaking never seemed to hurt them, and they swam when still tiny things.

We wanted to keep all the pups, but realizing that we could not set this precedent, we gave away as many as we could find homes for. Two or three were still left with us, and we all had a good time that summer.

The garden began to supply us with vegetables early in the summer. Green peas, lettuce, and spinach, from your own garden—here one can taste the springtime. Anna often made a salad of all the young, tender leaves in the garden, and beet and carrot tops from the rows that needed thinning. Soon the carrots were large enough to eat, and the tiny beets could be boiled with their greens. Encouraged by all this, we were anxious to do some fishing and take advantage of the food that swam under us. This would be as natural as gathering greens from the hillside and more direct than raising beans and potatoes.

I am not a true fisherman. Many are drawn to the river by a desire to fish, but this was not even a minor reason for my becoming a shantyboater. Perhaps it could be said, since I am not a thorough fisherman, that I am not a genuine river rat. I have become a consistent fisherman, but only because fish are so valuable to us. I enjoy it, too, but all the pleasure of fishing does not come from catching fish.

To make a beginning, our hopes lay in Andy. He was a real fisherman, and it was fishing that first attracted him to the river. This was in his early days when he was working in the coal mines, soon after his arrival in this country from Germany. At Brent he still used his bank cap and miner's carbide lamp for night fishing.

We were pleased when Andy promised to help us, and we bought the specified hooks and two sizes of cotton twine. After a long delay, waiting for the June rise to be over, and, I think, because Andy was somewhat reluctant, after all, to give away his secrets, we put out a trot line.

First there had been some preparatory work. Andy "stagin'd" about fifty hooks, showing us the clever way in which he tied each hook to a short piece of light twine he called a staging. Then we selected two

heavy anchor stones of the right weight and shape, for Andy was particular about details, cutting shallow notches in them so the line would not slip off. For a buoy, a square gallon can was preferred, though a jug or block of wood could be used just as well. A few small weights were the last requirement.

One evening Andy and I went out in our johnboat with this equipment and a bucket of live minnows for bait. One end of the heavy line was tied to a stone, which was dropped overboard some distance off shore. As I rowed out into the river, holding against the current, Andy payed out the line. He soon tied on another piece of heavy twine to which the buoy can was fastened. This was tossed overboard. When the other end of the main line was reached, it was tied to the second stone, and that was heaved overboard far out into the river. Thus the line lay on the river bottom, stretched between the two stones, at right angles to the current.

We now rowed over to the buoy can, and raising the line to the surface, tied on the "stagin'd" hooks, about three feet apart. A live minnow was strung on each hook in a peculiar way that was Andy's secret. Weights were attached at intervals to hold the line on the bottom. When all the hooks were tied on, the line was let go, and we rowed back to shore.

Next morning when we traced our line I was surprised to find several nice catfish on it. Andy took it as a matter of course. When we got back to shore, Andy began catching minnows, and putting them in a floating box, ready for use in the evening. We let our line rest during the day, for Andy's experience had been that not enough fish could be caught then to make it worth while to bait up in the daytime. The minnows were caught in a glass trap, a jug-shaped affair with a glass

funnel built into the large end. The trap was placed in shallow water near shore where the slow current fed out the bread crumbs which had been put in it for bait. It was quite effective if you set it out where and when the minnows were running.

This kind of fishing, with a trot line, is generally practiced around Brent. As we went down the river we found many variations of it, and also new methods of which we had never heard.

We were delighted to have some fish, and put into service a live box I had found in the drift, tying it to our boat in true shantyboat style. Fishing now became a daily chore for all of us, and a satisfactory division of labor worked itself out. Andy, or Sadie, caught the minnows, using their precious glass trap. They could not have been more careful of the Ark, removing all nearby stones, and sitting by in a shady place ready to snatch it up if threatened by waves from a passing boat. Occasionally the minnows must be emptied out and fresh bait put in. As this was often done by little Jerry, his grandson, Andy's contemplation of the river would be undisturbed for hours.

Our part was to supply all equipment and do all the heavy work—rowing, tracing the line mornings, for the fogs bothered Andy, and baiting the line in cool or wet weather.

The fish we caught were mostly catfish. There were channel cats, mud cats, and some light blue ones which Andy called, correctly, Mississippi blue cats. None of these were large, the average being a pound, perhaps. The largest we caught that summer weighed four pounds.

Fish became a main part of our diet. They still are. When they are available, which means a large part of the year, we eat them day after day, always with relish. The dogs eat fish, too, and the heads and trimmings cooked with vegetables and cereal. We soon experimented with smoking fish, making a smokehouse out of an oil drum. Smoked catfish turned out to be a delicacy, but perhaps smoked eel is best of all.

71

We canned fish for winter use, dried, and salted them. Anna has learned and invented many ways of cooking fish, and can even make a tasty dish out of gar.

From our observation, river people seldom eat fish. We never became acquainted with a boat which consumed as much fish as ours does. Farmers and Negroes seem to be the most fish-hungry. Our partners at Brent were no exception to the rule, and only now and then did Sadie cook a few perch for Andy.

Soon there was a surplus of fish in our box. We gave some to our friends, and Sadie, who was an old hand at the business, said we must sell some. When the word got around in the neighborhood, we soon had all the customers we could take care of. It was a nuisance at times, but we enjoyed our fish buyers, and made some good friends among the farmers, railroaders, and retired boatmen who came down to the boat. Sadie's salesmanship was worth listening to, over and over. If the fish were large, she praised their size. Of the small ones she would say, "Them's the kind we eat, sweetest of all. Hold him tight, Harlan, or he'll fin you."

At the end of the summer our share of the take was $67. We figured that by giving most of our time to the work, having four or five lines out instead of one or two, we could have earned, clear, more than $400. This would be a small income, but our overhead was small, and after all, $400 would last a long time on the river.

I enjoyed the fishing that summer. It was sweet to head out into the river in the summer dawn, through the rising mist, or perhaps a fog so thick that one must steer by the sound of roosters' crowing, or a Carolina wren, or a passing train. As we sat out there in the twilight, baiting up, shore sounds came to us over the water—children playing, their mother calling them in, the mooing of a cow, or barking of a dog. A steamboat comes up in the distance, columns of smoke rising from her stacks. You raise your eyes now and then, trying to judge whether you will be finished baiting before she reaches you. Or you see another fisherman tracing his line—a tall figure standing in the end of a john-boat, a boy with a steering oar in the stern. As the sunset fades, you smell the night coming on; the roar of water over the dam becomes louder, and the last evening song of the thrush comes from the hillside.

Life flowed back into Andy when he was out fishing. As he deftly baited hooks, he told many yarns about the river—about fishermen, steamboats, steamboat whistles, and some of his own experiences. He had traveled up and down the river, far up tributaries which were known to us only by name. He towed his houseboat with a little gasoline stern-wheeler, one of many he had built. One room of his boat was fitted up as a store, a sort of condensed dime store, with tin cups, dishes, notions, and such. He would trade with the natives for junk which he carried in a small flat alongside and sold in the first large city he came to. Andy had done much drifting and had a special little flat for his "beadle" hounds. One of these dogs, when he felt the urge, would swim ashore to hunt, and Andy would hear him as he coursed the hills. Later the dog would swim out to the boat when far below. We have often wished that our dogs would learn to do this.

Andy said that bigger fish could be caught by baiting up a second time after dark, and talked me into going out on the line during the night. All the rest of the summer I crawled out of bed at whatever time I happened to wake up, and rowed out into the dark. I picked up the buoy can by nocturnal landmarks, and took off what fish there were, then baited up in the light of a miner's lamp worn on my cap, for I had acquired one like Andy's. When finished, I put out the light, and rowing slowly back, watched Cassiopeia rising in the eastern sky. She seemed to draw up her fish line, which was Perseus, with the misty Pleiades as bait, and bright Venus caught. All was growing dim in the faint beginning of dawn. Then I felt I was fishing with the One who made the river and set it flowing. I felt its length and sinuous curving, fed by swift streams in the wooded mountains, and somewhere, after a long course through country unknown to me except by hearsay, past the mouths of new rivers and strange towns, it would at last enter an ocean and lose its identity, as I would, too, at the end of my devious drifting.

Fish have been a valuable commodity for bartering with farmers. All along the river they have served as an introduction in a new place, made friends for us, procured milk, eggs, bacon, and other country produce, the value of which seemed far greater than that of the fish we gave for it. At Brent we had already established such relations with a farm family. They lived in a gaunt, frame house which had looked out over the river for many years. It was of a type common along the Ohio. The broad side of the house faced the river, with windows on each side of a central door; in the upper story a row of five equal windows; a chimney on each gable end, the blank weatherboarding of which was broken only by the back of the broad stone fireplace. This, however, was flush with the wall. Such houses were often built of brick, handmade on the premises. As one goes by on the river, their simple dignity and beautiful proportions make them an adornment to the landscape, and they recall the days of the steamboat with which they were contemporary.

The Wilmer family, which lived in this house, was an odd collection of brothers and sisters. All were river-minded: they watched every craft that passed, and waved at many a friendly riverman. Tony Wilmer had worked on boats, sand diggers mostly. His voyaging had taken him as far down the Mississippi as Baton Rouge, and from him we had our first eyewitness account of the Father of Waters. Like river-

74

men we were to meet later, he spoke no good of the Mississippi. However, we felt the same attraction to it that had caused many a man, in the old days, to build a flatboat and drift down to that dread stream, and follow its treacherous course to the sunny land it led to, far in the south.

All through this summer at Brent I went daily to the Wilmers', riding up the road on my bicycle, a mile each way. After exchanging a few words at the barn or in the kitchen, I brought back a gallon of whole milk, and a carrier full of drinking water from their deep well. Once a week, or oftener, I took them a mess of catfish. One quart of the milk went to Sadie, but Anna and I consumed the other three. Having only the most primitive ways of keeping it cool, there was an abundance of sour milk for cooking and cottage cheese, and some for the dogs. This was country milk, of which town milk is only a weak and expensive imitation.

We feel close to farmers. They are often our nearest neighbors, since we seldom stay long enough in the vicinity of a town to become acquainted there. Some of the farm people we have met along the way have become our good friends, and our passage is marked by an increasing list of correspondents keenly interested in our travels down the river, which is a fearsome unknown to most of them. They write to us about their families and crops, changes in the neighborhood, all so intimately that we are sometimes confused as to where our home is.

It was fortunate for us that when we really needed help we were in a farm community. The kindness and hospitality shown then to the strangers who had drifted to their shores make an amazing chapter in our story.

Our gardening brings us closer to farmers, too. Through it we have become aware of the forces with which one must struggle in trying to raise any crop, however small. The earth prefers to grow horseweeds and wild sunflowers, it seems, and must be persuaded to raise cabbages and potatoes. The tender plants require protection from insects and animals. The weather is seldom right. We admire the patience and cheerfulness with which farmers go on planting year after year, in the face of all the hazards. They accept loss as a matter of course, and are content if, in the end, there is enough to carry them over until the next season.

It might be said that this is a dark view of farming, or gardening, but our gardening, at least, goes to extremes. At times, with disaster striking one crop after another, it looks as if there would be nothing to harvest. A few days later, after a rain, perhaps, or an unexpected recovery of some planting which had appeared hopeless, our spirits, and with them the whole garden, revive and flourish anew.

Fishing and gardening supply much of our food. There is another source—our foraging and gleaning of the countryside. This is a common practice of shantyboaters, who are like gypsies in many ways. Neither class is rated very high and some river people have been known to take more than the two rows next to the river which an unwritten law has allotted them. We draw a sharp line between taking anything the owner of the land might use to advantage, and picking up what he has left or discarded. I feel sure that no one ever missed the contents of our sack or bucket, and we should be credited with salvaging much that would have wasted except for our gleaning. If the rhubarb bed the farmer had plowed under put forth some shoots among the oats, or if the abandoned raspberry patch bore fruit, we gathered it up without compunction, and without asking any questions.

Most of the crops which we harvest abroad, however, are wild ones, flourishing with no man's care, on neglected and worn-out fields, along the roads and creeks. Our year is marked by their ripening. At Brent the first wild greens appeared in March. Wild asparagus early in April. We call it wild, but it might have escaped from cultivation, for it grew only along certain roadsides. Wild strawberries ripened just before the cultivated ones, late in May. It was past the middle of June before the black raspberries could be picked. Before they disappeared, dewberries came in. They in turn overlapped the blackberry season, which extended from mid-July through August. Blackberries were the most abundant berry crop, and we canned many quarts of them.

In the meantime we had picked apples under neglected trees. There was a scrubby peach tree in a thicket of sumac, along the railroad, near our log-roll garden. This year it happened to produce some beautiful peaches. We watched them anxiously, hoping they would not be discovered by strangers and picked while unripe. We knew that no one in the neighborhood would touch them for our right was acknowledged, since the tree was near "our" garden. Fortunately we were able to harvest the whole crop, about three pecks, picking each morning the onces that were ripe, or almost so. They were excellent fruit, of the same source, no doubt, as Thoreau's Railroad Apple.

It was not a good "plum year," when the wild plum thickets produce fruit, but there are always elderberries. Often neglected in the abundance of larger fruit, elderberries have undeveloped potentialities. Pawpaws, so aptly described by their family name, custard apple, were ripe early in the fall. About the first of October the winter pears matured, though hard as stones. They were abundant around Brent, lining some roads, to the advantage of the passer-by. For our pears, however, we went to the hilltop orchard of our friendly mail carrier, and picked several bushels of them. Carefully sorted, packed in an abandoned fish box, on the riverbank, and covered with leaves, they kept well into the winter. A ripe Kiefer pear is one of the delicacies of the earth.

Persimmons are the last wild fruit to ripen. There must be other crops that could be harvested all winter, roots to dig, acorns and nuts to gather. Walnuts have long been an important food with us, and hickory nuts when we can find them.

Donald picked up his walnuts along the river's edge, for many are washed down from the hills during the fall rains. Pumpkins are a freshet crop, and we retrieved a number of them as they floated by on their way down the river. Their native field was perhaps far up some unknown creek. One pumpkin was a prize winner, so large and deeply colored that I first thought it was a bushel basket as it floated toward us. Corn is another river harvest. If the river rises suddenly early in the fall, whole shocks are floated away to become the property of anyone who rescues them. In a flooded cornfield across the river, Donald and I harvested several rows from our johnboat just before the river covered the stalks.

Food that you have grown yourself, or that has some adventure or story connected with the procuring of it, has a spice and flavor that merely purchased food can never have. In actual quality, too, it is superior, perhaps not in size or perfection of growth, but in character. Think of wild strawberries compared with the commercial variety which is so large and perfect, and almost tasteless; or green asparagus tips; or freshly picked corn compared with what you buy. The apples we bring in might be wormy and imperfect, but they might also have the tang of an old variety which is no longer grown because newer kinds are better shippers.

This roaming over the fields and woods, gathering a portion here and there of the harvest, often so lavish, which no man has planted or cared for, relates to a state prior to the farmer. In so doing one approaches the natural man. The restrictions and divisions of society vanish. What paltry affairs to be concerned with on this wild earth, for the earth is yet as wild as on the day of its creation. Sometimes, it is true, my exaltation has been jolted by the appearance of the landowner, who wanted to know where I was going. I would quickly gather myself up, and such encounters were invariably friendly.

I made gleanings, too, which were far different from those I had set out to find. My eyes roamed the earth's uneven surface, feeling each slant and texture, or into the sky among its titanic sculptures. Nowhere was chaos, but all was bound up in a harmony which was so strongly felt at times that the scene before me seemed no longer earthly.

It was good to be among the hills and breathe the dry, scented air. We realized that the river world was not all. One summer twilight, when Anna and I were returning to the boat with our berry buckets full, walking down a road which descended the winding hollow to the river, we thought we heard a distant whip-poor-will. This was strange, for we had not heard a whip-poor-will in this section all summer. We stopped to listen, by chance under a tall pine before a gloomy house. Other bird voices seemed to come to us from far off, a cardinal, a jay, and a Carolina wren. Then we discovered that the source of all this music was directly overhead where a mockingbird was softly singing in the dark pine.

The change from summer to fall was marked in many ways. Coney Island became quiet and dark, the *Island Queen* appeared no more, and the little *Ferry Queen* went down the river to her winter quarters.

The river was deserted, these fairest days of the year, except by those who belonged there. We considered ourselves among the permanent residents now, since we had lived a full year on the river.

Out tracing our trot line, we watched the progress of autumn on the shores. The glowing hills up and down the valley were a spectacle we had missed the previous fall, being landbound. The johnboat would make the winter easier for us, too. And the cabin would be more comfortable with battens on all the cracks and a roof over the deck. Our hold was stocked with canned stuff, all from our garden and foraging. We liked to show this to people, raising a hinged section of the floor and revealing the ranks of jars.

The voyage down the river was ever in our minds. We had expected to be ready for it by this fall, but the time was not yet ripe. Another full year was to pass before our casting off. Far from being vexed at this postponement, we were content, even glad, to remain at our Brent anchorage.

Soon the geese were flying overhead, ducks and gulls appeared on the river. I helped the Detisches replace some of their old bottom planking. The sound of the caulking iron was heard again. Early in November there was a sharp freeze, and then began the rains of winter. The river became swift and muddy, the November rise was on, and summer far in the past.

4

It might be said that the river flowing by is the present time, upriver is the past, and downstream lies the future.

In the past with us was the country locked in the enfolding hills upstream. It had once been the promised land, the goal of many river excursions made when we were living on the hilltop. Our frontier had been gradually extended upriver as we sought new and unworn shores, until at last it was necessary to board a train at Brent and ride an hour to reach the place where our canoe was kept.

Through the metamorphosis of all things caused by our coming to live on the river, Brent had taken on a new meaning. We were content within its limits, and felt no longing to visit distant fields. Though we went no more to the beloved country upriver, we were reminded of it each morning by the passing of Number Eight. It blew for Brent with a soft-toned whistle that meant river almost as much as the steamboat whistles. The train passed on, and we followed it in our minds as it whistled its way up the valley, making all stops—New Richmond Station, California (Kentucky), Mentor, Ivor (across the river from Moscow), Carntown, Foster, Chilo Station, Wellsburg, Augusta, Dover, Ripley Station, and Maysville, fifty miles away. Beyond were faraway places like Cabin Creek and Vanceburg, out of our regular orbit.

Passengers were rare at the Brent station, and the agent, whose business was almost entirely with freight cars put off at the siding, made hard work of selling a ticket. Number Eight seldom came to a full stop. In winter, the station was not even open when the train came through. Once in the darkness of a winter dawn I flagged it down myself by waving a burning brand from a bonfire I had started by the track.

Before we became shantyboaters, Anna and I used to ride on Number Eight to Wellsburg, a remnant of a town in Bracken County. After a sail or paddle on the river, up Bullskin or Big Locust Creek, and a visit with some of Cord Smith's clan, all more or less shantyboaters, we returned in the evening on Number Seven, the westbound version of Number Eight. To us, weary and often cold, its obsolete coaches seemed to offer the utmost in luxury and comfort.

This train ride was a sort of condensed river trip. The tracks followed the river, which was often in sight. Sometimes we looked down on a towboat and barges which had passed Brent half a day before. At Foster on the outside of a curve, there was a long view up the river, beyond the low waterfall of the dam at Chilo, to distant blue hills.

Several ferries connected the railroad with towns on the other side of the river. The ferryboat might be only a skiff in which the mail was rowed across. There still survived two or three steam ferries, a type of boat almost extinct. The one at Augusta was a beautiful craft, having a tall stack, stern wheel, and steamboat pilothouse. This ferry landed broadside at a floating dock, and vehicles were carried on the forward part of the deck. At New Richmond was a side-wheeler with an open driveway down the center. Landing behind a point where there was no current, it lowered a sort of drawbridge over which the cars drove on board. They disembarked from the other end where there was a similar drawbridge. The boat was designed to run in either direction, with the forward apron raised, the after one trailing. Be-

81

cause of some mechanical deficiency, the boat would run in only one way, and on one trip across it must turn around twice, or else the cars would have to back off.

Most of these little river towns are today of no importance, are even without reason for existence. They dwindle with each flood, some having been almost destroyed in the disaster of 1937. In the days of the horse and steamboat, each town was a thriving, self-sufficient community with retail stores and local industries, a center for the surrounding farm country. Today most of the towns have moved to the highway which runs back near the hills. Still, off toward the river, among the massive water maples, stand the old buildings. They look out from their quiet and grassy streets on the empty river which was the highway of their day. To the traveler on the river, all that can be seen of these towns now are the ancient facades and cornices, a church steeple or cupola of the same period rising above the trees. It looks like a steamboat might still touch there daily. Only life is lacking, a busy landing with teams and wagons on the grade, a wharfboat, flourishing business. Yet in these latter days the weathered buildings, like old people resting, have such an air of contentment and repose that surely they have no regrets, no longing for the stirring times they once knew.

I was born with a love for the river. My earliest memory is the sight of it in winter, choked with grinding, convulsive ice. As soon as I was old enough I tagged after my older brothers to the river, whenever they would let me. Even then my thoughts turned upriver, perhaps because of my brothers' summer camp near Twelve Mile Creek. Too young to be a full-time camper, my mother took me there for single ecstatic days. Camp was near a station on the C & O called Oneonta, of which today perhaps only the memory remains. To reach it we boarded the morning accommodation, ancestor of Number Eight. The old train had bright orange coaches, but otherwise today's train is much the same—a light, graceful engine, cars with plush seats, and cinders coming in the windows.

A great moment at camp was the landing of the packet *Courier*, a thrilling sight as she rounded to, the bawling of calves on board added to the stirring, exotic noises of a steamboat. How proud I was to hear that the pilots used our campfire as a mark for landing at night.

It might have been the steamboats which drew my attention up the river. They passed upstream in the evening, bound for legendary places —Pomeroy, Charleston, Gallipolis, and Point Pleasant. Downstream they ran only to Cincinnati, which was then the end of the river to me. These boats could not be compared with the grand steamboats of the golden age. Though old and shabby, and fallen into unprosperous days, these last survivors of a proud tradition had about them a dignity and grace which are gone from today's river. The old packets have all passed away, cut down by ice, or decay. I cherish the early visions I had of them, and such names as *Queen City, Greenwood, Tacoma, Courier, Chilo* are hallowed ones.

My brothers once took passage on the side-wheeler, *Greenland*, and after a long, eventful trip up the river, reached Charleston on the Kanawha, called by rivermen "Kanoy." From this far-off point, it was nearly three hundred miles away, they paddled back in their canoe. This was a splendid adventure to me, and I looked forward to the time when I could embark on like voyages. The packets had ceased to run when I made my canoe trips, but towboats answered almost as well. Thanks to indulgent captains, I made some long voyages with my canoe on the boat's deck. The world is at its fairest when seen from a steamboat. The best vantage point, better even than the pilothouse, I say, is the head of the tow of barges. Far removed from the commotion of the steamboat, one glides over the water in magic motion, marked only by the hissing of the bow wave underneath. To ride there on a summer evening, to watch the sun set, and the shores lose

83

their detail as they fade into the simple masses of night, is a transcendent experience.

At Brent, in the absence of packets, the towboats were our consolation. From our shantyboat we became close observers of river traffic. We could identify most of the steamboats by their whistles, or even in the darkness by the heaving of their engines or the pattern of their lights. Passing at night, their searchlights often brightened our cabin like a sustained flash of lightning. A towboat with its two searchlights looks like some nocturnal monster casting its eyes about, each moving independently.

Most of the steam stern-wheel towboats were in the coal-towing trade between the West Virginia mines and Cincinnati. We often saw the big *Omar, E. D. Kenna, Sam P. Suit, Catherine Davis, J. T. Hatfield*—not the old one, *D. W. Wisherd, Kenova, Taric, George M. Verity* (which Sadie called the Variety). The *Robert P. Gillham* had passed away, but a few of the old-timers were left—*W. C. Mitchell, Julius Fleischmann*, the graceful old *Reliance* from Pittsburgh, the *A. C. Ingersoll*. When one of these boats went up, we almost expected to see a packet in its wake. Though towboats, they had indeed some packet character,—a graceful sheer, tall stacks, and some of the packet's ornamentation. The hog chains which braced their wooden hulls suggested the standing rigging of a ship. We watched the passing of these relics of another age with reverence. Each time we wondered if they would make it back again. In fact, most of these old boats were cut down by disaster while we were at Brent.

Some of the tows shoved by the larger boats were four barges wide and four or five in length. The whole tow including the towboat might be as long as an ocean liner. One marveled at the skill of the pilots who worked the tows in and out of locks with only a few feet clearance, and guided them along the narrow, crooked channel at low water. The stern-wheeler has not the rudder power of the screw-driven boat, and must round a sharp bend by flanking. This means reversing the paddle wheel until the wheel's wash against the rudder ahead of it swings the boat to the required angle with the bank. Then the engine room bells jingle and the wheel comes ahead.

The barges in the passing tows were a study in themselves. We still

84

saw an old-time wooden barge now and then, and remarked the character of line, color, and texture it displayed among the more prosaic steel ones. For some reason, an empty wooden barge arches itself slightly, and its waterline presents a slight curve, a sort of reverse sheer. On all barges, the underwater part is yellowed by muddy water, the part above the waterline is blackened by coal soot. This is a narrow band, for the deep-laden barges are almost flush with the water. The shining coal lies in heaps and ridges, as it was loaded from the tipple, each barge containing a single grade—lumps of different sizes, slack, or coke. In winter, all barges seem loaded with snow.

Sometimes we would wake on a foggy morning to find a steamboat and barges tied up to the shore below us, waiting for the fog to lift. I would walk or drift down past them, to be close to a steamboat again, to smell the hot steam and engines, cordage and oakum, and food cooking in the galley. The silhouette of the boat loomed amid the wraiths of fog. From within came muffled sounds, the breathing and clanking of an engine running, the jangle of a bell rung for breakfast, voices, footsteps. Suddenly a firedoor would be opened, a flare of red would light up the fireman. I might talk with some of the crew, possibly the mate, who would ask me if there were anyone in the neighborhood who would ship with them as deck hand. What a temptation that was!

The boats passed close to us in low water, since we were on the outside of a curve where the channel was not far offshore. The channel was constricted at this point by an old stone dike which curved out almost to mid-river from the opposite shore. When the river was low, two boats could not pass here. I woke up one night to find a big screw-driven diesel towboat close by, its stern just ahead of us. It was marking time, waiting for a downcoming boat to clear the narrow channel. When the diesel went ahead, engines at full speed, the wash from its propellers boiled past our boat like a millrace, carrying away the spars.

Our situation was an exposed one, and no experienced shantyboater would have lain there. Coming from the land, we had considered only the attractions of the place, and were lucky to find out the drawbacks without suffering any damage. In a collision with a towboat or a

runaway barge, a shantyboater always comes out badly, even if the right is on his side. The nearest we came to disaster from this cause was one summer night when the steamer *Taric* ran the head of its loaded tow onto the sandbar extending out from the dike. I was wakened by the rattling of heavy chains, and dashing on deck saw the *Taric* slowly sweeping toward us broadside. With the head of its tow fast aground, the current had pivoted the boat around in an arc which, if continued, would bring the *Taric's* great wheel into our boat. Before this could happen, the towboat cast loose from its barges, swung at right angles to them, and all passed by us, on down the river. The clanking of chains which woke me had been caused by the loosening of the ratchets by which the barges were made fast to the *Taric*.

The dike across the river from our landing, built of timber cribbing filled with stones, all worn and battered, scoured for many years by the current, ice, and drift, was one of the few, it might be the last remaining one, of the many that were constructed in an early effort to maintain a navigable depth in the channel. The dikes were to concentrate the current, making it swift enough to keep the channel from silting up. Evidently this simple plan did not work, for nowadays the river is kept from falling to a low level by a series of dams, nearly fifty of them between Pittsburgh and Cairo. This is supplemented by dredging at critical places, such as the narrow channel between our boat and the dike, which was cut out by a dredge soon after the *Taric* grounded there. The spoil from dredging is pumped out on shore, making a pleasant, sandy beach until the current washes it away in a year or two. The sand and gravel that pour through the pipeline are mixed with coal. Apparently much coal lies on the river bottom, lost overboard by passing boats and barges, or left there by sunken wrecks. The lumps of coal are clean as gravel and of the same shape and varied sizes, rounded by action of the current and sand. Many a shantyboater gets his fuel from the mouth of the dredge's pipeline. We picked up a sack or two along the newly made beach to carry as reserve fuel.

The dams are movable and their raising or lowering makes a sudden change in the river's level and current. Shantyboaters who are afloat must be on the alert to avoid grounding or loss of accessories, especially if their boat is not far below a dam, as ours was at Brent. We watched the dam always. If in a falling river the lock men began washing off the walls of the lock, and testing the gates, we knew they were about ready to raise the dam, and prepared to meet a sudden drop in the river. If when the dam was up, they opened both bear traps or sluices, got up steam on the monkey boat, the shantyboat name for maneuver boat, and moved it part way out on the dam, we pulled in close to shore and got all loose articles up the bank, for soon the dam would be thrown, causing a sudden jump of several feet in the river's level, with a swifter current.

The canalization of the river has made an unnatural thing of it in low water, and one will see no more the sandbars and riffles that should be there. This is partly compensated for by the opportunity afforded of seeing the boats close-up in the locks. Working the boat and barges through the lock is always a fascinating process. The locks necessitate much whistling of boats to our enjoyment, for this is the river's music. A few towboats carry whistles which were once on packets, or on a towboat of the old days. Their familiar chord belongs to the valley almost as much as the river itself. The whistle of the *Julius Fleischmann,* which the old boat had carried over various names for perhaps half a century, began with a shrill note. This was joined by a very deep tone in a weird harmony that ended with a falling cadence. There was the high, wailing, single note of the

87

Catherine Davis. Once a strange boat with a beautiful whistle passed at night, and I dreamed it was the ghost of a long-forgotten boat, making its old run unseen.

As we watched the towboats passing our windows we wondered, "How will it be to meet them on the open river when we are drifting? Will any of the pilots then recognize our boat as the one they used to see at Brent?"

This voyage which lay ahead of us was another of my boyhood dreams. It was always made in a flatboat, drifting. But the time for it then seemed as remote as life after death. Now, however, the boat was built, our departure talked of as a certainty. We felt a rising eagerness. However, since little in the way of actual preparation could be done in winter, we settled down for another season of boisterous weather and high water, of quiet days of work and pleasure within our snug cabin.

Our zest for the river did not wane, this second winter, even though it was not the new world we had entered a year ago. We went on in much the same way, in surroundings which had become familiar, with not even a flood to make the year memorable. Ruts, however, are worn only in traveled ways on land: a river life partakes of the freshness of the river itself. Each rise and fall affords a new outlook and gives to a well-known shore the feel of one at which you have just landed for the first time. The falling river leaves a clean bank from which all traces of your former activity there, the ashes of fires and chips from woodcutting, have been washed away.

Nor is the pattern of weather ever the same. Cold weather came upon us earlier this winter, and we were awakened on a December night by the dread sound of ice as it grated along the boat's side. This was unexpected, although the air had been very cold, the water low and clear. Except for a thin skim on the still water behind the dike, no ice had formed. Now it soon became heavier, and for a week was our chief concern. I again put a long, straight pole along the outside to protect the boat, and rigged a boom ahead to ward off the floating ice. The river boats had their troubles, too. Barges were brought through the narrows between our boat and the dike one at a time. At the lock they worked through the night. Strings of lights glimmered from the waiting boats, and their searchlights flashed over the snowy banks. For several nights, when darkness and heavy cold settled upon us, and when the ice floes seemed to move slower than ever, we were quite hopeless, expecting to find a solid, silent river by morning. Yet, as in the previous winter, it did not freeze over, and we suffered no damage.

The day before Christmas turned warmer. A freezing rain fell. We walked up the valley of Three Mile Creek a way to get a Christmas tree, through mud and icy fields. We brought back a small cedar, already lavishly decorated with glassy pendants of ice which bent and twisted its slender branches. In the warm cabin the ice soon melted and the tree regained its original symmetry.

Our boat seemed a more cozy place than ever, a warm spark amid the ice and snow. Preparations for Christmas, our first one on board, were most appropriate. We printed a woodblock to send to our friends, did some special baking, dipped tiny candles for our tree, and tied up some trifles in a fancy package to give Andy, Sadie, and Donald. Their Christmas tree was a much-used, artificial one, handsomely decorated, and placed before their middle window, where it could be seen from the railroad.

Some river people complain of the dreary confinement of winter, but we find it a season of special delight. The mere joy of being sheltered is magnified by our closeness to the elements: rain on the roof directly overhead, snow sifting on our faces asleep, the swaying and rolling of the boat, the wild and muddy world without. Our fires have the directness of campfires kindled in riverbank driftpiles for warmth on a winter walk. In bad weather, one can sit by the fire indoors without compunction, and not feel that he should be stirring about outside. It is then that we reap the harvest of winter, painting, writing, reading, making music. Our playing together has given us much solid satisfaction. Often we play two parts of a quartet or trio; incomplete music, to be sure, but the rich treasures of the inner voices, often lost in a complete performance, are realized. We were stimulated to practice by a session of quartet playing the previous summer when two violinist friends had come to stay with us for a week. Also, a lone violinist had at times strolled down from the hilltops, more, it might be, to watch birds along the way, then to play string trios on our level.

The strains of our Bach and Purcell, coming over the water, were somewhat bewildering to the natives and fishermen. Little Chuck and Jerry stationed themselves outside our window in a johnboat one day during a quartet. They were puzzled by the frequent breaks in our playing, and by one of us shouting, "Let's go back to K."

It was in winter that our best reading was done. The first session of the day came after breakfast. It might be only a few lines if there were a press of weather, or some affair needed immediate attention; yet we often lingered to read a whole chapter. To be read in the morning a book must be exceptionally good. Then we could take on some demanding, stirring volume like *Walden*. In the morning we liked to read poetry; it might be anything from Chaucer to Emily Dickinson. An honest, outdoor book of travel went well at that time—Hakluyt, *Two Years Before the Mast*, or Doughty's *Arabia Deserta*.

We read again during the noon rest, selecting something which called for both of us to read, often in French. Here I stumbled after Anna who is a proficient French scholar. Our range was wide—Racine, LaFontaine, Anatole France, Proust. A scene from some play was often our midday reading, each of us assuming a part or several parts. A one-volume edition of Shakespeare lasted us for years. When it was read through, we began again, with favorites this time.

In the evening our reading tended to relax a little, though if we began early enough we might undertake a chapter in a critical work like Schweitzer's *Bach,* to be followed by some slow-paced, gentle novel, or a book of reminiscences like Rothenstein's *Men and Memories,* or an article from an out-of-date *Atlantic* or *Harper's,* which magazines were sent to us in yearly batches by my brother, Frank.

Often in the wintry night, when the fire had fallen away to glowing coals, and all was silent save the voice which read, the words of the book seemed to speak directly to us; or we would come upon some ancient lines, like these which Thoreau translated from Pindar, whose beauty was enhanced by our peculiar situation—

"Honors and crowns of the tempest-footed
Horses delight one;
Others live in golden chambers;
And some even are pleased traversing securely
The swelling of the sea in a swift ship."

This winter marked the beginning of a new fireside occupation. It was netting, or knitting, as Andy called it, the making of fish nets from twine. Andy taught us the stitch and procedure, and I whittled out a wooden shuttle after his pattern. We first made a dip net, and were soon working on a hoop net for winter fishing. This work is good accompaniment for reading. Like picking out nuts, it is relaxing and occupies the hands only. The unfinished netting of white twine makes a pleasing and fit decoration on the walls of a boat.

On our boat cooking is a lively art. It, too, follows the seasons closely, and in winter we are likely to interrupt our playing to see if the beans baking in the oven need more water. Such long and slow cooking is easily achieved, with fires burning all day for warmth. Winter cooking is simplified by our stores of canned food. We regard summer canning as long-range cooking on a large scale, and in winter enjoy the fruits of our summer labor.

While much of our winter work and pastime is withindoors, the river and weather are always on our minds, subconsciously if not directly. How good it is to go into the open air again after an indoor hour or two. As I check the rise or fall of the river, speculate on the weather, and go about the evening chores, I look into the glowing sky of the winter sunset above the frozen, snowy hills, and am taken up again by the current of time and brought to the present moment.

Sometimes of an evening we abandoned our fireside, made our way either by boat or along the shore path to our good neighbors, the Detisches. Their boat had the homey air of an old farmhouse kitchen, and a quaintness all its own. Firewood was drying in the range oven, which never baked well since the stove was dropped when being carried off the boat in the great ice. On the bright picture calendar, the number of eggs the hens laid was marked against each day. Sadie drew the line at dogs—our own waiting for us on deck—but Patsy, the yellow cat, was privileged to come inside. There might be a litter of kittens in the woodbox, or in the springtime some peeping chicks, Sadie's biddies, behind the stove. All was so different from our spare, ordered cabin. Even the ticking of the clock was a novelty to us. Taking our ease, we talked back and forth. Donald and I might tell the details of a recent excursion on the river, how we gleaned corn from the field on the other side or what we found on the Coney Island dump. Perhaps we would listen to a long yarn of Andy's, into which Sadie inserted her personal comments. There was an intensity about Andy's quiet, exact talk, but Sadie's was unrestrained, compounded of laughing and gesture and pointed country words, so good-humored that one would not suspect she had a care in the world.

A few winter visitors stopped in "to chat us a while" as they passed our boat on some vague business in that direction. Old Bill would sit on the woodbox, his muddy feet planted on a newspaper by his request, and tell fragments of his tale of the river, of the terrible storm at Big Locust, how his wife sat in the middle of the floor, weeping through the night as she faced what seemed to her imminent destruction.

Sometimes Lou Gander would come peering in the windows. Only upon invitation would he cross the gangplank. He talked in his rambling manner about the old days in Brent where generations of his family had lived. Lou had once been an artist's model. The artist, a painter of Indians, had lived in an old hilltop mansion overlooking a vast sweep of river and country. We could see how Lou would make a good model for an Indian—he did look like one.

In the past, the bend at Brent was a favorite place for shantyboaters to lay over in their endless passage up and down the river. Here they were handy to town, yet not too close. A temporary job could be found at the log roll or at Coney Island, at Brent or on the hill. After a while their boat would be missed, and you would hear that they were fishing on the Kentucky, working in the mill at New Albany, or planting a crop on Brush Creek. Some of these river people had been difficult to approach from the land side. Now that we were living on a boat, a closer acquaintance with them could have been made. We often wished that Bob Wills or the Mortons would reappear, or some of the old fishermen on small boats, who were nameless to us. None ever came. Many of them are drifting about no more. The race is dwindling.

The winter is a short season after all, when you begin a garden in the first warm days, it may be at the end of February. This year we had not so much clearing of ground to do, but were occupied with the building of a fence to keep out the rabbits. The summer before, they had seriously damaged some crops, beans especially. Enough fencing material, however, would have cost as much as the beans were worth; so I looked around. Across the river I found a roll of rusty wire fence that had been discarded at Coney Island. This was half enough to enclose the log-roll garden, the one we planned to fence in. For the rest of the way, I made a palisade of orange crates which I found in almost unlimited number on the town dump. I clipped the wire binding, removed the ends, and opened out the boxes into flat sheets. At the garden I fastened them together by the ends of the wires. A few stakes held the fence upright. It kept out the rabbits very well, and in its protection we raised some fine crops.

Another event of late February was Skipper's second litter of pups, of which we kept the incomparable Buster, a sad-faced, long-eared hound. Over the winter we had lost two of our dogs who did not

93

learn in time the hazards of the railroad and highway. So the pups were fun all over again, and Buster, the sad clown, was a favorite with everyone. He was so likable and such a promising hunter that we felt sure he had been taken up by some sportsman when he suddenly disappeared late in the summer. Perhaps it was better so, since his talents would have gone to waste with us.

When spring was well under way we made a new acquisition, a swarm of bees. We had long been eager to try our hand at beekeeping, but since it seemed incompatible with a drifting life on the rivers, we had put this experiment on our list for the future. By chance it was decided otherwise. One Sunday in May, while we were eating dinner, with Anna's sister, Etta, a guest, the humming noise of a swarm of bees approached us from out on the river. It passed over the boat, and I dashed out to follow its course. The bees did not go far—probably the flight across the river was a long one for them—but settled in the thicket of small trees on the steep bank above us. I was about to try to get them into a box when I remembered a regulation hive stored away under the studio. I had acquired it long ago in a chance way and was keeping it for just such an occasion as this. So I rode up the hill on my bicycle to get it. Pedaling through the town on my way back, with the hive balanced on the handle bars, a police officer passing in his car motioned me to the curb. I tried to think of what ordinance I could be violating but found that my services as a handler of bees were required. A swarm had settled above the pavement in another part of town, and considering it a menace to the peace, the police force was out scouting for professional help. What a coincidence! A man with a beehive found in the nick of time! After some hesitation, considering my almost complete inexperience, yet attracted by the prospect of two hives of bees, I rode over to the spot. It was a street of residences, and the inhabitants seemed to have nothing to do this fine Sunday afternoon but watch the bees—from a safe distance. A murmur rose as I appeared with the hive. I went ahead as if I knew what I was doing. Indeed I did have a general idea, for I had taken a quick look at a government bulletin on beekeeping, another item I had picked up at the studio. From the cooperative neighbors I borrowed a saw, cut the limb of the low tree so the swarm would fall on some

94

newspapers spread underneath. The hive had been placed close by. All went well, the swarm dropped before the hive entrance, the bees seemed to be going in. Thinking then of the first swarm on the river-bank, I decided to take the chance that these would finally go into the hive. Accordingly I rode down to the boat, secured the swarm there in a wooden box with little trouble. Then I rode back up the hill to the street of the bees. What a shock! My hive was standing empty and forlorn. Instead of going into it, the bees had swarmed again. Nearby in a truck, equipped with all the accouterments, veil, smoker, gloves, and a suit of oilskins, a real beekeeper was gently driving the flock into his hive. I made an inglorious departure with my hive, and having had enough of bees for one day, I waited until another time to transfer the swarm at the boat from the box to the hive.

The bees became a prime interest for the rest of the summer. I bought a veil and smoker and at intervals opened the hive to see what was going on. The purpose of these inspections was uncertain, but they revealed a fascinating world. The bees did not seem to mind having their work temporarily interrupted. As the old beekeeper said, they realized I was a greenhorn.

We placed the hive at the top of our clearing. From out on the river, though only a white dot, it was a unique and significant mark on the landscape, giving a new tone to our landing.

Summer was now running full head, and we were as busy as our bees. Gardening, fishing, gathering in the wild crops as each one had its season, canning, smoking fish—besides such activities there must be time for some painting, music, and reading, and for the margin of leisure without which none of it would be satisfactory. All this, by good management, we were able to keep in hand. It is well that summer days are long ones.

Summer was the season for visitors, too. We were always delighted to have our family and friends, and strangers as well, come down to see us. We had given up trying to foretell how the different ones would react to river life. Sometimes the most unlikely person became a frequent visitor. From the most unsuspected quarters we have heard, when we told about our boat, "That is what I have wanted to do all my life."

Anna was a born hostess and entertained with the zest of a child giving a tea party. It did not matter who the guest might be—friend from the city, riverman, farmer, farmer's wife, boy or girl—nothing was spared to honor them, nothing held back.

Special attention was shown to all little girls who came on our boat. They brought out an elfin streak in Anna, and she would read with them from *The Wind in the Willows* about Rat and Mole on the riverbank and the fun they had "messing about with boats," or about Winnie the Pooh, taking it all as seriously as her young listeners. They were entranced with our way of living and understood its charm more than some adults whose minds were prejudiced and inflexible.

This summer we desired to improve on the makeshift way in which we had accommodated our overnight guests. After considerable thought and experiment, there was evolved a collapsible compartment on the roof. It was a low boxlike affair, just large enough for the mattress. A light cover of scraps and strips of sheet metal fitted tightly over the box. It was placed on the center line of the cabin roof with one end against the low bulkhead which extended from the cabin roof to the higher level of the deck roof. Thus it was compact and unobtrusive.

To use for sleeping, the cover was raised up, one end resting on the edge of the deck roof, the other supported by two small posts at the corners of the box. The sides were made of panels which could be inserted or left out as desired. The end panel and one on each side near the sleeper's head contained a small window. One could lie there and have a view in three directions and of most of the sky, by a turn of the head. Of course there was not enough headroom to stand up. One crawled in backwards, adjusting the last panel from the inside.

We called these quarters the texas, since it reminded us of the texas deck on a steamboat, the topmost one and smaller than those below. It was a delightful place to sleep, though a little out of the ordinary. Anna and I usually slept there ourselves, since it required a certain adeptness and experience, and it was novelty enough for an initiate to sleep in the rollaway bed in the cabin. Nights in the texas were delightful, so close to the stars and river. The slightest rolling of the boat was felt at the higher level. We did allow some of our special guests to enjoy it.

As summer ended and we folded up the texas after the departure
of our last guest for the season, our leaving Brent and the voyage down
the river became our prime concern. It was exciting business, preparing
at the same time for winter and drifting. It would be a new experience
for us, though a test run had been made during the summer when we
drifted down to the garden. A few days later I had hauled the boat
back to our old landing by a towline as I walked along the shore.

In the light of this experience and from Andy's advice and our
imagination we contrived, found, or purchased the equipment we considered essential. We knew, however, that only actual drifting could
give a definite answer to all the questions which were in our minds.
We hoped the experience might not be too dearly bought.

As we considered the unknown future, I looked back over the past
two years. The building of the boat and our living there successfully
in true riverbank style, fitting into the neighborhood so well, yet re-
taining our own standards, mostly, and our own pursuits which were
so different from those ordinarily engaged in on shantyboats, though
we fished and gathered up junk like a true river rat—all this seemed
a worth-while accomplishment, and we were proud of it.

We hoped to leave on the fall rise, which usually came in November.
There was still much to do, procure, and decide. One day we borrowed
a friend's car and traversed the city almost from end to end, buying
such unrelated items as fiddle strings and a tarpaulin. We were searching
for an anchor, too, following the advice, which turned out to be
valuable, of an experienced boatman. We saw just the anchor we

wanted in the boat store. It was an old style fisherman's anchor which had already seen service, though on what craft we never found out. The proprietor of the boat store was not in, and the price quoted by his deputy seemed too high to us. So we went about our other errands, buying some rough-weather clothing, some watercolors and paper, a few books, some reserve food. Then we visited our friend the violin maker. He had once been a fisherman and had told us how to make catfish soup, a river delicacy. He gave us the blocks on which he had made his nets. One almost knew from the wood and workmanship that they had been shaped by a fiddle maker. On our way home we stopped at the boat store again. The proprietor had evidently been in, meanwhile, for his man said as we entered, "Boss says you can have it for ten dollars." It was a deal. We also bought rope—what delightful stuff it is—some heavy oarlocks, and as a final touch a foghorn, which Anna persists in calling the fish horn.

The river rose on schedule, the dams were lowered, and the swift current and floating drift seemed urging us to come along. Yet we were not quite ready. When we finally were, the river had fallen again, and the dams were raised. We decided to go anyway, thinking that bear-trap water might be swift enough for beginners, with five bridges to run almost at the outset. So we set a day, even though snow lay on the ground and it was nearly Christmas.

What to do with the bees? This problem had been on our minds since we first secured them. Our final decision was to take them along, though there was much against it. One evening Donald and I plugged them up and shanghaied them aboard. We had decided to put them on the roof, but the hive was so heavy with the bees and their summer's honey, for we took none that fall, that we placed them on the main deck beside the door. This was alarming to some of our friends, but we figured the bees would be mostly quiet through the winter and could be kept confined.

Our departure was set for Sunday to allow George and Elisabeth to make the first day's run with us. It was a still, cloudy day, not very cold, but the banks were snowy. Our friends came down early, and we were ready—all but Skipper. She had no idea that such a radical change in her life was to take place, and had gone off somewhere on a scout. She sometimes stayed away until evening. To our relief, however, she came in, after much searching and whistling. At the last minute, another pair of faithful friends, the Dunlaps, came down the slippery bank, carrying as a bon voyage gift, a crate of oranges and grapefruit.

At last we took in our lines and shoved out into the current. Our familiar landing at once merged into the wild river shore. No trace of us remained behind. Looking back we saw Andy and Sadie waving to us from the deck of their boat. We blew a long blast on our foghorn.

5

This was the long-dreamed-of moment.

We worked out into mid-river and drifted slowly away from Brent. The place lost its significance as it faded into the impersonal river landscape, and we looked back no more.

It was a little bewildering to be out on the broad water with no hold on shore. Yet we were stirred with a vague sense that a new world was opening before us. It was river never before known. The familiar hills and reaches seemed almost a strange country. Our boat became more alive, turning round in the slow swirls of current, and rolling in the waves of a passing boat with a free motion we had never felt when it was lashed to shore.

Soon the first bend was rounded. There was now a light breeze, and we tried out our sweeps. These were crude oars, like those used on log rafts and flatboats of old times, though of course smaller. One sweep was mounted on each corner post of the main deck. Thus a person could stand in the center and handle them like a pair of oars. Further motive power was gained by towing with the johnboat. We soon found that our combined efforts moved the boat but slowly. Fortunately our first day out was mild and quiet with a slow current. At that, we just missed a channel buoy. In fact, I had to stand at the corner of the deck and shove it aside as we drifted into it. These heavy steel buoys were to become a menace in the swift river, where they seem to come at you under their own power.

We landed at the broad sandbar on the Kentucky side, relaxed, and ate our dinner of catfish which had been broiling in the fireplace. As we shoved off again the sky cleared and there was a splendid view of the city of Cincinnati and the bridges at the end of the westward reach. On the right the river was overshadowed by a crenelated hill on whose side the gray buildings seemed mere facades. At the distant point where this ridge dropped away to the city below it, an old-world church rose against the golden sky.

It was very pleasant drifting slowly along. The late afternoon sun shining in our windows was a new delight to us who had lived under a western hill until this day. At sunset we pulled in to shore on the Kentucky side, above the first bridge. Our departing guests boarded a streetcar and were soon back to Fort Thomas. Although only a few river miles had been covered on our first day's run, we felt it to be an auspicious beginning. Already we sensed that the joy of drifting did not depend on getting anywhere in particular. Just to have rounded that one bend brought us to as new a shore as could be desired. It was no longer the stony one at Brent, but a sandy beach backed by willows. Strange train whistles were heard, and constellations of city lights shone from the opposite hill.

Within our cabin, however, all was the same. There was supper by the fireplace, Skipper asleep underneath, all just as it had been. Nothing was left behind.

On the second day we must run the gantlet of five bridges bunched together on the winding river past the city. The fair, quiet morning after a frosty night was a good omen. When everything was made ship-shape within and without, and all hands were on deck, we pulled out into the river, hoping no wind would rise. We had decided to follow the channel, where the bridge piers were farther apart and the current steady. This meant the hazard of passing boats, but we hoped to slip through without meeting any.

It is exciting to drift under a bridge. The tremendous structure swings overhead in violent perspective, the crossing traffic unconcerned with its watery foundation. We could not know, intent on the second bridge close below, that George was looking down on us from a passing bus, with us in spirit, and pulling hard on the sweeps. We were being watched from shore, too, for a voice was megaphoned out from a boat harbor on the Kentucky side, "Need any help?" We appreciated this, but confidently shouted, "No." Soon the second bridge was passed.

On our left was the mouth of the Licking River. The dead, muddy inlet suggested in no way the lively stream of riffles and rocks we had once descended in a canoe almost from its mountain headwaters.

On the right bank was the Public Landing of Cincinnati. In the row of buildings at the top of the broad, paved grade were a few crusty survivors of the golden age of steamboating, when this shore was crowded with boats running to every river port in the midwest. The light, single-decker from the Big Sandy nosed in alongside the stately New Orleans packet. The tradition still lingered in the Greene Line wharfboat from which a daily freight boat ran to Louisville.

The next bridge was the old Suspension, a relic of the structural past with its stone piers and fine webbing of cables. In its shadow was the site of the building which had furnished the timbers for the hull of our boat.

We ran the fourth bridge in fine style, but before reaching the last one, a cross wind came up which forced us to the Ohio side. We passed close to the shoreward pier, and tied up just below the bridge to rest a while. We were relieved to be past the bridges, and would have been glad to call it a day. This place, however, in the very slums of the riverbank, made us uneasy and we decided to cross over to the Kentucky side. It was a hard pull against the wind, but we found there a shore more to our liking. The boat was moored to tall willows beyond which were houses and backyards, and after dark, lighted windows and street lamps. The river itself was unclean everywhere. Even the flowing water offshore, where I took the johnboat to wash out the mud, was foul. We learned at first hand what a city does to a river.

Next morning we cast off by starlight, burning our lantern for a running light until daybreak. It promised to be another day favorable for drifting. Since then we have learned how rare a thing it is, especially in winter, to have three such days in succession. Later in the morning we met our first boat. It was the *Chris Greene,* once a freight and passenger packet which ran to upriver points. Now it carried

freight only between Cincinnati and Louisville. To our relief, the pilot swung aside to pass us, and reduced speed. This consideration impressed us much at the time, but we have found it universal among the operators of boats which have passed us when drifting. On our part, we try to keep as far out of the way as possible.

The shores now, especially on the Kentucky side, were becoming more countrylike. The city had been an impressive sight from the river, with its towering bridges and waterfront structures of industry, coal docks, and barge terminals, but it was a relief to be through with it. Approaching the long-established Anderson's Ferry, we saw *Boone No. 6* laboring back and forth. It was a strange craft—steam, side-wheel, an open driveway through the center, a small cabin on each side. Above one cabin was the pilothouse and smokestack. The ferry landing on the Kentucky side was at Constance, a village strung out at the foot of a steep hill. The settlement below is called Stringtown. Coasting by, close inshore, I landed Skipper who was restless, thinking she would run along with the boat, as Andy's beagle hounds used to do. After half a mile, she was nowhere to be seen. We dropped anchor, whistled and waited, but no Skipper. I had to row back to where I had landed her and take her aboard.

In the afternoon a light cross wind blew us over to the right bank. We had already discovered that even a gentle breeze moved our boat more easily than we could with the sweeps and oars, and hard pulling was necessary to keep off a lee shore. This time we made no effort. We landed on an open gravel beach behind which rose a line of trees, some large sycamores and maples among the willows. The water was unclean, especially along the shoreline. The influence of the city extended farther than its limits, but we hoped that another day's run would put us beyond the evident pollution. Except for this disagreeable feature, it was an attractive place, and we did not mind when the increased wind made it impossible to leave that day.

This was Christmas Eve. In the flurry of departure, we had not provided a Christmas tree, trusting to get one along the way. I took a walk on the hillside, but came back empty-handed. In the twilight I saw what appeared to be an evergreen growing on the riverbank. It was a weed, green and flourishing in the wintry season, which resembled very much a small cedar in form and color. This became our Christmas tree. When installed in state, with a border of tiny hand-dipped candles, it performed its role very well.

We had a fine Christmas alone on that strange shore. It was good to relax, to forget about the river and drifting. There were packages to open. We thought of our friends, and wondered how they were receiving the gifts we had sent—smoked catfish wrapped in aluminum foil and tied with a red ribbon.

Tuning up our instruments, we played twice during the day. We took a walk ashore, and in the evening enjoyed some good reading by the fire. Our thoughts, though, were on the morrow's voyage.

During the night a towboat came in to the landing below us, and shuffled past our windows several times, close in. Much shoving and pulling, sound of engine-room bells, mate shouting, clanking of chains, as it sorted and shifted the barges. At last it departed upriver with some empties, leaving behind the darkness and quiet of deep night.

The day after Christmas promising fair, we cast off as soon as it was light enough to see. It turned out to be a fine day, indeed, one of those rare blue and gold days of winter when the sunlight is unbroken and warm, and there is not wind enough to ripple the water. With the sky reflected below us, we seemed to float in mid-air.

Our first concern was with Lock and Dam 37, not far down the river. The procedure of locking was well known to us—we had been put through many times in canoes and rowboats, and had often watched towboats and barges as they were warped into the lock, and

104

raised or lowered to a different level. We had seen with what care the pilots approached the lock from above, taking no chances with the set in the current which might carry the unwieldy barges to the outside of the lock and over the dam. So we too were cautious, and relieved to get a line to the guide wall. The rest was easy. The lock men had seen us approach, and had the gate open for us. I climbed up on the guide wall, the top of which was even with our roof, and hauled the boat into the lock, while Anna remained on deck. We were both aboard while the lock chamber was being emptied, holding on to the ladder rungs as the boat dropped slowly down. The dam at this time was partly open. The water passing through the bear traps and section of lowered wickets had raised the river below the dam higher than normal pool; thus the drop in the lock was only about six feet. When the lower level was reached, and the heavy gate slid open, we rowed out of the lock chamber and headed for mid-river. Soon our boat was caught up in the swift current pouring through the opening in the dam and we were again on our way.

We now began to taste new joys of drifting. I sat on the sunny roof for a while. The higher elevation gave one a better view of the river and the country behind the willows. We observed the life that went on there. Mostly it turned its back on the river, but there were frequent paths to the shore used by fishermen in summer, and driftwood had been collected in piles for winter fuel. Barge terminals were passed where coal and oil were handled. Above North Bend the old *Taric* was tied up. It had not made a trip past Brent for a long time. The Kentucky shore was entirely rural. We saw one old mansion facing the river, white with tall columns in front, and a low wing on each side. Situated now on no road, it had been built when the river was the highway.

We anchored offshore at North Bend, Ohio, to get drinking water. When we were drifting again, I washed the cabin windows on the outside from the johnboat. Passing the mouth of the Great Miami we remembered what an important junction this had been in the days of the birch canoe when it was a way to the north and the Great Lakes. Now, although a huge power plant stands on the shore above, it is a forsaken place almost as wild as in pioneer days, rarely seen except by rivermen, to whom it means nothing.

The town of Lawrenceburg, Indiana, which we passed in the sunny afternoon, seemed buried behind its new flood wall, only the steeples and chimneys rising into the air. The ferryboat here was another example of curious marine architecture. After the third and last of the red buoys in the Lawrenceburg reach was passed, we pulled in toward the Kentucky shore. The sun was setting as we tied up along a clean, gravel beach. Inland were some trees, mostly sycamores, and then a steep, clay bank, on top of which, though from the river there was no evidence of its existence, was the hamlet of Petersburg. We had drifted fourteen miles since daybreak, a good run, considering the passage through the lock.

We laid over at Petersburg for three days, for no particular reason.

One afternoon was still and warm, so we turned loose the bees. They swarmed forth in a cleansing flight, stained Anna's spotless windows. A few fell into the river, but we judged that most returned to the hive. After that we let out our flock often when conditions were favorable. On every warm day they buzzed loudly at the screened opening, but we thought it safer to keep them in when drifting. Luckily the weather was mostly cold, and then our passengers were withdrawn and content.

It was here that I made the sweep swivels that we are still using. The sweeps themselves, with light blades of white pine—which had once been door panels, and then leeboards—and spruce spars for handles, were good. However, the method I had tried of binding them to the corner posts with rope was unsatisfactory. I now made two swivels of blocks of wood and bolts, contrived in such a way that free motion was possible with no loss or friction. The sweeps could easily be unbolted and removed if in the way. The necessary material for this work was found in my stock of junk, which never lets us down. Indeed, an unconsidered piece often suggests a solution to some tricky problem.

Petersburg was not unknown to us, but to approach the town by water and moor our boat there made a new place of it. Strolling about the informal streets, we found old houses which belonged to the river

of the past. We were told that Petersburg was once proposed as the capital city of Kentucky.

Of more import to us was the forecast of much colder weather. Since our landing place was open to the northwest, we made ready to leave next morning, and were casting off as the Lawrenceburg clock struck five. When we drifted slowly away from our anchorage, the shores could hardly be seen in the darkness. After passing the Kentucky landing of the Aurora ferry, which was making its first trip of the day, we anchored, had breakfast, and watched the gray dawn reveal the city across the river.

At this point, the Ohio rounds a sharp bend to the south. Its general direction since we began drifting had been westward. From here on, its course would be west and south. Nearly five hundred miles remained of its winding way to the Mississippi, but its north bends lay farther and farther south. Because of this change in direction, the east and west land traffic no longer followed the river. Its shores became wilder, the towns smaller and less industrial. On our left was the bold coast of Boone County, its rough hills cut through at intervals by large creeks. Walls of bare rock, even rocky pinnacles, rose above the fringe of willows. Then, close to the right bank, the first island appeared, a thrilling sight to us who have no islands in our stretch of river.

Not far below was Dam 38. In the past day or two there had been indications that all the dams had been lowered: a sharp rise in the river, swifter current, and muddy water. Yet, approaching the dam, we could not be sure. From up the river, the water falling over the wickets cannot be seen. Whether the dam is up or down is indicated by a signboard placed on the lock building—a black and white sign if the dam is raised, giving the gauge reading, and a red and white sign marked PASS if the dam is down. This sign can be read only from mid-river, and we were unwilling to get far from shore since it would be a serious matter to drift into or over the wickets of the dam. As we came nearer, our belief that the dam was down was strengthened by the position of the maneuver boat, which was inside the lock chamber. At length I could see from the roof that both lock gates were open. This was positive proof that the dam was lowered. We pulled out into the stream, and a few minutes later drifted swiftly through the navigable pass. Crossing the submerged wickets of the dam, we felt a slight but definite drop.

Since then a plainer way of informing boats in the daytime of the raised or lowered position of the dam has been devised; so evidently other navigators have been in doubt.

Below the dam we pulled over to the Indiana shore and anchored off the town of Rising Sun. Beached out there was the abandoned hulk of the former Rising Sun-Rabbit Hash ferry. Other decaying remnants of river activities were noticed in the old brick buildings along the waterfront. We liked the stores here; farmers' towns seem always to have good ones. We procured some fresh provisions, and drinking water conveniently from hydrants standing in the yards of houses. We then hoisted our anchor and drifted around another bend or two.

On the outside of the curve there was always a steep hill close to the river, with low bottomland on the other side. We tied up for the night against one of these low willow shores where we would be out of the swift current and safe from passing boats. It was a remote place, and we enjoyed once more the darkness of a country night.

The next day was still drifting weather, but windier. All hands were called a time or two, and Anna must leave her morning chores for a spell at the sweeps. Rounding a bend, a new reach to the southwest was opened. In the distance lay Big Bone Island, standing boldly away from either shore, long and narrow as a ship.

Desiring to lay over a few days near the island, we kept close to the

Indiana shore, thinking to find a harbor on that side, since the channel
and the boats passed the other way. The anchor was dropped when
abreast of the head of the island. At once our mistake was evident. We
should have known the current would be too swift through the chute
between island and mainland. Raising the anchor with difficulty, we
dropped down to quiet water below the island, still on the Indiana
side, and tied up there. The view upriver was unexpectedly fine. The
island lay in the notch where Big Bone Creek cut through the high
range of Kentucky hills which stretched off above into the blue distance.
Across from us the hills rose from the rocky shore with no trace of
road or field on their steep, shaggy sides.

We remained here a good week. Winter storms swept the valley and
snow transformed the bleak landscape into a cheerful world of infinite
delicacy and grace. The muddy water of the river climbed the muddy
banks in a swift rise. So raw and boisterous outside, within we enjoyed more than ever our fires and lamps, music and reading, food and
sleep.

It was good to be out in the cold and wind, too. I went up to Big
Bone Island for dry hardwood to burn in the cookstove since our
shore afforded nothing but willow. It was something of an adventure
to land on the strange island—a wild, uncared-for place scoured by past
floods. In the driftwrack caught on the head of the island, I found a
dry walnut log, excellent fuel and a pleasure to work up. When burning, its fragrant smoke scented the wintry air.

I made another excursion into the Kentucky hills, and found a rough,
brushy country of worn-out and abandoned farms. Overlooking the
river was a tiny, forgotten burying ground. On one of the old, barely
legible headstones I made out a finely carved rose. I did not go far
enough up the valley of Big Bone Creek to reach the salt lick which
was so celebrated in early times, but would surely have done so if any
of the huge relics had remained—fossil ribs of which the discoverers
made tent poles, and vertebrae large enough for stools.

In contrast, the Indiana shore at this point was rich and prosperous,
with miles of cornfield in the bottomland. The corn had already been
harvested, but we gleaned as much as could be stored. The corn-picking
machine is a boon to shantyboaters, crows, mice, and such foragers.

109

The farmer who owned the land where we were tied up discovered his uninvited guests when he came down to see about the rising river. He was a jolly, hospitable sort, and in the course of our stay we visited back and forth. This was the extent of our society here, though some duck hunters occasionally passed by on their fruitless quest, a shock or two of corn in their boat making it a floating blind. An old, bearded man and his wife passed, too, bound up the river in a johnboat with a balky outboard motor. The patient lady kept her seat at the oars, poised ready for action. When the motor stopped, she rowed until the man could get it started again. But for her timely exertions, they would have made little progress against the current.

It was well that we could get within the willows as the river rose, for the boats now ran our shore going up, towering above us as they brushed the outermost branches. One big diesel running light came down the Indiana chute, making a great wash along the shore. I happened to be out in the johnboat at the time, and could see part of the bottom planking on our boat as she rolled from side to side in the waves.

Our first along-the-way washing of clothes was performed here. At Brent Anna had worked out a satisfactory procedure, and I had made a wash bench to her specifications, high enough for comfortable working and long enough to hold three tubs. This equipment, with a boiler for heating water on the bank, was carried along, stowed on the roof. So our clothes washing while drifting offered no new problems except a suitable place to string the clothesline. In this case it was along the willows at the edge of the cornfield, where the clothes were hung in one long line. Clear water was obtained from a nearby creek. We worked at it together, and as usual it was as much fun as labor. Our washings that winter, and always when drifting, were large ones, being far apart because of the difficulty of obtaining the complete combination of necessary conditions—clear water, a space for hanging out, and above all a sunny day.

It was January eighth when we proceeded down the river, a sunrise start on a clear winter morning. Before rounding the bend, we looked back once more at Big Bone Island standing forth in the morning light against its background of dark blue hills. On the next reach we were

faced with a wind, and took refuge in the mouth of a creek. The wind held us there all that day and the next. Drifting is like that—only a mile farther on after our auspicious start.

Creeks are to be trusted as harbors only in high water, when the runout after a rain is blocked or slowed up by the backwater from the river; so with no hesitation we pulled up into this one far enough to be protected from wind and waves. The boat was moored between two willows, one on each bank. Down through the arch of trees the river could be seen, flowing swiftly, and the hills on the far side.

We found ourselves in the town of Patriot, once called Troy. It was a very small place with two or three country stores, and even a horse and buggy in from some muddy side road. Its only connection with the river at present was an incline where an occasional barge of coal was unloaded. The steamboat landing, once paved, was grass-grown and neglected. Nearby was a long brick building, tenantless now, and of such a somber dignity that it was hard to imagine that it was ever busy and thriving.

On the first quiet morning we snaked the boat out of the creek onto the broad river, and drifted past the town. In the half light a few old buildings against the dark hill were all that could be seen of Patriot. It appeared as a true river town. We have often noticed that landmarks on shore which are survivals of river days are more plainly seen from the water than highways and more recent structures. Thus the shores still appear to the river voyager much as they did in steamboat days. The illusion is broken by a visit ashore where only a few shells and ruins of the past are found in the present scheme of things over which the river has no influence.

Later in the day, as we rounded the sharpest bend in that part of the river, the head of an approaching tow of barges suddenly appeared, close to the bank. We were farther offshore, and far enough from the path of the barges to feel safe. The tow was a long one, and the towboat still out of sight around the bend. Then the barges seemed to leave the bank, and I judged that the boat's pilot was about to make a crossing to the other side of the river. Calling all hands we made the best headway possible toward the shore. By this time the towboat had come around the bend, and it became evident that I had made a wrong decision, for the pilot blew two blasts on his whistle. This meant that he would pass to his left of us, still keeping close to shore, and that we were moving directly into his path. I was so delighted at having a steamboat whistle for us, even with two short toots instead of the long, spaced blasts with which another towboat is signaled, that even before turning around and rowing away from shore I dashed into the cabin, snatched a spray of bittersweet from our foghorn and from the deck blew two feeble notes which the boat's pilot could never hear. All this happened so quickly that we had not moved a boat's length in either direction before the tow passed by. Anna still laughs at my horn blowing.

In such incidents there is only a slight difference, a few rods of space or a few minutes of time, between comedy and tragedy. It was around this very bend and because of a misunderstanding of passing signals that the worst disaster of this section of the river occurred—the collision in 1868 of the U. S. Mail Line packets, *United States* and *America*.

At midday when we were drifting smoothly and figuring on reaching Warsaw, Kentucky, still several miles ahead, by evening, a cross wind came up, and our day's run was ended at once on the Indiana shore. Scouting behind the riverbank border I saw nothing but cornfield. It seemed to stretch miles to right and left and back to the far hills, a desolate plain of broken stalks.

We were by this time accustomed to yielding to the stronger powers and to adapting ourselves quickly to sudden changes of circumstance. This afternoon, instead of drifting, we had a busy time in the cabin. I got out my tools to work on a new chest which was to fit under the window next to the fireplace, and soon had the floor cluttered with tools and material. Anna managed to find a corner where she could do some sewing.

Next morning was windy, too, but the late afternoon calmed and we cast off. Soon a johnboat put out from a creek, a man hailed us when near enough, asking if we had any nets to sell. We had to disappoint him, as we usually do when taken for authentic shantyboaters or fishermen. We had many hails from shore as we went along. Most were, "Where're you bound?" To which we would answer, "New Orleans." It seemed to both parties as far off as heaven. Once or twice we were asked if we would sell our houseboat, and the johnboat could have been sold many times over.

We made little distance that short afternoon and did not reach Warsaw, which was to windward. We tied up in a rainy nightfall against the steep Indiana shore, watched and speculated on the town lights as they appeared across the river. I made a telephone call from a one-pump filling station on the road above, after much difficulty, first in finding a telephone in the darkness, then in getting a connection through the Patriot exchange. Mine host finally took over, and while he cranked and shouted, I played two or three hands of euchre in his place.

Our progress down the river continued in this manner, drifting by easy stages and usually laying over for more than one night at each place we stopped. The weather determined our schedule mostly, but we often cast anchor off some shore that appealed to us, even though further drifting that day was possible. Often we tarried through good drifting weather to do more exploring or sketching. There was no hurry, no desire to be farther on our way. We drifted a few miles, around a bend or to a different kind of shore, and there had a new outlook, new banks, and new inhabitants to become acquainted with, all as strange to us as a landing twenty-five miles below would have been.

There was one reason why we might have traveled oftener and

farther—the pure delight of drifting. Each time, it was a thrill to shove out into the current, to feel the life and power of the river, whose beginning and end were so remote. We became a part of it, like the driftwood. Of not so simple and trusting a nature as driftwood, we studied charts, kept an eye on wind and weather, observed each feature of the passing shores. Yet the driftwood was the better navigator for at times we had to labor with our oars and sweeps to keep off a lee shore while the logs and snags went on their way unaffected by the wind.

It was exhausting work, not the labor of rowing so much as the tension and excitement, the near ecstasy of drifting. We had to stop often and take it in small doses.

The weather became so cold that often the lines were stiff as wire cables when we cast off, and must be thawed out inside the cabin. There were nights when we closed the shutters for warmth, and kept the fire burning. We tried to tie up the boat so that the bees would be in the lee of the cabin on windy nights. When it was very cold we bundled them up in an old comfort. Even then one could hear a happy, summer sound within the hive.

Our first station below Warsaw was a stony shore that reminded us of Brent. A fisherman soon visited us, saying, by way of excuse, that he thought our boat was Clark's, a man who bought junk and sold crockery. A hunter strolled by, too, and asked if we had any hound pups to sell. We were acquiring quite a list of items which it would be profitable for a drifting shantyboat to carry along.

There was some bad weather here. One night a high wind blew across the river with such force that I expected to hear our deck load of tubs and bicycle carried away. I wished I had lashed the tarpaulin more securely, but it held, after all.

Fearing a southwest wind, which would have a long sweep at us on that dangerous shore, we dropped down a short distance to the mouth of Plum Creek. This was an isolated place—the highway lay a mile back, and our nearest neighbors lived across the river in Kentucky. Later on we met a shantyboater who had lain here for several years. When we learned that he had operated a still, we understood his choice of that remote place. He had made garden here, too, never raising corn, of course— "It grew everywhere." He had survived runouts and ice, being solidly frozen in, one winter, but at last the law caught up with him and routed him out, though the elements had failed.

We saw our first canebrake here, and became acquainted with the word towhead, which was applied to the point above the creek. To us it means an island lying close to the shore, separated from it only at high water by a narrow channel.

The river, which had been falling since our departure from Big Bone, now began to rise swiftly, and we could row around the towhead. At the upper end was a great pile of driftwood poised over our heads and almost ready to float away. To make us even more uneasy, the creek bank began to cave in, as the current flowed around the towhead. So we left there and drifted down, on a sunny day, past Ghent, Kentucky, pronounced Gent, and Vevay on the other side. A ferry crossed here, the first since Aurora. The old Warsaw ferry, like the one at Rising Sun, had been discontinued.

Some eight or nine miles below Plum Creek we made another stop, this time on the Kentucky side. The mouth of the Kentucky river, a good harbor, was less than two miles farther on, but this location and shore were so attractive that we chose to remain here. It was almost a disastrous choice.

Some tremendous sycamores lined the bank. At this stage of the water we were able to work in behind them and get a gangplank out on the gravel shore. When we climbed to the top of a high clay bank, we found a different world. The land was level, the hills far back and out of sight. Heavy traffic sped along a four-lane highway parallel to the river. The countryside was taken up with stock farms and estates, all so landscaped and artificial that one could hardly remember that the river was just over the bank.

On a rainy Saturday afternoon we rowed the johnboat down to Carrollton at the mouth of the Kentucky. Buying little ourselves, we watched the country people in town for the day. The place had a southern feel, different from the Indiana towns lately visited. The air was colder coming back and we were given some help against the current by a strong southwest wind. It blew hard all night.

The next day will always be known to us as the Great Blow. The weather became much colder, the wind shifted to west, clouds broke up. The wind was directly upstream and the swells in mid-river were the highest we had ever seen, long combers that broke in a smother of foam. It was a sight to see, but when they came closer, as the wind shifted to northwest, the situation became alarming. Soon the waves were rolling through the sycamores and breaking on the beach like ocean surf. I ran extra lines to a tree out in the river, which luckily was directly to windward. These lines and the anchor out in the river upstream held us offshore and away from a heavy sycamore tree which was but a few feet to leeward. Spars were carried away. The boat rose on the swells and each time gave such a jerk on the lines that we expected them to part. It was an anxious time. I said to Anna, "I don't believe we can hold it." She answered, "We've got to." Then somehow I knew we would.

The gangplank thumped the side so I cast it loose. Then, afraid of losing it, I went ashore in the johnboat and pulled the plank out on the bank. It was not difficult to get ashore; the waves carried the johnboat in; but the breaking waves nearly swamped the boat and I could barely make it back to the deck. Then the waves filled the johnboat completely. Since it was our life boat, it must be bailed out. I worked it into the lee of our boat, and after many trials with a bucket, gained on the waves and emptied the johnboat of water.

The worst was over now. The wind lessened in the afternoon, and at sunset the air was calm, the river smooth.

This experience taught us to be more careful of wind. Our future harbors were chosen with an eye to exposure and protection rather than for an attractive shore. We have never since come so close to being shipwrecked in a storm.

A spell of good weather followed the blow and we laid over another day, a Sunday, so that George and Elisabeth could drive down and spend an afternoon on the boat. They were eager to hear about our voyage since our leaving them that first day, and we were glad to have news from our home port. They had some difficulty in finding the exact spot where we were, and drove up to a nearby mansion to ask about our location. It was a big place between the highway and river. We had seen the back of it and the terraced riverbank garden when

116

investigating the shore below our boat. The owner, however, could give George no information about his shantyboat neighbors, and was no doubt surprised to learn that he had any.

We left next day, drifted past Carrollton and the mouth of the Kentucky river. A ferry operated here. The most striking feature of the landscape was a noticeable change in the formation of the hills. They had not the rounded outlines with which we were familiar, but rose abruptly from the river land, often showing near the top a naked cliff of rock. More evergreens appeared and formed a crest of dark green above the rock, giving a new boldness to the river scenery.

These rugged hills first appeared on the northern shore, while on the left bank, about the mouth of the Kentucky, was a rich plain where stood old plantation houses. The country, like the town, was southern. Thus it was in early days—the northern shore remained Indian country long after Kentucky was settled. Some of the creeks flowing down from the north have the prefix, Indian, to their names. The Indian Kentucky River is opposite to the Kentucky. An even more pointed example is found on the upper Ohio where Indian Cross Creek comes in from the north, Virginia Cross Creek from the south. A mere list of the Ohio's creeks and tributary streams is poetry.

As we drifted along, our life seemed most pleasant to us, out in the sun, on the golden water. The shores had the openness peculiar to winter, all their details sharply incised in the thin air. We tied up at midday for a leisurely dinner and a walk through the fields. We were making the most of this day in the open country, since if our plans survived the uncertainties of drifting, our harbor that night, and for the next few days, would be Madison, Indiana. We were going to try the experiment of living on our boat in town.

After the river was left clear by the passing of two towboats, one the small steamer *Kenova,* an old friend of ours, we crossed to the Indiana side, and approaching Madison, began to look for a harbor. Our desire was to be above the town where the water is always cleaner, but the shores there were so low and muddy, with no possibility of improvement from either a falling or rising river, that we went on down under the bridge and past the public landing. Here were two inclines, and coal diggers with some barges. Passing by all this, we dropped anchor close below the lower fleet, ran some lines to the scattered willows on shore, and tied up there.

We found ourselves at the foot of Broadway, about as near the center of town as a shantyboat could be. Along the shore was a riverside drive where cars and strollers and children on their way to school often stopped to watch the river, and us. Looking up from our playing, we might see quite an audience. It was all strange to us, the city noises, street lights shining in the windows. Somehow we did not feel as close to the river as we did in the country.

Madison delighted us. It was a clean, lively town, the people quick and energetic. There were many old buildings, but they were all kept up and used for residences and places of business instead of being neglected and left to become the mouldering ruins so often seen along the river.

There was much to interest us as we prowled about. Nearby was a mill and feed store to which farmers brought their grain to be ground. Here we bought our first wheat, which we learned to use in many ways. For instance, toasted wheat is delicious with walnuts, and ground with toasted soy beans it became a favorite breakfast cereal. We experimented with flour, and in the end ground all that we used. I had been grinding cornmeal for ourselves and the dogs in a small box coffee mill. It was slow work and I was on the lookout for a more efficient grinder. Thinking to save some labor, I took a sack of our corn to the feed mill to be ground. Their grinding included "free mixing," as some farmers brought in two or three kinds of grain to be ground together. Our little batch of corn went through the mixing machine, too, and came out mixed with some kind of feed which had remained from a previous grinding. We could not decide what the mixture was, but it spoiled our cornmeal, although Skipper relished it.

One day I rowed down the shore to look about, and came to the landing float of the Madison Boat Club. The watchman there had a rather lonely life in winter, I guess, for after a sharp look at me, he asked me to tie up and talk a while.

Thus began our acquaintance with Art Moore, the most thoroughly shantyboat person we had met. He was neither old nor young. Small and weatherbeaten, when you met him on the street he seemed to belong to the river more than ever. He had been raised on a shantyboat, and any one place between Wheeling and the Saline River was as familiar to him as another. He knew everybody on the river, he said, —"good, bad, and indifferent." A little apologetic about his job as caretaker, he was even then building a little flat which was to become another in his long line of shantyboats. We often wonder where he has drifted to.

Art soon returned my call, and with no hesitation accepted our invitation to dinner. He was a charming guest, good-humored and debonair. His yarns were fascinating. Later we found the tales which landsmen told us about him hard to believe. Art had been through storms and floods, in boats that leaked from above and below; he had known hard times, when "corn and punkins" were his food. Three times he had been cleaned out by the law. He remarked that he liked the Kentucky mountaineers, had known several from Harlan. We asked if he had been there. "No," he said, "I met them in Atlanta."

It was Art Moore who had made Plum Creek his hangout for a spell. Another of his haunts, his favorite spot along the river, he said, was Payne Hollow, not many miles below Madison. It was on the Kentucky side, a gap in the highland which there ran close to the river. No one lived at Payne Hollow, there was a good spring, an old root cellar. This was the sort of place Art would pick out for his purposes, but we gave it special attention on our own account. Though still February, our summer plans were taking shape: we would not drift much farther that winter, but tie up some place from which Fort Thomas could be easily reached. This would have to be in the next twenty-five miles of river, as any point farther down would be too close to Louisville to suit us. Payne Hollow sounded promising, and we kept it in mind.

We heard more about this section of the river and the people who lived there from Jess Singer, engineer of the small towboat, *R. W. Turner*, who visited us one Sunday while the boat was in port. His home was in Bethlehem, Indiana, seventeen miles downriver. Not a young man, Mr. Singer had been engineer on one of the last true packets to operate on the Ohio River, the *New Hanover*, which ran from Madison to Louisville. One of the lowliest of packets, not even a steamboat, the *New Hanover* had continued to serve the farmers and riverbank communities long after most packets had gone out of business. Trucks could not take away its trade because no road was ever built along the river between Louisville and Madison, except in short, unconnected stretches. Since this was because of the many steep hills which rose directly from the river, and because there were no cities to demand such a road, this section of the river became more attractive to us than ever.

Mr. Singer's present boat, the *R. W. Turner,* was a small, diesel stern-wheeler which we had seen pass many times at Brent with a single oil barge. She laid over at Madison on Sunday whenever possible since it was her home port. We had unknowingly tied up at her landing, a section of the river front leased by the boat owners from the city. The captain was not pleased to find us there, and shouted that he was coming in and we must take the consequences. To our relief, he changed his mind and tied up below us.

That Sunday was our last day in Madison. In the afternoon we walked down the driveway along the river as far as Art Moore's dock. He invited us into his living quarters, a small cabin on the float, which might have been transplanted from a shantyboat. Leaving there we walked a short distance to the Lanier house, an ostentatious mansion of the old days, a place of wealth and refinement then, now beautifully kept up by the state. What a contrast to Art Moore's shack, we thought, and were glad we could understand in each its own peculiar value.

The weather was uncertain when we cast off in the morning. Puffs of wind made it difficult to keep offshore, but we struggled along past the Madison marine ways where a small towboat and a barge or two were hauled out for repairs. It was an interesting sight—the boats perched in air, their hulls exposed. The heavy triangular cradles which supported them, the long skids, and winches at the top, were antiquated survivals of the days of steam and wooden hulls.

Not far below, a wind sprang up which was not to be trifled with, and we looked about for shelter. According to the chart, Clifty Creek was near, but it could not be seen as we skimmed swiftly along the edge of the willows. The opening appeared suddenly before us. Quick work was necessary. From the johnboat, I made a line fast to a tree,

Anna snubbed the line around a kevel, the boat swung out of the current into the still water of the creek.

It was a good place for us. The backwater was deep, of a clear green color in contrast to the muddy tide which rushed by the entrance. Tall trees arched overhead, the northwest wind now roaring through their tops. Somewhere on the charts we had noticed a little creek called Cold Friday. This was our Cold Tuesday Creek. The wind continued for three days, flurries of snow at first, then clear and bright winter weather. A skim of ice closed the creek above us to navigation. The wind was cold and strong on top of the bank. I kept close to the boat, cutting wood in a sunny, sheltered spot, in company with the winter birds. Indoors it was warm and cheerful. The bright sun through the large windows made little fire necessary by day. In the evening I piled on firewood, and we battened down for the winter night.

The wind gradually subsided, but it was still cold the morning we again launched ourselves on the swift river. We drifted through a white, wintry world. Not for long did we drift, however, for there was more wind, upstream. We crossed over to the Kentucky side, and just made Gilmore Creek.

A second section of the cold wave descended on us with even more severe weather. Our harbor was small; I could almost step to either shore from the deck. Ice made further entrance impossible, and the west wind swept across the river directly into the creek. We turned our back to it, and made out very well.

Partly for our amusement, we had listed the requirements for our summer location. First, it must be far enough below Madison to be completely in the country, yet not so far down as to be in the Louisville district. It is surprising how far the influence of the city extends and how subtly it penetrates the country. Also, we knew that down near Louisville there were no hills. It was strange to be thinking of summer gardens in zero weather and snow storms, but we got out our warmest clothing and explored the shores and back country, with a garden in mind. This was the upper end of Trout Bottom, which was not a low and level tract, but higher ground, rather broken and rolling. We liked the place, with its old farmhouses scattered about. I think the only definite objection was the distance from the river to the hills, but somehow the place did not feel right. We decided to go farther on when the weather permitted. Our choice would be made instinctively, in spite of our list.

This more or less abstract speculation about summer plans did not interfere with our enjoyment of those perfect winter days at Gilmore Creek. The place had such a polar look—the snowy banks, the fantastic formations of ice. Crystal pendants girdled the trees, and the over-hanging banks and roots were draped with icicles which lengthened to reach the falling water.

The cove was already inhabited by a solitary and contented coot, who paid no attention to our arrival. I observed that the coot snapped up small silver fish and took them on the bank to eat. Shoals of these fish could be seen in the clear water. Their dark backs seemed to make almost a solid mass as they all swam along together. With little hope of success, I thought I would try to dip some up. A grass sack opened flat and tacked across two sticks made a rude net. I reached down into the thick swarm, expecting them to vanish in an instant. When I raised up the net it held as many fish as I could lift. I was dumbfounded. "Annie," I yelled, and all I could think of to say was, "Bring the camera!"

We learned that the fish were called shad. One day in conversation with two farmers at a deserted house nearby, where we went to get drinking water, we mentioned shad and invited them to come down and get a bucketful. They laughed, said that they sometimes hauled up a wagonload for their pigs.

The shad remained in the creeks until the water became warm. Since our supply of canned, smoked, and dried fish was used up, and the catfish in the river had not yet begun to bite, the shad were very welcome. Some say they are too bony, but that did not bother us. These shad were smaller than your hand. I would prepare about two dozen of them by scraping and then cutting away head, underparts and tail by one curving stroke. Then they were placed on a wire rack and grilled over the coals until brown and crisp. In this state the bones did not matter.

Our harbor was becoming too small for us as the river fell. When the weather moderated we moved out and dropped down along the shore a mile or two. This brought us to the lower end of Trout Bottom, where the river curved in to meet the steep range of hills. As we were tying up the boat to some trees, a hunter sauntered along the shore and spoke to us. After some conversation he gave us a rabbit he had just shot, and departed. We had learned his name was Jesse Powell, that he had a small farm on the ridge, that he worked through the country as a carpenter, and that he was part Indian. From his appearance this last was easy to believe.

The new shore and its inhabitants soon became well-known to us. At the top of the path leading from the river, among some locust trees, was a small weatherbeaten building with an old signboard even more weathered, on which could be dimly read, "Groceries and Dry Goods." We were told that in the days of the packet *New Hanover* and its predecessors this had been an important landing. Farmers from Trout Bottom and the surrounding hills came here to ship their produce, and trade at the store. All that remained now was the shattered building and Cleo and Wilmer. Their father, once a pilot on the *New Hanover,* had established the store. With the passing away of the boat and the store's usefulness, the old man moved up Spring Creek to a little farm he owned there. The place on the river was left to his two sons, Cleo and Wilmer, who lived in peace and contentment amid the ruins.

They were the friendliest of people, and went out of their way to make us feel at home. In fact, they wanted us to stay all summer, offered us a garden spot, and proposed a joint crop of watermelons. We decided to lay over there at least until we could write some letters

and receive answers. The mail came down into Trout Bottom within a mile of the river, if the weather and road were not too bad. Cleo had no mailbox of his own, but the carrier put his scanty mail in Boulders' box, at the end of the route. Our mail reached us safely, after passing through all these hands.

We wanted to catch up with our washing of clothes, too, a chore which was some weeks in arrears. Clear water was available in a little creek close by. We picked a day which promised fair weather and set to work early. It was necessary to start early not only to allow time for drying, but to heat water on shore while the ground was still frozen. Later in the day, under the bright sun, it was riverbank mud at its worst. While Anna washed and rinsed, I slogged through the mud in rubber boots, hanging up the wet clothes which seemed like fair blossoms unfolding in the sun from plants rooted in the alluvial slime.

It was the muddy bank, as much as anything, that influenced us to leave this place. Also, we had kept in mind Art Moore's account of Payne Hollow, which was but a short distance ahead. We heard more about the Hollow from our new friend, the Indian hunter, who stopped by again, this time leaving us a wild duck. Since Payne Hollow was his favorite hunting and fishing ground, we thought our settling there might not be welcomed by him. Yet he urged it upon us, and said he was sure an arrangement could be made with the owner of the land there, who was very agreeable, and a good friend of his.

Next day I made a scouting trip in the johnboat to Payne Hollow. Its aspect was so favorable that I brought back an enthusiastic report. There were disadvantages, the most serious being the exposed shore with a long reach to north and south. Even a west wind, blowing across the river, would have a good sweep at us, as the river was very wide there. We decided to move down to Payne Hollow for a while at least and think it over. Yet I was so strongly attracted, I felt that it would take more than a wind to discourage us.

The evening before we left their landing, Cleo and Wilmer came down to call on us. They were accompanied by Wilmer's wife and some of his youngsters, and by Cleo's daughter. The party waded down through the mud by lantern light, and filed across the gangplank with enough talking for a score of people. For some reason known only to himself, Wilmer would not take off his galoshes, as the others did; so I scrubbed the mud off as he stood first on one foot, then the other. Finally all were seated around the fire. Cleo was a fast and endless talker—allegro vivace. Wilmer's tempo was largo, but he was persistent, and completed his exposition as if he were alone with you on a mountain top. Listening to both at once was almost too much for us.

We were interested in what Wilmer had to say about his lamp lighting, for he tended the Spring Creek navigation light. The fact that oil lamps were still used was a surprise, for so far we had seen only electric ones, fixed or flashing. The light across from Gilmore Creek had the soft yellow glow of an oil lamp, but though we watched every evening and morning, it was lighted and put out when our eyes were turned away. Farther down the river oil lights were common, and we met light tenders far different from Wilmer.

It was not a long voyage down to Payne Hollow, but we had never seen such a shore along the Ohio. It rose sharply from the river without the usual fringe of willows. The hardwood forest trees and stones of all sizes from the rugged hillside came down to the water's edge. The natives call such a shore the Narrows, rather "Narrs."

We landed at Payne Hollow with great expectations. How good it was to have a sandy beach, and solitude!

6

We explored our new territory with the eagerness of castaways on their desert island. The freedom of the river was still with us. We occupied the shore as naturally as the driftwood and river sand, though of course the land belonged to someone, and we were ready to decamp at the least suggestion.

The nearest road or house being a mile away, no one came to the riverbank in those inclement days of late winter. Powell, the hunter, in fresh clean overalls, stopped by on his Sunday forays into the woods, but he was the aborigine and disturbed the solitude no more than did the ducks on the river.

The small upland creek which came down Payne Hollow—it was never called Payne Creek or given any other name that we heard—had cut through a high range of hills which paralleled the river. At its mouth a narrow strip of sandy bottomland, covered with last year's broken cornstalks, extended along the river, tapering to a point above and below the creek where the Narrows rose steeply from the water's edge. Farther back from the river, against the wooded hillside and higher than the field next to the willows, was another strip of tillable ground, not recently cultivated. We thought this would be a good place for a garden.

Winding through the bottomland, the course of the creek was marked by two rows of water-loving trees, and where it entered the river a pair of cottonwoods formed a gigantic gateway. The creek had high mud banks at this low stage of the river, but its clear water flowed over shelving rock. A few rods from the river, under a tall sycamore whose exposed roots formed a wierd Gothic canopy, was the spring, pouring forth in great volume.

Downstream from the creek, at the higher level, was a stone foundation. The house which once stood there might have been carried away by some high flood. Prowling among the briars, we came upon the root cellar mentioned by Art Moore, its low door like the hidden entrance to a cave. Within it was a rather spacious dome, the stones well-laid, plastered and whitewashed. A stone shelf ran all around. There was an air hole at the top, which was at ground level. This cellar was enough to tempt one to rebuild there.

We followed the trace of a road along the creek which farther up ran over a shallow bed of broken stones. The hollow widened out into a level field in the midst of which stood a well-built fireplace and chimney of stone. Except for some unevenness of ground and a few scattered stones, no trace of a house remained. Against the hill was a tobacco barn, evidently of later date than the chimney and still in use. Here the creek divided and the old road, following neither branch, began its sloping climb to the ridge.

We, the latest inhabitants of Payne Hollow, came upon other sites of dwellings, perhaps a square of rough-laid stone overgrown with new forest, or an old well. Later the natives told us that there had been a small settlement at Payne Landing. The farmers used to bring their stock and produce down to the steamboat. Near the landing once stood a rude warehouse and a small corral. Many wagonloads of peaches had been brought down from the ridge and shipped from there. The road must have been much better in those days, for in our time it was too rough for even an apple.

In this year winter ran its full course. The smoke from our blazing fires was ever carried downstream with the south-flowing current. March was past the season for ice in the river, but the water was low and clear, the air very cold. One night we awoke dismayed to hear

the crunching sound of ice, made by the scattered floes as they crashed into our boat and scraped along its length. In a few days the river was nearly full of floating ice. A solid mass of it extended out from shore. I hauled the johnboat out on the bank, and kept a little duck pool open around the boat.

Remembering the advice of Andy, which was repeated by the local river authority—who was Cleo's father, the old pilot—we determined to pull the boat out on the bank if the river froze into a solid sheet of ice. Some straight young sycamores to be used as skids were located. No actual preparations were necessary, however, for the March sun checked the formation of solid ice. After a few days the running ice vanished as suddenly as it had appeared, and the river was again open for navigation.

Thinking that all danger was past, I took away the protecting boom from the outside of the hull. The nights turned cold again, and large sheets of very thin ice formed in the river. One morning in a stiff west wind, about an acre of this ice, as thin and transparent as window glass, was blown in to the boat, and as it drifted along, its saw edge cut a narrow groove the length of the hull, thus doing more damage than the heavier ice had. It was remarkable how fast this sheet ice was moved toward the shore and our boat by the crossriver wind. There was nothing on the ice to catch the wind, but the rippling wind waves at its edge, and friction of the wind across its surface must have created a continuous force which set the sheet of ice in motion.

These cold nights and thawing days made us think of maple syrup, or it may have been the hard maple trees we saw on the steep Narrows upriver from our landing. In a previous spring, living then at the studio in Fort Thomas, we had boiled some sap, and still had the wooden tubes I had whittled out and used as spigots. I now made a few more and we gathered together all available buckets, cans, jars, and utensils—there was no dump to draw on now, no gas station from which to get discarded oil cans. Nineteen trees were tapped and our makeshift sap buckets hung out. The hillside was rough and very steep; so the gathering of sap and carrying it in was a difficult and uncertain performance, even though the trees were concentrated in a small area near the bottom of the hill. The fire was built in the woods, close to the river, at the end of a little path which ran along the shore from Payne Hollow.

The season for syrup making did not last long. We continued our sugar camp for nine days, boiling down nine washboilerfuls of sap, each of which made about a quart of syrup.

These were special days. It was a joy to be working in the winter woods, above the river, building huge fires. I would roll in some logs and big chunks of hardwood on the last trip before bed time. Then I walked back to the boat through the dark, starry woods by a path soon well-known. In the morning the sap was still steaming, half boiled down. As we finished off this, the sap buckets were emptied into a wash tub for a new batch. It was convenient to take our midday meal up to the camp, to watch carefully the last of the boiling, exciting for us novices, and to start afresh. Our dinner was often shad broiled over the coals and potatoes and corn dodgers baked in the ashes. The new syrup was delicious with the hot bread.

While cutting wood near our sugar camp one day I saw, standing upright among the old leaves—it still seems the most unlikely object to find there—a grinder. It was just what we were looking for to grind our corn and wheat, an old hand-power coffee mill, the kind once used in grocery stores, with a wheel on each side to serve as crank and flywheel. The coffee beans were put in a hopper in the center. The hopper had a bell-shaped cover, missing in our model, as was one of the wheels. Originally a bright red, it had been repainted

gray, unfortunately. Yet it worked, and it was not too rusty. Our grinding of corn and wheat became much easier and faster, and the meal and flour finer. Later we found other things to grind.

Who left the grinder on that uninhabited hillside is still something of a mystery. Powell said that Art Moore had camped there, and had made the path to the spring. His campsite, close to our sap-boiling fire, was still marked. We thought he might have used the grinder in some process of his distilling.

During our syrup making we explored all the hillside. Halfway up, on a narrow shelf, was an overgrown clearing and the remains of a house. Above this the slope became even more steep, ending in a palisade of bare rock. It was more like mountain than river country. Almost at the crest of the hill a strong spring flowed out from under the rock. This water had been piped to the farm on the hillside clearing below by a rude aqueduct which we followed down through the steep woods. It was made of the trunks of straight trees, mostly ash, which had been split and hollowed into rude troughs with an ax. At the end was a large, hollowed-out log to receive the water. All this might have been done in pioneer times, or even in the stone age, but later we met the man who, with his boys, had made the clearing and piped the water.

Following the brow of the hill, thick with cedars, an almost sheer drop to the river on one hand, farm land on the other, past a log cabin in good condition but unoccupied, we came to a weatherbeaten farmhouse which had long stood on this windy point. With its cluster of pine trees, it was a landmark from the river, which was spread out before it as on a map. We wondered how anyone could live an ordinary life with such an outlook constantly before him, with so much of the world at his feet.

Hospitable folk lived in the old farmhouse. They were our first friends in the neighborhood of Payne Hollow, and we were soon making frequent trips, by an easier path up the shoulder of the ridge instead of climbing the steep face of it. We brought back skim milk by the gallon and often a jar of cream, taking up as many buckets of shad as they could use, and later an occasional catfish.

Stirred by a few warm days in early March, we pored over seed catalogues, and, though not assured of a garden to plant them in, sent off an order for seeds. By the time they arrived, by way of Cleo, the weather had turned too cold and wet for any thought of planting. Meanwhile we scouted about the countryside, though it might have been better to have let our exploring wait for warmer days. The wind-swept hills and roads gave no welcome, and at the farmhouses where I stopped, the inmates were gone a-visiting or still holed-up for the winter. We called at the house of Owen Hammond, the owner of Payne Hollow, but he, too, was away. A few days later we stopped by again and found the whole family at home. Owen and Daisy were themselves young, and had a family of four young children. Daisy's father and mother lived in the same house, though it was but a small one. All made us welcome in an off-hand manner, as if we were old neighbors. We did not say at once that we would like to stay all summer at Payne Hollow and make a garden on their land. We knew that country ways are more deliberate, and such a project must develop slowly.

Another matter we were anxious to arrange was our mailing address. A rural carrier passed Owen's house daily, but the mile walk up the rough road caused us to hesitate about receiving our mail from that direction. The Indiana side of the river was another possibility. Wide as the river was there—about half a mile—the row across seemed easier than the climb up the hill. Moreover, the voyage took us to a shore entirely different from Payne Hollow. It was a wide bottomland where even the birds were not the same. Thus our trips to a mailbox on that side would give us a wider range of country and also an opportunity to make new friends.

While these decisions were pending, it became necessary to make a trip to town for certain supplies which were running out. The last chance to buy anything had been at Madison, nearly six weeks back, and no great stock had been laid in there. Even so there was no lack of food. Much remained of the vegetables and fruit canned at Brent. It was an easy matter to dip up shad in the creeks. The skim milk from the Marshall farm was a boon to us at this time, for drinking, cooking, and cheese. An invitation was extended to help ourselves to their patch of winter kale. Our bean sprouts furnished salad stuff, and wild greens would soon be available. We had corn and wheat to grind, and plenty of walnuts. Our potatoes were all gone, but their place was taken by groundnuts which might be called wild potatoes. They grew along the sandy shore across the river, long strings of them often washed out by the waves. They were very good when boiled, of a more earthy taste than potatoes, the fresh ones beautifully white inside.

With all this to draw on, we need not go hungry. Some of the items lacking—bacon, butter, whole milk—were later procured from farms in exchange for fish. But in those early days the catfish had not begun to bite, and it takes time to become acquainted with the farmers who like fish and who have the desired products to exchange.

Town meant Madison, nine miles away. Not liking to ask any of our new neighbors to carry us along with them, we decided to take the chances of the road. Crossing the river early one morning we waited by the side of the gravel road near some milk cans. The milk truck soon came along, and the obliging driver took us with him as if he were accustomed to picking us up there with the cans every morning. The road followed the river even around steep Plowhandle Point, whose bold outline was a feature of the upriver view from our boat. A steep hollow beyond was called Big Six, the driver said. Two shantyboats were beached out there, all that remained of a former land and water community. One of the boats, a little one even smaller than ours, belonged to Bill Shadrick, known to be the best fisherman in these parts.

Before Madison was reached we had told our story to Jim, the truck driver—where we lived and what our errand to town was. To help us out, he informed us that another milk truck would be leaving Madison in the early afternoon. Instead of following the river road, however, it would take a route through the hills to the Saluda School, a point as far south as our landing, but some three miles back from the river. This looked like our chance.

We felt quite at home in Madison. After all we had really lived there even if it was for a brief time and with only one foot on land. Our good impression of the town was renewed in the little time there was for looking around.

When all the items on our list were bought and assembled, it was a heap of stuff. There were two sacks of potatoes, one to eat and one to plant in our hypothetical garden, and two or three boxes of groceries. We are always surprised at the amount of food we buy when we go to town. Before going there seems to be so little we need, and if the trip is postponed we get along very well for an indefinite period.

The young driver of the outbound milk truck, whom we found having lunch in a hamburger stand, agreed with no hesitation to take us and our goods. We loaded our sacks and boxes in with the empty milk cans. Then we sat in the cab waiting for the driver to complete his afternoon's business in town. We ate some lunch and read from our current pocket book, all the time keeping an eye on the procession along the sidewalk. So many people here, yet we lived a few miles away in almost complete isolation.

The return trip was through country new to us. The driver left us at the Saluda School, our sacks and boxes piled up by the roadside. Luckily for us, school was not yet out. We were hoping to get a ride to the river on the school bus, whose driver, Harry Schirmer, owned a farm on the river across from Payne Hollow. When he arrived with his bus, he took one look at our plunder and said there would be no room for us in with the school children; if we did not mind waiting, he would come back with his pickup truck and take us down to the river. This he did—surely the act of a good neighbor. He hauled us down the lane as close to the river as he could go. It was an easy carry to the johnboat, and we were back home before sunset, quite pleased

with ourselves for having managed to get to Madison and bring back
two hundred pounds of freight all in one day.

A few days later we crossed the river again to put up our mailbox
along the road. I had made one of a five-gallon tin can, and painted
it red like the hull of our boat. At one end was a hinged door, and
on the side the customary signal flag. This was our first mailbox and
we were proud to see our name along the road, and to send our new
address to our correspondents. The first time we looked in our box
there was mail—rural advertising addressed to "Boxholder."

It was not long before we came to an agreement with Owen Hammond. I think he was puzzled that we should be at all formal about it.
His attitude seemed to be that we would stay there as long as we
cared to, and the only question about a garden was where to put it.
The location he suggested was above the creek, on the upper level
next to the hill, the very spot we had picked out.

We now took formal possession of our new domain by moving our
colony of bees ashore. This was not easy, for the hive was heavy. The
bees had wintered well, and there must have been honey left over.
Making a litter of two poles and some cross pieces, we ferried the hive
ashore and carried it up to the edge of our garden. Soon the bees were
flying forth into their new territory.

The sweeps could now be dismantled, and the deck load on the roof
carried ashore. It was stored under a tarpaulin which we called the

bicycle tent, since my bicycle was one of the principal items unloaded from the roof.

We plunged into gardening, not spading or waiting to have it plowed. I broke up the surface of the ground with a heavy hoe, chopping up last year's weeds and leaves where they lay. Each section or row was planted when ready. It made a patchwork garden, but the method allowed us to plant early, and work almost between showers. Some of the potatoes were planted by the middle of March, before the last snow and frost. It is an unrivaled adventure, putting seeds in the ground, in this case intensified by the strangeness of our situation and our voyage to those new shores.

We had already become so attached to Payne Hollow that any objection to our remaining there would have been regretted. It answered most of the requirements on the list we had made out of desirable features for a summer location, and offered some advantages not thought of. As for the list, a better way might be to judge a place by its first impact. If attracted to it at once, even if for reasons not easily recognized, your choice will turn out to be a happy one, and hidden advantages of your new home will in time be revealed.

There are bound to be drawbacks to any place. One of these at Payne Hollow was its exposure to the south wind which had a long sweep against the current of the river. Already one day had been so rough that we were glad to spend it on land. The waves had carried away the gangplank and to get ashore we must row the johnboat into the sheltered creek mouth.

Another possible objection, which hung over us all summer, was the return of the sand digger. Some sand diggers are not bad neighbors. A picturesque sight is an old steam-powered one, anchored in mid-river, with a cloud of smoke rising from its stack above the haphazard pattern of screens, booms, and chutes with a sand flat or two tied at each side. The scene is enlivened by a small towboat bringing empties. It takes away the deepladen barges of sand and gravel, and the digger is left in its insular solitude.

However, the sand digger which had operated off Payne Hollow the preceding summer, Owen told us, was diesel-powered, and made a racket which was heard over the country miles back from the river.

This was a disturbing prospect; but we figured that since it was not already there, the sand digger might not come at all. This turned out to be true, and the sand fleets which came around the bend all passed by without anchoring.

The noise and vibration of a sand digger, besides shattering the summer peace, might have spoiled the fishing. Toward the end of March the test line which I had kept baited began to catch some fish, and soon there were more catfish in our live box than we could use. The surplus was easy to dispose of. Powell, too busy working at his trade to fish, would get a mess on his Sunday visit, bringing us perhaps a squirrel or two, or a piece of country ham, and later on young fryers. We took fish to the Hammonds and to the Marshalls, who would never let us pay for the skim milk which we got from them in quantity. Harry Schirmer was another fish-hungry person, and we were pleased to take him a mess now and then. Also to the Joe Montgomerys. Their mailbox and ours stood side by side, and our trips for mail came to include a visit or at least a passing word with them.

Once or twice I carried a sack of catfish up to the farms on the ridge, where they were eagerly received. If possible, I bartered them for country produce. A dozen eggs, a gallon of milk, or a piece of bacon was a good bargain for a few fish we could not use, and seemed of much greater value than money, even if the money would buy the same things, or more. Our neighbors liked this idea, too, and before long the demand was almost greater than we could meet. When the hens began to lay, and cows were fresh, so much milk and eggs were given us that we began to long for a mess of catfish for ourselves.

The game warden came up the river one day, and asked for a fishing license which I could not produce. He said I had better get one before his next trip. The nearest place to buy a fishing license was Bedford, the county seat, some miles back from the river. Perhaps it was the only place, for towns were so scarce in Trimble County that we could account for only two: Bedford, and Milton which was on the river opposite Madison.

I rode to Bedford on the bicycle one spring day. I did not follow the blacktop road which made a wide swing to the north along the ridge, but went directly eastward from the river. The first lap was push and carry up the old road to the ridge. Then down into Corn Creek, along an indifferent, muddy road, up toward the head of the valley. Happening to pass the end of the mail route as the carrier arrived in his jeep, I witnessed a strange ceremony. He handed over the last of the mail, a few letters and newspapers, to an old lady mounted on a red pony. She wore a long, black coat and a black stocking cap, her face barely peeping out between them. She tucked the mail into a canvas bag, and rode slowly up the hollow to the last houses, over a road too rough even for a jeep.

It was more of a walk than a bicycle ride for me. Corn Creek, high and icy cold, had to be forded twice. I wondered at some large, well-built, old houses, signs that the valley had once been prosperous. Near the head of it, the road left the narrow hollow and climbed to a higher level. The remainder of the way in to Bedford was smooth and level. Returning, I followed the roundabout, paved road, a quicker and easier way, though a more ordinary one.

When I left the road and began the descent to the river, glimpses of which, far below, could be had through the budding trees, it seemed that we lived at the end of the world, more remote even than the last farm up Corn Creek; yet I approached with an inward lifting, and when home again, our little Hollow seemed the center of the world.

These were full and busy days. The earliest-rising farmer was not ahead of us. Bluff Mr. Mack, when I met him on one of my frequent catfish-milk trips to the ridge, did not reply to my "Good morning!" directly, but merely said, "What time do you get up, anyway?"

One time, returning to the boat with the rising sun, I was surprised to see Art Moore step out from behind a tree, pistol in hand. He had been watching a ground-hog hole, while his friends, a couple from Madison, were after squirrels on the hill. They all had arrived, soon after I had left, in a motorboat belonging to one of the members of the Madison Boat Club who had trustfully left the key with Art. All was quiet in our cabin, where Anna had chanced to go back to sleep. She was wakened by the bang of a gun and a voice from the river saying, "I guess that'll wake 'em up."

After an unsuccessful hunt, Art and his friends had breakfast with us. They relished especially the pan of corn bread which Anna baked from meal ground in the grinder which we thought had belonged to Art. Though it was in plain sight, he made no mention of it. After breakfast we took a walk, with considerable proprietary interest shown on each side. The joke was that Art could not find his root cellar, and we had to lead him to it.

In the spring and early summer, much time and labor went into our flourishing garden. It was a good investment, in many ways. Perhaps the richest harvest comes in the beginning: the thrill of planting seeds, and the cherishing of great hopes for the sprouting plants. Soon there were more substantial rewards—lettuce, spinach, peas, and tiny carrots and beets, with a delicacy and tenderness in keeping with the wild flowers and song of birds.

Owen plowed the lower strip of bottom one day with his team of white horses. As we watched them from below, crossing back and forth against the green hillside, we admired the understanding between man and horses, working smoothly together, with only a few low-spoken words of direction. When the ground was made ready, an easy task in the soft, light soil, Owen offered us as much of it as we cared to plant. This was another instance of his unstudied kindness toward us. In a long strip next to the river, we planted crops which were still seasonable, and which needed space—muskmelons, watermelons, sweet potatoes, peanuts, sunflowers, late beans, corn, and tomatoes. Our operations now approached farming.

On some days we deserted the boat and rambled through the country, always followed by Skipper and Old Boss, the neighbors' dog who was spending the summer with us. We explored the hills and valleys, marked the location of crops to be gathered in their season—raspberry and blackberry patches, wild and untended fruit trees. We stopped to talk with farmers as they worked in the fields, became so well acquainted with some that they invited us to spend a day with them. We never knew just what this meant, but we liked to visit them at their homes, inspect their barns, have a good country dinner. The change was good for us, the society and conversation, the dry air of the hilltops, the smell of pines and hay. Then, too, we are ever curious about the way other people live.

Some of the farmers grew strawberries which they sold to a processing plant at Bedford. When they ripened at the end of May, we became strawberry pickers, crawling up and down the long rows with the crew of farm women and children. This was one time we had all the strawberries we could eat. We found by experiment that we could use up five quarts before they became too soft. In this we were different from the farmers, one of whom in his own strawberry patch, I heard asking about strawberry shortcake as if it were a delicacy heard of but never experienced.

The best came at the end of the season when Ansel McCord turned over an old patch to the pickers. The berries were small, down among the grass, but of a sweetness and flavor far superior to those on the new vines, which were cultivated and forced. They were like wild strawberries. Perhaps the so-called wild strawberries are merely abandoned beds or escaped plants. From them we made a store of preserves.

Strawberry preserves was but one item on Anna's canning record. The list, beginning with twenty-one jars of poke in April, became long and varied. If there was more of any crop, wild or domestic, than we could use currently, the surplus was put into jars and stowed away in the hold.

Blackberries were plentiful on the hills, and we picked gallons of them in the wooded pastures. Soaked with the dew of early morning, we returned down the hill with full pails before the sun became hot. After a swim, the berries were looked over and left to stand in sugar. The canning was done with the dinner fire, and the processing, my job, was completed on the bank over a blazing fire of driftwood.

With such good management on Anna's part, canning never became a tiresome or time-consuming chore. There was likely to be a touch of adventure somewhere along the line, in harvesting the crop, perhaps, or a storm might come up during the processing.

This busy life is quite different from the shiftless leisure that shantyboaters are supposed to enjoy. We became industrious and respected members of the community. I even cut corn in the fall to get our winter's supply. On Sundays we prepared for visitors. I kept myself presentable, and did not become involved in any work which could not be dropped instantly.

This placed us in a new position with regard to the river. Watching it from the shore, almost as a landsman, we might have felt a longing to drift with it again and, ever passing new shores, make only brief stops along the way. Yet we did not regret our present shore-bound life, rather we made the most of it; for the autumn and our departure would come soon enough.

Since there was no road to Payne Hollow, we had not expected many visitors. However, either from friendliness or a desire for fish, most everyone within walking distance came down to see us. The rough way was traversed one Sunday by a tractor-trailer with a load of visitors, and Daisy Hammond's mother came down in a wagon when the corn was cut. Others stopped by in boats, Bill Shadrick, and Mr. and Mrs. Tinus from Saluda Creek, and some who were strangers to us, on strange errands. It must be that some were curious about how we lived, and wanted to see the details of our boat about which they had heard— how the bed rolled out, how our floor could be lifted up, and the like.

Our old friends and family visited us, too. We made a rough map of the way from Madison to the landing on the Indiana shore opposite us, sent tracings of the map to everyone we thought might possibly come. Most of them did, beginning with George and Elisabeth in April. The texas was put in service when Anna's sister, Nell, spent a week with us just before strawberries were ripe. At the time, Skipper's Payne Hollow pups did not yet have their eyes open. They all slept in the cabin with

Nell, who was delighted with their company even though it meant getting up in the night to let Skipper out and in.

Entertaining our guests was an easy matter. There was an abundance of good food from the garden, the river, and our farm neighbors. We had our own honey and maple syrup. The boat never seemed small or crowded. Unlike most dwellings which enclose and shut out, it made no sharp division between inside and out. We overflowed onto the bank, and often cooked our meals there, broiling fish, roasting corn and potatoes, baking in an iron kettle with hot coals on the lid.

Much as there was to do on the long summer days, there was no haste or pressure about it. Time was never measured. The thread of our reading was unbroken; frequent hours were given to the playing of music together. I found much to paint.

We had said little about my painting to the natives. Anyone who lives on a shantyboat is at once and unchangeably classified as a fisherman. So I passed for a rather unsuccessful and indolent fisherman, one with some queer notions, yet, I think, likable. One of our friends, driving along the river road to Madison after a visit with us, picked up Bill Shadrick, the fisherman at Big Six. Bill thought this an opportunity to clear up a question that had been bothering him. "Is he a real riverman?" he asked.

So I was surprised one day, when picking strawberries on the hill, to be asked by a well-dressed stranger, "Do you paint pictures?" I guessed he was a preacher, and so he was. His son was picking strawberries in the same patch. When I admitted that I painted pictures, he said he wanted a picture for his church. It was to be a baptismal scene, a picture of a river rolling down from the far distance to the very pulpit. At this point I became interested, told the Reverend I would think it over, and also consider, as he requested, the matter of price.

We were puzzled as to the manner in which the church folk had learned that I was an artist. Up to that time I had imparted this fact to but one person, a young farmer whom I had met when walking through the fields. Our conversation that day, in that open, remote place, became frank and sincere. He was interested in our way of life, asked what my work was. Not to be taken for a fisherman was a

141

pleasant surprise, and I told him about my painting. He had remembered this when his church began looking about for an artist.

This picture would be a new venture for us, but after due consideration we decided to undertake it. I told the preacher as much, when we met in the berry patch next time, allaying his concern about price by offering to do the work gratis, the church to pay for all material. This was not a benevolent gesture on my part, but selfishly I hoped to work with greater freedom than would be possible with the suggestions and requirements of a paying client to consider.

Several preliminary steps preceded the actual painting. The preacher came down to the boat one hot afternoon, probably to see what manner of work I did. On another day we inspected the church, found it a white-painted wooden building in a grove at a crossroads. It had the air of sanctity and peace that country churches attain to, and was a real inspiration. I now made a sketch for the proposed picture. This we showed to the church committee at an evening conference at McCord's farm. McCords were not members of this church but the meeting was held in their house because it was about as close to the river as the committee could come, and not a long walk for us. The sketch was accepted with little comment. Size, proportion, and other details were discussed and decided. Now we could begin work.

Anna and I carried the panel on which the picture was to be painted down the stony trail to the river by means of a litter made of two poles. The panel was four by eight feet, too large to manage in our small cabin. Luckily one corner of the tobacco barn at the head of the hollow was empty. It made such a fine studio that I wished we had earlier thought of using it for that purpose. Light came through an open ventilator, a tall shutter such as tobacco barns have. Timbers and walls had a patina of age. The dim rafters overhead made an almost unlimited ceiling. One felt far away, there, deep within its comforting shelter. The barn was at its best in the mizzling days of autumn.

The painting went well and was a joy to do. When it was finished, the preacher came down to help us up the hill with it. It was transported to the church, and we alone set it up in place.

We liked it. The church folk did, too, when they saw it the following Sunday. It was not what they had envisioned. It was not the Jordan

of the Sunday School pictures, but the Ohio, its golden current coming forward from the distance, the landscape a patchwork of sun and shadow. The only ecclesiastical note was a white church spire in the little town in the foreground.

A week or so later we were invited to a church supper to be held at the Pleasant Retreat Community House. We did not know what to expect. On that evening Mr. Mack met us at the top of the hill in his car. At the community house, which was an abandoned rural school used for all such meetings, we were surprised at the number of cars parked outside. Within were seventy-five or a hundred farm people mostly members of "our" church. We were amazed to find that all this was in our honor, an appreciation of the painting. After a prayer, in which thanks were given for the new picture, we were the first to be served at the tables of food, good country food of a deliciousness and abundance that only farm women can achieve. Later there was singing, and Anna's playing of the accompaniment and of some solo pieces was the hit of the evening. As we walked down the dark road to the river we were a little dazed by our rise to such high estate from our humble beginnings there.

After the painting was completed we could give all our time and attention to the business of getting under way. We had arrived at Payne Hollow self-contained and unattached. After spreading out on shore and almost taking root there, we must again make ourselves compact and movable.

There was the garden to harvest, and its produce to stow away in one form or another. Potatoes were in such abundance that the middle hatch was nearly filled. Another year we would not be so reckless in the purchase of seed potatoes, a decision which was strengthened toward spring when the wrinkled potatoes had to be sprouted over and over.

After the strife of summer, when plants of all kinds struggle to grow and you help and protect the favored ones, the garden becomes a place of peace in the fall. A truce is made with the bugs; the weeds come into flower and produce their fruit or seeds. The tall sunflowers planted at haphazard, singly or in groups, gave a tropical look to our garden. The peanut vines were pulled up and hung on a stretched wire to dry. Herbs were drying, sacks of dry beans hanging about to be shelled out later. There was a heap of pumpkins gathered from the bottomland cornfields where they lay like boulders. Our melons lasted until cold weather.

Bushels of walnuts were gathered and hulled, then dried on the sunny roof. Kiefer pears from Mr. Mack's trees were spread out in the studio barn to be canned as they ripened. We gathered wild grapes, for jelly and juice to drink, from vines along the river. Another preparation for winter was the smoking of fish.

In August we had made an expedition down the river and across to Saluda Creek. On the hill above was an extensive peach orchard. Here we bought some fruit of the finest quality, at the same time keeping up the shantyboat tradition by picking from the ground a bushel or two which we got at a bargain price. We sailed back up the river with our cargo, and the next two days were busy ones.

Besides the corn cutting, I tried my hand at cutting tobacco. Here I did not do so well. There is a knack about it to be acquired only with long practice. I was a better hand at stripping cane, taking my pay in new cooked sorghum molasses. This was done on the hill farm of Owen's father, where stood an old log house, sway-backed and weatherbeaten.

While I was eating a good country dinner with all Mr. Hammond's boys, a meal spoken of as "beans and 'taters," Anna was entertaining unexpected guests. They had hailed from across the river. Anna rowed over in the johnboat, ferried them back to the boat, and later in the afternoon when they had waited as long as they could for my arrival, she rowed them across the half mile of water again. At this point I reached the boat, not a little surprised at the absence of johnboat and wife. I sounded the horn, and a familiar voice answered back from the twilit river.

The season was changing. Autumn brought a new sky, new air, a landscape unimaginably fair. The first frost was November eighth. Later, on a wind from the northwest, there were flurries of snow, melting on the ground but whitening the gangplank and the west side of the furrows.

We loaded the last of our plunder on board, on the roof, in the hold, behind the fireplace, wherever it could be stowed out of the way. A tarpaulin was stretched over the deck load; the sweeps were made ready. The last loading was the bees from whom we had taken a good quantity of honey. On November twenty-ninth 1947 we set sail from Payne Hollow on a light downstream wind. Old Boss was the only one to see us off.

7

Thirty-eight miles below Payne Hollow is the Falls of the Ohio. Had our voyage been made in the days of the flatboat, it would have been necessary to wait for a rise in the river to negotiate the rocky rapids. This obstacle to navigation has been gotten around by digging a canal at Louisville, and now, as far as steamboat men are concerned, the Falls of the Ohio is little more than a name. Yet to us drifters it was still a hindrance: the high dam built there for electric power backs up the water for seventy-five miles, and makes of that section of the river in low water a dead stream with almost no currrent.

Thirty-eight miles may be a short distance, but in slack water it seemed a long way to us, who in drifting from Brent to Payne Hollow had traversed less than a hundred miles. The easiest course would be to wait for a rise in the river: then the Louisville dam would be opened and the current swift. In so doing, however, we must forego our proposed Christmas visit to Anna's mother. To go away and leave the boat at Payne Hollow where no one lived to take care of it and the dogs was out of the question. If we could reach Louisville in time, we might find a boat harbor there in which our outfit could be left while we went on our trip to Michigan.

After all, there was nearly a month to make the thirty-eight miles, and we looked forward to an unhurried voyage. We had left Payne Hollow in the afternoon on a dying north wind, and were only a few miles below when we tied up for the night. To our surprise we were welcomed ashore by Old Boss who had followed us, unseen, down through the willows. We wondered how we could ever get away from him; at our slow speed he could follow us along the shore, and swim to the other side if we crossed over.

Next morning both Skipper and Boss had departed, probably for their old hunting ground. There was another dog to be accounted for, Susan, one of Skipper's last pups, now six months old. She had not gone off with the other dogs; she tagged along with us as we went visiting that Sunday morning. Our first call was across the river in Indiana, to the Tinuses, who had stopped at our boat several times when bound for Madison in their outboard. It was possible to row up Saluda Creek almost to their little hillside farm. Along the creek path we found some choice walnuts to add to our store.

Skipper being still absent upon our return to the boat, we walked down the Kentucky shore to the Corn Creek bottom. It was fun exploring new country since the paths around Payne Hollow had become quite familiar. At Corn Creek lived Mahorney, whose truck was an informal bus to Madison for the inhabitants of lower Corn Creek. We had ridden out from town with him once, finding a place for ourselves in the open truck body, as the other passengers did, among the empty cream cans, boxes of groceries and blocks of salt. Mahorney was an amateur evangelist; a "sanctified person" Powell had called him. In his house was a strange painting by a Trimble County El Greco. Mahorney was as scornful of orthodox painting as he was of the regular ministry. However, when he came down to our boat in the afternoon with two of his little girls, he liked some of my landscapes.

Soon after our guests left, Skipper returned alone, to our relief. Where she had been, and why Boss did not come back with her, was a mystery to us. Though it was already late in the day, we cast off. Calm weather must be taken advantage of, for the current was so slow that the slightest breeze ahead would stop us in our tracks.

We drifted into the night, tied up against the steep Indiana shore from which a cowbell tinkled in the darkness. There were lights in the Corn Creek settlement across the water. A church was brightest of all, but that beacon was extinguished while we watched, and the lights of parked cars flashed on as the congregation dispersed.

In the frosty morning, daybreak could not be distinguished from moonlight. I cast off and the boat slipped away as quietly as if drifting through the air. The dark shore was made real by the crowing of a rooster from an unseen farmstead in a hollow. Late that morning, after coasting a gravel shore lined with big sycamores, we landed at the town of Bethlehem, Indiana.

The postmaster here was a retired riverman. He had been master of the local packet, *New Hanover,* of which we had heard so much. Its picture hung on the wall of the tiny post office along with captain's license. He told us that at one time they made a daily round trip between Louisville and this town of Bethlehem. Madison was another terminus, up one day and down the next. The *New Hanover* was a most humble and unpretentious boat, having not even smokestacks, since she was gas-driven; yet everyone connected with her—crew and passengers—spoke her name with affection and regret.

As we were about to continue our voyage, a sudden breeze forced us to anchor off Bethlehem. Here we lay until the evening calm. Before nightfall Patton's Creek, in a lonely corner of Kentucky, was reached.

The narrow, shaggy valley of the creek was filled with morning fog as we drifted away. This was the last of the wild hills. Below here the shores on both sides were flat and within reach of Louisville.

Early in the day our progress was again stopped by a head wind, and we lay by. In the night I woke to find the moon shining in a dead calm. I dressed warmly, raised the anchor, and the sleeping boat drifted away. We voyaged through the night, quietly passing shores as unsubstantial as the clouds through which the moon seemed to sail. I kept watch on deck, wrapped in a blanket against the cold and dampness, with Susan curled up close to me. We both fell asleep for some unknown length of time, but the unguided boat made her way without mishap. Soon the dawn wind, blowing upstream, forced us to anchor. We tried to continue our way by hauling the boat along with a line run out to an extending willow on the bank ahead. This is called cor-

delling, an old flatboat maneuver. It is often successful, but in this case it was such hard and unrewarding work that we gave it up, and tied to the bank.

The day continued windy. Rocking gently in the waves, with drifting and even the river itself put aside from our minds, we engaged in occupations which had been neglected in recent days.

The next morning was different. On a light downstream wind we cast off at daybreak, and had breakfast by candlelight as we sailed past the first of the line of sand diggers above Louisville. The wind freshened, and our heavy boat skimmed along over the lively water. It sailed well, in its own way, always broadside to the wind, to which it thus presented its greatest surface. Once, carried near to shore, I landed on the gravel beach with the johnboat to give the dogs a run, while Anna sailed on alone. Luckily the dogs did not take off on a long rabbit hunt.

Late in the afternoon the wind died. A long row in the twilight, past another sand digger, brought us to Twelve Mile Island, the first island since Big Bone.

On the next day there was a cross wind. We lay anchored in the lee of the island, which I explored with the dogs, finding wild grapes, and corn to be gleaned.

Under way, there was so little current that I had to row steadily with the sweeps to make any progress. We finally reached Harrod's Creek, ten miles above Louisville. Our plan was to make this our Louisville harbor, but the entrance, with a beer tavern on one side, was so uninviting that we hesitated. Leaving the shantyboat offshore, un-anchored in the motionless river, I rowed up the creek to investigate. There I found the motorboat harbor of which we had been told, and a houseboat or two. It was a country-like place after all.

At first we anchored just inside the creek mouth, on the upper side where there was an open field. The tavern proved not such a bad neighbor, and we made some real friends at the boat harbor. Uncle Jim Meade and his wife were genuine river people, had experienced about every form of trouble and joy connected with a shantyboat. They had been on the Mississippi, and later, when navigating that river ourselves, we often said, "That's just what Uncle Jim told us."

There were duck hunters putting out from the creek every day, a watchful game warden, also a trapper, even as close to the city as this. He gave us our first muskrat, one whose skin was damaged. We ate it, and found the meat good, not at all strong or tough, for all its dark color.

There was a bus through Harrod's Creek to Louisville, and we made several trips to the city. All cities were one to us now, a place to buy things not to be found in country stores. The cities farther down the river would be even more strange to us than Louisville. We would arrive with a list of things to do and to get, eager to see a place of which we had so long heard. The list would never be quite crossed off, and our anticipation would be replaced by a longing to be back on the river again, away from the noise, smoke, and lights in the sky at night. Cities were hard on us.

On one trip to Louisville we bought mounting paper and envelopes for our Christmas cards. The woodblock print this year was of a riverbank church in the snow. To make a hundred and fifty prints, trim and mount them, write the addresses on the envelopes, and often a Christmas letter to go with the print—all this took time and application. However, in the bad weather which followed—it was rough out on the open river then—this quiet, indoor labor of the hands was pleasant to do.

Meanwhile we had become so well acquainted with the Meades, that arrangements for our trip to Michigan were easy to make. Mrs. Meade would feed the dogs, and Jim would look after our boat, which was moved farther up the creek into one of the motorboat slips. Tied up in a sort of stall, along a lighted boardwalk, it looked strange and out of place, as if its natural setting were some wild river shore.

Before we left I contrived a house for Skipper and Susan on the deck, a two-roomed affair to satisfy Skipper's demand for privacy. Another chore was to haul the johnboat out on the bank, so that it would be dry enough to paint when we came back. This painting was long overdue, but it had been impossible at Payne Hollow where the boat was in constant service.

All this done, we set forth with minds at ease, hoping to see much snow in the northern country. A journey on land was an adventure, as was living in a conventional house for a few days. Best of all was to be among old friends.

Back at Harrod's Creek, I painted the johnboat, and all was made ready for our winter voyage. The sunny fall days of our drifting down from Payne Hollow were no more. Harrod's Creek was covered with a sheet of ice. While Anna broke it up ahead of us with a pole, I towed the boat out to the mouth of the creek, walking along the gunwales of a string of empty barges which had been tied up in the creek for the winter season. It was the second day before Christmas. We hoped to make the steamboat landing at Louisville next day in order to pick up mail and supplies there. A favorable wind was blowing but, anxious as we were to be off, our departure was delayed until afternoon by a wandering Skipper. It was just as well, for the wind still blew so hard that anchor must be dropped on the first bend to keep off a lee shore—a bad one studded with rocks and piling.

The choppy wind, waves breaking over the deck, the irregular, sharp pitching of the boat made it an uncomfortable evening. Above us, at the top of the steep bank, was an elegant mansion alight with festivity. Downstream the light clusters of the city brightened the sky.

The wind decreased later in the evening and we had some quiet rest. When I happened to wake, about midnight, I guess, the moon shone through broken clouds, a light breeze was blowing straight downstream. Drifting at night is risky but we took this chance, desirous of getting away from an exposed position, and of reaching Louisville next day. We sailed slowly along the Kentucky shore which was indicated by car lights on the river road. After a while, Anna went back to bed.

A flashing navigation light marked the head of Towhead Island which lies close to the main. Not knowing what sort of channel was inside the island, I thought best to pass it on the riverward side. At this point the wind freshened suddenly and shifted its direction so that the boat was carried close in to the island, the shore of which extended out into the river. My hardest pulling from the johnboat could not hold us off, and the wildly-drifting boat crashed into the willows. No damage was done, the shutters having been closed against such a mishap. There was a great noise, however, which wakened Anna, asleep in the dark cabin. In the tumult of wind and waves, it must have looked like a shipwreck when she peeked out of the door. She manned the sweeps as quickly as possible, and we clawed off shore. When past the island, we came to anchor in its lee. Little of the night remained for sleeping.

Towhead Island, so near the city, was as wild as Big Bone. Skipper caught a rabbit in the morning which we cooked for the dogs' dinner. There was an old wreck of a barge nearby, out of which I got a few drift bolts. A small, tattered shantyboat lay behind the island. When its solitary inhabitant saw me, a stranger, he called, "What you got to swap?"

We soon got under way again, and in the murky dawn coasted the river front of the city. Here were the sand fleets, most of the equipment in for the winter—barges, sand diggers, towboats; on shore great piles of sand and gravel. There were coal docks; at one an old, partially dismantled steamboat, used as a landingboat. Passing the Greene Line wharfboat farther down, we came to the Coast Guard Station, a large two-deck boat like a quarterboat. We tied up to it, obtained permission to remain there long enough to take on supplies.

The supplies were not yet bought, so there was much running around town to do. Among the last-minute Christmas shoppers, we bought such items as a case of canned milk, oars, and rope. The boat store truck hauled it all down to the landing and we were away by late afternoon.

Ahead of us now was the canal around the falls, a two-mile haul in dead water, with the lock to go through at the end. As this was more than we could accomplish in the light which remained of that short winter day, we scanned the unlikely shore for a haven. Carried slowly along at sunset by the dying wind which had served us so well these two days, we neared the canal. At its very entrance, on the outside of the riverward guide wall, an unexpected harbor was offered. We cautiously worked the boat around the end of the concrete wall, always keeping a line fast to it, taking no chances with the current which was setting around the wall toward the dam not far below.

The end of the island between canal and river was a barren waste, an untrod shore, though the city lay just across the narrow canal. Overhead was a large sign which said, "Canal Entrance," and high above this a steel tower carrying power lines from the hydroelectric plant at the dam. The big towboats could be seen at close range now as they passed by, a few yards away, on the other side of the low wall. There were trains to watch, too, on shore and crossing the long bridges.

This was a queer place to spend Christmas; nor had a Christmas tree been provided, though cedars flourished on the hills we had passed on the way down. As a gesture we arranged two or three evergreen branches which I had broken off a tree in an estate on shore, that windy evening above Louisville. The feature of our celebration was the reading of a large bundle of mail which had been waiting for us at the Louisville post office.

One letter was disturbing. It informed us that Anna's sister was in the hospital. She was not in serious condition but Anna desired to see her. Accordingly, the morning after Christmas day we rowed across the canal, climbed the bank and crawled under a fence to the railroad.

Walking down the tracks we came to the station, found a train waiting to leave for Cincinnati in twenty minutes. A special train could not have given better service. Anna got aboard; and after filling the water bucket I had carried along at a hydrant used by trainmen, I returned to the lonely boat.

On the third succeeding night I met Anna in the same way. Then I was carrying an electric lantern and was mistaken for a trainman.

Next morning at sunrise we entered the canal, hoping to clear, that day, the last of the Louisville hurdles. The tow down to the lock was slow but not arduous. Luckily no large boats came along to shake us up. I walked along the top of the canal wall, which was partly over-grown with bushes, hauling the boat on a line, while Anna on board kept it from scraping. The U. S. Engineer fleet in winter quarters was strung out above the lock where the canal widened into a basin. We rowed past the line of derrick boats, dredges, and towboats, entered the smaller lock of the two, the gates of which had already been opened for us. The lockmen told us the drop to the lower level was about thirty-five feet. They warned us of a bad set in the current below the lock, saying, "You will think it is going to carry you into the bridge pier, but it won't."

In the narrow lock, when the water had dropped to the lower level, we felt we were in the bottom of a well. The gates, hinged at each side, and about the proportion of a page from a tall book, opened a crack, and it was almost a surprise to see daylight all the way down to the water. They swung open, and we rowed out, hit the current the lockmen had mentioned. It must have been the discharge from the power plant at the falls. Not trusting entirely the lockmen's assurance, we pulled our hardest and grazed by the bridge pier. The low sandy island on the right was passed, and at last we were adrift on the un-fettered river.

An extensive sandbar, often found below a dam, lay to the left. Across, on the crescent of the river, a few old brick walls and empty windows along the tree-grown shore recalled the busy river days of New Albany.

From this point the river trends south and southwest for some twenty miles to the Salt River, where it turns decidedly to the west. We drifted slowly down this stretch, the current slackening after the push it had received from the water over the dam. Gradually all traces of the city disappeared. Hills rose on the Indiana side, a cheering sight to us. On each eminence where a view was afforded up or down the river there was an old house, or the site of one marked by a crown of pine trees. On one such lookout was the tomb of an old riverman who was buried in an upright position facing a long reach of the river he loved.

Contrary winds halted us before we reached Salt River. Tied up along an uninteresting Kentucky shore, we set to and scrubbed away the worst of the Louisville grime. The coal smoke in our nest of railroads and factories had blackened every part of the boat—decks, floors, ropes, even the dogs. It was a satisfaction to see their white spots again.

Before we could get away, a moist warm wind sprang up from the south over a straight reach of river. It blew hard for a long day and slackened not a bit at nightfall. Standing or even sitting in the tossing boat became such hard work that we turned in early. The best way to take it was lying down.

The faithful anchor was our dependence in wind and waves. It kept the boat headed into the wind, which was important, for rolling broadside in the waves would not do. With a long anchor line there was no jerking, or slamming against spars.

At this point came the turn of the year, and 1948 was begun. Another change, more evident and significant to us, was a sudden rise in the river. When the weather calmed enough for drifting, we turned the boat loose on a swift and muddy current.

I was so eager to be adrift again, as if the river might fall and the current slow up before we could take advantage of it, that I cast off much too early in the morning. The dim light by which I took in the lines was not dawn but moonlight filtering through the clouds. When we drifted away Anna and the dogs were still sensibly asleep. How peaceful the cabin was, the fire crackling in the gray darkness; what remote, nocturnal thoughts to the lone watcher.

Later in the morning we entered the mouth of Salt River. This was easy to do, since the rising Ohio had blocked its current. Leaving the boat moored behind the upper point, we crossed Salt River in the johnboat to the little town. Returning, we decided to extend our stay there to include dinner. While Anna was busy cooking, I rummaged in the driftpiles and cut some firewood. After dinner we set sail down the westward reach.

Now came one of the surprises of our voyage. In our minds we had pictured the unknown river ahead as a wide stream flowing in long curves through a country of diminishing hills. Instead, at the bend below Salt River, the Ohio was contracted by steep, bold shores which rose into palisades of rock. The current was faster than ever as it swept around the sharp bends. We partook of the enthusiasm of explorers to whom an undreamed-of discovery was being revealed.

Looking up at the ragged crests, we saw many buzzards circling and roosting in the bare trees. Not known to us as winter residents, they gave additional wildness to the almost mountain landscape.

On the left shore, a single-track railroad, the Louisville, Henderson and St. Louis, made its devious way, now along the base of a cliff, now lost to sight in the woods. A train which passed, two or three coaches and a small engine, reminded us of our familiar Number Seven.

It was a cloudy, dark day. When time came to tie up, we sought a harbor on the outside of a bend, where the current swept along a steep shore under a cliff. It was easier water along the willows on the point opposite, but we wanted to be close to the forest and rocks, to make the most of them while they lasted.

At packet-boat speed we passed Rock Haven, a town which seemed to exist on the map only, where its population was given as forty. Perhaps it had declined since the map was made. The navigation light below was called Falling Spring Light, and there was the spring, a slender cascade spouting from the bare wall of rock. A short distance below, a small cove behind a rocky point came in sight. By some timely heaving, we managed to swing the boat into the small eddy there. It was a safe harbor even though the drift-bearing current swirled by close to the boat.

The pastoral Ohio River seemed almost out of character in this region. It was more like a mountain stream flowing through a gorge. We lay over at Falling Spring the next day to enjoy this novel aspect; also to celebrate my birthday.

The morning began darkly with a rain which at once turned to snow. It fell fast for a while, in great flakes. Then the wind rose, a wind not felt under the cliff, though it roared through the trees across the narrow river, and the boat was rocked by even swells coming from rough water around the bend.

Our special breakfast was pancakes, which we cooked and ate by turns before the open fire and served with maple syrup. Then, while Anna baked a chocolate cake, to my specifications, I explored the new shore. No farmhouse could be seen on our side of the river, but looking across from partway up the cliff, I saw a columned mansion which stirred the imagination. The land before it was cleared all the way to the riverbank, where instead of willows was a row of evenly planted cedars.

I worked on the bank for some time, cutting locust and oak for firewood. There were so many briars of wild raspberries that I wished we could be there in June.

In the intervals between this activity and feasting, we tuned our instruments and essayed the viola and 'cello parts of the easier movements of a Beethoven quartet. We read, too, from Jefferson's *Notes on Virginia* in an edition whose editor, to our disgust, had seen fit to delete the sections describing the Ohio River and its tributaries.

In the evening the cake was cut and found to be beyond improvement. The candles on our synthetic Christmas tree were lighted for the last time, and the day was over.

In the gray uncertainty of dawn we cast off again, had breakfast while drifting; then a stint of rowing, for the light wind and set of the current had taken us close to the Indiana shore. While at the sweeps we pulled all the way across the river to be in position for a landing at Brandenburg, Kentucky.

We had already learned how to use the assistance of the current in moving toward one shore or the other. Instead of rowing directly across, we headed the boat slightly upstream at an angle to the current. The current's force moved us sideways in the manner of a cable ferry operated by the flowing of the stream. Later we were to find out that a head wind made a crossing even easier for us by holding the boat more firmly against the current, thereby increasing its pressure.

From a distance the Brandenburg ferry, a flat towed by a motorboat, could be made out as it crossed the river back and forth. It was the first ferry we had seen since Carrollton, a hundred miles upriver. To keep out of its way we landed above Brandenburg in a small creek called Flippen's Run. Leaving our shantyboat tied to overhanging willows there, we rowed down to the landing, dogs and all, to see the town and refill our drinking water containers.

Brandenburg, a county seat, is built on rounded hills. Its courthouse, with a cupola which is almost a tower, overlooks the treetops and the river. The main street, which leads to the ferry landing, comes through a rather narrow gap in the hills, and we did not see it until almost abreast. The buildings, many with permanent awnings extending out to the curb, straggled down the slanting street, becoming more shabby as they approached the river. Along the waterfront were a few survivors of an older time, unpretentious, of simple dignity and gracious proportion.

The hill was a fine sight as we drifted past, again on our way. Below the town we coasted a rugged shore, where blocks of stone lay in the water, fallen from the cliff above. Similar rock bluffs were passed at intervals on down the river, their sharp contours contrasted with the brushy woods and unkempt fields of winter.

One such hill of stone was being leveled by blasting, loaded on barges, and hauled away to be made into cement. This was King's Landing, the only sign of modern industry seen that day; for even the railroad had taken a short cut through the hills.

Dinner was eaten while drifting, this time without an interruption. Anna was accustomed now to doing her work in midstream. It was disturbing at first, her attention divided between cooking and the passing scenery. Each time she looked out of the window, after having fired the stove, stirred the cream sauce, or checked on a dish baking in the oven, she faced a different direction. Sometimes it could not be seen at first glance which was Kentucky and which Indiana, their positions having been reversed since the last look. The river itself often seemed to be flowing in the opposite direction, and the sun played tricks on us by jumping suddenly to another quarter of the sky.

Washing dishes, however, occasioned no break in observing the slow passage of the shoreline. It was done at a table before the window, and by a system so perfected that conscious supervision was unnecessary.

Drifting this day continued well into the evening. Cold Friday Creek, a lonely place amid high, enveloping hills, was passed at sunset. Then came Upper Blue River Island, shaped like a ship and not much larger. Clearing it by the narrow chute along the Indiana shore, we landed in the mouth of a small creek below the island, called on the map Potato Run; colloquially, of course, it was Tater Run.

When the reckoning was made, the day's run was found to be twenty-one and a half miles, a record for our drifting on the Ohio River up to this time. It had been a memorable day, a rare combination of perfect conditions for drifting—swift current, no wind, and pleasant though cold weather. Add to all this the new country, which was most fair, and it was river wayfaring at its best.

We had pulled into Tater Run with no intention of making an extended stay there, but several considerations led us to lay over. One was the chance to do a washing, which was long overdue because of uncertain weather, muddy water, and rough shores along the way. Here was clear water up the creek, and an open, level place on the bank for the clothesline. The weather appeared to be fairing.

Our harbor in the mouth of Tater Run was an excellent one—deep, quiet water, protection from wind, and no hazard of loosely-rooted trees leaning over the boat. We might as well stay long enough to explore the inviting country—the two Blue River Islands, Blue River itself, less than a mile downstream, and the state forest which the road map indicated on shore. In that case, why not have our mail forwarded to Leavenworth, the town below Blue River?

Having decided on a longer stay, we postponed the washing a day and wrote letters. I started off to place them in the first mailbox along the road. It was a long walk through a thick woods in which there were no farms. The weather was fine for hiking—the air was sharp, a high wind from the northwest rolled white clouds across the blue sky, and cloud shadows flitted over the russet hills. Skipper and Susan had a great run. Over a slight rise we suddenly came upon some deer. They whisked off, dogs tearing after them.

At last inhabited country was reached, a road, farmhouses. I left the letters in the first mailbox and returned by a more direct way through the woods.

In the afternoon we prepared for the washing. Steps were cut in the clay bank to make toting easier. The weeds and tall grass were hacked down, branches trimmed so that the clothesline would be in the clear. A fireplace for heating water was set up. The iron rods for this, the boiler, tubs, rub board, and wash bench were gotten down from the roof. Then we rowed up the creek, breaking a thin skim of ice, to fill the tubs with clear water. We had to go a quarter of a mile to the transparent current of the creek, which held back, in a sharp-edged line of separation, the roily backwater of the river.

An early start was made next morning. It was a large washing, the first since leaving Payne Hollow, and we rubbed and rinsed through the short winter day. All went well, the weather was good for drying, and we enjoyed our task. It was a satisfaction to see the clean, sweet-smelling clothes and linen stowed away. The drying of the last heavy things, my jeans and the like, had to be continued the next day.

Now we could give more attention to our surroundings. A trapper had appeared, a onetime shantyboater who now lived in a cabin down the shore. He came in his johnboat every morning to run his trap line, and usually left a 'possum or rabbit with us on his way back. He was very friendly and told us about the country and river there, and below, too, for he had been down the Ohio to its end.

One day he asked Anna where we would be if we went ten miles down the river. She was ready for that question: we had studied the charts and knew that the course of the river below Potato Run is almost a circle. Ten miles of drifting would bring us within half a mile of a point directly across the river from our present location. The trapper told of a farm woman living on that shore who had once

tended the navigation light at the lower end of the curve. She climbed over the ridge and back each day, a mile trip by land. Down the river and back would have been twenty miles.

Three conservation officers visited us at Tater Run, with uniforms, badges, and weapons. They made it a social call, but no doubt had come to investigate this strange craft which had come within their jurisdiction.

A few days later, on an especially cold morning after a clear, frosty night, we shoved out of Tater Run, and dropped down to Blue River, a short distance below. It was a large enough stream to deserve the name of river. A dangerous place in a runout, we thought.

A little way up from its mouth was a shantyboat fleet—small house-boat, gas stern-wheeler, flat, motorboat, johnboats, and much fishing gear and junk. The owner soon came by, expertly handling his small motorboat, having with him a small boy on his way to school. This smiling, handsome young man became our friend. His name was Harvey Alcorn. He and his wife had come to the river ten years ago. In summer they moved out in the open river, where they fished and dragged for shells. Blue River was their winter station, and then Harvey worked in his crowded shop in the stern-wheeler, repairing guns.

Harvey Alcorn was not a born shantyboater, but had been led to the river by a pure love for it. His passion was music. He played the guitar and sang for us—songs about the river, which he had composed. In comparison, our own music seemed formal and irrelevant, lacking spontaneity.

Now it was time to call at the Leavenworth post office for our mail. On a dark, raw morning we started off toward some buildings a mile or so down the river. Coming out on a road, we refused a ride in a truck for that short distance. A near view of the houses revealed mail-boxes—this meant rural delivery. What! No post office in Leavenworth? Then no mail for us. However, we were told that this was not Leavenworth—it had been before 1937, but the record flood of that year had so ruined the town and discouraged the inhabitants, that rebuilding had been done on the hilltops. The post office and stores had all been moved to the new location.

It was a long drag up the hill, in falling rain. The new town was strung out along the highway, a collection of buildings without character. We found the post office; also the button factory, which was being operated in the corner of a garage.

"Shelling" was still a thriving business in the Leavenworth section of the river. The mussels, a sort of fresh water clam, are taken in the summer low water. They are caught by means of a brail, which on the Ohio River is a piece of pipe ten or twelve feet long having a row of grappling hooks attached by strings. The brail is dragged along the sandy river bottom and the mussels clamp on to the passing hooks. When the sheller has collected a quantity he boils or "cooks" the mussels in a shallow vat to get the meat out of the shells. These are sorted and sold at the factory. There, machines cut small disks out of the shells. The disks are made into the well-known pearl buttons. Harvey told us the factory paid roughly fifty dollars a ton for shells, that in a good week he could get out a ton, even a ton and a half. We were to see more shelling on the lower river.

We returned to the boat through the old town. Its streets were still lined with the great maples which had seen its rise and decline. Empty foundations from which the buildings had been lifted by the flood were more numerous than occupied houses. The inhabitants were fishermen or those whose homes had luckily remained in place. Some, no

doubt, clung to the old location because of their desire to be near the river. They accepted high water as one of the conditions of life.

The contrast between the two towns was striking. The old one was tattered, dingy, aimless—yet there still lingered about it the charm of the river of the past. The new town was out in the open, like a bare new house just begun to be lived in, whose trees were mere switches.

During these days at Blue River the Ohio had been falling, a result of the recent cold weather. As pool stage was imminent we determined to get on down the river while there was still a good current for drifting. Our departure was delayed for a day by a north wind, almost a blizzard, with snow and falling temperature. The following morning, in the sunrise calm, we ventured out into the big river. After passing the inactive lock of Dam 44, the wind rose again, as might be expected with the clearing sky. We tied up at the old Leavenworth landing. A fisherman there advised us never to cast off before ten o'clock in the morning: if no wind had come up by then, it would be a calm day. We thought this an extremity of caution—better to drift a short way in the morning calm than not at all. The risk is that a sudden wind might catch you in an exposed place.

Our course of action was never the most prudent. If safety and comfort were to be considered first, we should never have left Blue River in the face of winter. As it turned out, much strain and discomfort, even danger, might have been avoided had we remained in that safe harbor. Yet we would have missed some glorious winter drifting, and an experience which, rough as it was, revealed to us new aspects of the river and of the people who live on its shores.

There were no houseboats at Leavenworth, but hunters and trappers were abroad and at least one fisherman. He came alongside after raising a net nearby. In his johnboat, a little fire for warming his hands burned in a tin-can stove. It was cheering to see this winter activity. In the river at Brent, the small boats were all taken out of the water in winter or abandoned to weather and flood. Here many were in service. They were good boats, too, some being "yawls," which is an Ohio river term for a long skiff.

It was here we met our first true lamplighter. The oil-burning navigation lights seen above had been lighted and extinguished daily by nearby farmers. No one lived on this steep-sided curve, the horseshoe bend below Leavenworth. The series of five lights was tended every other day by this man who lived at Schooner Point. He had an outboard motor, but for some unexplained reason had rowed the five miles upstream on this rough day.

After the three days of wind, a fair, calm day could be expected. On that day we ran the thirteen and a half miles to Little Blue River. It was one of our best days of drifting on the Ohio. The narrow river wound among hills not so wild and forested as of Blue River; yet it was a remote, inaccessible country—no towns to be seen, no through roads. Land and river were of one spirit, of an undisturbed serenity. Some particular places attracted us, and we felt a desire to return to them sometime. One such was Cedar Branch, where a deserted farmhouse stood on rising ground, some cleared fields about it, and a little road winding up the ravine toward the ridge.

As we descended the river, marking off days and miles, the nature of the country changed. The hills flattened out and withdrew from the river. The stream itself widened, it flowed with a greater sweep to its bends. It was shallow, too, with extensive sandbars through which the channel, often a dredged one, was marked by long rows of buoys. We must watch the buoys carefully and keep clear of them.

The weather continued cold. There was ice on Little Blue River. The village of Alton, nearby, was numb with cold the morning we

strolled through it, the inhabitants kindling fires, or standing with their backs to stoves already burning red hot. They told us it was eight degrees.

Thereafter on the river itself ice was frozen each night along shore and wherever the water was motionless.

We drifted on with the usual attending circumstances—some hard pulls at the sweeps to keep offshore or to avoid passing boats; landings made on strange shores; much woodcutting, for both fires burned almost constantly. At Flint's Island we took a chance and went down the back channel, so narrow that the boat must be kept from turning broadside. Shutters were closed to protect the windows. One chimney was knocked down by overhanging branches. The danger in drifting down narrow channels is that you may find them blocked near the lower end. That means a tedious, difficult, perhaps impossible haul back up again; or in low water you may run aground and have to stay there until a rise floats you off. We have never had such ill fortune, but a back channel is seldom attempted without some assurance that it is open, and never on a falling river.

There were some long, straight reaches in this part of the river. Chenault Reach was nine miles, with no protection from wind. We entered these reaches cautiously, awed by the almost limitless downstream vista and fearful lest a wind should spring up.

Some lovely towns were passed. One little place below Oil Creek will always be remembered. It was built part way up a hill which lay fair in the morning sun. A white church and spire rose above the informal cluster of weatherbeaten houses.

One evening we anchored opposite Cloverport, Kentucky. It was a larger town, where the long-absent railroad reappeared. In the morning we rowed across, tied our johnboat in Clover Creek, and went up to the town to do some shopping. The stores were closed as if it were Sunday. We had not mistaken the day, but had arrived, by chance, on Robert E. Lee's birthday.

Towns were closer together now. There was a busy ferry between Hawesville and Cannelton. Then came Tell City, and Troy at the end of the long Troy Reach. One of our night anchorages was opposite Troy, whose lights were a cheerful sight. The Trojans must have wondered at our strange light at the water's edge. It was a cold night, and we drifted away with sheets of ice which lasted until melted by the warm midday sun.

This was a memorable day, fair and calm. Drifting slowly by clay banks and low sandy shores, Anna wrote letters and I made a new kevel, working on the deck, warm in the sun. At one point I took the dogs for a walk along the drift-littered shore while the boat sailed on.

That evening we reached Blackford Creek in Kentucky. There was barely room for us to nose into the small stream, which was blocked ahead of the boat by solid ice. At nightfall clouds filled the sky, the north and northwest became very dark. A gale sprang up, blowing straight across the river. Luckily our back was turned to the cutting wind and snow.

The wind lay before morning, but the weather had an ominous look. Snow began to sift down from the heavy sky. Our days of easy drifting were over. We considered what to do. The momentum of steady traveling was strong. Our next stop was to be Evansville—fifty miles downriver, where mail would be waiting for us. Looking at the slowly floating ice we realized that Evansville might be weeks away. Yet if ice conditions were to be serious the small creek we were in that morning did not seem to us a secure haven. We had heard tales of boats crushed between the solid creek ice and the broken ice in the river, and of sudden heavy rains and runouts. After some deliberation we decided to attempt another day's drifting. Perhaps we could reach Green River, a well-known harbor in times of ice, or at least the island opposite Owensboro, fourteen miles down the river.

We shoved out and drifted with the scattered sheets of ice. The open water became a thick slush in which the falling snow did not dissolve. An oar could hardly be lifted out of it, such a heavy ball of ice clung to its blade. Luckily there was a downstream quartering breeze which held us close to the sandy beach. By means of a pole, I was able to keep the boat from grounding. If there had been an offshore wind we could not have made a landing. And land we must, or be caught offshore by the freezing river. Picking out a spot where the beach was widest, the anchor was carried out on shore and additional heavy lines run to trees farther up the bank. There was no time for dinner that day. I placed the longer gangplank along the outside of the hull to protect it from the ice, hauled the ice-coated johnboat out on shore, cut a supply of firewood. By evening the ice in the river was heavy. The boat shuddered when the floes hit and ground along the side. Then, in the quiet, we went on reading until the next shock. Before long, however, there was unbroken stillness—we were frozen in.

The situation did not alarm us. There was solid ice for several rods out from shore, but beyond was open water and moving ice. The shore was a sandy, gently sloping beach, in a wide, straight reach of river. The winter weather was glorious. The river of ice sparkled under the bright sun and moon. There was a tall stack downriver on the opposite shore, and its smoky pennant lay always away from the northeast. More snow fell. Then came a day when the slow pace of the floating ice became halting and intermittent. At last all motion ceased. The river became a new creation, a vast snowy plain, its smooth surface broken by low heaps and ridges of ice. The dogs scampered about in this new field, and we walked far out; we could have walked across the river to the other shore. It was a Siberian landscape.

Our first contact with the natives was a visit from an old man who was as hale as winter itself. He was very friendly, offered his services, but his opinion was that we were in a bad spot. He told us doleful stories of previous runouts of ice; how a gorge in a narrow bend downstream had caused the river to rise overnight to the top of this bank.

Then the ice ground along with such fury that no boat could withstand it. This man became known to us as Uncle Bill Mattingly. His farm was up the road, the second house, he told us, the one with the windmill.

I had already seen the road when I had climbed the steep bank which rose perhaps thirty feet above the icy river. It was hardly more than a sandy lane parallel to the river, a hundred yards back. One could see a long way over the flat farm land. There was no house on the road directly in line with the boat. An eighth of a mile north on the road was a large white farmhouse which appeared to be empty. An equal distance down the road was a well-kept place to which we went for drinking water. There we became acquainted with young Murray and Marian Estes.

Later, our good fortune in landing at this particular spot became apparent.

On the first Sunday, we were amazed to have seventeen visitors on board. Other people came and looked down at us from the top of the bank. It must be a populous country, we thought. However, these people had come from miles around. The news of a boat caught in the ice quickly spread. It was a dull season in the country, no one was busy. Something new to see and talk about was welcome, and worth a long trip.

One who came aboard was an old man whose conversation was most lively and entertaining. This was Lawson Green. At intervals his family of grown boys came down. They were all familiar with boats, and Carl Green, who lived a mile downstream, was an experienced riverman. The general opinion was that our situation was critical, that we had made a serious mistake in leaving Blackford Creek, that our best chance of safety now was to haul the boat out of the ice.

At first we did not take all this very seriously. We enjoyed those quiet days in the depth of winter. Our reading, writing and playing were all caught up with. Cutting firewood was a chore never finished. The boat must not be allowed to freeze in solidly. This meant breaking the ice around the boat as it formed—another steady chore. The chunks of ice between boat and shore were removed, and piles of ice as high as the boat rose at either end. We became hardened to the cold. Un-

broken by a thaw, it became normal, and we were conscious only of the dry, keen air.

News came to us that the Ohio River was frozen solidly its entire length. The dams were lowered with great difficulty, and the water ebbed to low levels unknown in the days of artificial pools. We thought of beaching out on the sandy shore, but decided to keep afloat, not knowing what would be best for us.

At length the dire stories and predictions of the natives began to get under our skin. Perhaps it would be better to pull out of the ice. Many of the farmers had offered the use of their tractors, but we hesitated to entrust our boat to their jerking. I told one of the Green boys that I thought the steady pull of a winch from the top of the bank would be better. He said he would bring over a lumberman who had a powerful winch mounted on a truck.

To move the boat it would be necessary to lighten it as much as possible. Our new friends had already suggested that we strip the boat of all movables; that much would be saved, at least. They said we could live in the empty farmhouse, the one we had already observed a short distance up the road. This seemed a desperate move, and we hesitated. And would the owner of the farmhouse consent? We went to the Estes' to talk it over. About the range in the homelike kitchen were Marian, her aunt, and mother. I stated our case, our bewilderment and alarm. They were attentive and thoughtful. Then the mother spoke: we could move into the farmhouse, she said; the owner was her nephew; she would arrange it. Nearly all the community was of her family, and she promised that all would help us with the moving. We felt that the oracle had spoken in our favor.

On the appointed day a dozen men and boys straggled down to the boat. I had cleared a path up the bank, made steps and handrail in the steep part. Anna and Marian packed the loose articles in tubs— each jar of canned stuff wrapped in newspaper. The cookstove, bed and chests were carried up as they were. All of us, men and boys, climbed up the steep path time after time. At the top was Murray's tractor and open, flat trailer. Several trips to the farmhouse were necessary. It was amazing, even to us, how much stuff came out of that little boat. It was like opening a dry milkweed pod.

The jars of canned goods could not be moved into the frigid house; so a heating stove loaned by Uncle Bill was set up and fired beforehand.

By evening all our gear and plunder and our tired selves were tumbled into our new home. How desolate the boat was when we left it in the dark—dirty and littered, fires out, deserted on the icy shore.

The lumberman had been down to the boat that afternoon in the midst of our moving out. He thought it would be possible to haul the boat up the bank with his equipment, and set the following afternoon for the attempt. After this strenuous day, we would have been glad to rest a bit and settle down in our new home. However, it was too good a chance to pass up. Another day the weather might be unfavorable, our gang of helpers dispersed, the lumberman busy elsewhere.

We set about this new task early next morning. Carl Green was of great assistance. He said no timberhead could withstand the pull necessary to move the boat. Because of its position parallel to the bank, the boat would have to be pulled out sideways. Carl supplied some wire cables which were wrapped two or three times around each end of the boat, passing the stiff cable over the deck and under the bottom, clamping the ends. Boards were put between hull and cables to prevent their cutting in. Between the turns of cable at each end of the boat another cable was looped back and forth and clamped. This would serve as a bridle, distributing the force of the pull to either end.

Meanwhile another crew was clearing the bank above the boat, cutting brush, removing driftwood, and leveling off the worst bumps and holes. The truck arrived at midday, with the lumberman and two helpers. They brought several stout three-by-tens which we slipped under the near side of the boat for skids. A single, heavy cable was run down from the truck to our bridle cable. Lines from each end of the boat were made fast to trees up the bank. Slack on these lines was to be taken up as the boat was raised, so that it would not slide back if any cable parted.

Though it was a cold, raw day, with no ray of sunshine, a crowd of forty or fifty people was there to help or watch. For the most part they stood about a bonfire warming their hands. Nearly everyone had his own plan which he shouted out, never listening to the other fellow's. Only the lumberman was quiet. Anna, at the top of the snowy bank, and I, down on the ice by the boat, felt anxious, helpless, and could only hope for a successful outcome.

The first few tries nearly pulled the truck down over the bank. It was anchored at last by digging the rear wheels deep into the sand. Then another heave, and the boat came slowly out of the ice, like a huge turtle waddling out of the mud.

Above the sandy beach the way was steeper and uneven. Six-by-six timbers, also furnished by the lumberman, were laid to make a rude ways. It was a rough, jerky trip for the boat. We expected to hear the dread sound of timbers cracking or breaking, of spikes and bolts giving way, but the boat suffered no damage as it was hauled up as high as possible against the almost vertical sandbank at the top. The roof was even with the level field above. We estimated that the hull was fifteen or twenty feet above the ice. Then the cake of ice in which the johnboat was imbedded was hauled up, too, and the worst was over. The crowd departed and left us alone with the boat. It lay like a wreck, at a sharp angle on the snowy bank, but it was unharmed and out of the ice. Only in the most extreme conditions could it suffer damage now. We were relieved of strain, and thankful, and tired, tired.

Murray Estes and the others had offered their services so freely that I knew they would accept no money in payment. I asked Uncle Bill what to do. He said country people are accustomed to turning out and helping one another, so we must thank them heartily, and when the opportunity came, help them or another, a stranger perhaps, and expect no reward. His philosophy might have come from someone's Utopia, yet here it was, practiced in Daviess County, Kentucky, in the year 1948.

With the lumberman it was different. We expected to pay him for bringing out from town his equipment and men, for supplying planks and timbers. I was unable to make a definite arrangement beforehand, and after the job was done, he was even more evasive. At last he said we owed him nothing, that he was glad to help us out. He walked away abruptly and we never saw him again.

Our attention was now turned to our new home on shore. In a day or two Anna had made it clean and well organized. We used only two rooms of the farmhouse, but they were sixteen feet square with high ceilings. After the compactness of the boat, our new quarters had an air of spaciousness. The high walls dwarfed our little cookstove, which was set up in one of the rooms. The cooking equipment and water buckets were ranged about. The big chest from the deck of the boat was converted into a cupboard with shelves for dishes by turning it sideways and nailing legs under it; the lid made a hanging door which could be propped up level to make a large, convenient workspace. Most of the floor in this room was covered with our canned fruits and vegetables, which seemed to have multiplied in moving.

The other room was dominated by Uncle Bill's tall heating stove. We improvised a lounge before it of a porch swing supported by four of the storage drawers from the boat. The dining table was the tall wash bench which could be carried from the kitchen fully set and placed between the seat and stove. Our bed, carried up from the boat intact, was in this room, placed on the floor as usual. When we began to play and paint, instruments and stands were left in readiness and the easel remained set up. Because it seemed peculiarly appropriate here, we hung a painting, recently completed, of Chan Watson's Trimble County farmhouse which overlooked Corn Creek near Payne Hollow. When this picture was sent to the Watsons, it was replaced by a painting of Uncle Bill's farmstead in winter starkness, the view from our window to the north.

On that side the doors opened onto a long porch, convenient in

snowy weather. The windows on the other side looked over miles of flat, snowy fields with dark squares and distant lines of woodland.

More snow fell, renewing the whiteness of the landscape. Against the cold we bought a few bushels of coal since there was not enough wood around the house to burn, and the riverbank was too far away. The coal was hauled by one of the Green boys, who was a trucker, from a strip mine a few miles up the river. It was poor coal compared with that from West Virginia, a sack or two of which we had picked up on the spoil bank at Brent and carried in the hold thus far. We missed our open wood fire, but the coal stove had its points. It was delightful to take a bath by it, almost as tall as we were, and radiating heat all the way up and down.

Uncle Bill liked to come in and sit by his stove, ugly duckling though he considered it. It had once been his pride. All his children had been raised around it. Then, he explained, "I just got tired of looking at it, and got a new one." Yet he said the old one was better, for it warmed your feet.

Uncle Bill often came in the "evening," and before leaving at feeding time told us yarns of private and local affairs. There was an edge to Uncle Bill's slow and gentle speech. He spoke of "littling the fire along." On these cold days he appeared with a bandana tied under his chin and over the top of his head to keep his ears and face warm. His battered hat was pulled down over the knot. Prosperous farmer though he was, Uncle Bill went to extremes of thrift. He reversed his cotton gloves when the palms wore out; right on left, they did not fit, and gave his hands a crippled look. Yet he had bought a new stove before the old one wore out merely because it had become tiresome to his sight.

While Anna was busy in our new quarters, I went down to the boat, and with a borrowed jack raised up the lower side until it rested level and without strain. The bottom was exposed for the first time since the boat floated four years ago. Planks and seams were in such good shape that nothing need be done to them. The sides of the hull, however, and the rakes, I prepared to paint. It was good to be working on the riverbank again, and to be working alone.

Uncle Bill's windmill was his weathervane. If the wind shifted from north through west, all was well. If it went into the northeast, the rope which hung down to the ground became wrapped around the framework of the windmill, and the weather turned bad. In these days the rope was always tangling up. One cold wave followed another, and at last came a real snowstorm. In all this weather there were flocks of robins about, a bird we seldom saw on the riverbank. In the woods and brush were bluebirds, flickers, towhees, and some winter birds not identified.

In the evening we usually walked down the snowy road to the Estes', sat and talked with them in the warmth and brightness of a room which had two stoves, heating stove and range. It had the charm of country kitchen and sitting room combined. We read the latest weather and river reports in their paper, which carried daily pictures of the icebound river and of craft frozen in. We learned that one boat was caught about sixteen miles down the river. We had seen it pass the day before the river froze over, a large diesel with a tow of empty oil barges, on which was a load of new automobiles. This valuable cargo was now frozen in mid-river. Later we read of its release by boats driving up through the ice from Evansville.

After a lively visit with Murray and Marian we gathered up our mail, which was mostly letters of alarmed inquiry about us, took our quart of milk, roused the dogs on the porch, and walked back to our dark, silent quarters. On some nights the stars of winter were spread above the level earth in a magnificence we had never seen before.

In this period there was actually a day or two when we did not go down to the boat. We had moved ashore completely, and the river seemed far off. Yet there was work to do on the boat, and this took us often to the riverbank. The breakup of the ice was still a threat. If there should be heavy ice running when the river rose to the level of the boat, the inderpinnings on the lower side would be knocked out, the boat crushed against the bank. To save at least the wreckage, I strengthened kevels, made some new ones, bolted an iron ring for attaching cables on each side of the hull. The steel cables borrowed from Carl Green were kept in readiness.

We were optimistic, however, and while I caulked and painted outside, Anna was cleaning up within. Since the fireplace had not been dismantled, I could build a driftwood fire and keep the cabin warm and cheery. Walls and ceiling were washed down, some painting done, and all made ready for the return of our gear and stores.

After a while the cold passed away and the air softened. Rain fell on the bare earth and remnants of snow. We watched the river carefully. On the thirteenth morning after pulling out the boat, and the twenty-first after our landing on this shore, we awoke to see the ice broken up and moving. There was some open water. The next day was a violent one, hard rain and thunder. The earth was soaked and standing in water. The river, though it had risen several feet, filled again with ice; it became a turmoil of sheets and piles and cakes of ice, moving fast and grinding along the shore, piling up on the submerged sandbars until carried away by the rising water. We wondered if our boat could have survived this ordeal. It might have, but we were glad to be out of it, glad also to be out of Blackford Creek which was likely to be running out after the rain.

Four days after the breakup of the ice it became urgent that we move back on board. There was still much ice in the river, and the rising water had not yet floated our boat. The backwater, however, was flooding low ground between the ridge along the riverbank and the road. It would soon be impossible to reach the boat. We had to handle our return move alone since the threat of a flood was keeping the farmers busy. The task was much easier than the stripping of the boat, since, as if for our convenience, the boat had been lifted almost to the top of the bank up which we had toiled when unloading. Uncle Bill loaned us a team of mules and sled. A few well-organized trips were sufficient to haul our stuff to the riverbank. While we were loading it on board, the fast-rising river lifted the boat off the blocks, and we were again afloat.

It happened that Skipper was about to have her fifth litter of pups at this time. She did not like the present confusion and preferred to remain in the farmhouse even after we had moved from there. We had to carry her down to the boat more than once, and at last shut her in, until she understood we all lived there again. The pups came in the middle of the night. I woke Anna: "Skipper has a black puppy!" "Little Black Sambo," she answered sleepily. The black puppy was destined to share our later adventures. His name is merely Sambo now, and he is so big that no one can believe Skipper is his mother.

It was well that we moved back on the boat when we did. The next morning we found ourselves anchored to a long slim island, all that remained above water of the ridge along the river. Backwater extended from our island to the road, which was nearly awash.

On the river side of the island, a swift current swirled past. The ice had thinned out, but the river was still half full. At this point the ice was running near the far shore. Towboats were navigating again, and they sought the open water on our side, running so close to us that they appeared of giant size. Luckily we were inside the protecting willows.

It was no place for us to lay, yet there was still too much ice for safe drifting. We decided to drop down the shore a mile to Carl Green's landing, where the mainland was accessible and where we would be in a protected harbor. The remainder of the loading was quickly done, the deck load being carried over a plank laid from the top of the bank almost level to the roof. The bees were placed once more on the main deck, having survived the winter weather under a tarpaulin on shore. Just before our casting off, Uncle Bill hailed us, saying the mail carrier, on his last trip before being cut off by water, had left us seven packages.

To get the mail I waded through the icy backwater, swearing to get some hip boots. Some of the packages were Christmas mail catching up with us on February seventeenth.

It was a bright, mild day and we were all set for our short run. Some of the bees, however, had made an escape; so we turned the whole flock loose and canceled our sailing. Next morning we let go and skimmed along the willows. The cardinal practiced his spring whistle overhead and the meadowlark was heard in the fields. The woodwind notes of a dove came to us through the air of spring. How different had been our landing there, barely four weeks ago, in the ice and snow and Cape Horn weather!

We made a neat landing a mile below, snubbing on a tree and swinging into a narrow opening directly in front of Carl Green's house. Unfortunately the water was so shallow that the boat could not be brought within a plank's length of dry land: we had to paddle ashore in the johnboat.

At once we set about a grand washing of clothes. This had not been undertaken at the farmhouse because of the hard, discolored well water. Here good water could be had from Carl's pump, but it must be toted to the water's edge where it was heated over a fire, then transported on board in the johnboat. When washed, the clothes were ferried ashore and hung on a line stretched back and forth across the road which was unused because of the high water.

We walked back up the road to the Estes', fording some low spots where the water was deeper on the return trip. In each farm they were preparing for high water, patching up long-unused johnboats, contriving oars, moving stock and equipment to higher locations. This might be in their own barn where a false floor could be laid a few feet above ground. Except in unusually high floods this kept their feed and machinery dry, and even their cattle were installed on this higher level.

Carl Green was busy, too. He had a shop in which he rebuilt johnboats from wrecks picked up in the running drift. When the ice thinned a little he was out every day in his outboard yawl, "drifting," and towing in planks, timbers, and wrecks. Here was a man in his prime of life performing feats he would tell about in his old age. One of his prizes was a flat lost from some upriver boat harbor. Some of the wrecks he could not retrieve from the grip of the ice that had torn them from their moorings. It was dangerous work amid the shifting, swift-moving ice floes.

Carl's shop was in the basement of an abandoned country school which stood next to his house. The upper floor, formerly the schoolroom, was kept as a high-water refuge. In the yard was a onetime lifeboat, always held in readiness for rescue work. The community had learned in the 1937 flood that they could not depend too much on outside help.

We had much company these days, farmers come down to look at and speculate on the river which was rising but slowly now. Two of the boys made an overland trip to Maceo for mail in an outboard johnboat. They skimmed along flooded roads, jumped fences, navigated ditches, and pushed their way through treetops. Our portion of the mail they brought back was a large cloth sack of popcorn sent to us by Herbert Fall.

During these days the ice in the river had lessened until there remained but a narrow white ribbon of floating pieces which was shifted from one side of the river to the other by wind and current. We thought this could be avoided in our drifting, and made ready to cast off. True, the river was at flood, but it seemed to have reached its crest, and we were eager to be on our way.

When we worked out through the trees, we found that the current of the bankfull river was swifter than any we had experienced in our previous drifting. It flowed through a flat country, where water and land were now on one level. Thus instead of looking up at banks and hills, we viewed a limitless expanse of inundated land where trees rose from the water. In this low country, where floods are to be expected, the buildings are placed on the highest ground, which now appeared as low islands. Some farmhouses were built on artificial walled islands; others erected on piling, seemed to be wearing pattens to keep their feet dry. Immense corn cribs, which at first we mistook for barns, were raised above the fields by piers of concrete. They had a ramp at each end, and we pictured wagons of corn, in the sere autumn, driving in one end, and out the other, empty.

How good it was to be drifting again! At the head of Yellow Bank

Island, which was just about awash, we pulled into the chute on the Indiana side and had a fine passage down the narrow, tree-lined corridor. At the lower end we tied up to a line of trees standing on the flooded mainland. A graceful bridge arched its way across the river to the city of Owensboro, whose lights twinkled that night through the tall cottonwoods on the island.

In the morning we crossed over to Owensboro in the johnboat, rowing up through the slack water which covered the lower end of the island, so that the swift current of the river would not carry us below the city.

After dinner we cast off. It was a mild, sunny afternoon. Drifting past a wooded island called Little Hurricane, we pulled over to the right bank, and farther down, entered the long back channel of French Island. These narrow chutes were safe harbors for us. Toward the lower end of this one we caught on to a branch and manoeuvred the boat into an opening among some elms. Here the bank was above water, and the dogs had the satisfaction of going ashore whenever they desired.

Journeying down the river, or rather with the river, the most significant landmarks are the tributary streams. Thus it was in the early days, the first settlements having been made at the junctions of rivers. A succession of rivers, large and small, empty into the lower Ohio—the Green, Tradewater, Cumberland, and Tennessee from the south, the Wabash, Saline, and Cache from the north.

The first is the Green River, not far below French Island, a stream often mentioned by steamboat men and shantyboaters. We had once crossed it back in the Kentucky hills, and hoped some day to canoe down from its headwaters. Now we thought to pause there, perhaps laying overnight in its mouth. This did not work out. The land was low, the river distinguished from the flooded fields only by parallel lines of treetops. As we approached, it was to windward in a freshening breeze. We sailed by, the only land in sight a range of hills far back.

This was only a moderate flood, but the lowness of the land gave it the appearance of a drowned world. The suggestion of Noah's ark was carried further by the crate of chirping puppies in the corner of our cabin. For the first time, we drifted all day without touching land. Below Green River was a dry shore, but as it offered no shelter, we clawed off. All hands pulled hard to clear this lee shore, and to miss the piers of the highway bridge farther down. Some thrashing buoys were another hazard. After rounding a bend, we had a stern wind and sailed toward Evansville, Indiana. The city lies on the outside of a half-circle bend. The Kentucky shore within this loop was low and flooded, located only by the trees which stood in the water there. Across this watery plain we could see the stacks and smoke of the city. As we approached, the buildings of diverse shapes and colors seemed to rise from the water, a new, unheard-of Venice.

We steered for Pigeon Creek where, we had been told, a fleet of shantyboats harbored. The creek, just below the main part of town, was easy to locate by a railroad bridge crossing its mouth. From a distance we saw that the high water was almost up to the bottom of the bridge, and entrance to the creek was blocked off. Two or three houseboats lay along the river shore above. We prepared to land there, and pulled in close as we passed the walled city waterfront. Coasting by two sand fleets, we worked in as near to the bank as the shallow water allowed. It was not close enough for a gangplank, but this time we did not mind, glad to keep aloof from the city as from a hostile shore.

It was a rainy evening. After the desolate quiet of the island chutes, where only a wild duck's quacking might be heard, the city noises were disturbing. Switch engines banged their cars about, trucks rolled along the riverfront street. Below the creek was an immense river-rail-truck terminal.

Fog and more rain followed. It was no weather for drifting. We prowled about the city, which had the fascination peculiar to places in which one spends only a day or two en route. I was tempted to buy a farm bell from a junk yard, thinking it would make a good ship's bell, but it was really too big, out of proportion to the boat. We tried, unsuccessfully, to replenish our stock of soybeans. They are hard to buy even in sections where grown in plenty.

The upper part of Evansville along the river is an example of how a city should treat its waterfront, putting forth its best appearance there instead of making it a backyard dump. From the stone wall of the riverside park one has a splendid view of the curving river. Directly across, on what was probably a sandbar in low water, a sand digger was working, an unusual sight in winter and high water. We liked to watch a small steamboat towing barges to and from the digger. Another steam towboat was tied up close to us.

Behind the railroad bridge, on Pigeon Creek, was the largest fleet of houseboats we had ever seen. All sizes and conditions were represented, all variations of construction and design. Some were mere sheds kept afloat by oil drums, some were city houses on barges. The design of our own boat, with its large windows on each side and spacious main deck, suited us better than any we saw.

On the riverbank near our boat stood a squatter's shack, water halfway up to its roof. Its inhabitant, while waiting for the river to fall, sheltered himself from the rain in a discarded refrigerator crate of plywood, set up at the edge of the railroad. A piece of roofing on the top extended to make a little porch. Here a salamander burned, and the man inside must have been well toasted. The river had begun to fall now, and he watched with satisfaction as it receded from the walls of his cabin. One morning he pointed out to us with elation that his doorknob was out of water. We had supposed that the man lived in the little cabin alone, but when the weather cleared he was joined in his vigil by a wife and several children.

With the clearing skies, we made ready to shove off. Living so nearly in the open, the weather directs our course of action; also it affects our outlook. In a spell of rain and dark weather, like this one at Evansville, it does not seem possible that the sun will ever shine again for whole days at a time. We begin to accept the darkness and wet as normal. When at last the blue sky appears and the sun shines, it seems a blessing for which we should ever be thankful. This feeling lasts through the first glorious hours of fair weather. Then it soon wears away, the dark days are forgotten, and the sunshine accepted as a matter of course.

The exhilaration caused by the sun's return was increased, as we rowed away from shore and caught the swift current, by our joy at being afloat again and drifting on the broad river. Looking back, we saw the sunlit city, fair as the rain-washed landscape. Far in the east the curving lines of the bridge rose above the bare trees and flooded land. At an even farther distance could be seen the low hills through which the Green River flows. Above all this, against the dark background of the retreating storm clouds, a rainbow arched across the sky, a great span, its ends reaching almost to the earth.

Rounding a point farther down, we were surprised and alarmed by the sudden appearance, coming up around the same bend, of the *Clipper,* a large three-decked automobile carrier. We were drifting right in its path, but luckily the pilot saw us in time to swing out, so that we passed safely to the inside of the fast-moving boat.

We now hugged the shore in the slow current behind the point, looking for a harbor. The best we could do was to pull within the fringe of flooded willows, almost knocking down our chimneys. We were safe there, but the nearest dry land was a concrete road a hundred yards away, across a flooded cornfield.

That night a south wind sprang up, rolling waves in among the trees and booming through the branches overhead. After some rain, and a rough time for us, the wind shifted to west with clearing weather. It blew from off shore now, and our harbor became quiet.

During the two days we lay here, the dogs had to be ferried ashore. With the falling river we could not reach the road, and had to land in the soft mud of the field. Skipper insisted on going ashore one night. She could not be talked out of it, and even when put into the johnboat, which we thought might be an acceptable substitute for land, she merely stood up in the bow and waited for me to row her ashore. So I dressed myself, complete with rubber boots, worked the johnboat in through the trees, poled in as far as possible through the stubble. Susan, who was a delighted passenger, plopped into the mud and walked the rest of the way, but Skipper waited, knowing that I would carry her to dry land. As we strolled along the moonlit road, the whistling of killdeers came to us from the wet fields.

The boat lay swinging between the willows here for two windy days and nights. Firewood was picked out of the floating drift, choice pieces which would burn even though wet. One morning we crossed over to Henderson, Kentucky, whose waterfront buildings and courthouse tower were in plain sight. We desired to see this onetime home of Audubon. He seems not to have had a happy memory of the place, and in his journal expressed his feeling quite strongly as he drifted past Henderson in a flatboat on his way from Cincinnati to New Orleans in 1820. On our part, we found the city a delightful place. It was Saturday, and the lively streets added to the favorable impression. Here we bought some soybeans in a farm supply store, and a new lantern.

When leaving we talked to a man on the riverbank, a former shanty-boater. He had made one trip down the Ohio and Mississippi as far as Memphis. He shook his head, upon hearing we were headed for the Mississippi, and made some vague remark about, "Nearly lost everything I had." We began to wonder what was in store for us on that stream, whose reputation seemed to have improved little since the Indians told the first white men of a mighty and treacherous river to the west.

It was the last day of February when we got under way again, drifted under the Henderson railroad bridge, and passed a small, tree-covered island called Dead Man's Island. The weather was mild. The sound of peepers and redwings came to us over the water, and we noticed for the first time the reddening of the maple buds. It was a crooked stretch of river, divided often by islands. It must have been even more irregular in low water, with numerous towheads and sand-bars.

A stop was made at midday in a pleasant cove. For dinner we ate the last of the smoked catfish which had been prepared at Payne Hollow three months ago. Some small boats were out on the river that fine Sunday afternoon. One was a ragged shantyboater, who came alongside, anxious to swap something.

We tied up that night in the right-hand channel around Diamond

Island, against a solid bank on the mainland where locust trees grew. The island was a large one, of two thousand acres, we were told, shaped roughly like a diamond, with channels of nearly equal size on either side. It was a wild place, and many geese were about.

March came in like a lion, and the wind held us here for two days. It was a good harbor and the dogs had free access to shore, to the satisfaction of all. In the eleven days of drifting in the flood, on only one night, at French Island, were we close enough to dry land to have a gangplank ashore.

It was still windy when we drifted again, but the wind was mostly ahead, and the strong current carried us into it. On some of the sharp bends it was a hard pull to clear the point to leeward. Around the bend, the same shore might be to windward, and we would have to row in just the opposite direction to keep in the channel. As the current on a bend swings to the outside of a curve, we found it best to follow the inside, but far enough out in the river to avoid any slack water, or a possible eddy, behind the point. Drifting around sharp bends in a strong current, even when there is no wind, requires foresight and careful handling. We were gradually learning.

A brief stop was made at Mount Vernon, Indiana, an attractive place on high ground, with a big hominy factory on the waterfront. It is the last town in Indiana. The Wabash River, and Illinois, lay not far ahead of us, but they were not to be reached that day. A sudden gust of wind in the narrow channel behind Slim Island carried us crashing through the willow tops in spite of all we could do. It was a good enough landing place; we remained there the rest of the day and night. On the desolate shore the bedraggled cornfield of last year was level with our deck. Nearby a drab frame house, occupied only in the crop season, stood on stilts in the mud beneath a fine big elm tree, thick with mistletoe.

The next morning was still windy, but, as it blew in a downstream direction and not too hard, we cast off. It was a wild run. We managed to clear Cottonwood Point on the right, traveling fast and grazing the trees. Then pulling in the opposite direction we skimmed around Poker Point on the left. Passing Uniontown, Kentucky, on the far side, we rounded another sharp bend, and then made a landing to eat our dinner and rest a while.

Quick work is required to bring the boat to a stop in a swift current. This time a mishap occurred. From the johnboat I made a line fast to a tree, signaled to Anna, which meant to snub the other end of the line around a kevel. In doing this, she got her foot inside a loop, and when the line came taut, her foot was bound fast. She called to me to loose my end of the line, but this I was unable to do because the small tree to which the line was tied had been pulled entirely under water by the weight of the boat. She had to endure the pain until the boat swung into dead water and the tension was relaxed. No severe injury was caused.

The wind continued through the afternoon. We sailed past Dam 49, through some rough water over the submerged bear-trap piers. Wabash Island was just ahead. It must be the largest island in the Ohio. The Wabash River comes in to the right of the island. The left channel, to leeward and thus easier for us to make, was narrow, and would afford a good harbor. In fact, there was another boat of some sort in there already. But we chose the right-hand passage in spite of the wind, in order to see the mouth of the Wabash. By pulling hard we kept clear of the island shore, which was a thick forest. The Wabash flowed in through low ground, and again we had the feeling of limitless inundation. The Indiana side of the Wabash was marked by a navigation light on a pole standing in water, far from any land. We were thrilled to see the Illinois shore. So accustomed were we to having Ohio or Indiana on the right bank, this seemed far in the west. Appropriately it had a half-cleared, forested appearance.

The current swept us quickly past the Wabash and around a bend. Here the wind was downstream and the boat moved faster than ever. We were ready to call it a day now, having had enough of wind and rough water, of rowing, and of constant alertness. The chart showed a small island on the right. Hoping to find shelter behind it, we ran close to the shore. The island turned out to be merely a wooded point with no inside passage. The current flowed over it and was carrying us into the big trees which stood there. Prompt heaving on the oars and sweeps kept the boat from crashing, though it brushed through the outer branches. Farther down, in an opening where the water was quiet and deep, we tied up between the trees. There was little protection from wind, and the distant shore was screened by flooded woods.

We lay there the next day, enjoying the long view downriver. A few small boats passed. One was a weatherbeaten, homemade cabin boat, the U. S. Coast Guard Lamplighter, *Billie Z II*. We had wondered how the lights were tended in this flooded land. Some of them were under water. In such cases, the lamplighter had hung a lantern in a tree nearby. The river at this high stage seemed to have no definite shores. Sloughs and "ditches," as the creeks were called there, intersected the land like canals.

One of the passing boats was an outboard johnboat with nets. Another fisherman, who appeared to be tracing a line, tied up at our boat for a talk. No doubt he was surprised to find a strange craft in that unlikely place at that season. He was a shantyboater temporarily displaced, a true man of the river, come down from Pittsburgh some forty years ago. He seemed to have laid over at every town along the way. It did not take him long to learn that we were not real shantyboaters according to his notions—our boat was not quite right, we knew little of fishing, trapping, junking, or trading. Yet to our mind, we had our points, and knew a thing or two which he did not.

Following his advice, we dropped down two miles to Millrace Slough where he promised us a dry shore in a protected harbor. We laboriously cordelled in for several hundred feet against a current, worked through a line of trees, rowed across another channel, and entered a woods, nearly losing our chimneys. It was a beautiful shore, dry and firm, covered with crisp leaves of hardwoods—but the trees prevented us from quite reaching it. In the swamp were some cypresses, unfamiliar on the upper river; on shore, many pecan trees, and oaks with dry leaves still clinging. In the evening an immense flock of crows gathered in the woods, and at night owls hooted overhead.

We were still upriver from Shawneetown. I rowed down to it through the fields one rainy evening. Here for the first time was a real levee. Climbing to the top, it was a shock to see the town at such a low level. There was a block of old brick buildings in true steamboat architecture. One was a bank building no longer used, of brown stone, with broad steps and a row of columns. The aspect of the place was puzzling, it seemed incomplete. Later we learned that Shawneetown, even with its levee, had been ravaged by the '37 flood. The discouraged inhabitants moved most of the town back three miles to higher ground.

This old part by the river was left to fishermen. Here was Ohio River fishing on a scale unknown to us. Nets, seines, mussel brails, fish boxes, and boats were scattered along the levee. There were fishermen's cabins and houseboats, and a floating dock where fish were bought and sold.

On another day we both went to Shawneetown. In the hardware store the arrival of our shantyboat in these parts was already known. The proprietor owned the riverbank above town, and a passing fisherman had reported our appearance immediately. It was Logsdon's hardware store, and we had noticed Logsdon Landing on our chart.

There was a busy, well-equipped ferry operating at Shawneetown, where a main highway crossed the river. We touched briefly at the landing on our way down the river. When we asked some fishermen where to get drinking water, they seemed surprised that we did not drink water from the river, as they did.

This was a near-perfect day for drifting, without wind, and sunny. A low range of hills lay ahead, which we found to be at the mouth of the Saline River. How satisfying to see the rocky bluff rising almost from the water. We tied up in the mouth of this small stream, just to look at the hillside. Thoughts of Art Moore came to mind. The Saline was the limit of his boating westward. When he had told us of the "S'leen" at Madison, it sounded as far off as the Missouri. Now it was at hand, and we looked ahead to the Cumberland, the Tennessee, and beyond.

Down from the Saline was a beautiful reach of river. Battery Rock Towhead stood out from shore in the wide stream. The shores were rocky all along. Caseyville, Kentucky, was a little town on the hill. Along the shore below were a coal mine, tipple, and barges. This was the West Kentucky Company, which had operated some notable steamboats. One, the *Charles W. Richardson,* was perhaps the largest Ohio River towboat, to be compared with the *Sprague,* the giant of the Mississippi. I had seen the *Richardson* pass Brent one time; its stern wheel was almost as high as the upper deck. I had also seen the *Marcia Richardson* on the upper river, and some stray W K barges.

Farther downstream was the Tradewater River, a companion stream in Kentucky to the Saline in Illinois. It came down through the hills in a narrow valley which we longed to explore.

The Ohio now turned for a long run to the west. Kentucky was flat, but the Illiniois shore was a bold one, high and rocky. On the bend we passed the forgotten town of Weston, Kentucky. Not far below, after a twenty-mile run, we entered Crooked Creek—another one—on the Kentucky side. When the river is high, many creeks are obstructed by the tops of trees which in low water arch over the stream. Crooked Creek was open, however, and we pulled into it for a few rods, to a suspension footbridge, now at water level. The bridge afforded a walkway to shore from the boat, which was tied up to trees on either bank. This place was Ford's Ferry, in early times an important crossing for settlers moving into the northwest country. I walked up to the only house in sight to find out if anyone objected to our laying in the creek. It was a gone-down place, but the people were friendly and came to the boat for a visit. They told us that this had once been a town, in their own time, I think, with stores and a post office. No doubt our guests will long remember us, for strangers are rare at Ford's Ferry, and these people had never been on a houseboat before. They supplied us with eggs, rounding out the dozen with two duck eggs which were especially mentioned.

Ford's Ferry was but a one-night stand. Next morning, late, we drifted down to Cave in Rock Island, two miles below. We tied up to the Kentucky shore in the island chute, near the lower end. There was an open view of a long reach of river below, and of the Cave in Rock ferry crossing back and forth.

The famous Robbers' Cave was not to be seen from our landing. We knew it was on the Illinois shore, and started out in the johnboat to look for it. When we cleared the island the cave was in plain sight in this leafless season, a large gaping hole in the rock face of the bluff. We landed directly at its mouth, found it empty: not even a sight-seer was there. It was a good cave, dry and commodious, commanding the river, and well fitted for the grisly work of piracy. We appreciated

the cave more for its own merits and unique situation, and for the sheer rock walls of the cedar-crowned bluff along the river, than for the legends connected with it. Yet the legends are essentially true, no doubt, though Cave in Rock is but one of several places along the river which were pirates' hangouts in the old flatboat days.

We went to the town of Cave in Rock, too. Not much was going on there on that cold day in early March. It was an important fish market. The fish buyer there went up and down the river roads in a truck, and the fishermen sold their catch to him. Later we were to see this trafficking at close hand.

We wished to phone Anna's mother in order to wish her a happy birthday. Cave in Rock was not the best place to make a long distance call. The local telephone system seemed to be privately owned and we found the telephone office only after a long search. The exchange was in the owners' bedroom. While the man tried to make a connection through "E-town" to the outside world, we conversed with his wife who in the same room was altering and fitting a dress for herself.

A north wind held us close to shore behind the island for two more days. It became quite cold and there was a skift of snow on the ground.

Nothing more memorable happened except that I fell into the river when reaching for a piece of driftwood from the johnboat. I was out of the water so fast that it hardly soaked through my clothes. Each winter I managed to fall overboard. The previous year it was in extremely cold weather at Carrollton. It was at night, that time, and the flashlight I was holding still burned when I came to the surface.

We have learned that after a north wind, one from the south can be expected. Usually there is a quiet period between. This we try to make our sailing day. Sometimes we start a day too soon, misled by the quiet of early morning, and the wind comes up later in the day. The calm interval varies in length, or there may be none at all—the north wind ceases and the south begins to blow at once.

We left Cave in Rock Island on the last day of the north wind. It was only a light breeze but, since the river continued its westerly direction, it meant steady pulling to keep from being blown ashore. The same range of hills formed the northern shore, with frequent palisades of rock, always with a crest of cedars. Islands and towheads lay along the flat Kentucky shore. These we avoided because of the slack water there, although the cross wind was determined to blow us into them.

At Big Hurricane Island, a large one, we gave way to the wind and took the left channel. This was once the main one, but now the boats go around the other side. On this course we did not pass Elizabethtown, Illinois, before which the island lay. E-town is the center of the fluorspar mining district. Some of the mines could be seen from the river, and docks for loading barges. "Spar," we understand, is used in the making of steel. The upbound Pittsburgh towboats pick up a barge now and then and take it to the steel mills along with barges of scrap iron, and sulphur from Louisiana.

After passing Hurricane Island, Elizabethtown could be seen upriver, a white village on a hill. Then came Rosiclare—a smoking stack, a coal digger unloading a W K barge, and the sound of a locomotive. On a sharp bend below, rugged hills faced us from the Kentucky side; in a notch lay the village of Carrsville. We searched for a harbor there, but the current was too swift along the rocky shore. The river turned southward in a long bend where the bordering willows, standing in water, made an impenetrable hedge. Darkness began to fall as we coasted along looking for an opening. Of course we could have tied up for the night at any point. However, there was always a danger of wind—it might spring up unexpectedly in the night and give you two or three rough days. So we did our best to follow the rule of seeking a sheltered harbor each night. We almost gave it up this time, for it became so dark that we could not make out Golconda Island which was supposed to be ahead of us. At length an opening in the trees showed against the sky. We stumbled into it, tied up against a mud bank.

The morning light showed our position as abreast the head of Golconda, or Rondeau, Island, which lay close to the Kentucky shore. We dropped down to the other end of the island, and moored in a small creek, Love's Branch, above the ferry landing. The ferry was no more than an open scow for foot passengers. One of these, tired of waiting for the ferry, decided to go across with us when we started to row over to the town of Golconda. He called our johnboat a "dog-boat," a name new to us and never repeated. Because of the falling river, the landing at Golconda was a field of thick, soft mud, a wide interval between river and levee. We admired and were grateful for the excellent board walks which someone had constructed through the mire. The town, a county seat, was gathered behind its flood wall, like an ancient walled city. It was a bustling, cheerful place on this Saturday morning. "Condy" is another fishing town. We met some of the fishermen down the river, out running nets in excellent johnboats, larger than those used on the upper river, with a built-in well to hold the live fish.

The river flows in a southerly direction from Golconda. It was a noble prospect, down toward the hills at Big Bay Creek, where the ridge appeared to leave the river. The light wind was ahead, having already shifted to the south. Once all hands were called to pull away from the head of Pryor's Island, and the cook had to leave her work in haste. Susan took advantage of the situation, helping herself to an unprotected pan of cinnamon rolls just ready for the oven. We pulled in at Big Bay Creek, intending to tie up there for the night, but the banks were so muddy that we dropped down a short distance to

Barren Creek. It was no better, but we worked in there, and moored the boat offshore.

For the past week or two we found ourselves examining the shores with more than a passing interest. The idea of making an end to this season of drifting and of laying over for the summer became more and more insistent. It was too early for gardening, but the swelling buds were coloring the woods, and green grass showed on the hillsides. Drifting was as fascinating as ever, but we might have been getting a little weary. Looking back, it seemed to us a long time ago that we left Payne Hollow and made our way past Louisville; then after a long stop at Blue River came the strain and excitement of ice, and flood. A quiet harbor for the summer began to have its appeal. Another factor urged us in this direction. The river country we had just passed through was the kind in which we would like to spend a summer —rolling hills and small farms, with the requisite waste land and forest. But the wide river ahead of us seemed to flow through a flat country where there would be large farms and intense cultivation. The map showed a highway not far down which followed the river into the city of Paducah. In the face of this, we remembered with some regret the Tradewater reach and its empty hills. But upriver was as irretrievable to us drifters as time past. We must make the best of what was at hand and ahead of us, knowing that the right place was waiting for our recognition.

Looking about, we found that Bay City, at Big Bay Creek, was a country store, a good one, and two or three houses, with a gravel road leading back through a gap in the hills. A likely place, yet, for some reason, it did not appeal to us. Perhaps only in Kentucky would we feel thoroughly at home. Across the river from Bay City, on the Kentucky side, was a little circle on the map marked Bayou, near the mouth of Bayou Creek and at the end of a side road leading up the river from the highway. It looked like a possibility we should investigate. Looking across the river, we thought we could see the creek, and wondered if we would be able to row the houseboat over there before the current carried us too far down. The wind being in our favor, upstream and toward the Kentucky shore, we decided to try it. We pulled our best, heading the boat slightly upstream, to have the assistance of the cur-

rent. In mid-river the wind was stronger than we had thought. As we neared shore, the momentum of the boat and the wind slammed us into the willows just above the opening we were aiming for. This opening was not Bayou Creek after all, but a small ditch we could not enter. The creek was two or three hundred yards downstream. Meantime, the wind had increased. It pinned us to the willows and tossed us about for the rest of the day. Toward evening, almost dark, a brief lull came, and we made it into the mouth of Bayou Creek. Immediately the wind began again, and reached almost a gale that night.

We lay here for a week. I made a driftwood walk through the mud and we roamed about the countryside, found few houses except the little settlement of Bayou, a mile away. We caught a few cold-water fish in a net of chicken wire which I had recently made. We had an eel to eat, too, which a fisherman had caught and scorned. Also we found some wild greens. How good this fresh diet was after our winter fare! The dogs had a treat, too—a large, fat chicken came floating down the creek. It was so fresh that we almost cooked it for ourselves. One day we did a washing, stringing the clothesline down the muddy cornfield next to the willows.

While Bayou Creek had its points, it did not strike us as a place to stay all summer. For one thing, we met with no cordiality from the inhabitants. At the Bayou store we fancied, even, that we were rudely treated. This would never do, since it was the only store in that vicinity.

Eight and a half miles below Bayou was the mouth of the Cumberland River. If the Ohio offered no suitable location, why not go up the Cumberland a ways? To take our boat up one of the larger tributaries had been in the back of our mind since we began drifting down the Ohio. This might be our chance. I unlimbered the bicycle one day and pedaled down to Smithland at the mouth of the Cumberland. It was a quiet, old town, but I saw no place for us there nor in the Cumberland near its mouth. I fell into conversation with a man, while we looked at the river. He told me about his farm some twenty miles up the Cumberland. It sounded like good country for us, and there was at least one houseboat fisherman on the river up there.

We determined to drop down to Smithland, and from there investigate the Cumberland, also the Tennessee, which was but a day's drifting farther on. The short run seemed longer, the weather being so uncertain. We passed Stewart Island, which lay in midstream, and Birdsville, Kentucky, a little village on the lower slope of a spur of the hills which came out to the river. The Illinois shore was flat as far as one could see.

The threatening weather did not develop, and we reached Salt Point at the Cumberland without difficulty. Salt Point received its name from the quantity of salt which used to be stored there for reshipment. Around the point was an eddy in which we worked the boat up the Cumberland a short way to the unused ferry landing. It was with some regret that we said au revoir to the Ohio, knowing that it might be several months before we floated on it again. On the other hand, the Cumberland lay before us, offering untold adventures.

8

The Cumberland rises in southeastern Kentucky, in those mountains which are a nest of rivers. It is known to the world chiefly by Cumberland Falls, where, a mountain stream, it pours over a ledge of rock to drop sixty-eight feet. Immediately below the falls the river enters a high-walled gorge, through which it has been followed by only a few people. On leaving the gorge, the river becomes a navigable stream, at Burnside, Kentucky, five hundred and sixteen miles above its mouth at Smithland. All this will soon be changed by the high dam being constructed at Wolf Creek, forty miles below Burnside. The dam will back up the water as far as the falls, making a deep, still pool through the gorge. Also, the new dam will become the head of navigation for what traffic there might be on the upper river. A hundred and thirty miles below Burnside, the Cumberland leaves Kentucky to make a long sweep southwest through Tennessee. Nashville, the state capital, is on its banks, a hundred and ninety miles above the Ohio. Farther along, it turns toward the north, crosses the narrow western end of Kentucky to enter the Ohio at Smithland.

Smithland was once a place of importance and much wealth was concentrated there. It is said that at one time Chicago came to Smithland to borrow money In later days the new railroads and factories were established elsewhere, and Smithland relapsed into a small country town. Some of the buildings of its prosperous days still remain. From our landing across the Cumberland we could see the tree-lined river street, where there was one especially fine old brick, unadorned and severe in design, yet gracious and inviting as a building should be.

Many fishermen lived at Smithland, possibly because there were two rivers to fish. They were active in those March days, catching buffalo and carp in nets. The Cave in Rock fish buyer came through once a week. It seemed strange to us that none of the fishermen lived on boats. One family dwelt near us in the ruin of a farmhouse: their name was Hedgepath. We became acquainted with Grandfather Hedgepath, too. He was a veteran of the woods who had moved to town in his old age. A gunsmith, he still went to the woods for walnut to make his gunstocks of.

As soon as we were settled there in the mouth of the Cumberland, I began scouting around for a location which would be suitable for the summer. The Hedgepaths, and other neighbors who visited us—for our boat attracted so many that we had to keep open house on Sunday—urged us to remain in their midst, setting forth the advantages of our present location. But even Smithland was too populous for us. I made a bicycle trip to Iuka on the Cumberland, the place we had in mind, but was not much attracted to it. The river was swift, too, and the twenty miles to Iuka against its current would be a long tow. On that same excursion I pushed on farther south, heavy going on soft roads, to Grand Rivers, where the Cumberland and Tennessee are close together. Cutting over to the Tennessee, I came to the immense Kentucky Dam. One glance at the lake above it showed me it was no place for our boat. Nor was the Tennessee River below the dam inviting as it wound toward the Ohio through flat fields. After a fifty-mile bicycle ride, drenched by a terrific windy rainstorm near its end, I arrived at the boat feeling a little discouraged.

Some warm, sunny days followed. The green hills showed the flush of blossoming peach trees, and the Smithland gardens began to sprout.

196

We gathered wild greens and became anxious to plant our early garden. My next excursion was up the Cumberland in the johnboat, the dogs streaking along the shore. After a mile and a half we came to a low bluff on the right bank, where the shadbush bloomed and the redbud was beginning to show color. This place might do, I thought: here was a possible garden spot, and I found a spring under the rock. Climbing to the top, I saw that the river curved sharply to the north. On the right were all flat fields, the left bank was hilly. On that side, as far away as I could see in the hazy spring air, a stone cliff rose sharply and continued around the next bend. It was the highest land to be seen in any direction. On the boat that evening we looked at our maps and identified this ridge as Barrett's Quarry and Bizzle's Bluff. Next day I rode on the bicycle in that direction, following the highway to a side road which led toward the river. Within a mile, the road crossed a ridge, a fitting place for the church which stood there, I thought. I knew the river was near, down the steep hill on the other side, and I soon came out close to its willows. An old frame house stood there, a stone chimney at either end and a long porch toward the river. The little road continued up the river, past a shantyboat beached out—there to stay, it was evident, for an entrance way had been cut through the rake to avoid climbing over the deck. Farther on, the road ended, and the rocky cliff which I had seen from down the river rose to almost a sheer precipice. I was surprised and puzzled by the group of houses among the trees on the slope away from the river: two suburban places with well-kept lawns, and rows of frame cabins above, perhaps a dozen. No life stirred. Approaching one of the large white houses, I was met by a ruddy old man. He was a strangely busy and hurried person to be found in this place where time seemed to have stopped. I learned from him, in the scanty conversation he could afford, that this was Barrett's Quarry, ten years idle now, and in the small cottages once lived the quarry workmen. I told him what I was looking for, and he recommended a place half a mile up the river, a narrow shelf of bottom land under the hill, where the river began its turn away from the bluff. He said a little cabin, untenanted now, stood there. The owner was J. A. Joiner who lived at the top of the ridge near the church. One look up the river convinced me that

197

this was the place we sought, and I went no farther. Returning, I stopped at J. A. Joiner's mailbox. There stood Uncle Jim in his yard, smiling and affable. A tentative agreement was quickly made, and I rode back to Anna with the good news.

Our departure was made urgent by the rising river, which threatened to cover Salt Point and leave us without protection from the Ohio River current. Yet it was not easy to find someone to tow us up the Cumberland. The two most likely boats, small sturdy workboats, were off on the Tennessee, towing logs. We had noticed a small flat at Smithland used as a ferry by the man who farmed Cumberland Island, out in the Ohio. We hunted up this man, and he contracted to tow us the seven miles up to Bizzle's Bluff with the motorboat used to tow the ferry flat.

The Hedgepaths, meanwhile, had spoken for our black puppy, and we had just about decided to leave him behind. We couldn't support four dogs. Yet it happened just at this time that Susan was hit by a car on the highway where she was trying to pick up my bicycle trail. The loss of the lighthearted companion of our winter's drifting, and doubts as to the happy future of Sambo among the Hedgepaths, their four children and foxhounds, led us to decide to take the black puppy with us. Our dogs were now three—Skipper, Sambo, and his brother Chip, so-called because he was like his mother.

It seemed that we had been at Smithland a long time, but the spring morning at the end of March on which we started up the Cumberland was only the eighth day after our arrival there. The motorboat which towed us was handled by two country boys for whom this was an unusual outing. The voyage turned out to be an unexpected pleasure for us, and as we sat on our forward deck, enjoying this apparent reversal of natural laws, we thought it might be fun sometime to make a cruise under power. After a morning's run past rural shores, where a few old farmhouses showed through the trees still almost bare, for the willows are among the last to sprout; past an abandoned spar mine and the old house at Rappolee's Landing where the road had led me to the Cumberland; past the white houses, the cabins, and unused store building at the Quarry, and the long idle quarry itself, whose weathered face looked like a natural cliff, we reached our destination and headed into the bank. The river was so high that the old corn-field where we hoped to garden was mostly under water, and the little cabin at the base of the steep hill, seen for the first time, was not far above the river's level. The summertime shore was marked by some trees standing several rods out in the water.

The crew of the boat had dinner with us. It was an excellent meal with some flourishes, very cleverly planned by Anna so that it could be served at any time with little preparation. Thus she could enjoy the voyage without the distraction of cooking. The country boys were a little puzzled by our food, and passed up anything strange to them, thus losing a chance to experiment with some new dishes. They shied away from the tomato salad and freshly baked brown bread, and ate mostly of baked beans and the casserole of baked sweet potatoes. After dinner they departed downriver, and we were left alone in the new land.

While greatly pleased with this section of the river and country, we did not decide at once to remain at Bizzle's Bluff. One objection was the lack of a drinking water supply. The nearest well was at the quarry landing, more than half a mile down the river. Also, we hesitated to settle down near the quarry because of a rumor that it would operate later in the summer. In that case it would be a noisy, dusty place. So in our first days we made trips up and down the Cumberland to other

199

likely spots. One was the old spar mine passed on the way up, under which, we were told, was a fine spring in low water. There was another spring, a mile up the river at a long-abandoned quarry. We visited this place too, found three or four houses there and another houseboat, a large, fine one which could never be called shantyboat. It was the home of Walter Berry, who became our neighbor later in the summer. While these places had their advantages, we did not like them well enough to move the boat there. We decided to remain at Bizzle's Bluff.

Once this decision was made we wondered why we had hesitated in our choice. A deal was soon made with Uncle Jim Joiner: we would pay fifty cents a week for the cabin and as much of the field as we could use for a garden.

On the fourth day after our arrival we took possession by setting the beehive ashore. Also we planted some early seeds in patches of high ground, and made a few rows for potatoes next the woods. The potatoes we planted were of our own raising at Payne Hollow, and enough remained to last us until the coming crop should be ready.

How good it was to be at work again in the sun-warmed earth! The joy of it was heightened by our planting in a new field, by the new country which surrounded us.

One of our first acts was to set up a mailbox at the quarry, where the road ended. Leon, the carrier, refused to accept the improvised box we had used the previous summer. Only an approved box would do. We took down our red can and replaced it with a store box loaned by Uncle Jim. A batch of delayed mail arrived, the reading of which lasted several days. Some of it was Christmas mail. There were reports of severe winter weather from many sections of the country. Yet who had been exposed to the elements as much as we? A dread of cold in cities is largely due to the shortage of fuel, its high price, and to newspaper reports which are worse than actual contact with cold and wind.

To pay rent might be unethical for a shantyboater but having rights on shore gave us a new standing in the world. We were delighted with the cabin, though at first it seemed a useless acquisition. It served us in many ways during our tenure, however. At once it was used for storage, supplanting the tent we had set up on shore at Brent and at

Payne Hollow. It soon became my studio. It was our guest house during the summer.

We often left the boat to sit on the cabin porch. Upstream it overlooked an unusually long reach of river for the winding Cumberland, past the mouth of Bizzle's Creek to the cedar bluffs at the next bend. Downstream the river curved along the base of the quarried hill whose bold silhouette was our western horizon. Across the river were level fields, pasture, grass and crop land, cut off from us in the early spring by long canals of backwater.

The porch was large in comparison with the one room of the cabin. The whole was on a small scale; yet its placing and roof line could not have been improved by the most accomplished architect. Perhaps the one who had done this so well had also planted the flowers which grew there. These, having survived years of neglect and struggle with weeds, were already sprouting forth—narcissus along the stone wall and iris bordering the path.

Behind the cabin a rough trail angled up the hillside through the trees to the top. From here was a splendid view of miles of country, unknown hills rising in the distance, the winding course of the Cumberland below, and a glimpse of the Ohio far off to the west.

Our first acquaintance was Whistlin' Ike, the fisherman who lived in the shantyboat beached out along the road. He was open and cheerful, obliging no end, as upright a man as could be found. He came up the river every day in his outboard johnboat, whistling and singing like the very mockingbirds. He probably thought his caroling was drowned out by the buzz of his motor, but at a distance the motor was only a subdued accompaniment. Ike had set out a string of nets behind the willows across from our boat. We had never had a chance to see how these big nets were handled. We wondered how they got the fish out of them. The small nets, two and two and a half feet in diameter, which Andy had showed us how to make, had a slit in the end which could be unlaced for removing the fish. Ike's nets, with a four-foot front, were rolled over the side of the boat, a trick requiring strength and skill, then collapsed with their open end downward. The fish— carp and buffalo at this season—simply fell through the reversed throats, which were so large that even the big ones slipped out easily.

Ike also had lines out among the trees in the backwater of Bizzle's Creek, where he hoped to hook some big catfish. He sold his catch to the Cave in Rock fish buyer, who came on a certain day each week in a truck. We passed Ike's landing one day when the buyer was expected. The fish were all ready, the carp and buffalo in a heap in the grass, the catfish in a tub of water. Ike had been told that carp might not be accepted because all the fishermen were catching them and the market was flooded with carp. Sure enough, the fish buyer left them behind. Ike invited us to help ourselves, and we rowed home with the bottom of the johnboat covered with big, flopping carp. I spent the afternoon cleaning them, and next day we canned carp steaks. The backbones were cooked to get meat for fish hash, one of our favorite dishes; the heads, of course, made dog food. When we tasted the canned carp next winter, its quality was a surprise: the long processing had softened the troublesome fine bones, and the flavor was excellent.

When the river went down, we caught an abundance of catfish on trot lines. I made a smokehouse to handle the surplus. It was a queer structure of boards, which no one could figure out. Good wood for smoking was plentiful—some hickory already cut, to which I added green sassafras.

With all this fish, plenty of potatoes, grain to grind into cereal and flour, wild greens and poke, our canned fruit and vegetables from Payne Hollow, not to mention walnuts and popcorn, sorghum and honey, there was an abundance of food on board. We longed for country milk, however; so one evening I scouted on the hilltop to see if I could find some. The farmhouse directly above was vacant. From it a small, unused road led away inland. I was tempted to go that way, but as it passed no houses, I followed another lane parallel to the river, and came to a small farmhouse where Ellis Lytton lived. With three children and some calves, they had no milk to spare; their next neighbor might, however. Walking down there, I found the man in the act of milking, yet he had no milk for us. As I was leaving, he called to say that his brother, who lived nearly a mile back from the river, might have more milk than he could use. It was getting rather late for exploring farther, but I walked on down the rough dirt road as directed. The farm I approached was a promising place—well-kept house and yard, and painted barn. The people who lived there were friendly, and readily supplied me with a gallon of fresh milk and some eggs. I promised to bring them some fish the next time I came. Striking across the fields I returned to the boat in the twilight, feeling that this acquaintance with Ted Mitchell, his wife and father, was a fortunate one.

Later on the Champions also supplied us with milk whenever we desired it, and best of all with country butter. Oleomargerine was put aside for the summer. We value margerine, however, for its own merits: it keeps fresh in hot weather for months, while the life of butter without refrigeration is a matter of days. As a tasty food, margerine should not be compared with country butter such as Mrs. Champion made.

The Champion farm was along the river, across from the quarry landing. Their house was a ruinous old brick of forbidding aspect which deceived the visitor, for within were only mirth and good humor, and shining cleanliness. They were the jolliest people one could find, father and mother, a long line of husky boys, and one flower of a girl.

It was convenient to call at the Champion's as we made a trip every second or third day to the quarry landing for drinking water and for mail. This oft-repeated trip never became tiresome. A rough path through the woods and quarry followed the river but we seldom used it: the short voyage was so easy and enjoyable. First the steep, wooded hill was passed, with its lower trees extending over the water. The hillside leafed out as we watched through April and May, concealing the evergreens which had furnished such a fine contrast to the flowering redbuds. Then came the bare face of the quarry. From the water's edge rose a steep bank of loose stone which Uncle Jim called the "sprawl" bank, which I suppose should be spall bank, where the broken stones too small to use were dumped. The quarrying had been done on a level shelf above the spall bank. Steam, mules, and men had supplied the power. The intricate system of small rails for the mule-drawn cars remained, and many of the little dump cars. Some crumbling shacks and long-unused derricks and boilers gave to the place an air of peace and retirement. The stone quarried here had been loaded on barges and transported down the Mississippi River for revetment work. Walter Berry showed us a snapshot of the quarry in operation. It was hard to believe that this ancient ruin was ever so teeming with industry; yet the busy derricks in the picture were these same rusty ones which still stood in their original position.

On our trips for mail and water we became well acquainted with the Howards who lived in the two white houses with gardens and lawns sloping toward the river. It was Captain Jonas Howard whom I had met on my bicycle trip to the quarry. Both he and his son, Ray Howard, were connected with the quarry company. Mrs. Jonas Howard, a rare person of old-world charm, was a favorite of the whole countryside. To the Howards we will ever be grateful for their hospitality and kindness shown in so many ways to the strangers who chanced to live near them that summer.

It was in this setting and among these people that we spent the second summer after leaving Brent. This particular bend of the Cumberland soon became as well known to us as Payne Hollow. Indeed, home was wherever our boat was tied, since our lares and penates were always aboard, and no essential left behind. This new country did not seem strange to us. It was still Kentucky and a part of the Ohio River—more southern than Brent or Payne Hollow, with cypress trees and pecans, strange wild flowers, and other signs of a climatic change. It made the greatest difference to be on a small river. We missed the breadth of the Ohio, its long vistas, the feeling that the river was a creation separate from the land. Yet no river, however small, is entirely overwhelmed by the land. The Cumberland had its own character, and if spaciousness and sweep were wanting, there was a sense of intimacy and protection to be found only on a smaller river.

This intimacy included the passing boats, but there was no protection from them. They ran by so close to us that we came to know the features of the crews and their domestic arrangements. They could look down into our windows, and no doubt knew many details of our way of living. The danger was that a towboat would lose control on the bend, and smash into us lying on the outside of the curve. As it happened, not one boat ever came too close to us, but often their waves were bad. Most to be feared was the *Frances M. Hougland,* a large diesel powerful enough to shove her loaded tow against the Mississippi's current. She drove full head up and down our little stream, and plowed a deep furrow. Our boat was in deep water, and we made it a point to be always ready for waves; thus they never caused any serious trouble. Oil barges were most commonly towed, but some covered barges passed and now and then a barge loaded with fluorspar, bound for the Ohio. The towboats were standard diesels, most of them of smaller size. Two or three were stern-wheelers. These were old-timers, one of which, the *Stanley Petter,* we especially liked to see go by. It was relaxed and shabby, a homemade, small-river job, whose irregular, staccato exhaust echoed from the bluff.

One or two new towboats came down, fresh from the builder's ways at Nashville. Diesel driven, of course, they were vessels which even the most ardent lover of steamboats must admire and respect. The handsomest craft of all, we thought, were the new oil barges. They came in pairs, their huge size augmented by their being coupled tandem. The joined ends were square, giving the effect of one long barge. Bow and stern had a fine sheer, which, when the barge was loaded followed exactly the contour of the wave of water pushed ahead of it. Their rake was not the usual plain sloping barge rake, but a graceful spoon bow. The lines of these barges resulted not from a desire to make them beautiful, but from the advantages gained by making them run easily. If only the superstructure of the diesel vessels were dictated by some such natural law, as in the case of the old steamboats, instead of by the designer's fancy!

A few log rafts passed down, shoved slowly along by a small motor-boat or two. In old times many rafts of logs were floated down the river, and many flatboats of settlers who had crossed over the mountains from the southern seaboard states, through Cumberland Gap to the Cumberland River.

There was little drifting after the building of the locks and dams. Nowadays these structures of stone have an antique appearance. The small locks are inadequate for barge traffic. If a tow contains more than a barge or two it must be broken up and locked through piece-meal. The boat crews have to get out and help with the hand-powered windlasses. The deck hands get little rest, since the dams are close to-gether. It is a trying river for pilots, too—narrow, with some sharp, swift bends. The boats run at night even though there are no naviga-tion lights. Thus steamboat men, both pilots and deck hands, have no love for the Cumberland.

One night we were wakened by a sound which might have been dreamed. No, there in the darkness was a stern-wheeler steaming up the river with all the lovely sounds of a packet. It might have been one of the old Cumberland River steamboats—the *R. Dunbar, Will J. Cummins, Grace Devers*. On its return trip it passed in daylight, a small tramp excursion boat which was making the scattered towns along the Cumberland. This was the only steamboat which passed all summer.

One circumstance which made this summer different from last was our association with Phil Howard. Later in the summer he returned home from the college where he taught music. He was an excellent pianist and a very obliging one. Many times during the summer we loaded the 'cello and violin into the johnboat and rowed down to the

206

Howards' for a session of trios. The opportunity to play and talk music with a well-informed and capable person like Phil Howard was a great joy for us. The pleasure was mutual, for Phil no more expected to find that a violinist and a 'cellist had landed near his home than we expected to find a pianist on the Cumberland. One never knows, and must be always alert.

In one point this summer was a counterpart of that at Payne Hollow —we were very busy. Not that time was lacking for rest and leisure, reading and visiting, and work in the cabin studio, but all this and the gardening, canning, fishing and the like, accounted for every minute of the long summer days. Much time and labor went into the garden, which was as large as the one at Payne Hollow. Again the ground was prepared, the crops tended, by hand labor. We ate our bread in the sweat of our brows, entirely happy with our choice, and thankful to be free from that voluntary slavery which most accept in order to earn a living.

Much attention was paid to gardens in that region. Our garden compared well with others about us, and we were proud of it. We were able to supply beans and tomatoes to some of our farmer neighbors. A garden is always a chance and an experiment, even if planted year after year in the same piece of ground. To plant each year in a different place, where changes of climate and soil must be reckoned with, gave to gardening a touch of adventure. Uncle Jim and Ellis Lytton, who had planted corn there last year, advised us about the soil. Up near the woods it was very soft and friable, almost like powder. Here it dried out very quickly. The lower part of the field, when the river went down, was not the rich sandy loam of the Ohio River bottoms. The sun baked the three or four inches of sediment into a cracked, bricklike

207

substance that no working or subsequent rainfall would pulverize. We learned that the sedimentary deposit of all rivers is not alike, due probably to the nature of the soil through which the rivers flow.

We planned a garden such as we were used to, but discovered that here some crops new to us were raised, new varieties suited to the more southern climate. We even found seedsmen who more or less specialized in seed for southern gardens. One vegetable everyone raised was okra. It was not until another summer that we learned the value of okra, but we did plant here some black-eye peas from seed given us by Mrs. Wharton who lived in one of the cottages at the quarry. She had saved the seed from her last year's garden, and the peas were riddled by weevils. They came up well, however, and were truly prolific.

Canning, an important feature in our system of getting together a living, was continuous through the summer, beginning with the canned carp and poke in April. Every jar was filled before the season was over. When the hatches were raised to stow more away, or to show our visitors, the ranks of jars gave the impression of tremendous labor. However, done little by little, and by Anna's well-developed system which fitted the canning into the other household chores, it was not a burdensome task. Here again we were earning our living in the most delightful and interesting way we could imagine, and would not be likely to complain of attendant labor.

One of our household chores, the grinding of flour and meal, was made easier by the acquisition of a new grinder. Though with not so much character, it was smaller than our old coffee mill, and turned out a finer product. In it we could also grind fresh hominy into a substance from which tortillas could be made. The old grinder was kept, in spite of its size and weight, because we could not carelessly part with it, and because it would shuck out sunflower seeds, a task which the new grinder was unable to perform.

When at last the river receded into its banks, it was with a sudden drop which left a shore of soft, bottomless mud which was too much even for us. We were forced to abandon the landing for a week or two until it hardened somewhat. For that period we moved our shantyboat down the river about two hundred yards to a steep slope covered with broken stone, another spall bank, the remains of an old quarrying

operation which had been given up before the forest on the steep hillside was destroyed. There was not a level foothold at the water's edge.
I cut some steps in the slope where good-sized sycamores had grown
up since the stone was dumped there. When one went ashore he must
ascend this zigzag stairway, which was more like a ladder, to the level
shelf about three stories above. The woods were thick there, a pleasant
place in the early summer.

From this landing we walked back to the garden over a wood path
where we watched for birds. Besides the familiar ones, we saw, appropriately, the Nashville warbler, and identified another with staccato
notes, heard often in other springs, as the Tennessee. Some of the birds
we saw and heard had a southern range and were unknown at Brent
—the chuck-will's-widow, for instance, instead of the whip-poor-will.
The prothonotary or golden swamp warbler frequented the river shore,
nesting in overhanging willows and even in an oil can on the deck of
Walter Berry's boat. This bright bird we had never noticed at Brent,
though one of our familiars at Payne Hollow. On the other hand, the
yellow warbler, so common at Brent, we never saw in numbers again;
and the song sparrow and catbird, numerous along the water at home,
were rarely heard down the river westward.

There were strange wild flowers, too. We had been disappointed in
the early spring not to find the accustomed bloodroot and wild lark-
spur. This was atoned for in early summer by a brilliant flowering in
the woods. We saw for the first time a trumpet vine which bloomed in
May with flowers of yellow and red. In the damp mold we saw a delicate short-stemmed flower which we called a wild iris. Later, wisteria
bloomed untended in trees along the shore.

We had been curious about fishing on the Cumberland. It held up well all through the early summer, and we caught more catfish than we could use along the spall bank. When we moved back to our own landing, after the mud had dried so that we could walk on the shore and the low river became clear, the catfish ceased to bite, or perhaps left the river. Then we fished for carp, baiting a trot line stretched from shore to shore with kernels of green corn. Carp are often despised, but we found them something of a game fish. They were of good size, from two to fifteen pounds, and when you picked up an end of your line with a carp on the far end, you knew it at once. We ate them with relish, too. Anna broiled the steaks, seasoning with sweet basil, lemon juice and butter. We have little patience with those who consider carp inedible. However, we do not go as far as the Mitchells, who prefer them to catfish. It was lucky for us they liked carp: thus our trading of fish for milk and eggs went on through the summer.

Ike called them white carp, with now and then a big-scaled German carp. He had no use for them since they were worth little or nothing on the market. Ike had done well with his fishing. One day in May he told me he had caught over a hundred pounds of catfish that day. They brought twenty-two cents a pound. We saw him take a thirty-five-pound yellow cat near our boat, after playing the lively fish for half an hour. When the fishing slacked off with the falling river, Ike tried all the methods and bait which he knew of; even soap, as a last resort. He was always cheerful, and never discouraged. Early in June, however, he gave it up, and, as was his custom, went down the Ohio to shell. He had built a little cabin there, below Paducah on the Illinois shore. It was his summer home, and the rest of the year it housed his equipment, cooking vat, brails, and the like. We invited Ike to dinner before he left. He arrived at eleven o'clock in his outboard johnboat, dressed in fresh clean work clothes, and shelled the peas for dinner. We had that day the first mess of green peas from the garden, and the first new potatoes. The rest of the dinner was fried catfish, cornbread, tomato and cottage cheese salad, and a magnificent lemon pie. Ike was a perfect guest, and his conversation entertaining. He was a man to be believed, and when he told us of taking nine hundred and eighty-four pounds of fish at one raising of one net, we had not the least doubt that the statement was true. The fish were buffalo, ninety-eight head of them. The net had been placed in the middle of the Cumberland River, in the spring during the spawn run.

We were interested in what Ike had to say about his shelling, not of peas, but of mussels. We learned that there are many classes of shells, of different value. Those called sand and niggerhead shells bring the highest price; then muckets and pigtoes. Butterflies and eggs are sometimes accepted with the higher priced shells. Ike said he would try putting them in, for the first time anyway, when the shell buyer's boat came around. He also mentioned washboards, river run, blues and culls, all of lesser value. Some shells are worthless. The names of shells are no doubt derived from their shapes, and an experienced sheller classifies them at a glance.

Fresh-water pearls are often found in mussel shells, occasionally one of considerable value. The pearls are nearly always found in muckets, especially in shells with a crook at the end.

The low water which sent Ike away brought us a new neighbor. Walter Berry moved his handsome boat to the mouth of Bizzle's Creek when the banks dried up. There it became part of the upriver view of which we were so fond that we turned our main deck in that direction. Walter's boat was twice as large as ours. It was not its size but its neatness which overawed us. Even the gangplank was painted and scrubbed. At its landward end were two stakes on which Walter impaled his muddy shoes before stepping on the plank. The boat had elegant furnishings and an oil stove such as steamboat galleys have. When we returned home after a visit on Walter's boat, our own outfit seemed very shantyboat. Yet it was always clean and strictly in order. How could our decks be kept spotless with three dogs running back and forth? And Walter did no fishing.

Walter Berry, a native of Paducah, had first come to the Cumberland as a camper. Long canoe trips had made him familiar with the river as far up as Cumberland Falls. Three times he had come down through the swift gorge below the falls in a canoe. In later years he had been in charge of a manned oil barge. Living alone in a little cabin, neatly kept of course, on the end of the barge, he had been towed by various towboats on most of the rivers of the Mississippi system, on the Alabama, and to Florida as well. When, still a young man, he gave up his barge, he bought this houseboat and took it to the Cumberland, considering it the fairest river of all he had seen. He could live there in peace, he said, with plenty of room. It was even "outside the United States."

Walter was the best of neighbors. He often stopped at our boat, in passing, and several times we rode with him to Smithland in his outboard johnboat, which was as neat and shipshape as his houseboat. We are especially indebted to Walter for teaching us to make deck mats of rope yarn, a steamboat handicraft.

Our landing was an old camping ground of Walter Berry's; so he and Jim Joiner were good friends. We became well acquainted with the old man when in June he came down to plant corn in the remainder of the bottom, our garden covering only half of the acre of tillable ground there. He did his plowing with a whimsical mule named Kate. It was a long trip for them through the woods on top of the ridge and down the steep, stony trail to the river. On those days Jim had dinner with us on the deck of the boat. He liked the attention we paid to him. We listened attentively while he talked in his queer, high-pitched voice, telling us the lore of the country he knew so well, and how it used to be when he was young. He was a keen observer, sensitive and original, a little shy. His quaint, good-humored talk often revealed a poetic and thoughtful mind.

The old man came on our boat one day when we had our 'cello and violin out. He asked us to play for him, and said polite words of praise after our little duet. Asking to see my fiddle, he took it in his hands, began to finger it. Then to our astonishment he tucked the instrument under his chin and began to play. He soon warmed up, giving a lively rendition of *Arkansas Traveler*. Then followed *Soldier's Joy, The Eighth of January,* and many old dances we had never heard of and could not distinguish one from the other. One would never have suspected it of Uncle Jim, with his weatherbeaten face and crusty hands, but the violin fitted naturally under his chin, and his fingers were nimble. He had been a country fiddler in his youth. The young people in those days, he told us, would clean up a man's field or help with his haying, to be allowed to hold a dance at his house that evening.

On another day I showed Jim my viola. That took his eye, and afterwards he often asked to see my big violin, and tried to make a trade for it.

Uncle Jim had lived in the farmhouse, now empty, which was on the ridge directly above our boat. He raised a large family of boys, and said there was a brush field on his farm which had made steamboat men of three of them. Jim and his boys had made the rough trail from his house down to the river. It had required much labor and patience, and some crude engineering, to lay out and build a passable road on that steep hill, cutting into the rock on one side, laying up a rude wall on the other.

From the old man we heard the legend of Bizzle's Bluff and of its lost cave which contained buried treasure. Later we heard more of this story from a Paducah dentist who was native to this region and still rambled through it on days off. There was another cave, not lost, down the river near the spar mine. It was once considered worth running Sunday excursions by boat from Paducah to see this cave. Nowadays the farmers stored their sweet potatoes and apples in it over the winter.

Uncle Jim took an interest in our garden, and we were able to supply him with hot peppers when his crop failed. When the ground hogs became troublesome, he brought down his shotgun for me to use. The ground hogs living in the rocky hillside threatened at first to ravish our garden. One day Anna went to pick lettuce, found the whole row eaten to the ground. Going to the head lettuce, she found all of it was gone, too. The ground hogs nibbled half the peas and started on the beans. I borrowed some traps of Ellis Lytton, but the animals were strong enough to pull out of them. I did manage to shoot one or two, but Skipper turned out to be more effective and satisfactory than the gun. She put in long hours snooping around, and having located the ground hog, would call Sambo, who had not her patience or skill. If I did not come at once at their barking, Sambo would come back for me. They trapped several in the stone wall where I could be of assistance by moving the stones away. The ground hogs were good eating, and were our supply of fresh meat all summer. Especially good in the fall were the half-grown ones who fed in cornfields. We intercepted several as they swam across the river, dipping them up from the johnboat with a dip net.

On the Cumberland the blackberry season came earlier than at Brent by nearly a month. Many mornings through the sultry weather of July we made the rounds of the fence rows, across the river and up on the hill where the berries were abundant and of large size. There were other fruits which were faster picking. A neglected plum tree on the old Joiner farm atop the hill yielded a third of a bushel. This pleased us, but Uncle Jim said, "Miss Annie, as a crop, I consider that a failure."

The old farm had the wistfulness of deserted country homesteads, and we lingered there at every chance. In the flat meadows across the river was a place of like character, a small farmhouse which ceased to be tenanted when the land was absorbed by a large holding. Its small orchard apparently meant nothing to the present owner, but it was a rich harvest for us. There were apples enough to experiment with drying some. Our success was encouraging. The process was not difficult, and we discovered that dried apples were not merely something to eat after the fresh fruit was gone.

Bizzle's Bluff was not the coolest place in summer. The hill kept away the north and west winds, and reflected the sun's heat. It was seldom uncomfortable on the water, however. We swam often, diving from the deck into the clear water which became colder farther below the surface. Cooking over the wood fire was a hot job, but Anna usually managed a plunge just before serving dinner. Dinner was carried across the gangplank to a table and bench which I had made of some old boards and driftwood. It was under a bushy maple tree above the boat, high enough to catch any breeze there might be. We could enjoy the open view up and down the river while we ate and lingered there to read a little. By midafternoon the table was in the sun. Our supper and breakfast spot was a little way down the bank, shaded by willows except in the middle of the day. Here was a fireplace for the simple cooking of those meals.

The riverbank paths were bordered by little zinnias and marigolds. Another path led to the cabin through Jim's cornfield. He had said, "Cut you a path wide enough to let you carry a basket on your arm." The path continued along the side of our garden, a safe distance from the beehive, past a bed of zinnias which bloomed so large and brightly colored that all the farm ladies who visited us asked for seed. Our other flowers were all sunflowers except a bizarre spider plant transplanted from Mrs. Mitchell's garden. The sunflowers were planted about in the garden where other seeds had not come up; also in a long row facing the river, below the boat, where there had been a bank slide. These made a fine showing when seen from the river, and might have led to the name "Sunflower Bend" for this spot.

Our landing and our boat attracted nearly everyone who lived on the bluff. The Ellis Lyttons, our nearest neighbors, came down often, and with them, Marjorie Mitchell who lived on the next farm. The Lyttons had three little girls. The youngest, Pauline, was so fond of dogs that when Skipper had her Cumberland River puppies, Pauline would sit on the floor with the tiny things, jerking in their sleep, and endlessly arrange them in patterns about her. The Lyttons had already acquired Chip, Sambo's brother. Marjorie Mitchell had taken Sambo at the same time, carrying him, a heavy burden, up the steep path to her home. We missed Sambo, and were quite satisfied when next day Marjorie's brother returned him to us explaining, "My father says he is going to be too big a dog."

We often heard voices in the woods above, and made hasty preparations to receive visitors. Once it was the minister from the Dyer Hill Baptist Church and his family, escorted by all the Lyttons and Marjorie, with whom he was having dinner that day. The Dyer Hill Church was out on the highway, a pleasant walk over wood paths. Near it was Uncle Bud Lloyd's little store, painted bright yellow trimmed in red. We had first made this excursion in April through moist woods open to the sky. Going into Uncle Bud's store, more to get acquainted than to buy any necessity, Anna thought of asking for tapioca. Uncle Bud, the true storekeeper, said he was sorry but he was just out of it. Then his curiosity got the better of him; he broke down and asked, "Say, what is that stuff anyway?"

We attended services at the Dyer Hill Church with Ted Mitchell and his family. After church they spread a country picnic dinner on the table built in the churchyard for that purpose, near a fine spring. In the afternoon we all went on to the town of Burna to a "sing." The structure in which it was held—a low roof without walls—and the wooden benches reminded us of a camp meeting. The music had a revival fervor. Vocal quartets or trios representing different towns about the country performed one after another in a sort of tournament. The music, which would be called sacred, was puzzling to us. We had read in music histories that popular tunes were incorporated into early ecclesiastical music; this singing reversed the process, not only in regard to the tune, but also its delivery.

Through the summer the original contract with the Mitchells, of bartering fish for milk and eggs, had grown into a lively friendship. We often walked across the fields to their farm, picking berries in the fence rows, or on our way to help with the haying. The warm welcome and country fare were in the best Kentucky tradition. They shared with us anything we could use, and we always returned with a load. When our watermelons did not turn out well, they gave us several at various times, which I carried down the trail in a sack, a load which grew heavier and heavier as I neared the river. The peaches, however, had to be transported around the road to Howards' and up the river. One tree in their flourishing new orchard had been reserved for us, and it is still called, they tell us, the Hubbard tree.

Ted Mitchell farmed with imagination and foresight, eager for new ideas and willing to experiment with new methods. His farm was not merely a number of joined fields for raising crops, but it was their home, and his aim was to make it the best possible place for his family to live. He was in sympathy with our experiment in living, though so different from his own way, and we discussed our aims and hopes with frankness and understanding. A rare trait was his deep-felt appreciation of painting. He had lived briefly in a city, and he still remembered and intelligently discussed the paintings in the museum there. To have a painter come into his ken was a windfall for him. He came often to see my pictures and work in progress. Once with some hesitation he proposed a portrait of Martha Ann, his three-year-old daughter. With even more hesitation I undertook to do it. By the end of the summer I managed to produce an acceptable likeness of this vivacious young lady.

Rewarding in many ways was the small stint of haying I did for

Mitchell and Lytton. This was not modern high-pressure farming but leisurely work done with mules and by hand. On Ellis's farm we pitched the hay into the mow of a log barn roofed with hand-hewn shingles. Also I watched closely Ellis's planting and tending of the large piece of bottom land up toward Bizzle's Creek, which he rented that year and put into corn. It was excellent corn, white, open-pollinated, and as good to eat, we thought, though not so sweet and tender, as garden sweet corn. Ellis told us to help ourselves, and as it was planted late, we enjoyed steamed corn for breakfast for a long time.

We dried corn, too, not slowly in the sun but with a low heat and sun combined, after a preliminary steaming. The idea of dehydrating appeals to us. The success with dried corn, apples, and herbs has encouraged further experiments.

I helped Ellis snap a load of corn in the harvest. He gave us a bushel or two for "bread corn" saying the open-pollinated corn was softer and sweeter than the hybrid. We were amazed that a wagon could be driven down the steep, rough trail, but as at Payne Hollow, the descent was managed by chaining a rear wheel. Going up with a load was not possible, however, and Ellis hauled in his corn the long way around.

Ellis and Uncle Jim were pals and they often worked together. It was good to see the young man's admiration and offhand watchfulness for his old friend. He liked to quote Jim. About elections, he had said, "No matter who is elected, all we get out of it is beans and overhalls." In blackberry time Uncle Jim told a story of a thrifty farmer, one who had cleaned up all his woods and fence rows, who went on his neighbor's place to pick berries. The neighbor was a shiftless fellow who farmed only the middle of his fields. He chased the berry picker off his land, saying, "If you took care of your blackberries the way I do, you'd have plenty of your own."

Our knowledge of the country was extended by a Sunday drive with the Howards. We went north, stopping to see some rock formations called Mantle Rock. The country still kept a backwoods savor. We saw bees kept in gums made of hollow logs. In a cleared space along the road was a rude structure of poles and branches— no walls, merely a roof thatched roughly with twigs and dry leaves. We were told that a brushwood meeting had been held there. The limit of our trip was the top of a bluff from which we looked down on the Ohio. The blue water of the summer stream, narrowed by sandbars curving far out from the willows, the slow current—we could hardly believe that this was the wide and muddy river on which we had drifted swiftly past this very hill.

Because of this intimacy with the people who lived about us, we felt no longer that we were drifters, but settled residents. Of course ties with family and old friends were close as ever, and we welcomed those who could make the long trip into western Kentucky to see us. Not entirely to see us, but to have a few days afloat, and to be close to the river. Our most faithful guests have the makings of shantyboaters in themselves. All who came were taken with the Cumberland. George and Elisabeth were surprised to hear that towboats ran on such a small river. As if to impress the fact, a steady procession of boats and barges passed while they were with us, all the regulars, down and back, and some which were strange even to us. Etta and Fran enjoyed the swimming especially. During their stay, Herbert Fall appeared, unexpected and grinning as usual, having found his way along the shore from the quarry. Since the texas was already occupied, a bed was made for Herbert in the cabin studio. Other friends appeared through the summer, sometimes arriving by water. One day we saw the Howards' boat coming upstream. This time it was not Mr. Howard out fishing for bass, but a boatload of people, friends of the Howards, we thought, to whom the well-known voice of Phil announced the points of interest. As the boat approached we were surprised to hear a voice call to us across the water, "Hello, it's Warren and Patricia." These good friends had visited us at Brent and Payne Hollow, and we were happy to see them and their party, even though we were in the midst of bean canning and cleaning out the between-deck section, a chore which littered the deck with boxes and cans.

Walter Berry's guests came by river, too, and he brought them to our landing to see our boat and the pictures in the studio, but most of all to climb the bluff to the local Lovers' Leap. In the willow grove at his landing, Walter built huge campfires of logs, scientifically designed and constructed. He had made his riverbank quite like a park, with a garden and an outdoor cooking place in which he burned only cedar.

Toward the end of the summer, my brother Frank came for a few days. He had lived with us briefly each summer and this time as always gave an aura of refinement to our boat and our river life, which, stimulated by his letters, lasts through the year.

Our guests were easy to take care of, since they took care of themselves, mostly; and easy to feed, with garden produce, fish, and country milk and butter. When the last guest had gone, we folded up the texas and did a nine-sheet washing. Then it seemed that summer and our stay on the Cumberland were coming to an end.

The hottest weather of the summer had come late in August. Days of unbroken sunshine withered the garden. Thunderheads rose but passed around us, often to the south, which led Uncle Jim to bewail the unwanted rainfall in Kentucky Lake. At last our turn came; the long-awaited mud rain fell at the beginning of September, and a new season commenced.

Now the potatoes could be dug, what was left of them, for the crop was short compared with Payne Hollow's abundance. The peanuts yielded well, however. Ellis wondered what we would do with all of them. Few people realize how important such foods as peanuts, popcorn, sunflower seeds and walnuts are to us. We began getting in apples, pears and walnuts, provisions for winter and for the voyage alike. I cut some new sweep poles, straight and strong, which Uncle Jim said were slippery elm. It was not the best wood, being heavy and of short life in the water.

The approaching voyage was thought of more and more. Before we could leave, however, we must make a trip to Michigan to see Anna's mother, who had not been able to visit us on the Cumberland. We left the boat as it was. Walter Berry would stop there once a day to see that all was well and to feed the dogs. Getting ready was a busy time, and as usual with us, complicated by some irrelevant activity. I delivered the last three of Skipper's pups to their new homes on the ridge farms. Happening on some fine wild grapes, I brought back a sackful of which we made juice. This had to be done along with the cooking and baking which are necessary preparations for all our trips. At the last minute, the johnboat was hauled out on the bank, to be dry enough for repairs and paint when we came back.

Walter took us to the quarry landing in his boat. On his return, he would release the dogs who had been shut up in the cabin to prevent their following us. The Howards assisted greatly by driving us to the bus at Burna, since it was now after dark. There was little to see on the night ride, but with no light in the bus, one could look out over the nocturnal landscape. It was chilly weather, and we watched carefully for signs of frost. There was none in Michigan, and we congratulated ourselves that our garden, far southward, was safe. It was therefore a surprise to find, on our return, that the temperature for two nights had been 29°. The sweet potato and tomato vines were frozen black.

Persimmons were ripe now, and for dessert Anna served persimmon pulp with cream and walnuts. The summering egrets had departed, and more ground hogs than ever swam the river, always toward our side. We thought that perhaps they instinctively left the low shores to hole up in the rocky hillside. Another sign of fall was the return of Ike Jones from his shelling. The river being still low and clear he set out snag lines, which were merely long strings of perhaps several hundred unbaited hooks on close-spaced staging. On these lines he caught many spoonbills, a singular fish which was ranked by the fish buyer with catfish. Of large size, they might be called a cross between a sturgeon and a catfish, with a tail like a miniature whale's. It was good to hear Ike whistling and singing again as he came up the river, his music echoed by the bluff which had now blossomed out in the richest colors.

During the long summer the bees had done well, building up a strong colony and making an excess of honey. With some reluctance we decided not to take them with us. It might be warmer this winter, when we turned south at the Mississippi River, and the bees would be troublesome. Accordingly we took for ourselves most of the honey, gallons of it, leaving just enough for the bees to winter on. The hive was left under the little peach tree by the stone wall. Here the bluff afforded protection from north winds, and the sun would be warm. We told Uncle Jim how he could manage to get some honey next year,

but he was afraid of bees, and dubious. Whatever became of them we do not know.

The final preparations were under way. The last sacks of apples and pears were toted from the old orchard across the river. Turnips, parsnips, and carrots were pulled up and packed in baskets. The sweet potatoes—undamaged by the frost since the vines had been cut away at once—were carefully dug. We think this the most exciting harvest in the garden. Our crop, spread out on the cabin floor to dry, made a good showing and we were proud of it. Even now we regretted leaving our garden. The tomato vines which had been protected from the frost by weeds and grass continued to bear fruit. We picked them all, even the green ones, which filled a wash tub. Much of this we gave to our neighbors at the quarry.

The recent rainfall caused a rise in the river, and the muddy current seemed to have come just to carry us away. The last loading was done, and on the fifth of November, 1948, a Friday, we stood out into the stream. It was not a spirited send-off. Heavy rain fell in a thick mist, and there was no one to hear the blasts of our horn.

This was not our real departure, however. We tied up at the Champions' landing, and that evening entertained all the family, a lively time. Next morning we crossed to the quarry landing. We lay there over Sunday and kept open house, visited by all our old friends and some new ones who had not been able to make the trip to Bizzle's Bluff.

It was with regret that we saw these good people for the last time There was no similar feeling about the place, however. In the last days of summer had occurred the long-expected opening of the quarry. It was not to remove stone, this time, but to crush it into a powder which sifted the green earth with desolation. There was much noise, strangers had come in, and the peaceful serenity of the valley was no more.

While Anna entertained our visitors, I made a final trip back to the deserted landing. I dug up the flourishing parsley plants and potted them to take along. Then I made three more trips to the big walnut tree which stood in front of the old farmhouse across the river. The nuts, while not large, were of the finest quality, and we decided to get our winter's supply from this one tree. I began by hulling them, but this took too long. It was heavy work, packing across the soggy autumn fields. In my eagerness to get back to the boat, I left the parsley on the bank, after all.

Next morning, before anyone was up to see us, we were gone. The current was slower now, and even Smithland seemed a long way off. We could not imagine that this slow movement was the beginning of the longest and fastest voyage we were to make.

9

Before us always since the voyage began, and before that in our minds, was the mystery of the Mississippi River. What was it like? We had read books about it, and accounts of the earliest and latest navigators. People who had been on its waters told us about the river, and we questioned them further. No clear-cut impression resulted. Perhaps it was a different river to each man. One fact was certain—it was different from the Ohio.

Reports about the Mississippi River were nearly all unfavorable and discouraging. When anyone heard that we proposed to drift down it in our small boat without power, he shook his head and did his best to dissuade us. We had lately received much advice of this sort. Walter Berry was the most violent. He pictured the Mississippi as a raging, mad river with caving banks and dangerous eddies, and he gave us little chance of success. Captain Jonas Howard had come down to the boat that last day especially to warn us, from his own experience, of the hazards we were sure to encounter. Even mild Uncle Jim, who himself had been partway down the Mississippi on a derrick boat, urged us to stop at Cairo and turn back. He told us of a whirlpool under a cliff which was so terrible that the greatest drifting trees, when caught in it, stood upright, whirling, until sucked beneath the surface never to reappear.

A few accounts of the Mississippi were more encouraging. One of the Joiner boys, who worked on a towboat on that river, said that our trip was feasible, that safety depended on our skill as navigators. We were further reassured, on that first day of drifting down the Cumberland, by a fisherman who came aboard for a talk. Between various propositions to swap with him, one of which was to trade our Sambo for a dog of his that was "one-quarter police," he told us that he liked the Mississippi. There were bad stretches of caving bank, he said, but then you would come to a safe shore with quiet water. This was the sort of thing we wanted to believe. After all, it was no more than a river, and one that had been descended by hundreds of flatboats similar to ours. Many of them were lost on the way, it is true, but most of them made it. We believed that we could.

Before the Mississippi could be essayed, there remained sixty miles of the Ohio, including two locks and dams to get by, and a stop at Paducah. First came Smithland, which we reached after a day of slow drifting down the Cumberland. Anchoring at the old ferry landing again, we remembered the spring days there before our ascent of the Cumberland. Bizzle's Bluff was only seven miles back but we felt now as if we had drifted down from the mountains. We looked the part, too—dogs barking, hulled walnuts spread out on the roof to dry, corn and pumpkins peeking out beneath the tarpaulin, a ground-hog skin tacked on the cabin.

The Ohio River could not be seen from our landing because of the long island which lies off the mouth of the Cumberland. The actual nearness of the big river was brought to us the first night we lay there when one of the largest Ohio River towboats nosed into the Cumberland with its whole tow in order to drop off a barge there. As it glided slowly in, a deck hand standing on the leading barge with a line was picked out of the darkness by the boat's searchlight. A voice called from shore, "What boat is that?" The answer came back, *"Tenaru River."* We were to see this boat more than once far down the Mississippi.

In the two days we lay at Smithland the stowing of our cargo was completed and all made shipshape. It was the heaviest load yet, even without the bees. Decks and cabin were unincumbered, but all available storage space was put to use. The excess load on the roof made the boat roll heavily in the waves. We had stowed there, in addition to the usual plunder, two boxes from the beehive containing honey in frames, several pumpkins from Uncle Jim's cornfield, the baskets of root vegetables and green tomatoes, sacks of sweet potatoes, the tin lard cans in which grain and soybeans were stored, bushels of walnuts. In the water floated the fish box, a nuisance while drifting and a drag which canceled the efforts of one rower. It paid its way by supplying us with fresh fish for two weeks. Had there been a crate of chickens on the roof or some ducks perched about, the shantyboat picture would have been complete.

We left the mouth of the Cumberland early on a frosty morning, drifted past the quiet little town before sunrise. The island chute was so long that it seemed to be part of the Cumberland River. It was not until we cleared the end of the island that the full expanse of the Ohio was realized. It was good to be afloat again on its wide current.

Early in the afternoon we were abreast of the mouth of the Tennessee River, a dozen miles below the Cumberland. It was a surprise to find this river clear and without current. Tennessee Island, a mile and a half long, lies below the river mouth. To pass outside the island would have been easy for us, since the Ohio's current was trending that way. This course, however, would take us below Paducah, which lay behind the island. It was a question whether we could pass inside the island or not, since in addition to the unfavorable current, a light wind was blowing out of the Tennessee. We made a try, rowing as hard as we could toward the mainland while the current carried us down. We failed to reach the point of the island, but landed to the right of it in a swift current setting out into the river. From here we were able, by two or three hitches on trees ahead, to cordelle the boat into easy water, and at last into the current which flowed inside the island.

The boat drifted slowly down the narrow channel, the uninhabited island on the right, while on the mainland to the left were the harbor industries of Paducah, a river city. The shore was lined with docks and fleets of barges, towboats, marine ways, piles of coal and sand. A towhead in the upper end of the chute makes a protected harbor behind the long island, in which all manner of boats and barges take refuge in times of ice.

We watched all this with great interest as we drifted slowly past but found no harbor for us. Toward evening we anchored below a boatyard, almost down to the lower end of the chute. We obtained a ready permission from the owner to tie up to his barges. It was an excellent berth for us. Boat and dogs could be left here with an easy mind while we went about our business in Paducah.

It was here we rounded out our supplies. Our list included such unrelated items as soybeans from the seed store and pressed wood panels for future paintings. These we bought at a lumberyard and lugged down to the boat. Though all storage space seemed to be filled, the new purchases were neatly tucked away.

The fair weather held during the two days and three nights we lay at Paducah. The river continued to fall and was at pool stage when we rowed out of the harbor into the current outside the island.

Less than five miles downstream was Dam 52, the lock being across on the Illinois side. Five miles is a long way, but the river was a good three-quarters of a mile wide, and under unfavorable conditions we might not have been able to cross to the other side before reaching the dam. Then one of our bad dreams—being carried over a dam—would come to pass.

On this day there was little wind and current. We reached the Illinois shore too soon, and had to row back into the river a way to find moving water. After passing safely under the Paducah highway bridge, a wind sprang up which held us to the bank, a long gravel bar above the lock, for the rest of that Sunday afternoon.

After listening to the roar of the dam through the night, we entered the lock next morning at sunrise, and were put through. This was our first locking since Louisville, more than ten months ago. The one previous to that had been at Dam 37 nearly two years before. All the other dams, ten of them, were passed on an open river, and no locking was necessary. Because of the width of the river at Dam 52, and perhaps to take care of the runout of the Tennessee River, this dam has three

226

bear traps instead of the customary two. These were all open this morning, and some of the short wickets also, so that much water was pouring through the dam in mid-river. This caused a strong backlash up along the shore below. When the lower lock gate was opened we towed down along the guide wall to the end, and then, knowing we could make no headway against the backlash, rowed straight out into the river. It was a long, hard pull through turbulent water, in which the boat seemed to stick fast. Once in the power of the water coming through the opening in the dam, we were whisked down the river at a fast rate.

Ike Jones's summer camp and shelling ground were soon passed; then Fort Massac, where a state park perpetuates the name of one of the earliest posts on the river. We drifted past Metropolis, Illinois, slipped under a railroad bridge, and met several large tows coming up, all without touching an oar. Below Metropolis is a long, straight reach of wide river flowing northwest, the location of Little Chain Bar. From the railroad bridge light to the Joppa lights is seven miles. The Joppa lights are range lights, one higher and half a mile behind the other. The two lights enable pilots to keep a straight course down the long reach at night. The Metropolis bridge was in plain view from even farther down the river. It made us uneasy to think of wind on this long reach, but even though we traveled until dark, we could find no harbor. We anchored along the shore, having opened the long Grand Chain Reach to the southwest. The night became cloudy, and we heard rain. No wind rose, fortunately, and we shoved off in the wet daybreak. Geese and ducks were about, and we saw killdeers, and a great blue heron. From Paducah down, gulls had been frequent.

The weather faired later in the morning and we drifted along clean gravel shores. Just above Post Creek, wind and current carried us too close in and we ran fast aground on a submerged sandbar.

It was urgent that we get the boat off at once. The river might fall and leave us beached out there for weeks; or a wind might rise, while the boat was in shallow water, and the waves give it a pounding. With this in mind I set to work with poles, wading bare-legged in the cold water, prying and shoving. These efforts failing, we carried the anchor out into the river, and rigged up a block and tackle through the cabin.

227

Instead of pulling the boat off, we dragged the anchor toward us. If only a fast-moving towboat had passed, we might have pulled off when its waves lifted us. Instead, the river fell a few inches and we ceased our useless efforts.

Late in the afternoon rain and mist swept in. Perhaps it was a change of wind, but by one of those sudden fluctuations of the river our marks were covered by rising water. This time we successfully pulled out into deep water where our anchor was set. A violent rain came up. I ran a long line to a snag on the bar, and slacking off on the anchor line we worked the boat into the mouth of Post Creek. It was a good harbor —unless there should be a runout.

This was our first and only grounding.

The Ohio was a wide river for the remaining course of twenty-three miles to its mouth. Its width appeared even greater because of the low shores. The moon rose as out of the ocean. We imagined the Mississippi to be like this, but it was not, as we found out. Nothing is like the Mississippi, at least not the Lower Ohio with its parallel shores, even width and depth, slow-curving bends and steady current.

Dam 53 had not been raised. Next day we drifted past the inactive lock and tied up for the night below it. Now there remained no obstruction in the river, not a riffle, between us and the sea.

The weather became unsettled and that night white clouds raced across the moon. Surface wind could be expected to follow, but since the morning was quiet enough we cast off. A gusty wind soon rose from the south. We dropped anchor just above America Point, on the Illinois side. The wind increased and blew directly at us with great force from a point across and down the river. The anchor held the boat safely and kept it headed into the wind; yet it was an anxious, uncomfortable time on the tossing boat. The river was rising now, and we were shoved this way and that by the opposing forces of wind and current. We almost envied the dogs, who unconcerned with wind and river, blithely irresponsible as always, were chasing rabbits through the bare cornfields. After a rough, stormy night, through which we slept nevertheless, the wind gradually shifted to west with clearing weather. It blew harder than ever but now we were in the lee of the shore. Great combers were running in midstream. The sandbar at

America Point protected us from the direct force of these, but a kind of ground swell rolled in. It was not uncomfortable on board now, and we went about our indoor work—baking, a haircut for me, sewing of shoes, grinding meal.

It was here we dressed and ate the last of the Cumberland River fish. The fish box was abandoned on the beach without regret.

The third morning was as calm as if there had never been a wind, and cold enough to freeze ice on deck. We gauged our time by the height of the morning star, and cast off. It was quiet off America Point, the bar nearly covered now by the rise. We thought what a rough and stormy place this must have been the past two days.

On the straight reach below, for all the width of the river, the channel is narrow. It is marked by two lines of buoys which threshed about in the current disappearing sometimes beneath the surface to rise some distance away, or so it seemed, as if they had swum under water. Soon we were passing Mound City, Illinois, a true river town with an active marine ways on the waterfront. It was the first place of any size since Joppa, twenty-two miles back. The Kentucky shore is even less populous, there being no town at all between Paducah and the Mississippi River, a distance of forty-seven miles.

Our destination was the Cache River, a little stream flowing down through southern Illinois. It is said to have once harbored a band of river pirates. The man we found living there in a shantyboat might have been a descendant of the outlaws, such a wild strain was in him. He was friendly enough, towing us into the harbor with his long motorboat after he had met us out on the river. His family was more respectable, the bright-eyed little girls attending school in Mound City.

Everything on board was put in the best of order to facilitate our winter drifting. Screens were taken down, rolled and stored away. How much more light came through the windows, and how neat the boat looked without them—yet how necessary they had been through the summer.

We did a washing here, and wrote letters, since Cairo was to be a mail stop. The city was four miles downstream. Its smoke could be seen, and also the many-spanned Illinois Central Railroad bridge which crossed the Ohio.

Thanksgiving Day was celebrated in Cache River when Anna baked our first sweet potato pie. In the evening our river neighbors came to visit us, and as usual the children were intrigued with our boat. They never take it seriously.

We left the next day, and, in spite of gusty and threatening weather, made it down to Cairo where we tied up along a steep shore of broken stone. At one time it must have been the steamboat landing; now one would hardly know there was a city on the bank, so completely is it hidden behind a concrete sea wall. Cairo has every reason to shrink behind its levees: the low point on which it is situated is menaced by the Ohio on one side, the Mississippi on the other. We found Cairo a charming, friendly town, a good place for rivermen to buy. The stores give special service to towboats which put in for supplies. In the Boat Store Anna was amazed at the huge cans of pepper and syrup, gallon jars of mayonnaise, and other supplies proportioned for steamboat galleys. The store maintained an informal post office with pigeon holes to receive mail and messages for the different boats.

The choicest store we found was run by an old German and his partner, both of whom might have been characters in a fairy tale. Their chief business was harness, which they made in the rear of the store and displayed in front, though the whole establishment was more workshop than salesroom. The various kinds and parts of harness, the hardware and tools appertaining to it, were beautiful to look at. What

230

fine sandals we could have made! Besides harness, almost anything a farmer or boatman might want could be found—as well as some old buggy accessories which could be classed as antiques. We bought some rope—four hundred feet of quarter-inch Manila line for cordelling, and two hundred feet of half-inch, since our present lines were shorter and heavier. We were amused at the roundabout way in which the old fellows measured the line, stretching it back and forth from one end of the store, whose length they knew, to the other. Then they began coiling it up on their elbows from each end, finishing with a kink in the middle which it took us a long time to straighten out. A tarpaulin was another purchase. I asked if they had a machete, a tool I thought would be handy for clearing landings and paths in the riverbank brush. To our surprise, a genuine machete was produced. On their recommendation, however, I bought a domestic corn knife, as efficient a tool and much cheaper. As a bonus we were given some strong thread and a needle for sewing leather. One item they did not have; we bought a pair of hip boots at another store—no more wading bare-legged in icy water.

The Ohio bade us a rough farewell, as we lay on that rocky shore which became as dreary as the coast of Maine in the November gale. A fine, cold rain was driven through the air by the northeast wind, a downstream wind which kicked up a choppy sea. The waves gurgled and sloshed against the boat all day, splashing up through the drains, seeping in through unexpected places far above the waterline. For the first time in many months I had to pump out the hull. The boat jerked and pitched as if it were being hauled down a rough road. It was cheery within, storm or no, as we read our recent mail before a blazing fire of driftwood which we fished out of the river as it floated past.

By the next afternoon it was quiet enough to drift again. We dropped down along the shore, and moored the boat above the highway bridge. This was shantyboat town, the boats beached out in a grove of cotton-woods, many of them afloat now on the higher water. We paid little attention to them, our thoughts were directed forward. Cairo Point was but a mile below, and beyond, across the Mississippi, lay the dark Missouri shore.

After a clear wintry night we awoke to a morning of riverbank cold, the air heavy with fog, smoke, and frost. We built fires and made preparations for the day's voyage with a new excitement—this was to be the day of our entry into the Mississippi River. That we might be able to give our whole attention to this momentous event, departure was held up until breakfast was over and everything made shipshape. The sun was shining through the mist by the time I took in the frosty lines and pulled out into the fast current amid the wrack of driftwood which seemed to cluster about us. The silver bridge swung overhead. Then we grazed by the lines of barges tied up at Cairo Point. Here is a sort of clearinghouse for barges. Like freight cars in a railroad yard, they are transferred to different routes—up and down the Mississippi, to the Missouri, Illinois, the Ohio and its many branches. Beyond came the last point of land—nine hundred and eighty-one miles from Pitts-burgh, five hundred and nineteen from Brent, and nine hundred and sixty-four to the Head of Passes into the Gulf of Mexico. We shot out into the Mississippi River, a larger chunk in the long line of drift pouring out of the Ohio.

Our immediate concern was to pull over to the Missouri shore in order to be on the inside of the first bend. Even had there been time for it, there seemed to be no occasion for any ceremony. Out here on the broad, ruffled water, the names and arbitrary boundaries found on maps had little significance. The Ohio did not end, nor did the Mississippi, at first, seem to be different. It was all water merging and making its way down to the sea, carrying us along with it. As for maps —if we had been the first explorers, the map we made would have indicated the Ohio as the main stream, not only because of the water and drift running out, but it looked bigger than the Mississippi, which is divided above the junction by a large towhead. Also, the river downstream carries out the contour of the Ohio, while the Mississippi seems to come in from the side.

Had it been a time of low water, the effect would have been otherwise. Even then the Mississippi is swift and muddy, while the Ohio becomes the limpid stream which Audubon compared to a youth losing his innocence by contact with the world, just as the Ohio's clear waters gradually disappear into the muddy current of the Mississippi.

Skirting the Missouri shore, we had a sensation of being in a land new to us. It was strengthened by the sight of a bald eagle sitting in a treetop. We were becoming aware, too, that this river was not the familiar Ohio. The current had a new force to it, almost a willfulness and driving purpose. A piece of driftwood floating in the swiftest water—for the stream is made up of many currents of different velocity—seemed to move under power, as if towed in some unknown manner. The Mississippi's course is angular, shifting from one side to another, bouncing off points behind which are eddies where the current, just as swift as in midstream, is reversed. It has a wildness compared with which the Ohio's flow is a sedate rounding of smooth curves.

As we drifted along, unexpected areas of slack water were encountered. These gave us a welcome chance to relax. Below the head of Island Number Two we dropped anchor in slowly moving water for a midday stop. The islands are numbered, though a few have names, from the mouth of the Ohio downstream. Island Number One lay so close to the Kentucky shore, or rather to Cane Island, that we had not been able to make it out. The map indicated the site of old Fort Jefferson just above Island Number One. Many islands were missing, we soon found, washed away, or left far inland by the ever-changing river. Going ashore with the dogs on this particular island, which was really Islands Number Two, Three, and Four, combined, I found that a large cornfield was being harvested. A chute had been built down the bank for loading the corn into a barge. The loading must have been done carelessly, since bushels of corn lay underneath the

233

chute partly in water. We would have liked to take it all with us, but could salvage only part, since our storage space was already filled.

Drifting until nearly sunset, we eased in to the shore below the landing of the busy ferry that crossed to and from Columbus, Kentucky. We were delighted with our first day's run on the Mississippi. The distance was eighteen miles, no difficulties had been met with, the night's harbor was a good one in easy water.

That fair evening we watched the red bluffs across the river, called the Iron Banks, glow and fade as the sun set. In the morning we started off again, rowing a little to counteract a light cross breeze. The chute to the right of Wolf Island Bar was swift. Formerly, before this channel was dredged out, boats passed eastward of the wide bar, along the famous Chalk Bluff, which, jutting out into the river, causes a whirlpool dreaded by all navigators. We saw this cape shining dimly in the morning light, over a wide expanse of water and sandbar. That was close enough. No more would I wake at night to think of Chalk Bluff, after hearing its dangers recounted by old timers, or by people who had never been there.

The easy drifting below was suddenly interrupted by a wind from the southeast which carried us in toward the revetment at Beckwith Bend. This was the first of our struggles to keep free of those dangerous shores where the current races along the asphalt slope like a galloping horse. Often there is dead water along the shore, or a vicious eddy. You are dizzy with the roaring water's changing pace and direction. You pull your limit, not knowing whether it helps much. We never crashed on such a shore, nor did we succeed in moving away from one; we just scooted along the ragged edge until the bend was rounded. To Anna, rowing alone on the main deck facing the shore, all this was especially vivid—I was out on the river side, rowing in the johnboat.

The rest of the day was rough going. As we approached Island Number Six it seemed like a good idea to take the narrow chute behind the island, if it were open. The wind would carry us into it, and Hickman Bend, a sharp one, could thus be by-passed. The chute appeared to be narrow but unobstructed. We rowed toward it, thought we were in, but the current broke suddenly to the left and carried us into the wind and around the outside of the island. We saw Hickman

234

after all, and were glad of it: the last river town in Kentucky, built on a hill, it brought to mind the lovely towns on the upper Ohio. We would like to stop there, we thought, but must be content with what we could see as the current swept us around the bend—almost into a swaying buoy, and into the path of an upbound *Clipper*. Luckily the pilot held to the outside of the channel, and all we suffered was a shaking up as we dashed through the boat's waves which were breaking on a submerged reef extending far out from the Kentucky shore above the Reelfoot revetment.

After dodging the Hickman ferry, we looked for a harbor in which we could end this wild ride. Possibly because of our anxiety, we bungled our first try for a landing: I had run a line to a tree, but the shantyboat was carried by the current below the short eddy in which we hoped to tie up. I was standing in the johnboat on the wrong side of the line which, becoming taut, carried me overboard. I waded ashore, cast loose, and retrieved the johnboat. An easy landing was made farther down. We had learned another lesson—not to try to land on a shore where the current is swift.

A daybreak start was made next morning. The previous day had been a hard one, but any temptation to lay over was counterbalanced by a desire to get away from the open shore where we had passed the night. Ahead lay Island Number Eight, around which the river circled in a wide bend. It was a large island, seven miles around on the river side, four miles through the chute which cut off the point. This chute was shown on the chart to be open and wide, but after some deliberation, we decided to go the long way around, since we could not be sure of the inside passage. Accordingly, I rowed with the sweeps out into the river, and thought we were passing the chute safely, when to my astonishment, the boat began to slip the other way, drifting fast into the chute. It turned out to be a safe passage through a channel, itself wide enough to be a river. We stopped halfway through, had breakfast while the dogs raced about the sandbar. The immense sandbars of the Mississippi were beyond our conception. Even in moderately high water, they extend for miles, not only along the river, but inland. They are sprinkled with snags left by past floods. Tall grass, even willows, grow on the higher parts. These might be shores of an ocean,

235

or one can imagine, far back from the river, that he is in the midst of a desert.

A south wind was springing up, and we considered staying in that quiet, sunny water. Outside lay a ten-mile southward reach. However, this was one of those days when my urge to keep moving is stronger than caution or reason. This time it turned out well, and we had a fine run for the rest of the day. In the head wind we used a contrivance called a mule, or mud sail. It is really an underwater sail, used by shellers to drag their heavy brails over the bottom. Our mud sail was a square of canvas as wide as the boat. It was lowered into the water, over the end of the boat, an iron pipe on the lower edge to hold it down, the upper edge fastened to the deck. Lines extended from each end of the pipe to the corners of the other deck. The boat was kept parallel with the current which exerted its force against the sail just as a wind would do. The mule carried us into a head wind very well. Another advantage was that it kept the end of the boat into the wind and waves. Without it our boat always turned broadside to the wind.

Thus we sailed down the long reach, waves slapping against the rake. Our course followed the channel, which was then over toward the right bank. The map showed that the channel made a crossing over to the left, at Island Number Nine, which, for all we could see, was part of the Kentucky shore. Two towboats were coming up below the crossing. We expected to drift down along the right side, giving the boats a wide berth, but the Mississippi had another lesson for us. Reaching the crossing, marked by a navigation light on each shore, to our surprise we were carried over toward the boats, following the course marked on the chart as if we had steered it. A little rowing held us out of the way of the tows, but after that, the line marking the channel had more meaning for us.

The river rounded another bend at Island Number Ten, which had been a fortified place in the Civil War. This island lies at the beginning of the famous New Madrid Bend. There the neck of land is less than a mile wide, but the river flows nineteen miles around the bend, in almost a circle.

For several miles we drifted northeast, back toward home. It was here a small towboat with an oil barge overhauled us. It blew a passing signal, a mark of attention we seldom received. Of course we answered with our foghorn. When the boat passed, the pilot blew a long and a short, the crew came out and waved. It was the *Bullfrog,* which had often passed our landing on the Cumberland.

When the river began to swing northwest we made a crossing, taking advantage of a set in the current that way. This put us in position to land at Morrison Towhead which on the chart appeared to be a good harbor. We worked into the narrow chute there and to our satisfaction found it was well protected. This was the third day of fair, calm weather, and in December one could expect no more.

Three days of drifting are about all we want in one stretch, anyway. Then we begin to think how pleasant it would be to moor the boat in some quiet water and forget about current and winds for a spell. Like the dogs I get restless for a good run on shore. Anna and I both had chores to catch up with, and we would enjoy some extra reading and music. Drifting, especially in the swift current and around the sharp bends of the Mississippi, is strenuous work. Added to this is the alertness inspired by a new country. We have wondered about the old picture of the drifting flatboat, a scene of jollity and leisure. Perhaps the passengers can spend their time in music and dancing, but, from our experience, the crew has little time or energy left for such frolicking.

Accordingly we welcomed the following blustery and threatening day. The shore at this point was heavily wooded. The banks of the Mississippi generally form an almost continuous forest. Sometimes, on the outside of a bend, the levee is close to the river, where it rises like a smooth grassy hill. A cabin, like as not deserted, shows occasionally in an old clearing, but often for many miles there is no break in the trees. Few towns are close enough to the river for even their water tanks and church spires to be seen. If there were no revetments, which are paved shores to prevent erosion, and no navigation lights, one would think he was drifting down a wilderness river. It stirred us deeply to come down from the hills and find that the river became more primeval on its way to the sea. The reverse might be expected.

In the woods at Morrison Towhead was a little cabin which suggested the dwelling of a pioneer, even though it was covered with tar paper. The man who lived there, a fisherman, came to inspect us

237

when I was tying up the boat. After some talk I invited him to visit us. That very evening he and his wife came down the dark shore to our boat. At such meetings there is much to say provided the local people are at all talkative. We are ever curious about new places and people and while poor conversationalists we like to tell about where we came from and what we saw along the way. Not all strangers are interested, however, being so concerned with themselves and where they live that their minds seem closed to new impressions and ideas.

When we returned the Haycrafts' visit next day, they showed us their newly built house with pride. It was a small cabin, neatly made and neatly kept. The feature that interested us most was the foundation of logs. It was really built on a log raft, huge cypress logs, worn and weathered, pulled out of the driftwood. When the river rose and covered the shore, their house would float up into the branches of the trees. The chicken house had logs under it, smaller ones, and the doorstep was a block of wood. A wide swath had been cut in the forest through which they could move their floating house back into smooth water where the levee was accessible.

While we were there, some friends came to call on the Haycrafts. They had lived on a houseboat until its destruction in a runout of St. John's Bayou at New Madrid. This and other disasters they related to us in detail, trying evidently to dissuade us from our venture, which they considered a foolhardy one. After they were gone, Mrs. Haycraft made light of her friends' croaking. She herself was much in sympathy with our voyage, saying she would like to go, and would not be afraid "even in a paddleboat." While we were not alarmed by the reported dangers ahead of us, we could not disregard them entirely, and Chalk Bluff was superseded by the whirls and eddies of Fort Pillow and Richardson.

On the following morning we dropped down the long chute behind the towhead, a winding passage like a narrow, sandy river. It took us almost to New Madrid. Leaving the boat anchored offshore there we landed and climbed over the levee. It is always a mild shock to look down from the levee into the squared-off town, to see the inhabitants going about their business unmindful of the river, a wilderness within a stone's throw. We had a walk through the streets of the well-built, busy place, which the natives call New Mad'rid. We mailed some letters, bought a few articles, and returned to the levee. On the outside of it were the fish buyer's establishment and some shacks which could find no place within the levee's protection. We looked out over the crescent of the river, the sandbar opposite, and the wooded islands downstream, eager to shove out into the current again, our eagerness tempered by a vague inward sense of dread, like a boy ready to start down a fast and hazardous track on his sled.

We did not get far that day, however. The gauge reader, who passed in his boat when we were about to raise anchor, told us that strong southerly winds were predicted, and advised us to get in somewhere, pointing out St. John's Bayou near town. His advice seemed good, but the bayou, along the backyards of New Madrid, did not appeal to us; so we drifted and rowed to the islands which began below town and extended around the bend for three miles. No name was given them on the chart where they were indicated only as sandbars. However, we found them well above water and covered with tall willows. They would afford good protection from a south wind, and we liked it out there in the open. Across the inside channel was a big sawmill whose smoke was our weathervane. A short walk across the island brought us to the swift edge of the main river and a long view downstream. The wind came in, that night, moaning through the tall willows with a foreboding sound. Rain followed, then a shift to the west, and clearing weather. We were glad to be in protected water, for it was rough on the outside of the island.

It was not too rough a day for a sailboat which came down the inside channel. It was evidently on a long voyage; the mast had been lowered, the boat was running under power. A woman steered while the man made soundings. He must have decided it was not deep enough, for they turned and went back around the island and down the outside. We had seen the same boat come into port at Cairo, and later we saw it again at Memphis. At least two other sailboats passed us later on, making their way under power to the Gulf.

On stormy days we studied the maps of the next section of river. Its direction was noted, the kind of bends it took, the location of possible hazards like revetments and piling. We tried to pick out places

239

which would be safe harbors. This was a fine game to play, with a large element of chance in it. Although we learned considerable in our passage down the river of its nature and most likely course under given conditions, we could never be quite sure, by looking at a map, what a certain bend or island would be like when we reached it. This uncertainty gave a zest to our drifting, and to our map reading as well, which would be lacking if the river ahead were always a known quantity.

Our maps and charts were publications of the U. S. Engineer Department. Those of the Ohio, while they gave all the required information about the river, did not go beyond the river's edge except to locate the towns. Each one of the Mississippi River maps covered nearly two hundred square miles, through which meandered a section of the river varying in length from ten to thirty-five miles, depending on how crooked it was. Much information of the terrain away from the river was given—elevations, old river courses, lakes, creeks, roads, railroads, schools, churches, plantations, and, of course, the levees. We liked to pore over these details, seeing it all in our imaginations, even if none of the flat country behind the levees was visible from the river. These maps were necessarily large, and bound in a book, so that they were not as convenient for posting on the board in our "chart room" as were the loose-leaf Ohio River charts. Anna, who was chief navigator, managed it by cutting out a sheet or two at a time, matching them up carefully, and tucking in the edges.

The Mississippi River maps made no attempt to keep up with the frequent and sudden changes of channel, crossings, lights, and buoys. Navigators obtain the latest reports on conditions of this nature from bulletins issued by the Engineers which contain information gathered by their boats on frequent trips over the section of the river assigned to them. We had already met the steamer *Jupiter,* a fine boat, an old, single-deck stern-wheeler, which ran in the Memphis District. These bulletins were available at convenient locations along the river—in this section, according to the Engineers, "at the Boat Store and Barrett Line, in Cairo; mailbox on bank foot of Ward Av., Caruthersville, Mo.; Warner and Tamble wharfboat, Easyway Grocery Store No. 12, Paul Martin's Boat Delivery Service, and C and B Grocery, Memphis, Tenn.;

Helena Terminal and Warehouse, and Project Five oil docks, Helena, Ark.; and mailbox on bank at Terrene Ldg., Miss." These bulletins were good reading, and some of the facts were valuable to us. They kept us posted as to the location of lights. Often at the distance from which we saw them the only light we could distinguish was the one with a daymark nearby. The bulletin told us which light this was, and thus we always knew our position. When we read, "Eddy makes well out into river below Reelfoot Light," we tried to pass Reelfoot Light on the other side of the river, or if the bulletin said, "There are several snags between Tamm and Nebraska Point Lights 150 yards out from shore," we at least knew they were there, and navigated accordingly.

Another source of useful information was the bulletin boards, at intervals along the river, which give river stages. At New Madrid, for instance, the board read 21¾ R(ising). This meant a good stage for drifters, about halfway between extreme low water and bankfull. We had already met the gauge reader at New Madrid in person. He changed the figures on the large black board according to his daily reading, and pilots ran whatever course such a stage called for. It is impressive to observe the sailing line of boats, to see how it changes with the rise and fall of the river, each pilot following in the path of preceding boats as if it were marked. At some points, however, there is a difference of opinion, and one boat tries for easier water on one side, the next one follows the other shore; or they will make crossings at different points. The fact that the pilots know where and when there can be a deviation from a strict course makes their knowledge and skill even more to be admired.

The river stages were significant to us, in our own way, helping us to decide whether the chutes and shallow places were navigable for our craft. A chance could be taken on a rising river, which would float us eventually, even if we ran aground.

All this might be called finicky, to be sure, and one could drift safely down the river by rule of thumb. But we liked the maps and calculations, we liked to know just where we were, what we were passing, and to some extent, what was ahead. This knowledge, without doubt, made our navigating safer and less dependent on luck.

241

After two days in the lee of the New Madrid Islands our voyage was continued—a day too soon, as it turned out, for on the open river a stiff upstream wind was blowing. There was no turning back, by the inexorable law that governs drifters; nor was there any protection along shore. We set our mud sail and were carried along by the river into the wind and waves. I had been experimenting with some rigging which would carry the heavy gangplanks partly in the water. The waves broke this up, and I lashed the planks, one on each side, under the guards, where they have been carried ever since, weight or no. The johnboat while drifting had always been a problem, too. The wind and waves affect it differently than the heavy, deep hull of the larger boat, and it was always bumping, or getting crossways, or hooked under a corner. The best arrangement, after trying others, was to tie the johnboat alongside the houseboat by each end, with fenders made of pieces of tire along the guard between the two boats. Though tied fore and aft, the johnboat was ready for instant service. When I stepped into it, casting off the painter, the stern line remained tied to the afterdeck of the houseboat, and I was all set for towing.

When we saw that all was going well, the breaking waves and the roll of the boat were fun. There was enough creaking of gear and flapping of canvas for us to imagine that this was sailing; and so it was, with the sail under water. The boat must be kept headed into the wind by a pull on one of the sweeps now and then. This made it necessary for us to eat dinner by turns.

It was a bright day, and as we looked back on the sunlit ranks of trees and gleaming sandbars, the splendor of the winter river was revealed to us. The willows were reddish tawny, the young shoots, in a lower band, a brighter red. Above, the gray of the cottonwoods feathered into the blue sky. These horizontal bands of color extended for miles, broken only by the purple shadow in a slough, or by a white tree trunk.

This was our last view of Kentucky, which had been on our left hand ever since leaving Brent, nearly six hundred miles. Of this, seventy-seven were on the Mississippi, and in all, we had dropped a hundred seventy-two feet nearer sea level. With Tennessee on one side,

Missouri on the other, it seemed a strange, far-off land. Yet the river went on its way unchanged.

Then the river curved, narrow and swift on the bend, spreading out below to a mile and a quarter in width. The wind, offshore now, carried us into this slackwater bay, and it was a hard pull back into the current again. Soon we were slipping past a low shore where the trees stood in water. A bank appeared, and we made a landing. The low ground just passed, we judged, was the foot of Island Eleven, and in the narrow chute we found an indifferent harbor, the bank on one side, no land at all on the other, only a screen of trees between us and the open river.

Nearby was a houseboat beached out on top of an old levee among the cotton fields. A truck load of cotton went by, the Negro pickers riding soft on top, joking and laughing. We visited at the houseboat in the evening while the family who lived there were eating their supper of fried potatoes and eggs. The young man was a fisherman in summer. The old father had come from central Kentucky, in which state, he said, this rich riverbottom soil would be used as "fertilize." He had nothing but discouragement for us, telling of boats wrecked on his shore, and saying over and over, "The Mississippi is a fools' graveyard."

The morning was overcast, and it looked like the stormy prediction which the old man had made last night would come true. We pulled out in the cloudy sunrise, entered a narrow pass between Williams Point and Marr Towhead. Three heavy boats passed us, two on one side and one on the other, this last running very close. Since it was going up the river its waves were high and prolonged. I took my place in the johnboat to keep the houseboat from turning sideways in the trough of the swells. These were so great that our two boats seemed to stand on end as they rose and fell, one up while the other was down. It was all I could do to prevent a crash. On future occasions I used a longer towline.

Quiet drifting followed. There was no wind, and the sun came out bright after the cloudy indecision of the early morning. The Tipton-ville ferry was operating, but the town, in Tennessee, was out of sight. Three and a half miles behind Tiptonville is a shore of Reelfoot Lake,

243

that strange body of water formed during the convulsions of the great earthquake of 1811 which centered in this area.

Next the river rounded Merriweather Bend to the right, and Little Cypress Bend to the left, flowing so calmly that we could eat dinner without interruption. At the head of Island Number Fourteen was a perfect harbor for us, of easy entrance, but we passed it up, since it was early afternoon. Moreover, the quiet weather afforded a good chance to run the bend of Island Number Fourteen, which was a bad one. The bend was sharp, with a revetment on the outside, and immediately below that, Reelfoot Point, where a dangerous eddy was to be expected. Nevertheless we rounded the bend easily and cleared the point. Then, at the beginning of a ten-mile reach to westward, a sudden wind sprang up from the north. We had to abandon an attempt to reach shelter at the lower end of the island, which was to windward. Even with all hands rowing their best, we were carried gradually toward the left shore, a mean-looking caving bank. We could not have drifted another hundred yards before grounding, when a small cove opened before us. We ran into it, and found deep water, the shores sandy and firm. It was open to the north wind which was by then blowing hard, but this crossriver wind we did not mind. East or west winds were the ones to be feared midway of that long reach, and the cove would protect us from them.

The north wind was the beginning of a spell of cold weather. The bright sun moderated the air by day, but the nights were so cold that the sweet potatoes, pumpkins, and carrots had to be removed from the roof to a warmer place. Wintertime fires were kept burning, the drift-piles supplying an abundance of fuel. It was good to be out in the sharp air, cutting wood and exploring. These might have been the shores of a desert island. There was not even a levee. Yet we found an abandoned house or two, a soybean field to glean.

Coves like this, formed by a circling eddy, are frequent along the Mississippi. In some of them the whirling waters are dangerous. Here the anchor had been set out in the middle of the cove and we were puzzled by its shifting about. We knew the current could not move the heavy anchor, but we did not know that in such places the sandy bottom itself is in motion. The swirling current cuts it away and piles

244

it up, and it was this action that shifted the anchor. Lucky for us it was not buried in the sand and lost.

The anchor was raised and we left the cove after a layover of three nights. The north wind had lessened each day, and we hoped for a calm spell before a wind sprang up from the south. Drifting around Little Prairie Bend we entered another reach of ten miles, to the southeast past Caruthersville, Missouri. The waterfront there was a busy place, and signs of industry rose above the levee. A ferry was crossing over to Tennessee, and in a towhead below town were several shantyboats.

We drifted past all this close to shore, making good time, and soon closed it behind the bend. Ahead lay an even longer reach, this time to west of south. The low shores diminished from one headland to another until they faded into the sky and there was no horizon. Sky and water were one substance; we floated in an aqueous blue vapor. The river might be entering the sea, all maps to the contrary. The awe we felt at this sight was intensified by an uneasiness caused by a rising south wind.

Drifting far from shore we had no sense of motion; yet the speck in the distance loomed into the Cottonwood Point ferry. This was the last outpost in Missouri and, they say, nearly beyond the reach of the law. Then the right bank became Arkansas.

Ahead was Island Twenty-one, standing boldly out in midstream, in contrast to most of the others, which lay close to shore. Though the main channel was to the right, the left one was nearly as wide. We considered going down this more protected way, but the entrance, around a dike, appeared too difficult for us. We took the main channel, were overhauled by the big steamer, *Missouri,* and tried for a landing on a stretch of sandy beach along the island shore. Here I made some blunders and awkward moves which might have ended in disaster. Seeing that we were not going to make the beach, but were drifting past, I dropped the anchor, intending then to run a line to shore, and by it haul the boat in. But I misjudged the distance from shore, and also the current, which was suddenly very swift. The boat seemed to be anchored in a millrace. We must get away, but it was out of the question to raise the anchor by hauling in the line, which was rigid as an iron rod. The anchor might possibly be raised from the johnboat; so I got into it and loosed the anchor line. This line, due to my haste and awkwardness, became fouled around the kevel, and the boat was hauled up short again, with me in the johnboat twenty or thirty feet away, hanging onto the anchor line. Here more bungling, for I was in such a position that I could not let go and return to the deck, being in a tangle of my own in the johnboat. I yelled to Anna, "Cut the line! Get the hatchet!" She could not find it, came out with the handsaw. The line was so taut that she was able to cut it even with this tool, and she and the houseboat shot off into the twilight. I was able to pull the johnboat against the current, and to my relief heave up the anchor. Soon I was back with Anna, and we made a landing farther down on the island.

One more alarm before the day was ended. The shore at that point was screened by a hedge of willow shoots growing thick as grass. I was trying to tie up the boat at an opening which had once been cut through by a surveying party, when Sambo, already on shore, began to scream loud and piteously. I leaped through the brush, filling my boots with water, and in the woods found the dog with his foot caught in a steel trap. He yowled until released, but his big paw was uninjured.

That night we heard the wind in the tall trees, a portentous sound, and the slapping of waves, felt the thrust of the boat. The south wind blew for two days while we lay on the open shore against the springing willows. Yet the waves were not high. This wind at Payne Hollow would roll up breaking swells, larger than any we ever saw on the Mississippi. The swerving current of this river, crossing back and forth, its irregular shoreline, break up the waves, while on the Ohio, whose bottom and shores are more even, the current steady, the waves roll on unhindered, piling up into cresting swells. This is our observation, at least; maybe we have just been lucky so far.

Anyway, we paid little mind to the rough water, sometimes deserting the boat to ramble over the sandy island, half expecting it to be rolling underfoot, too. No fields or houses were discovered. To our surprise we found a little cedar tree growing among the soft maples, willows, and cottonwoods. It may have fallen into the water from some bluff, or perhaps it had come down from the hills in a runout and had floated with the driftwood until cast away on this shore where it took root. We appropriated it for a Christmas tree and carried it on the roof, roots in earth, until the time came.

On the day we had drifted to Island Twenty-one we had been in hopes of making the Obion River, five and a half miles farther. It was then too much, in the failing light, with thirty-one miles of river already behind us. We had to wait until the second afternoon before the wind allowed us to make that five miles to the Obion River. The short run was not easy. We never like to start late in the day, and to make a definite objective is sometimes difficult. You never know what kind of water or shore will be found there, and the current may carry you past. In this case, one difficulty was to find the Obion River. It could not be located by the navigation lights, one or two of these having been moved since our bulletin was issued. The shore ahead appeared to be an unbroken willow forest. We coasted along, wondering if every notch in the bank could be the small stream we were looking for. All the way our attention was divided between this search and the view upstream. The sun through broken clouds made the island we were leaving glow with color in that quarter of the landscape, otherwise darkened by the retreating storm clouds. The red and orange and gray trees rose from the water in distinct level bands, and the long triangular point of the island reaching toward us was given form by the deep blue shadow on one side.

A motorboat approached from that direction, and when near we made it out to be a lamplighter's boat. He asked if we were going to the Obion River. When we nodded yes, he offered to tow us in.

Shortly we were moored in the narrow stream, closed in by an overhanging wall of trees on each side. After the openness of the cove and the island, we felt hemmed in, and missed the sweep of river and sky. However, as the weather turned bad, and dark days of fog, rain, and wind followed, it was good to be in a sheltered place.

One bank of the Obion River was rather high. On that side were cotton fields, houses scattered about, and a small local schoolhouse. A road led back to a town in the interior, but there were no levees. Cotton picking was still going on, and we were offered work. We thought that

the lamplighter, who was a cotton planter as well, might have towed us in as prospective pickers. This job we declined: cotton picking did not appeal to us and we were already busy with projects of our own. One was the annual Christmas woodblock. Its beginning went back to a sketch of the Ohio made at Cache River. The block was whittled out at odd moments on the way down, and now we made some prints. These we prepared for mailing, since a mail route came in to the river there.

The lamplighter at Obion River was the first one with whom we became acquainted, though we had seen some lamplighters' boats out on duty. The Mississippi River navigation lights, maintained by the Coast Guard, are nearly all oil-burning, such a light being the easiest to move and thus more practical on a river of shifting channel and caving banks. The lights are serviced every third day by the lamplighter, in the employ of the Coast Guard, who fills the lamp and trims the wick. If the bank is caving, he moves the heavy light standard to a safer place, or, in high water, to its regular high-water location. In an emergency he hangs the lantern on a tree, for the light must be kept burning. He must go out in all states of weather and water, climb the treacherous banks, and do much ax work. It is a tough job, and a serviceable boat is required. Most of these are homemade affairs with a closed cabin and a dependable motor. The length of each lamplighter's run varies, and the number of lights in his charge. The Obion River lamplighter had eighteen lights, some upstream and some down. It is a part-time job with most light tenders, and some are fishermen, drifters for floating timber, farmers, or cattle raisers.

Another acquaintance we made at Obion River was Ted Leman.

He was not a riverman by heredity or circumstance, but had some-how, in his youth, been possessed with the ambition of living on the river. He had come from the west after a career so exciting and adventurous, according to his own account of it, that one would think that a river life would be too tame and monotonous for him. His little boat, a jerry-built affair, so low that even he could not stand upright in it, he had constructed himself on the upper Missouri. He began his voyage with a big outboard motor, found it unsatisfactory, and traded it for a skiff with an old-time, slow-speed inboard marine engine, a beautiful and practical boat. He had tried fishing at Cottonwood Point, and had done a spell on the river towboats, where he had gathered more adventures to tell us about. The past summer he had fished, with no great success, laying with his boat in an eddy below a revetment on the Arkansas side. It became a bad place in the autumn storms and current, and he moved into the Obion River. When we were there he was cutting cordwood to sell in town, thinking this work more profitable, at least more independent, than cotton picking. We have often wondered what became of Ted Leman. We enjoyed his society for those few days, and admired his coming to the river by choice from a background so different.

The rains had set the Obion River a-flowing, so that when we were ready to leave, it was just a matter of casting off and drifting out into the Mississippi. It was like putting forth to sea, after four days in the straitened and closed-in Obion. We were given a rough welcome by waves from the U. S. Steamer *Arkansas II,* whose downstream approach we could not see until out on the river. Then a light wind sprang up from the northeast, and I had to row to clear Nebraska Point on the Tennessee side. Meanwhile, Anna had prepared breakfast which we ate in peace while rounding Barfield Bend. The Arkansas shore was now on our lee, the long sandbars of Island Number Twenty-five. Across was the mouth of the Middle Forked Deer River, which the lamplighter had called "Fork-a-deer." It flowed through a wild country of forest and water, an intricate maze of lakes and pockets, old river beds, swamps, and connecting water courses, a region abandoned to the floods, yet threaded by a few roads marked on our map by dotted lines. No doubt there were deer in there.

Although our stay between the close shores of Obion River had lasted but a few days, we were thrilled anew by the expanse of swift water that was the Mississippi. Drifting was becoming a passion. Though there was nothing new, nothing changed, we looked around each succeeding bend with undiminished interest. No prospect was quite like any we had seen before; no landing was like another, each afforded new problems in handling the boat; and when on shore, we climbed the bank or threaded the woods with keen expectation—of what, we could not say, but our zest for new shores and reaches of river was sharp as ever. The details of drifting and landing, of each shore we explored, of towns, boats, people, even of the weather, remain vivid in our minds.

On this particular day we made a landing on the point of Island Number Twenty-six, and ate dinner while moored there. I cut firewood from the drift and snags scattered about over the waste of sandbar. One could see the effects of what might have been a powerful wind continuous from one direction, but it was the action of that more solid wind, the river's current. This was the river bottom in flood, when the swift water polished the skeletons of trees and shaped the sandy surface to fit its flowing.

Leaving the island, we clawed off the bar, watching for submerged snags which were revealed by ripples on the surface even when at a considerable depth below it. The shore gradually turned more eastward until it lay with the wind, and then it was easy sailing. As it happened, a straight reach of fourteen miles lay ahead. The boat was driven fast by wind and current, past Lower Forked Deer River and Ashport, Tennessee, one of the few towns which lay close to the river. We sailed by close in, waving to the ferryman. Below, a big diesel passed us, bound up for Pittsburgh. It was the *Reliance,* carrying an old name, and one of the most handsome of the newer boats, we thought.

All this time there was nothing to do but watch the river and scenery, but our easy course was interrupted by a hard pull to clear some piling below Gold Dust, which we came upon suddenly and almost crashed into. Piling is a fence of timbers driven into the river bottom to prevent erosion, and extends far out from shore. It is frequent along the Mississippi, and is one of the drifter's worst hazards.

Near the middle of the river now, we crossed over to the Arkansas shore, after waiting for a large downbound tow to pass. It was time to tie up for the night, but there was no harbor in sight. We determined to run for shelter behind Island Number Thirty, even though it lay so far ahead that darkness might fall before we reached it. It was a big island extending for five miles along the river. On the narrow back channel was the city of Osceola, Arkansas. This channel extended even farther up the river, a network of passages around towheads and islands, past Luxora, Arkansas, an old haven for shantyboaters, almost as far up as Ashport. We had been tempted to enter this channel at its upper end, but were afraid to try it because of a series of dikes along the shore, and not knowing whether the channel was open at this stage of water. The middle entrance, however, showed plainly enough on our map. All we had to do was follow the right bank past two lights and into the chute before reaching the third light, which was on Island Number Thirty. It might have been as simple as that in daylight, but darkness overtook us and we were lost. The lights were not where they should be; there was slack water along the uneven shore. Yet we must not get out into the current lest we be carried on down the river. The searchlight of a towboat far downstream helped some. I went ashore and towed the boat with a line. The bank trended to the right, which was what we wanted. Suddenly the boat was carried forward by the swift water. I moored it to a snag, walked ahead on the sand to see what we were coming to. A light appeared in the darkness, and I hailed it. A man answered from across the water. He said that this was the entrance to the Osceola chute, and that it was open all the way through. I went back to the boat, found Anna alarmed at the shouting in the darkness. We drifted in, rowing over to the light of the man's lantern. He helped us tie up behind his gas boat, saying, "You'd never catch me out on that river after dark with no power."

The man lived on the island, but his business there we could not determine. The owner of the island visited us next morning, a hale old man who had been a log rafter in his young days. He told of the heavy sweeps they had used on rafts, compared with which ours were in miniature. I asked him if he had ever had any trouble in controlling

251

the raft. He laughed, and said, "Yes, but I always made my landing."
This became a byword with us.

Next morning we followed the swift and narrow channel farther
in, winding around the head of the island, past the Luxora chute
which turned off to the right. We landed at the first fleet of boats—a
houseboat, lamplighter's boat, the usual collection of motorboats,
johnboats, and fish boxes. In the afternoon we set out on foot for
Osceola. It was a long walk to the main part of town, along a straight
concrete highway through the cotton fields, fringed with miserable,
patched-up houses standing in the mud, where lived both white and
black families. It was dark, sodden weather. The depressing picture was
completed by the cheap tinsel of Christmas in the crowded business
streets. We mailed the last batch of Christmas cards, bought a little
fresh food, and trudged back to the boat.

On the following morning, cloudy and uncertain, we got under way,
but thought better of it and tied up while still in protected water, to
see what the rising wind would do. We remained at anchor all day,
off the lower end of Osceola, which was a section of comfortable and
well-kept homes. Several small boats were out this Sunday afternoon,
duck hunters, mostly. We spoke with one of them, and to our surprise,
he knew where Brent was, the first and only person who did. He knew
the place very well, having operated the ferry there when the owner of
it was in the Navy. We remembered having heard of his rebuilding a
boat on the Brent shore and setting off down the river. This was not
long before we began the construction of our boat.

The weather cleared during the night and we got away before sunrise. Breakfast while drifting down the remainder of the chute, which
we had come to regard as the river itself, forgetting the broad stream
which flowed outside of the island. Soon we were out on the main
river. In the distance lay the line of blue hills which is called Chickasaw Bluff Number One, or Fort Pillow of the Civil War. It is part of
the high land which extends from Kentucky south into Louisiana,
forming a high wall at many points on the eastern side of the river. It
was thrilling to see a hill rising above the water, after the miles of low
shore. Here, as in most places where the river approaches the bluff, it
is turned aside in a sharp angle, and a wide whirlpool is set in motion.

We had been warned of this bluff particularly. Nevertheless, I let the boat get too far out in the river when rounding the sharp point, and without knowing just how it happened, we saw ourselves going back upstream close to the bluff, to which the eddy had carried us, though we had been rowing away from it all the time. The circling water was not swift, but we were unable to pull out of it, though almost reaching the sharp line beyond which was the main current of the river. Always we were sucked back to the bluff, and up past the Fort Pillow Light, which we saw many times that morning.

A light, upstream wind made our task more difficult. I was ready to give it up and lay over in Cold Creek under the bluff until the wind was favorable. Anna suggested one more try, at a different angle. All this time we saw a small towboat with a barge of gravel at the lower end of the eddy. He was making no headway; so we supposed that the current was too much for him. Now, however, when we were pulling our best hoping to break through, this boat came up the eddy to where we were and offered to tow us out. I carried a line over in the johnboat, and this small, nameless craft shoved the barge of gravel and pulled us along out of the eddy. Before they had turned us loose, almost over to the Arkansas shore, I went aboard and thanked the two men of the crew, but their friendly talk was unintelligible as a foreign language, because one man had an impediment of speech, the other no teeth, and the engine made too much noise. I did make out, however, that they were not being held up by the whirlpool, but were standing by to help us if we failed to make it. We had no further trouble with that whirl, and looked back with satisfaction at the last of Fort Pillow Light.

After a breathing spell along an easy shore, the current picked up on the bend, and I had to man the sweeps to keep away from the caving banks. When dinner was ready—a fine dinner, too, of baked beans, baked sweet potatoes, and turnip greens—one of us ate alone while the other rowed. The wind increased around the bend and a mild sandstorm was raised in the air above the bar at the head of Island Number Thirty-four. This island is seven miles long and shaped like a crooked sweet potato. At the end of it the river meets another bluff, Chickasaw Number Two, and turns right, to the west. The bend is not so sharp as at Fort Pillow, but it was said to be a dangerous place—a large whirl circling under the bluff, where the river widens out to more than a mile. We kept on into the wind, passed the broad mouth of Hatchie River on the Tennesee side, always pulling the other way, toward the island. We hoped not to repeat our experience at the first bluff, but for a while it looked like it would be two in one day. Rowing as hard as we could, the boat was carried slowly to the left bank as we drifted through the choppy water. Off toward the bluff we could see driftwood behaving in a strange manner, seeming to move back and forth. Then we saw it was circling round and round in the whirlpool. We were not carried into it, however: as we rounded the last long sandbar of Island Number Thirty-four, the boat moved in the direction we wanted it to go, and we neared the safe shore. A landing was made on the mainland, a bank on which tall trees were growing. Across the narrow lagoon was the flat, reedy shore of the island.

The evening after a day of drifting is a busy time. Now Anna can take her mind from navigating and watching the passing shores, and attend to household chores, mopping the floor, preparing supper. I tie up the boat securely, get a gangplank out to shore if possible, pick up loose ends. The dogs are ashore at the earliest moment, usually standing poised in the bow of the johnboat when I run a mooring line to a tree on the bank. They leap ashore, dash off to explore the new territory, often routing out a 'possum from his peaceful den in a hollow log, or chasing rabbits. This particular evening Sambo again stepped into an open trap and remained there, howling, until I could get to him. On a new shore, I always reconnoiter to get some idea of the lay of the land. I cut firewood if the daylight allows it. Then we have a bath by lamplight and supper before the fire.

Our thoughts this evening were on the next day's run, which, if conditions were favorable, would take us close to Memphis. We desired to stop somewhere near the city to lay over for Christmas, and for mail, which had not been sent to us since Cairo. After carefully studying the charts, we picked out the Loosahatchie River, a small stream which came in on the Tennessee side, as a desirable and convenient harbor. It lay above the city—a point in its favor, since the water would be cleaner than below—and it was only five miles from downtown Memphis. When we saw that it was thirty-five miles from our present location we doubted if we could make it in a day. Then we noticed that the mileage included Centennial Bend, so named because a natural cut-off had occurred there in 1876. Now the channel was even shorter because of a more recent cut to the left of Brandywine Island. This shortened the distance to Memphis by six miles, leaving twenty-nine, a possible day's journey.

Before our departure next morning we took time to gather some of the mistletoe which grew above the boat in great clusters of green. To reach it I climbed a tall maple at the water's edge, and while carefully lowering the mistletoe to Anna by means of a line, I could look over the long island and curving river. We saw mistletoe in sycamores and other trees than the conventional oak; the thickest in elms perhaps, which trees often resembled evergreens because of the thick growth of mistletoe.

When under way we kept close to the right bank, for the treacherous water along the bluff was just opposite. We overdid this a little and were almost carried around Island Number Thirty-five on the wrong side, a distance much longer than the main river in a narrow and tortuous back channel. It was nip and tuck for a while, in shallow water among the snags, but soon we were drifting free down the main channel in a fine stretch of river.

As we neared Brandywine Island we wondered if it had received its name from the steamboat *Brandywine,* which was destroyed by fire a short distance above Memphis in 1832, with great loss of life. The country at the end of the huge island was like a desert. Brandywine Chute lay not far ahead. We had been warned of this swift and narrow reach, a bad place in which to meet a large tow. One shantyboater who often traversed the river from Cairo to Memphis said he always shut off the motor of his towing launch when at the end of Brandywine Chute so that he could hear if there were any towboats in it; if so, he tied up and waited. We listened, too, but heard nothing, and could not have tied up in time to do any good if we had heard a boat coming up. As usually happens, a fact which Audubon commented on, these places with an evil reputation or an awesome name—the Devil's Racecourse was the one he was referring to—are not nearly as bad in the encounter as in anticipation.

We ate dinner together as we drifted swiftly along, spinning around in the boils and whirls. There were even some quiet places along the shore which would have been good harbors. The country was wild and desolate as it usually is when there are no levees. None were needed on the Tennessee side because the bluff still followed the river at a few miles distance. The Arkansas shore was a confusion of towheads and islands and old, closed-off river courses, far back from the present channel. Island Number Thirty-seven is now four miles inland. On the map one could follow the changing course of the stream, at least through the nineteenth century, the successive meander lines and old river beds being marked. Happy Valley and Devil's Elbow were intriguing even to read about.

The weather became a dead calm now, and under the heavy sky a winter mist began to form on the water. The veiled shores became formless, all sense of motion was lost. It might have been a painted ship upon a painted ocean, the picture a harmony of blue, gray and silver. By the time the main river was reached visibility was so bad that it was unsafe for us to be out in midstream. Nevertheless we kept on because the Loosahatchie River was but seven and a half miles farther. The Mississippi at that point is divided by a wide island, or series of islands, called Redman Point Bar. A few years ago the channel was to the left of the islands and passed close to the mouth of the Loosahatchie; now it followed the right bank. Before reaching the islands, the current around a wide sandbar on the left carried us into mid-river. Now we could see through the mist the old daymark at the mouth of the river we were aiming at. We began to row toward it, got into dead water. It was a strange situation, motionless in mid-river. We pulled back into the current, drifted farther down, then made another try for the shore. There was now some current flowing in our direction, and by drifting and rowing we made land just above the Loosahatchie. I ran a line to a tree, the boat swung into the quiet water of the little river. We were glad to be there, glad to be off the foggy Mississippi where the early darkness was beginning to fall. At first we landed on the open left shore where stood a queerly built, deserted house. Some goats appeared, and we hastily embarked to avoid a battle between them and our dogs. The other shore was just as good, after cutting some brush, and we were soon at home there.

The Loosahatchie River is two hundred and thirty miles below Cairo, and we were twenty-three days on the way. This distance is half that from Brent to the Cumberland, a voyage which had taken us two winters. Drifting on the Mississippi was fast traveling for us.

Now for a spell we put aside the maps and turned our attention to the shore on which we had landed, to Christmas, and to communicating with our family and friends. There was one houseboat already in the harbor, a little farther up than ours, a permanent resident there. He kept cattle on the islands, and ferried hunters over. At first it seemed a poor combination, but since the hunters could not get back except in his boat, it would not pay them to shoot a steer if game were scarce. He kept goats over there, too, and sometimes had a customer for one, bringing back man and beast in his motorboat. One day it was a cow, and the boat was not a large one.

We soon became acquainted with this man's vivacious four-year-old daughter, Beverly. She liked to come over to see us, especially for lunch. She was quite mature and up with the times; ahead of us, in fact. Yet with childish simplicity she brought her pet goat one day, a wobbly little kid for whom she made a warm bed before our fire. Beverly examined everything in our cabin and asked many questions.

"What is that?"

"A fish horn," said Anna, referring to my foghorn.

Beverly thought a moment before replying, "I wouldn't know how to call a fish."

The only other inhabitant here was an old man who lived in a tent on stilts, a type of dwelling new to us.

A dirt road led from this tiny settlement back through low, brushy land, then climbed the bluff. The first thing we came to on top was an immense new manufacturing plant in which, so we were told, mechanical cotton pickers were made. Beyond was a suburban area, then a through highway on which was a shopping center, and a bus to Memphis. This was all we required. We considered ourselves lucky

to have it within two miles of the river, and still be on a clean, unspoiled shore.

Christmas came soon after our arrival there. The little cedar was
brought down from the roof, trimmed with hand-dipped candles, red
berries from the woods, and strings of popcorn. Mistletoe was hung
outside, and the tree was kept on deck in daytime. On Christmas morning we walked over to the highway and tried, unsuccessfully, to telephone Anna's mother. It was a cold trip in the rising northwest gale,
and we were glad to get back to the riverbank, where it is never so cold
as inland, to warm fires and our Christmas dinner.

In the fair weather following we had a washing of clothes, infre-
quent in winter drifting, and worthy of mention—the previous one
was at Cache River a month ago.

On another day, we put on town clothes and made our way by bus
to Memphis for mail and a few items to be purchased in the large
stores. The post office is on the riverbank overlooking Wolf River, a
small stream which empties into the Mississippi there; so we need not
go out of our way to see the river.

On the last day of the year we moved our boat out of the Loosahatchie. The plan was to tie up for a few days at some point on the
lower side of Memphis, stopping at the post office again on the way
down. This short trip worried us a little—the hazardous drifting by
a large city was complicated by the stop en route. Nevertheless it was
made successfully. The current allowed an easy landing on the outside
of Mud Island, a fitting name for this waste land across a few rods of
water from the imposing buildings of the city. I moored the boat, one
line to a navigation light standard and another to a geodetic survey
marker, since no trees were handy, and set the anchor out in the river
in case there should be boat waves. Leaving Anna on board, I rowed
around the point of the island into Wolf River, landed at the boathouse
of the Memphis Yacht Club. It was a short walk up the bank, all lawn
and trees, so different from the river approach to most cities. Returning
from the post office, I filled the drinking water containers at the
Yacht Club, and rowed back to the boat. All was well there, but Anna
said that a small boat passing had warned her that this was a bad spot,
since towboats often landed barges there.

258

We were soon away, drifting past the city. We thought it made the finest appearance from the river of any we had seen. Farther down was the bridge, and a new one under construction near it. Watching all this, we came unawares on a small area of rough water, probably caused by the swift current over a shoal or sunken obstruction. I was in the johnboat ready for the approaching bridge pier. Seeing the waves, I tried to pull the boat to one side, but all I did was to turn it broadside before we went into them. The waves washed up to the windows as the boat rolled heavily, but we were soon out of them, drifting smoothly under the bridges.

Below, the river makes a long swing to the right around President's Island. There is a channel to the left, large as a good-sized river, called Tennessee Chute. The course of the main river around the island is eight miles, and the chute is about the same length. We chose to go down the chute as it offered a good place to tie up within reach of the city. At its entrance, along the mainland, was a huge Engineer fleet—quarterboats, dredges, and revetment equipment—tied up for the winter. We dashed by at a great rate, to the astonishment of those watching. The current slowed up farther in, and about two miles down, an opening in the bank suddenly appeared on the left. We were ready for it, and quickly pulled the boat in. It was Nonconnah Creek. Northwards were an oil dock, refinery, and an immense whirling crane used for loading scrap iron into barges; beyond lay the city. To the south were cornfields and woods. This was our place.

There was one houseboat in the creek, another beached out on the north shore. The one in the water was large, almost new, the cabin painted white and the hull red. Children were playing on the big porch, which had a railing. There was a floating dock alongside, to which the small boats and fish boxes were tied; on shore, chicken coops, net-tarring vat, and assorted plunder. We spoke to the man who lived there as he went by in his motorboat with a load of hunters bound for the island. Soon the little girls came over with an invitation from their mother to spend the evening with them. This we were glad to do. Their name was Story, Henry and Lou, both of them river people by birth, ancestry, and inclination. Originally from the Ohio River below Paducah, they knew Whistlin' Ike from the Cumberland; they had shelled together. The river between Memphis and Paducah was their home. Their boat was built at Paducah in the very boatyard which had been our mooring place there, on our way down. It was like a battleship compared with ours, twice as long, divided into three large rooms with high ceilings.

New Year's Day followed. We made a visit then to some cousins of mine living in south Memphis whom Anna had never met. It had been years since I had seen Elsie and Grace, and many changes had taken place. We recalled the old days, and the people we knew then and lived with. Anna played their unused piano and sang the old songs. The day was a vignette from the past inserted among our present days of constant change, of making new friends and at once leaving them behind, bound for shores we had never seen.

During the week we lay in Nonconnah Creek we visited back and forth with our new neighbors, the Storys. In one conversation Lou remarked that she was the mother of fourteen children, and Henry the father of sixteen. I think this included the present four, three girls and a little boy. Peggy, the oldest, went to school, a trip which she began each morning, in rain or fair weather, by paddling herself, standing up, across the creek in a heavy johnboat. This was the manner in which she came to visit us, too, tying the johnboat neatly to the deck and helping her younger sister, Irene, whom her parents called Dago because of her curious speech. The girls were entranced with our Christmas tree and came over at dusk one evening to see the lighted candles. This was its final illumination.

We went in to Memphis from this direction, to get the last of our delayed mail and a copy of the latest navigation bulletin at the Barge Line wharfboat. On this trip we saw the southern city we had expected Memphis to be. The north side and downtown district had suggested a northern or western city.

Early one morning we let go our moorings, blew the horn in farewell to the Storys, and drifted down the Tennessee Chute. The shores bore no mark of the city, at whose door the wilderness always begins if you go in the right direction. Entering the main river, we felt anew the power of its current which shunted us over to the far shore, close to a barge being loaded with saw logs. Then came Cow Island Bend,

a narrow place in the river where it turned sharply to the southwest. On this bend, the Tennessee line was passed, and the map called the left bank Mississippi. An Engineer fleet was at work on the long revetment. Meanwhile a south wind had sprung up and the sky clouded over. We let the wind carry us across to Cow Island on the left, to be in position to enter the lower end of the chute if it should be a good harbor. We drifted along the low, wooded shore, looking for the opening. It came suddenly, and I just had time to make the johnboat painter fast to a tree limb. This swung the houseboat around the point of the island, and we worked it far enough into the chute to have a dry landing. There are two Cow Islands, Islands Number Forty-seven and Forty-eight. We figured we were in Rock Chute between the two islands.

The wind rose during the night, and we were glad to remain the next day in this sheltered place. Our first act was to plant the cedar which had been our Christmas tree. It was green as ever, after its hundred and seventeen mile voyage.

The river was rising again. The stage at Memphis had been eighteen feet, the lowest it was to be all the winter. The prediction was for twenty-eight to thirty feet, but after that had been reached, it never went back. A bankfull river, swift current and bad weather were to be expected from now on.

261

The low shore at which the boat lay was about to go under in the rising river. On the second day, though the early morning was threatening, we ventured out. It became a warm, sunny day with a light breeze from the south. This called for frequent turns at the sweeps, but this kind of rowing is a pleasure—it does not require all hands, nor last too long, and there is a satisfaction in keeping the boat on a desired course. After rounding Cat Island Bend, we came to a long reach into the southwest, nearly fifteen miles without a bend. It might have been the earth's edge that we looked toward, past islands and wooded points, until the horizon became such a thin, faint line that we could see it no more. Off Basket Bar we ate our dinner, creamed smoked fish on baked potatoes, string beans, blackberry cobbler, the courses interspaced with rowing. At the end of the reach before the bend shut it off we had a long view back of a golden river in the full sun under great white clouds.

The second bend was called Mhoon Bend. The town of Mhoon could not be seen but the levee was close to the river there. The bulletin board read 22¼ R. Two upbound boats passed us on the bend, the *Ashland,* a familiar at Brent, and the steamer, *Jack Rathbone.* Among the other boats seen that day was the *Amos K. Gordon,* also a steam stern-wheeler. These two steamboats were soon to come to the end of their careers in quiet southern waters where there was no river's current.

The river was wide below Mhoon Bend. We let the dying wind take us over to the right bank which on the map was miles of forest traversed by old river beds. We read on the map "State line indeterminate," and no one cared, I guess. As we moved slowly along, the sound of wild fowl and little frogs came from the dark recesses of the woods whose outside trees glowed in the low sun. Before reaching Walnut Bend we towed into a narrow opening which might have been Old Walnut Bend, or Whiskey Chute, or Old Bordeaux Chute. We could not go far in because of the thick trees, and the shore was blocked by a solid line of driftwood. I rowed down the river a quarter of a mile to see if a sheltered place near shore could be found. One must be careful rowing down the Mississippi, not to go around a point where the current is so swift that you cannot row back against it. On this wild shore was a fisherman's boat beached out in the woods. Smoke rose among the trees from a fire which was heating his tar vat. A pulley creaked, and the new-tarred net was raised from the barrel. In a clearing was a little farmstead, a rude house, two or three cedars, surrounded by thin rows of corn. All this could have been the riverbank a hundred years ago.

That night our boat swung between the willows in deep water. In the morning there was a light fog, but since the sky was clear above and windless, we put forth thinking the sun would quickly burn away the mist. At sunrise we were pulling away from the Walnut Bend revetment, in fast water. The fog, instead of vanishing, grew more dense, a level stratus of impenetrable mist close to the water. The current bore us to midstream, the shore was lost. From the roof I could see the tops of tall trees, but even these came to an end, and there was nothing but fog below and sunshine above. We might have been at sea, out of sight of land. Luckily no boats came along, and there were no buoys to crash into.

Under these unfavorable conditions, we entered our first artificial cut-off. The old river lay to the left, somewhere, in a twenty-mile bend, while we were going through the mile-long cut. At least, we hoped we were going through it, and not drifting into the old bendway. After some time a line of trees appeared. We were moving fast; it must be on the main river. The fog began to thin, and the Arkansas shore came in sight at close range. We did not get our bearings until the mouth of the St. Francis River was reached. It was an inviting place, a narrow entrance between high banks, but we had no chance to stop there, even if we had made up our minds to. The succeeding shore was a cypress forest, and the song of birds was in the springlike air.

Ahead lay the Helena Bend, a bad place where the narrow river makes a square turn to the right. We were coasting the sandbars of Prairie Point Towhead now. A motor skiff was going up close to shore. We would have liked to ask him about the best course to take around the bend, but he was too far away. We held close to the point, as the safest way. Across the river we could see the rip of the current over a reef and hear the roar of water. This sound was lost in a great boiling up of the water around us. In these boils, common on the

Mississippi, the water seems to come up from underneath and spread out over the surface in an oily slickness about which circles a mild whirlpool. They are usually not as dangerous as they sound, except to a very light craft. In this place they were so frequent as to make a continuous noise of broken water, like a cataract.

The city of Helena is but three miles below the bend, but it lies on a bay, out of sight behind the islands and towheads. Far upriver, however, we had seen smoke rising, and heard a deep-toned steamboat whistle. This was the railroad car ferry, which was crossing as we approached the city. The river widened out now. We were at the edge of the current, and a good half mile of slack water lay between us and the shore, through which we would have to row to reach Helena. We were afraid of being carried too far downstream, and, as usual, pulled out of the current too soon, so that in addition to crossing the bay we had to row downstream. It took us a long time. As we rowed, the man in the motorboat, whom we had seen going up, came in sight. He was drifting down now, in midstream, alongside a driftwood log so large that he could stand on it. He was sawing it in two. We did not know what to make of this, but later saw many timber drifters, who salvage floating logs and trees and sell them to sawmills.

At last we reached shore and dropped anchor. It was not Helena, for the city lay on a narrow channel which we did not like to enter without scouting. I rowed in with the johnboat. The right side of the channel was low woods; on the left lay the city behind a levee, a small settlement of shacks and boats before its gates. Along the shore were some docks at one of which was the steamer *Wacouta,* an old friend from the upper Ohio. It was being used as a landing dock, but appeared complete and in good condition.

Even farther up the narrow channel was the landing place of the car ferry. It was an old-timer called the *Pelican,* a steam side-wheeler. It looked as if the boat had been cut in half lengthways and two tracks for cars inserted in the middle. The tall stacks were far apart, the pilothouse and texas on a sort of bridge over the tracks. After looking about and talking to some men on the bank, I decided we could find a berth for our boat farther up, beyond the *Pelican*. One of its crew assured me that they had made their last trip for the day. We

towed in, with barely room between the huge side wheel and the shore. A hundred yards beyond we tied up on the right, where there were trees and bushes and no houses, a good place for the dogs, and for us too. On the left was the grassy levee, the tracks from the car ferry sloping up to a gate on top. Over the levee rose the upper parts of the Helena buildings. When we saw our boat tucked away in this little pocket, far from the river, it was amazing, even to us, how it got there.

The first evening in Helena we called on the Nelsons, friends of Phil Howard. We were all complete strangers, but that was forgotten at once. How good it was to talk to such people again, and hear their fine records. Adolph was a pianist of exceptional ability, and we were delighted when he agreed to play trios with us. He took such an interest that he canceled his teaching engagements to make these sessions possible. On one evening the Nelsons came down to our boat for a dinner of 'possum, Skipper having treed one on the island.

At the time we were sorting through the paintings on hand to select those that should be sent to Richmond, Indiana, for a one-man show at Earlham College. This showing was encouraged and arranged by our friend, Warren Staebler, who was a professor there. It went back to his seeing the paintings at Brent and on the Cumberland. All the paintings were to be of the Ohio River. We found nine suitable ones, to which would be added several others done at Brent and left there. The frames I made of some sections of an old white-pine door, picked up in a driftpile somewhere along the way. Once painted white, it had a beautifully weathered surface which went very well with many of the paintings. The rest were framed with the bare wood, with perhaps a little of the white left on; or of dark wood if more suitable. This was nice work to do, though it littered the whole cabin and crowded Anna into a small corner. Material for crates and packing was obtained in the alley behind the furniture store, and the two crates were sent away at the express office, conveniently located just over the levee. The packet of watercolor sketches which were to round out the exhibition could be sent later from some place down the river.

Helena was the first completely southern town we had ever been in; we prowled about observing the houses and yards, struck by the contrast in the way different people live. We visited the library, some of the stores, and the river landing from which a steam stern-wheel ferry made hourly trips to the Mississippi shore. Nearby was a barge line terminal where we again procured the latest navigation bulletins.

On our boat we never tired of watching the *Pelican*. It came in to the landing with much exhausting of steam, whistling, and bell ringing, the wheels backing and coming ahead, the locomotive on board smoking away as it was fired up to pull the grade. A dozen or so assorted freight cars were carried each trip, on the two tracks. When the boat was finally moored, the locomotive pulled off one string of cars. Then the *Pelican* shifted sideways to line up her other track with the single track on shore. After an exchange of whistles, the engine coasted down for the remaining cars. The *Pelican* began operations about one A.M. and was as noisy by night as by day. We came to know the crew by sight, and they probably knew us better, there being only two of us. The captain talked with us one day as he went ashore, asking where we were from, how long on the way. At our answers, he exclaimed, "That's a real odyssey!"

At last we were ready to leave Helena. The framing of the pictures had taken time, the weather delayed us, and there was always "one more go at the trios." Thus it was ten days after our arrival that we worked out into the open river, one fair morning, on the last breath of a north wind. As we passed the *Pelican,* its captain megaphoned from the pilothouse a warning about a bad set in the current toward the Arkansas shore. He added the river forecast, and "Good luck!"

He was right about the current: we just cleared the oil dock below town. It was fast drifting, and so close to shore that we could speak to some men who were cutting timber. On their advice we went behind Montezuma Towhead, although our low-water map showed the passage dry. This is one of the advantages of high water—the drifter can often follow back channels instead of the main river. They may be shorter, and by-pass a troublesome curve. Best of all, some of these narrow, winding waterways take him into an unmarked wilderness where he has the feel of a primitive river. A higher stage of water is safer, too, in that the towboats are not held to a narrow channel, and can give the drifting boat a wide berth. This the pilots did without exception, often swinging their heavy tows out into the swiftest water to give us plenty of room. Also, when the river is up, many new harbors are accessible to a small craft. Naturally, the increased velocity of the swollen river was manifest in the increased length of our daily runs. From now on, we made thirty-five or forty miles, while on the Ohio, even at flood, our best day's run was twenty-five.

On the other hand, high water makes the acute bends even more dangerous. The whole current of the river pours along the uneven shore, which is often a revetment, or caving bank with fallen trees and snags in the water, even standing trees, which have slipped down in an upright position. We tried always to keep near the inside point on a bend, but our efforts amounted to little if the river had other ideas. It usually carried us over to the outside of the curve, where there was often a strip of dead water along shore, separated from the racing current of the river by a series of whirls and sucks. The water along shore was at a higher level, as if squeezed against the bank by the thrust of the stream. It was this fact, more than our rowing, which kept us offshore, for the boat would have to go slightly uphill to get out of the current. The places we feared most were those where the water rolled on through standing trees, which do not deflect the current like a point of land. Some of the trees were leaning, and disappeared

267

under the surface and rose above it with a slow rhythm as if worked by a giant machine. These are called sawyers; the stationary ones are called planters. We managed to miss all of these hazards, but had many close calls.

This is the kind of drifting we had for the rest of the winter. Cut-offs became frequent, often two successive ones on an S curve of the river. Our first night out of Helena we tied up in Jackson Cut-off, with Mississippi on the right where Arkansas should have been. Next morning we went on into Sunflower Cut-off, and there Arkansas was on the left. The state lines are never changed by a cut-off, either a natural or artificial one.

That morning was wet and misty, but we drifted a short distance to Jug Harris Towhead, behind which we lay to. The following morning being fair enough, we set forth again. At the end of the towhead was an eddy, not large, but spinning fast. We tried to avoid it, but our boat was soon going around with the rest of the driftwood; nor could we pull out, handicapped by an onshore breeze. I ran a line to a little sycamore tree fortunately placed in the water below the eddy, but our arms had not the strength to haul the boat against the reverse flow. By running a line from the same tree to each corner of the boat, however, we were able to seesaw our way out, taking up slack on one line or the other as the boat swung from side to side in the current.

A few miles farther down, we directed our course behind a fairly large island called Cessions Towhead to avoid a sharp bend on the main river, around Australia Point. The current was swift through the chute, and the banks were sloughing off into the water with a sound like the random firing of a distant cannon. We closed the shutters to protect the windows from overhanging branches. I was rowing at the sweeps, facing the bank. Directly in front of me a wheelbarrow-ful of earth slipped from the roots of a cottonwood, one of the largest size. Looking up, I saw the tree lean toward the water, then fall into it with a great crash. It struck the water where we had been a few seconds before, and its top was twice as far from shore as we were.

About halfway through the chute we decided to try for a small branch to the right, the beginning of the back channel around a large island, Number Sixty-nine, which lay next to Cessions Towhead. We approached this opening as close to the bank as possible, and pulled hard into it at the right moment. This shove, and the current which was diverted that way, carried us into the narrow, swift-flowing chute. Some sharp turns were encountered, but the force of the water carried us around them. Soon it was quiet drifting, though tree limbs nearly carried away our chimneys. It was a long passage, and so straitened that a fallen tree or a long drift log could block it. This back channel led us through a wild section where it was difficult to find an opening on shore at which to land. At last we nosed the boat in among the trees and lay there two days in a solitude which we felt could go on endlessly.

There came a springlike morning, the song of chickadee and titmouse in the trees, and white clouds blown from the south across the blue sky. We drifted on through the silent forest, ready to take our chances when we came to the windy river. It was good to be out on the open waters again, after two days in the woods. The cross wind kept us rowing off the lee shore. Then came a short revetment with a bad eddy at its end. We shot along the edge of the boiling, whirling water, our speed seeming doubled by the counter current up along the bank.

The next point was one of those rare open and treeless ones, with sandy shores. The current was easy along it, the swiftest water having crossed over to the other side of the river. We could barely keep off-shore now against the increasing wind, and after skirting a long sand-bar gave it up. At that point, the bar trended to the right, one shore of a large bay, while the river below turned sharply left around Scrub-grass Bend. It was a long way across this area of slack water to the distant trees on shore, and we did not care to be blown so far from the river's current. By chance there was a small inlet in the sandbar, just about large enough for us to enter. This little pocket, almost land-locked, would be a safe place if the river became rough, but there was not a tree or mainland bank for miles.

The map called this Henrico Bar. At first it was a little disturbing to have the boat moored out in the open, the tallest and largest object in the miles of surrounding water and sand. But this uneasiness soon passed away and our days there, for thick weather detained us, gave us a chance to know aspects of the river which had hitherto been only

glimpsed in passing. We roamed far along the curving beach, marveling at the grotesque snags half buried in the sand, like huge bones bleached and weathered. The contour of the land was slightly rolling, the higher areas, away from the water, covered with tall grasses of winter grayness. Here, in decaying logs and stumps, the dogs routed out several 'possums, a supply of fresh meat for all of us. What became of these animals in a flood, when the river covered even the highest parts of the sand? I walked back over the moorlike waste to a low ridge covered by willow saplings. Beyond was a quiet arm of water where many ducks were swimming and diving. I could walk no farther for the low land was interlaced by bayous and lakes formed by the shifting river. We were "forty miles from nowhere," as the lamplighter said.

The lamplighters came by the next day to service the Henrico Bar Light which stood near our cove. Their boat was a well-designed craft, suited to its work, its somewhat rough and homemade appearance more appropriate than paint and finish. I hailed it, and asked the two men on board to take some letters to the post office for us. They willingly did this, a part of the light tender's duty, it may be, for they already had some mail from a towboat which was tied up in the fog. They said they would be back in three days, and asked if they could bring us anything from town.

Besides the light near us, three others could be seen at night—the Smith Point Light across the river, Little Red and Little Red Lower Lights on the bend. We looked for them each night, as for known stars. Their mellow beams twinkled forth one at a time, of different magnitude, and were cheerful company. By day we watched the passing boats. Those upbound ran close to the far shore, but even there the current was so strong that you had to sight carefully to note any progress. We have been told by a sometime pilot that a boat working up against a stiff current might be stationary for hours off a swift point, with engines running full speed—for a whole six-hour watch, the man said. Then would come an easing of the current, like a lull in a wind, and the boat moved ahead around the point.

We were surprised to see another motorboat put into the bay. It was old and battered, small openings in the sides of the board cabin for windows, a hand windlass on the forward deck, heavy towing post on the stern. It was a drifter's boat run by two Negroes from Greenville, Mississippi, sixty-six miles downstream. They gathered up logs here and there, from the running driftwood in midstream, or near shore where they were floated by the rising water, sometimes waiting for a choice one on the shore to come afloat; for it is unlawful to pull them into the water. They hauled several logs into the bay, the beginning of a raft, to which they would add others on their way back to Greenville. Some were escaped saw logs, or sawn timber, others whole trees which they must trim and saw up. Some of the logs seemed too rotten to be of any value, but these, called "blues," are sold to the box factory. A crusty snag might be cypress, sound as ever within. I was attracted to this work, where a man could be master of his own vessel, one he could build himself, and make a living combing the driftwood, which is fun to do anyway. It is hard work, though, and one must be out in the winter when the river is high. Also it requires experience and knowledge to know what is salable, and to identify a low-floating log from a distance.

After the fog came some bright days when the sandbar shimmered in the sun, an unsubstantial golden plain amid the dark blue water. The sun rose over one low horizon and sank behind the opposing one.

At night the canopy of stars was revealed down to the lowest ones, in all quarters.

This gave way to foul weather in which every wind seemed to blow in turn, driving rain clouds across the sky with blasts of thunder and lightning. The weather was so rough that even the lamplighters skipped a day. We looked that night, and all their lights were burning.

The men came on the following day, which was colder, and gladly accepted our invitation to come in by the fire. Their home port was up the river, in Mississippi, at the bend of Island Sixty-nine. This made their run eight or ten miles each way. They told us that in low water the Henrico Bar Light stood way out on the point of the bar now covered by water. Until recently, the present location had been the year 'round one, and in summer they had to trudge a long way through the burning sand to reach it. These fellows enjoyed their work and made a sort of picnic of their long run. En route they patrolled the shores in the interest of the owners, watching out for timber poachers. Yet they had their eyes on a certain caving bank, waiting until the trees on it should fall into the river—for they were drifters too.

A northwester followed the thick weather and swept all before it. Snow fell for an entire day. A new earth was created outside our windows. On that day some birds appeared we had never seen before, Lapland longspurs. They walked in flocks about the boat, in the slushy water, picking up seeds of grass and weeds, quite at home in the blizzard.

In the week at Henrico Bar the river had been creeping up on us. The lamplighters said that much more water was on its way down from the Ohio, which was ten feet above flood. Our harbor had already expanded into a small lake, and the additional rise would drive us off the bar into some channel far inland. To avoid this we got under way early in the morning following the snow, on the last day of January. As we rowed out toward mid-river, the sandbar behind us was a long wedge of white above the water which was the color of dull copper, and the snags lay stark against the snow. Overhead, blue and golden light filtered down through the opening clouds. The whole effect was so striking that I must stop at this critical moment of getting away, to make a sketch of it.

It was not easy to reach the dashing current, for the intervening water, though almost motionless, was slowly seething as if in a pot about to boil, making it difficult to force the boat through. At last the swift water caught us, and we were again on our way down the river. Our plan to go through a chute around Montgomery Island into the White River and continue down that stream to the Mississippi had been abandoned after the lamplighter's report of a runout on the White. We soon went by its mouth, and around another bend was the entrance of the Arkansas into the Mississippi. This point was the limit of the first exploration of the Mississippi from the north, by Marquette and Joliet in 1673. We had expected this important tributary to be wider than it was. At closer range it might make a better show-ing, but we saw it from the far side of the Mississippi, to which the current had carried us. As we drifted by, we thought of the town of Napoleon, once situated at the mouth of the Arkansas, the very land on which it stood long since washed away. We remembered also the evil reputation of the spot today. More than one person had warned us that the Arkansas harbored a gang of desperadoes who were un-molested by the law. We were advised to keep clear and not linger there.

At this point Anna announced that dinner was ready, and as all was going well, we sat down at table. We never lose sight of the river, even when inside, because of the view in all directions through the big windows and glass doors. Thus we saw a motorboat when it came out of the Arkansas River and crossed directly toward us. It was a crude, mean-looking affair with a small cabin. Could this be one of the Arkansas River outlaws? The boat kept coming, so close at last that I went on deck, which caused it to sheer off. After some parley, it came alongside, and we discovered that it was just another crew of timber drifters, as civil and friendly as could be. They had thought that our boat was a runaway from the White River, since it was merely drifting with the current, and no one could be seen on board.

It was easy going the rest of the day, with but one short pull off Catfish Point, to keep out of the slack water. Above this bend, as at Henrico and others, the river widened out into a bay of still water along which the current raced as along a shore, with nearly as sharp a line of division. The boat was always swung against this rip current, and we rowed to keep it from going into the still water beyond. On later occasions, however, when the situation demanded that we pull out of the current into the slack water, we found it almost impossible to accomplish.

We made forty miles that day, harboring for the night behind Choctaw Bar, a wide expanse of sand and willows even at this water. We tied up at the old Arkansas City ferry landing. The snow lay on the levee, and in the morning every twig and weed was white with frost. A heavy fog and breathless quiet added to the ghostly effect. The sun broke through as we drifted down the intricate passage behind Choctaw Bar, and burned away frost and snow together. We went through more cut-offs that day. The cut-offs are partly responsible for the swift current; in fact, this is one of their purposes—to run the water off in a hurry and lessen the possibility of flood. Another benefit is to navigation, by making the river straighter and shorter like an express highway. In the nature of their shores and in width the cut-offs can hardly be distinguished from the true river. Yet we resented them and each time, as the current swept us into the new course of the river, we looked down the old bend with regret, as a stretch of fine river never to be seen.

The wind was against us, but we chose a favorable point and made it over to the Mississippi side of the river, holding that shore on down that we might land at Greenville. This city is no longer on the main river, a cut-off having left it on an old bendway called by the fancy name of Lake Ferguson. The upper end of this is blocked off by a levee, but the lower connection with the river is kept open to allow boats to reach Greenville. In spite of all our care the shantyboat was nearly swept past this side channel, and we made it only after a hard pull to break through the confused water at the edge of the current. Inside we tied up to willows at the upper point, to get our bearings. The land on that side was under water. Across the channel it was higher, and we saw boats and fishermen's shacks. An old levee covered with green grass stood a way back, and in the distance the immense new levee. Four or five miles up the channel could be seen the buildings, stacks, and tanks of Greenville.

We were anxious to get away from that exposed willow point before nightfall, but a light wind off the other shore made it next to impossible to row across. I was just about to run out a long line and cordelle farther up on the same side when a man came over in a motorboat to see about some logs tied up near our boat. He offered to tow us across to the other side. There we found a good anchorage at the site of a sawmill which had burned to the ground. The muddy shore was covered with dry sawdust, like sand, and much charred wood lay about which we burned the rest of the way in our fires. Close by, a road came down to the water, once the landing place of the ferry to Arkansas, discontinued when a bridge was built several miles down the river. A few fishermen and drifters lived along the road and shore.

It seemed best for us to lay over in this safe place until the crest of the rise should pass. For all we knew, a major flood might be on the way, in which case we had no desire to be adrift. So we made our landing as convenient as possible, and settled down. It was not long before we became acquainted with our neighbors. The only orthodox house belonged to Joe Huffman. It was behind the old levee, with some chinaberry trees in the yard, the name of which I had to ask. The levee was no protection at all, being washed out farther down. Joe's son, Snap, had solved the flood problem by living in a trailer which he could haul to higher ground. The trailer was barely large enough for Snap's wife and baby; so his mother-in-law lived in a tent nearby. There was another tent farther back, with a smoking chimney sticking

out the top. An old river rat named Sam—the man who had towed us across—lived in a tiny boat beached out under a pecan tree near the water. His only family was a pair of handsome young dogs. One drifter had played safe by placing his homemade trailer atop the old levee, though with water on both sides of it he would be marooned there. Farthest down the shore was a confused collection of sheds, boats, junk, dogs and children, where dwelt some very amiable people. The most curious dwelling contained cows and goats beside the humans, and we could not decide whether it was a house or stable. The only other inhabitants we knew of were a farmer, and some Negroes who lived near the dump, in toward Greenville, who came to the riverbank to cut wood.

These people were fishermen and drifters. The drifters went out on the river every day and brought in logs to take up to the Greenville sawmill. The fishermen were busy repairing and tarring nets to be ready for the spring fishing. They had nets out already, but were not catching much. We liked to talk with them when they were at work out-of-doors, or in their homes where they made us very welcome. Some of them came down to the boat to see us. The conversation was mostly listening on our part, and we learned much about the country, climate, what grew there, how they fished and what they caught, much local and river history. Always on the lookout for new words, we heard bateau and pirogue, which Old Sam called peerow, for the first time. They called our johnboat a bateau.

276

Joe Huffman was the best of neighbors, though he had spoken sharply to me when we first came in, because he thought we were going to tie up at the old ferry landing and be in the way of their boats. He took us to Greenville one day in his car. It was a very pretty town, we thought, comfortable houses and yards where the grass was getting green. Some trees and flowers were beginning to break into color. There was an air of neatness and progress about the whole place. We were surprised to see a number of Chinese storekeepers. One day I rode in with a stranger, and walked back on the levee, discovering what a splendid place that is for walking: the elevation gives a wide view over the flat country and the river.

Among our visitors on board was one of the Henrico lamplighters, who was in Greenville for a funeral, and had come out of his way to see us. On another day the man who owned and farmed the bottom land extending along the water came aboard. We had noticed some winter vegetables, and were glad to talk with him about his crops. He specialized in raising vegetables in midsummer when they were scarce and the market high. The idea of a summer being too hot for tomatoes and beans was a new one to us. The situation of his land near the water was favorable, and he added to the natural moisture by pumping water from a small lake. Since his farm was not inside the new levee, the old one was valuable as a pasture and a refuge for stock in high water. Another new fact we learned was that all alluvial soil is not the same. Some of it, which he called buckshot, was so hard in summer "you could not drive a steel spike in it." Later we were to learn about buckshot land at first hand.

Before leaving, the farmer casually remarked that we might as well help ourselves to any vegetables then in the fields, because the high water would soon cover them. We had made out very well since leaving Bizzle's Bluff, with the fresh carrots, parsnips, and pumpkins, white and sweet potatoes, all from our garden, and our large stock of canned vegetables.

Our fresh vegetables being nearly gone, the farmer's offer came at a good time. We hurried out to the fields and found turnips and beets, a few carrots, and much collards, spinach, mustard and turnip greens. The turnips and collards were good keepers, we knew; so we packed several bushels of them in sawdust from our landing. Beets were canned, or rather pickled, twelve quarts of them. It seemed strange to be canning in February. Also from the beets Anna devised a fresh beet salad—ground beets, a few tiny beet greens, walnut meats, mayonnaise, and a touch of lemon. Thus replenished, our stock of green vegetables lasted far down the river, until poke and wild greens were available. The pickled beets went even farther, to the end of the river, and beyond.

There was an interesting side light to this episode. When we mentioned to some of our shantyboat neighbors that the farmer had invited us to help ourselves to the vegetables in the fields, they interpreted the "us" to mean not Anna and me but the whole shantyboat community of which we were a part. They acted accordingly, and none of the crop was spoiled by high water.

We had a big wash day at this location, under favorable conditions, using river water cleared by settling two or three days. It was well into the afternoon when we hung out the last jeans and corduroys. All was not work, however, for I completed several paintings begun at Henrico Bar. We got on with our reading, and inspired by the Helena trios, practiced our instruments. There was much to watch from our windows, too. The boats on the big river could be seen, often tying up their tows to double trip up through the cut-offs. Many boats came into the Greenville lake, some of the largest ones. Frequent passers-by were two small boats towing sand and gravel from the sand digger we had passed on the way down. The boat we observed with most interest, however, was the *Sandford E. Hutson,* a small old steamboat, side-wheel, with one stack. It came pounding down from Greenville in a cloud of steam, with a log barge and derrick, went out into the river and we never saw it again. This boat was a survival of the past, like the *Pelican* and *Jupiter.*

There was a big sawmill in Greenville to which several log rafts were towed in by drifters. One rafter misgauged his course and was carried past the mouth of the lake by the current. Landing his raft farther down, he had to break it up and bring it in one log at a time. While we lay there the boat belonging to the drifters at Henrico Bar, assisted by three other motorboats, brought in a large raft of assorted logs and timber, their whole collection on the down trip. All the boats belonged to Negroes, which one would know at once by their queer construction, their unexpected colors, shapes, and proportions. It was a lively fleet while they tied up the raft opposite us. At night they burned dim lights for a while, but in the morning all were gone out on the river again, except one left to tow the raft up the dead water to the sawmill.

During this time the river had not risen much. No one we asked could tell us much about what it was going to do. The official forecasts were limited and noncommittal. The natives took it for granted that the river would keep on rising, and prepared for high water. At the time, we thought this was looking too much on the dark side, but they knew the Mississippi better than we. As there was no talk at all of a serious flood, we decided to continue our voyage. It was well into February now, the grass was green, the elms in flower, and some spring songs of birds could be heard. We wanted to get in some more drifting before the gardening urge became too strong.

It was remarkable how we had settled ourselves at Greenville in nine days. We felt we had known these people for years. Yet, as always when leaving a familiar place, it became strange in the first minute of drifting and our thoughts turned to the river ahead. The business in hand was the Greenville bridge which loomed up around the first bend. Not long ago the big towboat *Natchez* had crashed into a pier of this bridge and sunk. It was a tough place, close to the bend, in a narrow, swift river. As we approached it along the right bank, a U. S. Engineers workboat put out from shore either to rescue or assist us —we could not understand their shouting—but seeing we would miss the piers, it went back. The first pier was on the shoreline. Against the second, the water and driftwood were piling up with a fearsome noise. We shot through without even time to look up at the bridge. The water below was like a rapids. In the johnboat it was all I could do to keep out of the way as the whirlpools swung the two boats around like balls on a string. I could see the hull of the houseboat settling down in the sucks, almost to the guards. It was soon over, and we were drifting easily again.

A winding river lay ahead of us, cut-offs and crossings to run, towboats to keep clear of, sandbars, dead water, and buoys to miss, but that day the boat drifted through all the hazardous places as if handled by some invisible crew. We, almost as passengers, had an easy time of it.

Early in the afternoon we began looking for the night's harbor. This problem had become more acute with the river over its banks. Dry land near the water was limited and often inaccessible because of thick-growing trees in the water before it. After shooting through the turbulent Sarah Cut-off, we worked over to the left bank through Opossum Chute, drifting close to Duncansby Towhead. At the bottom of it was a small inlet, on the lower shore of which we could see a high bank. We pulled in, crashed through a barrier of willow switches, and moored the boat. There was still time to look about, and the full moon rising extended the daylight. Although an easy day's run, we had covered thirty-eight miles.

Since this was the lower end of the towhead, an outward flow could be expected. For some reason, perhaps because there was another outlet farther down, the current was setting in. This was very well when we entered, but getting out the next morning was a tough job. We cordelled as far as we could, but there was nothing to tie the line to for the final haul out into the current. With considerable difficulty we worked the boat upstream behind the trees and broke through at a point where the river's current was close in. Soon we were drifting in midstream past the sand digger we had heard rumbling through the night, past the Arkansas-Louisiana state line. Louisiana! We were in a strange land now.

Although the day before had been such an easy one, this day was the most trying of the whole winter's voyage. Nearly all the morning had been taken up by the exhausting work of hauling the boat out of the chute against the inflowing current. There was more trouble off Lake Providence, the first town in Louisiana. The river was about two miles wide there, the sandbars all covered, much slack water off to leeward. We had to row steadily against the cross wind to stay in the current. We finally made a small island, Stack Island, where we had a breathing spell. When we were past it, the wind blew us into dead water off to the side, and it was only by the hardest labor that we got the boat back into the flowing channel. We might have let it go and sailed to the lee shore, but it was far off our course, and no dry land showed in that direction. We finally worried around the bend and could put up our oars as the boat drifted down the straight reach.

About five miles farther, the river turned right. The outside of the curve was an open shore along a levee and a houseboat could be seen in some backwater. We made a try for a landing there, since the wind, now ahead, seemed to be increasing. When we pulled out of the current, there was slack water again, or perhaps an eddy. To our dismay we started to sail upstream, bound for Lake Providence. Another laborious heave put the boat back in the current, which carried us down the river, close to the levee. On the bend we managed to make a landing behind a small point, but were unable to work the boat around it into a promising harbor above—the same in which the houseboat lay. Not trusting the open shore we set ourselves adrift again, made another attempt to land at the lower end of the bend, but could not break through the current.

It was at this point that I saw the first Spanish moss hanging thick on some cypress trees near at hand. Anna, on the other end of the boat, facing the river, did not see it; so I shouted, "Spanish moss!" Now, one of our weak points in drifting was communication between the johnboat and the main deck. Anna could rarely hear what I said, and if she left the sweeps to look back along the side of the boat, I was most likely off the other corner. So she took every shout to mean "Pull hard," though pulling her hardest all the time. As I kept hollering on this occasion, she left the sweeps to see what was the matter. "Spanish moss!" I shouted again, and she saw it too.

In the next several miles, by rowing and by lowering the mud sail, which at least served as a sea anchor, we managed to hold our position in the flowing water, the wind being across our course now, and were carried at a fast rate toward Alsatia Bend. This was a setup like that at Lake Providence, the river even wider, the widest we had ever seen. Cottonwood Bar, off the point, was all under water, though we did not know this and several times made for breaks in the trees which we thought might be the chute behind the bar. By steady labor at the oars we were able to round the bend, and began drifting down the next reach close to the right bank. It was nearly sunset now, we were tired and anxious to make a landing. Try our best, we could not break through the boiling edge of the current into the still water beyond. It was tantalizing to drift past quiet harbors among the trees and not be able to reach them. We got so close in at one place that the boat nearly crashed into some trees standing in the racing water. Two DPC's shoving a single tow, were coming upstream toward us, close to our bank, but when we showed a light, for it was dark now, they whistled a passing signal and veered way out into the river to avoid us.

We drifted as fast as a man can run along that shore until the full moon began to show. Then at another opening in the trees, which appeared to be our last chance, we tried again. "Pull hard, I think we can make it," I shouted. My optimism seemed to inspire Anna, tired as she was, with new strength. We both gave our best, and after a few uncertain moments had the satisfaction of seeing the boat lose its forward motion as it glided into the quiet water. A beacon light gleamed on a spur of the levee immediately below us, and on the shore the levee's mass could be seen against the sky. We made no attempt to reach the land in the darkness, but were content to tie up between two trees for the night, and make an end to the weary day.

It was a windy night, and shreds of white clouds sailed fast across the sky all pale in the moonlight. We lay awake listening to the moaning of the trees, the chirping of frogs, and the lashing current out in the river. It had been a good day after all. This is what we were on the river for—to feel the power of it, to see it in action, to be near to it with as little as possible between us and it, to know it as an elemental force stripped of names and associations. The hard work and aggravation, the unwieldy boat, stubborn as a mule, water like glue, all this was good, too. What true understanding of the river could one acquire by a fast trip in ease and comfort? And now, after such a day as this, it was good to be at rest, sheltered where wind and current could not reach us.

A warm gusty south wind can be depended on to blow day and night for a few days and end in bad weather. Therefore in the morning we moved our boat several hundred yards upstream through the backwater, letting the wind blow us along, keeping a safety line on a tree all the while lest the current or a flaw in the wind carry us out into the river. Squeezing through an opening narrowed by driftwood, we entered a small placid lake and tied the boat to the outside shore which was a narrow strip of grassy land atop a revetment. It was along this shore that we had drifted the previous evening, and we saw now that it was the bounce of the current off this submerged revetment that had made it impossible for us to land. In landing where we did we had crossed over the revetment where it was lower, or perhaps broken.

This strip of land was nearly awash, and we could look over it at the turbulent river only two or three rods away, and across the river to the distant, low shore. Inland, the green levee lay beyond the smooth water.

We soon discovered that this was the harbor of two fishermen who went out to run their nets in a bateau powered by a big outboard engine. They stopped a few times to talk with us, but since they worked hard and fast, as most fishermen do, their visits were brief. They gave us a nice buffalo to eat, and some shad and cold-waters for the dogs. The cold-waters look like small carp, and are caught chiefly in winter net fishing. These men also mentioned "gaspar" or "goo," a fish we had called perch; perhaps this name is a corruption of the French *gasparot* or *gasperau,* a kind of shad. Our status puzzled these fishermen, as it did most others, and they probed us indirectly to find out our business. As a feeler, they asked Anna if she would make some nets for them. This was a joke, as it would take us the rest of the winter and spring to knit even one. They said they could complete a net in one evening. Other fishermen have made this same statement. We wonder if any of them have ever done it; or is this one of those accepted standards never put to the test.

The dogs had an exciting time here, chasing rabbits whose escape had been cut off by backwater. I crossed the levee and had a short walk, but the country was so dismal that I was glad to get back to the river again. One chore here was to replenish our supply of firewood. Finding no hardwood in the drift, I cut down a honey locust, which burns well even when green. What could not be stored away inside in the woodboxes I piled on the roof in long pieces since having cut it, I would leave none behind. There happened to be plenty of even better

283

wood at succeeding stops, and the locust was carried until we tied up for the summer.

The south wind ended in rain and colder weather, and it was not until the fourth morning after our landing at Alsatia Bend that drifting was again possible. In the frosty sunrise we worked the boat through the narrow outlet of the backwater lake and set off down the river. All went well for some ten miles, when rowing was called for to keep out of slack water above Milliken's Bend. On the bend itself the river was flowing right against the bank from which an oil dock projected. Because of the set of the current and an onshore breeze, our passing around some barges at the end of the pier looked doubtful. We rowed hard, kept the boat at just the right angle to the current. A deck hand watched us from the outside corner of the barge. A small towboat came out from behind the dock to help us, but by that time we had grazed by the barges and dock. After some conversation with the operator of the boat, the *Buckhorn Sun,* he shoved us out into the river, saving us further rowing, and we drifted on our way.

After our boat had followed its own course for another ten miles we began to get into position to land at Vicksburg by holding close to the Mississippi side around Brown's Point. Down the straight reach, the distant bluff lay like a barrier wall across the course of the river. As it came nearer, white houses and streets and patches of grass shown forth, a most pleasing sight in the thin spring sunshine.

The river flows straight to the bluff where it turns sharply right. At one time it bent left before reaching the bluff, made a hairpin turn, and ran along the foot of the bluff for a longer distance than it does today. The center of Vicksburg is on this old course of the river, so that today the main part of the city does not lie on the Mississippi. The river broke through the narrow neck of land in 1876, another Centennial Cut-off. Thus in the Civil War the entire city of Vicksburg lay open to the river.

The Yazoo, an important tributary entering the Mississippi at Vicksburg, has had to accommodate itself to the shifting bed of the big river. The old meandering of the two streams is hard to trace. Now the Yazoo flows into the Mississippi through the Yazoo Diversion Canal, part of the old bendway along the bluff. We heard of an older

Yazoo canal, somewhere back in its delta, which was cut during the famous siege of Vicksburg.

Our plan was to enter the mouth of the Yazoo. We closed with the left bank half a mile before reaching the bluff. Along the shore there was no current at all for that last half mile. We pulled partway out into the river to let it carry us a little farther down. It was slow drifting at first, but suddenly we were caught by the main current shooting off from the point on the other side of the river. In no time we were off the mouth of the Yazoo, and we began to pull out of the current into the band of slack water which still lay along the shore. We began —but could not make it. Skirting the very edge of the quiet water, we bent the oars in our efforts, but we were unable to break the boat from the grip of the current which slowly boiled and circled as it rolled along. It was not a serious matter to miss our landing and be carried past the Yazoo, but a short mile and a half below was the Vicksburg bridge. If we were lucky enough to run by its piers safely we would be far down the river before a landing could be made, too far to be within reach of the city.

A motorboat happened to be going up along the shore while we were trying to reach land, and when I saw we could not make it, I waved my hand. The man in the boat was watching us; he came out at once, turned around and tied the painter of the johnboat, in which I was rowing, to the stern of his boat. Thus the three boats were in line. His was an old tub with an engine about the size of a quart can. He could not get it started again, and it looked like Anna and I might have to tow him in. At last he got his engine to pop, and its feeble power added to our rowing dragged the shantyboat in to shore. He guided us to a cove just above the bridge, which he said was a safe anchorage.

We all relaxed now and had some talk. The man who towed us in was a fisherman from the Yazoo River, and this was his "line boat," meaning that he had another, larger one for net fishing. He told us he had been one of the crew of the towboat *Natchez* when that boat struck a pier of the Greenville bridge and sank. The *Natchez* was proceeding up the river at the time, as we understand it, had passed under the bridge, when the tow was swung around by the current and the boat carried into a pier. It sank at once, and some of the crew were drowned. This man happened to be on deck, grabbed a life belt and jumped into the water before the boat struck. He swam ashore, landing five miles downstream where, having some waterproof matches with him, he was drying himself by a fire when a rescue boat picked him up.

He pointed out a smudge of oil on one of the piers of the Vicksburg bridge. This he said was made by one of the twelve barges in tow of an upbound boat, whose tow got out of control and broke up against the bridge.

The roar of the deep and swift-running river against the bridge piers was insistent and neverending. All the time we lay there it reminded us of the gantlet that must be run in leaving, and what would happen if we missed the opening. The towboats ran the bridge with great caution, shortening their tows coming down, and double tripping upstream. Even so, they had to inch along, and we saw a big diesel actually dropping back with the current.

It was exciting to have the bridge in the sky above us, the bluff rising to an even greater height, after weeks in the low country with nothing higher than the levee on shore, and only treetops and sky overhead. The bluff rose steep from the water, grown over with trees and vines, its top crested by a highway and the old battlements. The bridge carried highway and railroad across the river. It was good to see some trains again. The freights hauled many logs cut into short lengths like cordwood and neatly stacked on special flatcars. The trains entered a short tunnel on the bluff side, the only one, probably, for many miles, and then coasted down a long cut to the bank of the Yazoo in Vicksburg.

We made two or three trips in to the city. To scale the bluff it was necessary to row down to the bridge, being careful not to pass under it, for the current was too swift to row back again; then we followed a path to a landing where two small boats were moored, the homes of two lone men who were fishermen and drifters. Though our only neighbors, we did not visit them often because of Sambo's trouble with a dog there. A trail led up the bluff from their boats and on top ran the Vicksburg bus. It was worth the climb to view the river from above, to see it rolling down from far off in the flat country, a restless, troubled tide of muddy water. Our boat below looked small indeed, and had we seen the river from this viewpoint before starting out, we might have hesitated to cast ourselves adrift on it. On the bend we could see the long line of eddies and boils at the edge of the current where we had failed to break through. Looking directly across, we thought of Walter Berry, who had told us that his barge had been one of a fleet tied up there behind the point for ten days while the Mississippi was full of heavy running ice.

Vicksburg is built on the bluff, on its steep side, and below it. The sloping streets and houses stepping up reminded us of Cincinnati.

We visited the Mississippi River Commission where we looked at the photographs of Engineer activities and bought a new book of maps to replace the one we were cutting up.

The part of Vicksburg the most fascinating to us is under the hill, along the Yazoo, where stand some of the old buildings of steamboat days. The shore is lined with river terminals, barges, railroads and freight cars, small boats, houseboats, fish dock, and farther down a big sawmill. Unexpectedly we came upon the towboat, *Sprague,* tied up there, all complete, but out of service and never to run again. This boat, the largest river towboat ever built, became a legend in its own lifetime. Many stories were told us of the waves she rolled, but we would have taken our chances with them if we could have seen the boat running. As it was, we looked on it as if it were an old lion in captivity.

A special trip was made while at Vicksburg to the Waterways Experiment Station of the U.S.E.D. There, small-scale models of waterway projects from all over the country are built and tested. We studied with interest the model of the Mississippi River, amazed at the variation of depth. Our special attention was given to the seventy-mile section of river between Vicksburg and Natchez, for we hoped to find a place near Natchez where we could tie up for the summer.

The run from Vicksburg to Natchez was made in two days, with a rather long halfway stop at Bayou Pierre. It was all easy drifting, in quiet, warm weather, along shores increasingly green, for the young willows were sprouting. Great quantities of mistletoe and Spanish moss made the country look more southern, though essentially it had not changed all the way down from Cairo. Nevertheless we felt that in our southward drifting we were advancing to meet the spring, and entering new regions.

On our departure from Vicksburg we took no chances with the bridge piers, but cordelled to the upper point of the cove. Rowing out from there, we were midway between the first two piers when we passed under the bridge. The rough water below, which was tame compared with that of the Greenville bridge, was soon passed through. The roar of water died away as we drifted down the southwest reach, but the shining framework of the bridge remained in sight a long time.

We passed the entrance to Palmyra Lake, an old bendway twenty miles around, and entered Diamond Cut. The other end of Palmyra Lake is ten miles below, off Big Black Island, where, rounding close to the point, we came suddenly on some approaching barges. As soon as the towboat, the *Davy Crockett,* came far enough around the bend to see us, it sheered off, but even so, we passed close. This is another of the drifter's bad dreams—to meet a long, wide tow on a sharp bend where it appears so suddenly that he has no time to get out of the way, and the pilot of the towboat is still around the bend where he cannot see ahead.

Beyond the point was the Big Black River, an important tributary from the east, but we could not tell just where its mouth was, in the confusion of backwater islands. This river comes in parallel to the Grand Gulf Ridge which could be seen from the river. This is a favorite territory for fishermen, and we saw several houseboats, all of them beached out in the woods. Some of the meager establishments looked so primitive that they might have been the miasmal riverbank clearings and woodyards described by the early travelers.

Off Hard Scrabble Bend, the *Raccourci,* a buoy boat, as the river people call her, passed inside of us. It was a small, yachtlike craft towing a barge of newly painted red and black buoys. Her work was to make soundings, and keep the channel buoys set in accordance with the shifting channel and fluctuating river.

Farther downstream we pulled over to the slow current along the left bank, drifting among snags, and entered the channel around

Bondurant Towhead, which lies at the mouth of Bayou Pierre. We found a night's harbor in the woods below the point of the towhead, but next day moved down a mile to a landing on the mainland below the mouth of Bayou Pierre but still behind the towhead.

Here the boat lay in deep water close to the bank which was just even with the deck. The shore had once been cleared, though now overgrown with weeds. Farther back was a cypress swamp. Beyond that rose another bluff, the Petit Gulf Hills. It was a wildernesslike place where we did not see, or expect to see, any people. This harbor being away from the river, not even a lamplighter came by. Only far-off reminders of human life reached us, the barking of a dog, the noise of a truck as it made its halting way along the road—it must have been a poor one—atop the ridge. Through the towhead chute was a distant view of the river and passing boats. Once, standing quietly in the woods, I was startled by a sudden splashing as several deer ran through the shallow water. The dogs were out hunting most of the time, but the only game they caught were some very large rats. These rats would climb into a tree to escape, and Skipper showed herself to be an agile tree climber, actually scrambling up one leaning vine-covered tree trunk. The dogs would not eat the rats raw, but after I had cleaned and cooked some they ate them readily. It looked like good meat.

We washed clothes again, setting up the tubs on deck for the first time since last summer. Some rain water caught in a shower was used, and some water dipped up in the swamp, which was perfectly clear, though it had wigglers in it.

We liked the place so much that we considered settling down there for the summer. The old clearing would make a good garden, and a trail led back through the swamp to the bluff. However, we had to remind ourselves that this was high water, nearly a flood, and in low water this fine harbor might be a muddy ditch. Also, the ground was at an elevation likely to be covered by higher water as late as May and June, as the records proved. So we made the most of it on those four spring days, and on the first of March, a fine morning, we pulled out into the river.

It was windier in the open than we had expected, and after eating our breakfast of fried mush, I had to row away from shore as the boat was carried around Spithead Point at a fast rate. Then the wind died and we could take it easy. A handful of buildings at a place marked Ashland made a great show from the river. We were reminded again of how few towns or even houses we had seen in the nearly six hundred miles of the Mississippi which we traversed that winter.

The river now flowed a more or less straight course to the south, or west of south, for the remaining fifteen miles to Natchez. The Natchez bluff extends six miles up the river from the city. As a good harbor was not likely along the bluff, we had it in mind to stop before we reached the beginning of the hills, and accordingly held to the left bank. At Coles Creek, in the mouth of which we saw two large houseboats, a submerged sandbar forced the current and us out to mid-river. We rowed back toward the shore, which appeared to be an unbroken forest of cottonwood. Just then a motorboat, which from its cabin we thought to be a lamplighter's boat, came up along the bank. Seeing us pulling for shore, the boatman ran out to where we were and offered to tow us in. He came at a good time, not because we needed help, but he could tell us about the river and shores below. He said there were two inlets on the left bank, the second one just above the beginning of the bluff.

After he turned us loose, we drifted slowly along the shore looking for the openings he had mentioned, ready in our positions to pull the boat in. At the first one, no dry land could be seen. The second one we did not see until right there. Back through the trees I glimpsed a bank. "Pull hard!" I shouted. A few strokes of the oars cleared the branches of a big willow standing in the water. We slipped through a narrow opening and tied the boat among the trees standing in the calm water within. A few minutes later, the current, shifting its path as it does on the Mississippi, was racing past the entrance, breaking against the willow with a roaring noise. Had we come along then, we could not have made the harbor, and our history might have been different, for though not at all sure of it at the time, we were to remain there, under the bluff, until the next winter.

10

Magnolia Bayou—this we called it at first, because of Magnolia Bluff which rose above it. It is a most fitting and obvious, almost inevitable name for the bluff, since according to our observation nowhere along the Mississippi are the dark green domes of the magnolia trees so conspicuous. The real name of the little stream in which we anchored is Bisland Bayou, which goes back to the original Spanish grant to the Bislands, descendants of whom still own the land and live in the house begun by the first Bisland in the eighteenth century. So that is an appropriate name, too. Bayou, however, we think hardly correct: it is rather a creek flowing down from the hills, subject to treacherous runouts. A bayou is more placid and even-tempered water.

The lamplighter, who stopped by on his return trip down the river, told us about the runouts, but with the river as high as it was the rush of water down from the hills after a storm would be checked by the backwater from the river long before it reached us. With no uneasiness we moved the boat inward through the treetops to the bank seen on our first approach.

Not then, nor for some time afterwards, did we have any fixed notion about staying in Bisland Bayou for the summer. The place had
an immediate appeal, but there were serious objections to it. While
making up our minds, we became used to living there and lost the
momentum of traveling. In fact, having stopped a while we found
ourselves a little weary after our winter's struggle with the river and
glad to give it over for a spell. Our thoughts turned to the land which
was blossoming into spring.

For all this, our stay in Bisland Bayou might have been a short one
had not Alfred Smith happened to take his fish to Natchez on that
first day we pulled in through the fringe of trees. After tying up the
shantyboat, I had left Anna on board and gone downstream in the
johnboat to look for a possibly better harbor. The river skirted
the bluff, flowing swiftly along the ragged shore. It was no place for
us. I gave it up after a mile, landed and scrambled upward through the
dense growth to the top of the bluff. Here was a splendid view out
over the river and the flat country beyond. Inland were rolling pastures
in which stood great pecan trees, like pasture oaks in the Blue Grass
meadows. In the surrounding woods redbud bloomed among the pines
and hardwoods. It was attractive country.

Rowing back to the boat against the current and a sleety rain, I was
overhauled by a motorboat, a long trim johnboat. The young man
slowed down, took me in tow and stopped at our boat. He said he was
Alfred Smith, a fisherman, that he was returning from Natchez to
Coles Creek, six miles upriver, where he and his family lived in a
houseboat. His was not one of the boats which we had seen when
drifting by the mouth of the creek—they belonged to cousins of his, he
said. He was anchored farther up the creek.

Alfred Smith knew much about Bisland Bayou, having lived there
two years with his parents, who had made garden and fished. It was
an experience of theirs which gave the place a bad name. A sudden
runout had carried away two or three motorboats, washed them out
into the river where they were sunk and lost. Luckily their houseboat
was beached out on the bank at the time. The exact details of this
catastrophe we never could make out, the several stories told to us of it

being considerably at variance. Nevertheless, this ever-present danger of a runout made us a little shy about staying there.

Before Alfred left, he said that he would stop on his next trip to Natchez, in two or three days, and take us with him, if we cared to go. The offer was accepted at once. Meanwhile we looked about in the new territory. For some two hundred yards back from the riverbank, which was marked by the beginning of the trees, the land was under water. Then came another bank which, we were told later, only the highest floods had surmounted. On this higher level was a long narrow field extending from the bayou in an upriver direction, northward. Cornstalks of last year's planting, and a fine stand of Johnson grass covered this field. Beyond rose the bluff in a long line which approached the river in a downstream, southward direction. Thus the area of low, flat land between the bluff and river gradually diminished until at a point only a quarter mile below Bisland Bayou the escarpment rose directly from the water's edge.

Alfred Smith had told us that the land belonged to Doctor Shields who lived at Pine Ridge, four miles inland, and that it was farmed by a Negro called Tomcat. We thought it would be wise to find out how welcome we would be as squatters; so I walked back to Pine Ridge one day. We had already climbed the bluff, to which a path led through the cornfield, passing the site of an old house marked by some scattered bricks, a fig tree and some budding iris—traces of an inhabitant prior to the river people. How many even earlier residents there, no one will ever know.

The road, or what was left of it, began at the foot of the bluff. It was a kind of road we had never seen before. The soil being fine and soft to a great depth without clay or stones, the wear of traffic on such a yielding roadbed, and in this case erosion by rain, had lowered the road gradually until it ran between high, almost vertical walls. Even the banks along the modern paved roads in this region are cut and remain nearly perpendicular. The famous sunken roads of Natchez are sections of the old Natchez Trace, a pioneer road which led overland to Nashville. Our road was as good an example of a sunken road as any. We saw none whose banks were so high, so beautifully draped with vines, and laced overhead with the arching branches of trees.

293

A deserted cabin stood at the top of the bluff, and a winding road led off through groves of pine. There were a few old clearings, one of them said to be the site of a plantation house. If the road up the bluff was impassable for any vehicle it was not much better on top. It threaded its way along the ridge, circling deep, sandy chasms, in some places but a narrow bridge between two steep-sided ravines. The country was a wilderness, almost impenetrable if one left the road because of ravines, undergrowth and tangled vines. I expected this to give way to cultivated land farther from the river, perhaps to farms such as were atop Bizzle's Bluff, but it was a sort of pine barren all the way to Pine Ridge. Here were some fields and a few houses. Back from the road in a grove of live oaks was the old Bisland plantation, now the home of Doctor Shields, whose wife was a Bisland.

Considering our best approach to be through the tenant who farmed the river bottom, I inquired of a Negro boy on the road where Tomcat lived. His name was really James Carter; to us he became Tom. His wife—they were young people—came out to the gate. Full of curiosity she was a little put out because I did not tell her my business, saying, "He's down at the barn, but I am his wife."

Our experience with Negroes in the south was very limited. Tom understood this at once and made allowances. He went about harnessing the mule, his face expressionless as he considered how to answer my sudden proposal to settle in his territory. He made some noncommittal remarks, and came to no decision until I had left. I think it was my mention of fish that weighed the scale in our favor. He called and came after me to say that he would try to get Doctor Shields' permission for us to stay in Bisland Bayou. I left it in his hands, and went back to report to Anna.

A day or two later Alfred came by as he had promised. In the hatch in the forward end of his boat was a large heap of buffalo and goo, perhaps two hundred pounds. We thought it a large catch, since he had taken fish to market so recently, but Alfred said he often had as much as six hundred pounds. On the way to Natchez, six miles, we observed the river carefully. It was very wide off Bisland Bayou, a mile across to the distant wooded shore which was well above water. The river narrowed as it ran along the bluff. In its original course there was a bend to the right, a fifteen-mile circle which returned to the bluff at a point above Natchez. A two-mile cut-off had been made along the bluff in 1933, which eliminated the bend and shortened the river distance from Bisland Bayou to Natchez by thirteen miles. On this high water a current still flowed through the old bendway, but Alfred said that in low water both entrances to it were cut off by sandbars and a new growth of willows. The cut was narrow compared with the river above. We could see Natchez now, buildings on top of the bluff, a sawmill by the water sending steam and smoke high into the air. The stern-wheeler *Chisca*, an old Engineers' boat, lay at the waterfront, and the *Raccourci* was in port. We passed all this, a houseboat or two, a derrick boat unloading steel pipes for oil wells, and landed at what must have been the old steamboat and ferry landings. Here to our delight were a few ancient brick and frame buildings, some in ruins, the last remnants of Natchez-under-the-hill. It was hard to believe that it had once extended several blocks out into what is now deep water. All these buildings, and even a race track, which was said to have been under the bluff at one time, have caved into the river.

Alfred delivered his fish to the buyer, whose establishment was in one of the oldest buildings, and we went up the hill by the road which slanted up its side. At once the dual nature of Natchez was apparent. Roughly speaking, one main street was given over to the Pilgrims—tourists who came to see the old houses—and another to the stores and business one would expect to find in a small southern city. We liked it all, and would be well content to be citizens for the summer, if our random trips from a six-mile distance would entitle us to that standing.

On our way back, we noticed with surprise that there was no current along the Natchez shore even up through the cut. Around its upper point, however, the full force of the river was sweeping along the shore, made irregular by landslides and fallen timber. Here the current boiled and eddied and fought against itself. Alfred, calm as if in still water, said it was even worse along here when the river was low. He also told us that in low water Bisland Bayou ran dry, that a wide sandbar extended along that side of the river from the bluff up to Coles Creek.

By this time we had pretty well lined up the conditions which faced

us at Bisland Bayou. On the whole, we liked the place. We were glad to be near the high ground; there was a good place for a garden; a short piece down the river was a fine spring, according to Alfred, though now under water. The fishing along here was said to be good. Natchez was not too far away, a pleasant city of just the right size for us. Against all this was the almost complete isolation of the place; no passable roads; a current too swift to row back against, if we went to Natchez in the johnboat; no neighbor for four miles inland and six miles up the river; no farmers from whom we might get country produce, milk and eggs. There was also the danger of a runout, and in summer low water, no harbor at all, only an open sandbar.

Mulling over these considerations, we awaited word from Tom. He came down shortly and, with a broad grin, said, as nearly as Tom's speech can be written down, "Rosy says that Dr. Shields says you can stay here if you want to, and make a garden, but don't shoot any deer." Rosy worked part of the time in the doctor's house. We suspected that it was she who had managed the affair. On my leaving, the day I had talked with them, Rosy had said in a low voice, as if hardly addressing me, "If you catch any gar fish down there—."

The satisfaction we felt at finding no obstacle in the way of our staying at Bisland Bayou we took as an indication of an inward desire to do so. We realized that we would have been disappointed if Tom's report had been negative. Bisland Bayou was turning out to be an even better place than we had first considered it. The objections remained, but we could think of ways around them, or perhaps they were not so bad after all. It might be years before the recurrence of another flash flood; we could be careful always, and move out into the river if a heavy rain fell back in the hills. If the bayou went dry, with a sandbar offshore, there was a harbor half a mile downstream, in a pocket behind a tiny island which the lamplighter had said would appear in low water. This place was a little removed from the garden, but not too far, and it would be close to the spring. The lack of neighbors did not really concern us; better so than to have people nearby who would disturb the peace. As for getting to Natchez, it looked like Alfred might be a solution to that problem, since he would be going back and forth all summer. We did want it possible for our friends to reach us, in case any of them made the long trip. Here our hopes were that Tom could really grade the road and keep it open, as he claimed he was going to, though it seemed too big a job for one man and a mule. There was one shortcoming for which we could find no answer—the surrounding wilderness, no farms, no fresh milk and eggs to be had, no Hammonds or Mitchells with whom to form the satisfactory relations enjoyed by both parties at Payne Hollow and Bizzle's Bluff. We accepted this as inevitable, and made the best of it.

Now we could take possession with a free mind, and establish ourselves on land. The unshipping of the sweeps marked an end of drifting for the present. There was no beehive to place on shore to mark our claim, but we soon unloaded plunder enough. I emptied the big woodbox under the step to the afterdeck in which fireplace wood was stowed away. Putting this space to summer use was a sign that winter was over and that we lived partly on land where some reserve wood could be stored. The woodbox contained pieces of driftwood picked up along the way, a few of them coming all the way from Brent. In firing up I had laid the best pieces aside, either for their sentimental value or because they might be used to make something; or maybe they were just nice to look at and handle. Thus the box contained many souvenir pieces, and I remembered where and when nearly every one had been picked up. When the voyage was resumed, some of the choice pieces were reloaded and carried on to the final port.

The river was still rising, so slowly that one could hardly notice a change, but this condition allowed us to pull the boat close in to the bank. Our landing was an open space sloping up to the higher level of the cornfield, surrounded by trees, one a tall pecan from whose exposed roots the dogs at once routed out the polecat who lived there.

The gangplank lay between the stumps of two gigantic cottonwoods which had long ago been cut for timber. On cleaning up the ground I unearthed various relics—scraps of iron, brickbats, rusty remains of tools and utensils, broken crockery, bits of tar—testifying to the life that once went on in the shade of the cottonwoods, and what work was done there. The skeleton of a Model T Ford came to light, and in making garden most of its parts were found—hub caps, steering wheel, springs of cushions, mud guards, axles—everything but the engine, which might have been installed in a boat or used as net anchors. The rusty iron brought forth as many speculations as Yorick's skull—how and why the automobile ever got there, what its use was, most of all how it was possible for five people at once to ride on that small, light frame. Such a simple, honest piece of machinery at that, so cleverly made.

Part of our dooryard was left as a space for woodcutting and other work, and for hanging up clothes on washday. The rest was put into early garden. It was a good spot, protected, the soil rich. Here we planted the seeds which our foresight had led us to buy way back at Vicksburg; or perhaps it was rather that we could not resist the seed store there. The season was almost too late for peas—English peas, Tom called them—and potatoes, in that climate. Nevertheless we planted some on the upper level, at the base of the bluff where the Johnson grass was not so thick. In working the ground, we found why this grass is so hard to eradicate: its deep roots are tender and break into sections which at once begin to grow into new plants.

We thought it best to buy new seed potatoes, though some of our Cumberland River crop remained. Parsnips and carrots had lasted until this time, also; and sweet potatoes, which had kept so well in the hold that not one was lost. To get the seed potatoes, another trip to Natchez was made with Alfred. On that same day, we mailed to Richmond the thirty small watercolor sketches selected from those made while coming down the river. These would be shown with the paintings already sent from Helena.

Alfred came into the bayou on every down trip and no doubt he enjoyed the halfway stop. Some of his family were likely to be with him on nice days, often his wife and two boys, one of whom, though an infant, was a second Alfred, burly and energetic. Alfred was so big that his clothes, even his hunter's cap, always looked too small for him; yet he had an athlete's grace and agility. It was a pleasure to watch him handling his boat or the big nets with swift, decisive motion. Nothing slow or slack about any of the Smiths, no drawl in their speech. Mr. Smith was a wiry old man who looked like a daguerreotype. He had originated in the Ohio valley, perhaps Illinois, like so many river people on the Lower Mississippi, drifting farther and farther down, never to return. His wife had not been raised on a boat; indeed the old man joked about what a landlubber she had been when he first saw her, a young lady, back in Louisiana some place. One could hardly believe this of her now, she was so thoroughly of the river, helping Alfred daily with the fishing, and running a little motor scow of her own. At one time the Smiths had been fish buyers, and Alfred's mother liked to tell how for a while she had carried on the trade alone, making long boat trips up and down the river, dealing with the fishermen on the way.

A week or two might pass in which we saw no one but the Smiths and Tom, who came down once in a while to work on the sunken road, making ready to plant the field below it. Even the lamplighter no longer passed by, having altered his course to the other shore when the Magnolia Bluff light was moved downstream a way and a new light set up across the river. There were a few rare visitors like George Inman who had a fish market in Natchez. He made a weekly trip up the river, to buy fish, in his fast scow which he drove like a racing boat. Though he seldom stopped, it was good to know we could flag him down if necessary. Ed Wilkinson, whose logging camp on the old bendway was closed down during the high water, came to see us; and Willy Fitt from Natchez set out some lines in the bayou, an old fishing ground of his.

We tried fishing in the local manner, tying short lines from one branch to another among the trees in the bayou and backwater, baiting with cut shad which Alfred gave us. No results at first, but the catfish began to bite when the water became warm and we caught some fine ones. It was a novel way to fish, paddling the johnboat back into the woods around logs and vines, with the sweet fragrance of wild grape blossoms in the air. Approaching the line, you might see one of the branches to which it was tied swaying back and forth as a big one struggled to get loose. In this shallow water we caught one blue cat that weighed twenty-two pounds. This fish we traded to Alfred for buffalo, a much cheaper fish, which we canned. Though considered a more desirable fish than carp, the canned buffalo had not as fine a flavor as the Cumberland River carp we had processed at Bizzle's Bluff.

Poke was canned, too, after some hesitation, for considerable old stock remained. It was well that we did, for the canned poke came into its own much later in the swamps and prairies of southwest Louisiana, where no fresh vegetables were to be had.

Since the dogs had little success, as far as we were concerned, with their hunting, we rarely had fresh meat. We caught some turtles on our lines, and after Alfred had taught us how to prepare them, we learned how good fried turtle is. Tom brought us part of a young goat he had butchered, in return for the fish we were giving him. Tom and Rosy were most generous and thoughtful. She would send down a quart of milk, or perhaps five eggs with a warning that they were from a nest the hen had hidden away. One time Tom brought us a chicken, suggesting that we feed it two or three days before killing it.

In these first weeks, we systematically explored the vicinity, that is, as much as could be penetrated. Away from the watercourses and trails there was a jungle growth through which one could hardly make his way. I never saw so many vines, and one steep ravine succeeded another. On the high water our johnboat would take us far up the bayou into the hills, into flooded ravines among great sycamore and magnolia trees. The bayou to the north of us was called Green's Bayou. There we found a more open country since cattle wandered about and kept the paths open. Still farther north was a cypress swamp where white spiderlike lilies bloomed. We walked back to Pine Ridge one fine day, eating our lunch along the road. Dogwood bloomed everywhere, and spreading bushes of wild rose having large white flowers without fragrance. The air was dry, scented with pine, and reminded us of southern mountains. We had a glimpse of some deer on this trip, which furnished great excitement for the dogs. Tom said he often saw deer in the woods, and that a bobcat prowled about. He called it a "pant" for panther. Many of his words he thus made into one syllable, like "by" for bayou—this word, by the way, is pronounced by'-o.

These active and varied days moved quickly on, and it was full summer, though still spring by our Kentucky calendar. The garden had been expanded—another section in the upper field planted in potatoes and peanuts and sugar melons. The soil, of a red color, was easily worked, being soft as flour. There is a name for this dirt—"loess"—and they say it is wind-borne, that the Natchez bluff was formed in this way. Under the bank at our landing was a black soil, and no Johnson grass—Tom said it does not grow on land which is often flooded. All available space there was planted: okra—the seed from old stalks at Greenville—sweet corn, Anna's herb garden, sweet peppers, and red peppers requested by Alfred. Tomato plants were set out early in April.

About the middle of April the long, slow rise of the river, begun the first of the year, when we were at Memphis, came to a stand. It might rise even higher in May, June, or July, but now it began to ebb, and our landing between the big stumps had to be vacated. It had been a secure harbor. Even a terrific rainstorm had failed to make a flow of water in the bayou. This rain had come in the evening and, happening to look out of the window, I saw not water but a surface solid as land. Even though the runout had not reached us, it had pushed out all the drift, which covered the water around the boat completely. There was no danger, but we were made uneasy in the dark silence after the rain had ceased by the roar of water up the hollow, the crash of falling trees, and of land sliding into the water. I was able to clear a path to the river by sweeping the surface of the water with a line tied to the johnboat. I made a boom of long trees fastened end to end to hold back the drift, which after a while dispersed into the backwater.

By the end of April we had moved down toward the mouth of the bayou, though still in protected water. The river was in plain view now, not seen through the trees as it was from our first landing—a view which had been nearly closed off by the expanding leaves. From our new position the Louisiana shore still seemed a long way off, but the booming sound made by great chunks of it falling into the river could be plainly heard. The first crossing of the river was soon made, to see about dewberries. They were beginning to ripen, and Mrs. Smith said

301

that they grew over there in abundance. The crossing of that wide, swift river in a rowboat was not to be lightly undertaken. When we had rowed so far out that our houseboat looked even smaller than it did from across the Ohio at Payne Hollow, there was a wide river ahead still to be crossed. The trees which had appeared so small loomed up into a tall forest of cottonwood, gum, pecan, and oak. By the time a landing was made, we had drifted a mile downstream. To return, we had to row two miles up against swift water along the uneven shore to a point from which a crossing was made, right into the mouth of Bisland Bayou. Few ripe dewberries were found on the other side, few bushes, in fact; so it was more a voyage of discovery.

With the lower water, the catfish had left the woods, so Alfred said. He set out twelve nets along our shore, which was supposed to be a good fishing ground. As he would not have left them unwatched so far from home, had we not been there, we felt that at last we were of some use. He picked out the swiftest places for his nets, just below a small point of land if possible. First he tied a three-eighths-inch line to a tree on shore. This was the tail line of the net, a hundred feet long, with a heavy iron weight about twenty feet from the net, so that the current would not swing it in toward shore. The current, however, kept the net stretched out and on the bottom. To raise it, Alfred ran his boat in to the bank, and cast a grappling hook out over the net, or rather over the tail line between net and weight. When this was caught, he pulled the boat over it, and raised the line, then the net, working the boat alongside it; the net was rolled over inboard, a feat of strength and balance.

A net with a four-foot front was as large as could be handled in the current. The fishermen used larger nets in the still water of the woods. These were set out facing each other, perhaps fifty feet apart. Between them, leading to the center of each net, was a fence of twine netting, kept vertical by floats and sinkers. This was called a lead, and the fish swimming against it were diverted into the nets.

Every other day, ordinarily, is "raise day," and it might seem an easy method of fishing. The nets, however, always need attention: they must be moved in or out, set in a new place, the holes made by snags and gar fish mended. Tarring and repairing are continuous jobs, and

the fisherman is always building new nets. He, or his wife, or the old people, usually do the netting, a winter occupation. The old-timers made their own net hoops, but nowadays they are usually bought. Most net hoops, handmade of white oak, seem to come from a place in Arkansas. We have seen a picture calendar from the hoop-maker hanging in a fisherman's boat.

Net, boat, tarring vat and other necessary equipment run into quite an investment. Operating overhead is not a little. The fisherman's return must be considerable to cover all this and losses from accident, wearing out of boats and nets, and to carry him over times of poor fishing. Still it takes more than a good outfit and hard work to be a first-class fisherman: he must know how. It is an art handed down from father to son, usually, and to this must be added long experience and a real feeling for it. With all this, plus good luck, and a certain amount of thrift, a fisherman makes a good living.

We had a chance to try some net fishing of our own. Tom brought down two nets which had never been used. Stowed away in his barn, they had been damaged badly by rats, but Tom thought we might make something of them. Anna undertook to reweave the nets, which meant knitting half of one of them anew, and filling in large and numerous holes in the other. All neatly done, of course, for could not Anna knit a new heel into a wool sock?

I set about making two sets of net hoops, one of white oak and another of pecan. I picked out the trees, not too large, with the longest trunk and straightest grain I could find, cut them down, and split the logs into sections. I rived strips out of these, using the froe which Powell had given us at Payne Hollow. Next step was to dress the strips to size, about three-quarters of an inch thick, a little wider. This was done with a drawknife, working at a rude bench of planks set up on one of the cottonwood stumps at our old landing. The first hoop was four feet in diameter, the six others decreasing so that all nested together. A four-foot hoop requires a strip nearly thirteen feet long, next to impossible to get in one piece, so it was made of three sections spliced together. This was all nice work, but much more difficult than it sounds. The next step was to hang the nets, that is, lace them to the hoops. Then they were stretched out on the bank and I crawled inside to form the throats—no job for a fat man. Alfred tarred the nets for us.

As soon as the water dropped away, we began clearing on the lower level for another patch of garden. Here was a surprise for us: the ground which we had expected to be soft and mellow, was a tough clay which dried in the sun like brick. It was even worse than the made ground along the Cumberland River. The edge along the bayou was easier to work; there we planted sweet potatoes, cucumbers, and some melons. The rest Tom called buckshot ground and gave us little encouragement. About all we could do was make holes and set out tomato plants, plant a few seeds experimentally, and hope for the best.

From this new garden a path was cut through the vines and brush to our landing at the mouth of the bayou. We made the path very wide so as not to be ambushed by any snakes. Moccasins were common in the woods, and both the Smiths and Tom had warned us of rattle-snakes. We saw none of these the whole summer, but became well acquainted with the moccasins. There is a harmless water snake which resembles the moccasin so closely that it is almost necessary to have the specimen in your hand to be sure. We were always careful in the woods; not so Skipper, who attacked and usually killed every snake she saw. Twice during the summer she was bitten on the face and neck by moccasins, and these parts swelled to enormous size. She be-came quite well and normal after a day or two of misery, during which time we could hardly keep from laughing at her comical appearance. She did not look like Skipper at all, but like some new breed of dog.

Now befell a most unexpected mischance which broke up, for a time, our whole pattern of living. One would expect a ruptured appendix to cause more disturbance than it did, happening six miles from a doctor, with no way to get to him except in a rowboat. Had we known that this was what ailed me, our course of action would have been different. As it was, I waited two days, hoping for some improvement in my condition.

It was midafternoon when I decided to go to a doctor. This meant a trip to Natchez. We scanned the empty river from the top of the bank like castaways, looking for a passing boat though there was little hope of seeing a fisherman on his way to Natchez at that time of day. The sound of a motor was heard from down the river. We hoped it was Willy Fitt coming up to bait his line just below the bayou. It turned out to be the Truits, homeward bound to Coles Creek with groceries and ice. They said Willy was dipping for shad a mile downstream. Intending to get him to take me in to Natchez, I went off down the river in the johnboat. Before reaching Willy's boat, however, I was dismayed to see it crossing over to the Louisiana side. Already too far from Bisland Bayou to row back, weak as I was, I went on alone, drifting and rowing five miles to the sawmill landing at the upper end of Natchez. Here the Negro watchman was a Good Samaritan, giving me a drink of water and calling a taxi.

When at last I found a doctor, he could not tell just what was the matter, but advised me to remain in town that night and see him again in the morning. A message which I tried to send to Anna by means of George Inman was never delivered, through no fault of George's. Thus Anna had to spend the night alone, not knowing what had become of me. She did not worry, realizing that I might not have been able to find anyone that evening to bring me back up the river. She prepared for an uncertain tomorrow by a good night's sleep. In the evening and early morning she set out the two hundred sweet potato plants which, as my last act, I had temporarily heeled in. When George Inman came for her next morning with the news that I had been taken to the hospital in the night, she was ready to go with him. They arrived after the operation was over. Groggy as I was, I remember how their river

305

appearance impressed me. Its mark was on all of us. I had gone to the hospital in my fishing clothes.

After we had adjusted ourselves to this completely new environment our stay in the hospital became almost a holiday. A cot was set up for Anna in my large room. Our windows looked out on the lawns and garden surrounding an old plantation house where magnolia trees were opening their great white flowers and the mockingbirds sang through the night. This hospital had not the air of tenseness and solemnity which pervaded the hushed corridors where I had occasionally visited friends. There was talk and laughter; everyone was friendly, relaxed. It was a fine place for reading. The little Natchez library furnished the books which Anna read aloud while I looked out of the windows. What a treasure *Pride and Prejudice* was, a book we had never appreciated before.

On the second day, Anna had gone up the river with George Inman on his regular trip, stopping at our boat while he went to Coles Creek and back. Luckily both Alfred and Tom came down to the boat, and they promised to feed the dogs. Skipper was raising her seventh litter of pups at the time, and to her credit not one of them fell off the deck, or if he did, a rescue was effected.

Alfred came to see us at the hospital and reported that all was well, plenty of water under the boat though the river was falling. Even so, we were relieved to get back home before the boat had to be moved into deeper water, and before the June rains began. The return trip was a little unusual for the convalescent, who had to sit upright on a hard seat in Alfred's vibrating motorboat. A stop was made at George Inman's for our johnboat, another at the sawmill for the oars. Farther on a mired cow was passed, and Anna and I waited on shore while Alfred hunted up the owner.

On our return to Bisland Bayou we conducted ourselves very much as if no hospital sojourn had intervened. I found I could be quite active without becoming tired. Our first job was to move the boat into deeper water at the very mouth of the bayou. Here it was almost like being out on the river, a long vista up and down, and a fresh breeze which sometimes rolled waves into our harbor. On several days we picked dewberries along the sandy ridge near the river, enough to can many quarts after eating all we wanted. Of course there was much to do in the garden where the weeds had flourished during our absence. We worked there together in the early morning, hoeing, breaking new ground, and planting. Anna often kept at it after I had gone back to the boat.

All went well for twelve days. Then I developed another fever. A second time I went to the doctor alone. He sent me back to the hospital at once. No doubt the previous treatment had not entirely cleared up the infection, and my activity caused it to break out again. On this day, luckily, one of the fishing boats was at Natchez to take the message and the johnboat back to Bisland Bayou. Anna came in next morning, and we were soon at home in the now familiar surroundings.

This return to the hospital was a hard dose to take, at first. We were cheered by the warm welcome from our friends on the hospital staff; and another armful of books from the library, one of which was Darwin's *Cruise of the Beagle,* consoled us for having to stay indoors. The five days passed quickly enough. Desirous of turning them to account by producing something positive, some fruit which would never have ripened in ordinary times, I began the writing of this narrative of our river life. I had no hopes of any reward other than to be able to say, "That stretch in the hospital was good for something, after all."

The writing continued after our return to the boat, for the doctor's orders were to rest in bed for a week. I can't say that I did this, quite, but at least I never left the boat during that time. It was a most strange existence for both of us. Usually on the go from daybreak until dark, I now lay around on the deck like the traditional shantyboater is supposed to. Anna, besides caring for me and doing the housework and cooking, had to rustle up her own firewood since the reserve was all used up. She did this very handily, sawing blocks and splitting them with a hatchet. Even with all this to do, she set about singlehanded to reclaim the garden which was overrun with weeds and burning up in the dry and hot weather. Late in the morning Anna would return, red-faced and weary, from her bout with the weeds. At least I could shell out the lima beans which we were having then nearly every day.

I also managed to snag a few catfish from my deck chair, and catch shrimp in the net.

After a week I seemed to be perfectly well again, but continued to run at a slow bell for some time. The burning heat of the sun made it almost necessary for anyone to rest in the shade during the hottest part of the day. In the long, still afternoons we retired to a tiny clearing in a willow thicket on top of the sandy bank, where the sun never penetrated. Except at the top, the tall, close-growing saplings were bare of leaves, and the air circulated freely through them. Here we read and wrote until the sun lost some of its power. These days set the pattern for the rest of the summer. Our work was done in the cool and shady morning. After a bath, or swim, and dinner, always on deck, we remained quiet like the birds in the thick covert.

I was soon able to do my chores again and a share of the garden work. That we had any garden at all was due to Anna's patient and determined attack on what had seemed a hopeless mess. After she had weeded those crops which had thus far survived the drought, heat, and neglect, it looked like we might have something of a garden after all. There were beautiful tomatoes ripening, a full month earlier than we had ever expected them in Kentucky. The okra, bush limas, corn and peppers were doing well. There was plenty of collards and mustard greens. The sweet potatoes and peanuts showed great promise. There had been nice snap beans—the only ones we were to have that summer —when we were not there to enjoy them. Most of the early stuff, peas, cabbage, beets, carrots and lettuce, planted too late, never came to maturity. The potato vines withered early. We soon learned that few vegetables could stand the Natchez summer. Our later plantings of green beans, lettuce, corn and lima beans had no chance against the sun. Even the sunflowers did poorly. We had expected to find them everywhere in the south, but the ones we did raise at Natchez were looked upon as curiosities by the natives. The early cucumbers and melons did fairly well. We were lucky to have tomatoes all summer, though none to can.

There were some vegetables, however, which seemed to thrive in the heat. One was field peas. Of the many varieties, we planted black eye and crowder peas. Tom brought us some of his own seed, white lady peas of delicate flavor, and an earlier, darker kind which he called gentleman peas. They all prospered, and, with okra, were our mainstay for the summer. The okra, planted in the rich soil under the bank, grew as tall and sturdy as young trees. At the end of summer, the twelve-foot stalks had to be bent over to reach the pods at the top. We had a northern prejudice against okra, but when Anna learned from Rosy how to cook it properly—fried in butter even when used in gumbo —we became very fond of it. Well that we did, for it came on so fast that it must be picked nearly every day.

The peppers were another bright spot in the garden. Planted around the old stumps, they grew shoulder high and bore heavily. We used only the sweet green ones; the red peppers were for Alfred. In the end he could not keep up with them, and others had a share.

The prodigy of the garden, however, was the sweet basil. The single row in the herb garden crowded out everything else. Cut down, it sprouted again more abundantly. Plants pulled up and thrown away took new root. It sprang up on the riverbank, and bushels of the fragrant stuff went to waste. Another herb which did well was fennel which Anna used in many salads and cooked dishes. Our customary zinnias, planted from seed we had saved from the year before, flourished here as well as at Bizzle's Bluff and Payne Hollow.

On the whole, the Natchez garden did not come up to our previous ones, for reasons evident. Sometimes when we went to town and saw the rows of huge watermelons brought in by the Mississippi and Louisiana farmers, and thought of the care and effort our few precious ones had cost us, we wondered if it would not be better to buy them and all our vegetables from the store. Yet when we entered our garden again it was all so exciting, the little encouragement we had from some crop or other such a joy, and our dinners of fresh vegetables, potatoes and fish, all of our own procuring, so satisfactory, that we would not change our way for the other, even if a life in town did not incur its tremendous price.

In the beginning of the season Tom had said, "I hope us has a good crop year." In his riverbank farming, however, Tom's hopes were not realized. He had early put the sunken road in fine shape with a ditch on each side to carry off the rain water. He had brought down a borrowed tractor and disked the whole long field until not a spear of Johnson grass remained above ground. All this he planted in corn and soybeans, both in the same rows. His road survived the spring rains up to the cloudburst which had pushed the driftwood out of the upper bayou. After that his road looked more like a wild ravine choked with fallen trees. Before he could get down again the Johnson grass had sprouted, and soon it was a solid field of waving green, no corn to be seen. Even Tom was discouraged and long-faced. He managed to clear the road enough to bring his mules down. Breaking up a small part of the field he planted corn again. This did better; he and Rosy hoed it once or twice, and it made some corn late in the fall. For some reason they neglected to harvest it, and the 'coons took the greater part.

We were often puzzled by Tom's erratic motives and procedures. He was our good friend, however, and always welcome at the boat. We liked to hear him talk, though his involved narratives were hard to follow. He himself was often so amused by them that his laughter made the story even more unintelligible. Then his face became, in a flash, grave and determined, the impish wildness gone from his eyes and voice. Tom and Rosy taught us much—about the country, about gardening, about the woods and snakes, about southern cooking, and, most valuable, something about the make-up of the Negro. This we learned indirectly, but on other matters, realizing our ignorance, they did not hesitate to tell us the proper way to do things. Anna wisely followed Rosy's advice in the cooking of new foods, like gar. This fish is usually scorned, but when boiled a long time, as Rosy recommended, and then baked with the proper tomato sauce, it is very good and we had it often.

One day I found a strange fruit, like a small plum or a large grape, under an elm tree. I asked Tom about it. He said it was a muscadine, and showed me the vine high in the elm. I found more in the woods, ripening always in tall trees. We canned some of them to take with us. The vine peach, or as Tom called it, "plumgranate," was another wild fruit new to us. It ripened late in the sandy fields, about the size and color of a small yellow tomato, and could be made into a thick preserve. Ripe figs were also unknown to us before this summer. These untasted flavors, the muscadine especially with its wild tang, gave an

aura of strangeness to this country. We felt, in a very small way, like the discoverers of a new continent who taste unheard-of and exotic fruits, and learn their names from the aborigines. We had lost out on the first crop of our misshapen fig tree, which grew almost inside of a larger hackberry, but when it put forth another harvest, late in July, we gathered in every fig. The canned figs went a long way with us.

There was an abundance of dewberries and elderberries in our range. The dewberry season was a long one, lasting all through May and June, because the vines which had been under water early in the season ripened long after those on higher ground. They were not quite like the Kentucky dewberries. We have noticed much variation in both blackberries and dewberries growing in different parts of the country, or in different soils.

Elderberries are usually passed up, but since it was the only fruit we had in the late summer, Anna found many uses for them. She made elderberry muffins and elderberry cobbler which is even better than pie. They are good cooked with apples. We canned them and made them into juice for the winter. Of other fruits there were only a few wild grapes, pawpaws and persimmons. Not a long list compared with the plentiful harvest of other summers, but all that we really missed were apples.

The summer rains did not come until mid-July when storm after storm rolled over us and we were made uneasy by the threat of wind. The rains kept the river up and we were able to stay inside the bayou until August. Then the river began to fall. The Engineers made soundings, put out red buoys to mark the shoal water. Sandbars appeared even in midstream; these were called by fishermen, the Middle Ground. To everyone's surprise, however, there was no sandbar along the shore below the Coles Creek bar. Off our bayou was deep water where last year the sandbar had extended far out. When the water at last drained from the bayou we had only to move the boat around the point. It was a short distance, but a significant change. The Mississippi River shanty-boaters never lay out in the open. After our long stay in the sheltered bayou we were very conscious of this new exposure to wind and current, but we became accustomed to it, and no disaster befell.

How different it all was from our first landing there. Only the velocity and color of the water were unchanged; it never cleared or slacked its pace. The banks which were under water in the early spring, and the willow whose branches we had barely cleared when entering the bayou, now rose high above us. The bayou had become a dark tunnel with high walls of clay and a roof of heavy foliage, lit up only by the last level rays of the sun which transformed it into a cavern of gold.

The spring was accessible now, and its copious waters most welcome in the dry heat of late summer. It never failed nor became muddy. An even larger spring poured forth from under the bluff farther down the river, a stream of water like a small creek flowing out beneath a layer of living rock. This was the only rock I found on those sandy shores.

Up to this time we had used rain water caught from our roof and stored in jugs and various containers. None of the native river people made an effort to get any water other than that of the Mississippi River which they drank straight, without any question. It shocked us to see the Smiths dip water from alongside the boat to give the baby a drink. It never seemed to hurt any of them, and on occasion I drank river water myself. It was very handy when hot from rowing to lean over the side of the boat and drink. The water, to my surprise, tasted like chemically treated city water. Perhaps that is the natural flavor of river water.

The fishermen complained of the poor season. They take up their nets and depend on line fishing in the low water of summer. Their lines are rigged according to the water they are fishing in. The art lies in this placing of the right kind of line, and in using the right kind of bait.

One of their methods of fishing was called blocking. It was Ohio River jugging on a grand scale. The fisherman sets adrift in midstream fifty or seventy-five blocks, which might be tin cans, jugs, or pieces of lightweight cypress root, each with a short piece of line and a single baited hook attached. He drifts along in his boat, watching all the blocks. When a fish takes one of them he chases after it. They caught some big ones in this way, but often drifted for miles without a strike.

There was one old man who lived alone in a little boat at a place up the river called Lyjohn. We made this out to be the L'Argent on our charts. Mr. Warner was accounted the best line fisherman on that part of the river. He had nothing but a small outboard johnboat but he caught more fish than the rest did with their highpowered equipment. He sent his fish in to market by Alfred, who became bored with explaining, when we saw the fine catfish in his boat, that they were Mr. Warner's. The old man made a trip to town once in a while, and always stopped at our boat on the way back. This was not entirely to see us, but to refill his motor which always ran dry at that point. He had begun his life on a farm in Iowa, and knocked about over much of the world, it seems, before settling down on the river as a fisherman.

Our own fishing was both good and bad. Sometimes we had so many fish that Alfred took them to market for us, and often our box was empty. We fished only a few short lines along the bank, called drop lines. They had a light weight at the end, which was raised when running the line; it would be impossible to keep a fixed trot line across that current. When tracing the drop line, you keep the boat at an angle to the current which swings it out into the river like a kite on a string. When there were no fish or turtle, we could depend on shrimp. The shrimp were caught in a round, shallow net which you raised whenever you thought of it. We also used a floating trap, made

313

of a wooden box with an inverted V bottom. At the top of the V was a slot into which the shrimp went to get at the bait. It was well that shrimp were easy to catch, for they were small and tedious to shell out. Shrimp gumbo with our own okra and tomatoes, and shrimp salad, we thought delicious food. Like the figs and muscadines, the shrimp made the Ohio River seem a long way off.

Alfred made a trip to Natchez every Saturday whether he had any fish or not, and he always stopped for us. We went along about every other week. In town, as a respite from the hot streets, we often went into the little park behind the cathedral. With crackers and cheese and cold milk for refreshment, and a packet of new mail to read, we lingered there until it was time to meet the Smiths. The rendezvous of all the fishermen was the C & G Grocery. We had a common interest with Elmer, the suave proprietor, for he, too, had drifted to Natchez in a houseboat from the Cumberland River. When everyone's groceries were bought, they were loaded into the grocery truck in which we all rode to the landing, stopping on the way for Alfred's ice. Sometimes Anna and I walked down to the river ahead of time to read in the shade, or chat with Louise in her tiny store at the end of the street. She said once that when she first saw us she thought we were poor folks, but now she knew better. We wondered what made her change her opinion. We were puzzled, too, by her insistence that my picture was in the newspaper every night. Perhaps I resembled some writer whose photo appeared with his daily column. At last Alfred's boat was loaded and we were homeward bound on the cool river. We picked out the familiar landmarks ahead in our eagerness to get back to our quiet haven. Often, however, our attention was held by the spectacle of sunset over the Louisiana shore. Its sunsets alone should make the Mississippi famous.

With the waning of summer and its fiery heat we stirred about more and often left our caves and shady groves to make longer excursions. One Sunday we rowed up to visit the Smiths. The first stop was made at the Truits' boat which was then in a small cove at the foot of Coles Creek bar. We were surprised at their menagerie—birds roosted in the cabin, a tame dove for one, and little eyes peeked out of dark corners. Even a stray rat or mouse was tolerated, almost welcomed. Ducks swam about the boat, and on shore barnyard fowl made themselves at home, and three small pigs. The Truits had once lived in Cairo, had built their boat at that place and had some notion of going back up the river in hope of finding better fishing. This was a startling idea to us who had been told all the way down the river that the best fishing grounds lay ahead.

When we had drifted past Coles Creek in the spring there was more water than land. Now, as we found when we pursued our way up-stream from the Truits', a mere trickle of water came out of the dry creek bed, before which lay a vast sandbar. As we slowly encircled its edge the dogs forayed about on shore, swimming across the inlets and chasing flocks of "sandbar gulls."

The harbor of the Smith clan was a narrow slough between the sand-bar and the shore. It was like the street of some watery city, the three large houseboats moored in a line, children playing about, dogs, chickens on shore, piles of gear and plunder, everything but fences and pavements. We had a good visit with them, were especially pleased to listen to the old man's river lore. Also, we had a chance to inspect the boats under construction, for the Smiths turn boatbuilders in the slack fishing season of late summer. There was a large new cabin scow built for the landowner who had a ranch on the island. Alfred was building

a new launch for himself, with a model bow, and a cabin, since he often had to make the long trip to Natchez in bad weather. During the summer, he had replaced in his johnboat the simple marine engine we admired so much with a brand-new automobile engine. Since this engine was too powerful for the old hull, he planned to install it in the new boat. These men were good designers, workmen, and mechanicians, with an honest love for a good engine.

There was no resemblance here to the shiftless hand-to-mouth river rat so often pictured. The Smiths' standard of living was high—fresh meat and milk, ice, and store bread, a gasoline-powered washing machine. Their roomy boats were furnished much like town houses. No bartering or bank trade in fish, no gardening, all so common on the Ohio among river people. It was easy to understand this—no one lived near them on the riverbank, garden land was not always available and gardening not so easy in that climate. Anyway, fishing was more profitable, like the town man's job.

The Truits, however, had a garden on shares with a Negro farmer. They picked cotton when fishing did not pay, and their raising of pigs is an idea we might try for ourselves.

After glimpses such as these into other households, we looked at our own more critically. In comparison it seemed bare and meager. Even Tom and Rosy had an electric refrigerator and an oil stove. Yet we were in no way roughing it—our guests will vouch for that. Surely refinement of living does not consist in gadgets and machinery, but in such elements as leisure, contentment, lack of confusion, small niceties.

Anna cooked on a wood stove. The two were in rapport, and turned

316

out the best of food. It was a hot job, but Anna wore the most comfortable clothing, and there was the river in which to cool off. We ate our dinner on the shady deck, and by the time the meal was ended, with some reading together, the almost unfailing river breeze through the big windows had cooled off the cabin.

As for refrigeration, there was little to keep cool, with vegetables brought from the garden as needed, fish and shrimp fresh from the river. Not even milk this summer, except for a few jugs of it which Tom brought down when his cow was fresh. Canned milk and especially powdered milk, our great discovery that summer, were just as satisfactory as store milk.

I do not mean that our way was better, and do not recommend it. To most, it would mean deprivation. To us it had an honorable simplicity and independence. We were living as we desired, and put out less than most, to get what we wanted.

One September day we were surprised to see Old Jasper rowing up past our windows in his battered skiff with a load of blocks to fish on the way back. If he could row up from Natchez, why couldn't we? The upstream trip was found to be not so difficult as anticipated, though at some points along the bluff where the bank was scoured to the bone by wind and current we could barely inch our way past. These trips under our own power took away the feeling of dependence on others, even though we continued to ride now and then with the cheerful and willing Alfred. The greatest reward, however, was an understanding of that section of the river never achieved in our skimming motorboat rides.

There had been one disappointment this summer—no music together. It must be put aside when I was out of action, and a proposed visit at that time by Warren and Patricia Staebler, the other half of our string quartet, had to be canceled. In the heat and dampness of summer all our instruments had come partly unglued. I now undertook to repair the viola and violin; the 'cello could still be played, though the top was loose in two places. Finding no cabinet maker's glue in Natchez, we had Frank send us some from New York. I made clamps of bolts with two small blocks of wood on each one. The tops and backs of both instruments were loose in several places; also the fingerboard of the viola and the neck of the violin. When all was made ready, however, the actual gluing was not difficult.

Later we tackled the 'cello, with longer clamps. All the instruments remained perfectly tight, having adjusted themselves to the new climatic conditions. We ourselves, no doubt, went through a similar period of adjustment, for this summer was different in so many ways from those on the Ohio and Cumberland.

The solitude of the place did not bother us; we can take that in unlimited quantities. But we did miss the visits of our regular guests of other years. A few of them were able to make the long trip to Natchez. First came Nell, Anna's sister, who reversed the customary summer migration by coming south from Michigan. It happened that the two weeks she spent with us were rather cool with frequent rain. For Nell, we used Alfred's transportation.

Joe and Naomi were not so lucky when they came. They had written to us, but the letter still lay in the post office when they arrived. Joe spent two or three days trying to get out to our boat, and stirred up the whole town in his behalf. None of the fishermen happened to come in, but at last one of the Natchez amateur boatmen brought our persistent friends out to Bisland Bayou. The owner of this boat—he was its builder, too, a protégé of Bill Smith—became a new friend whom we often saw during the remainder of our stay.

Frank made it again this summer but only for a brief visit. He and Frances, Uncle Jack, and a friend, Mrs. Mitchell, came through Natchez on their way home from a long motor trip through the west. We went in to meet them, leaving early in the johnboat and having a drifting breakfast on the way. The trip out to the boat would have been too much for Uncle Jack, but the rest of them were eager to come. We had not been able to get word to Alfred; so it was Willy Fitt who towed us out. It was a slow trip in his slow boat, our johnboat loaded with passengers trailing behind. The ladies returned to Natchez that evening with Willy, but Frank stayed on with us for two days.

Before we left there happened an unexpected incursion of strangers into Bisland Bayou proving it to be not so isolated and forgotten as we thought. They were oil prospectors whose trails, marked with streamers of colored paper, lead into the most inaccessible places. We had con-

318

sidered the sunken road impassable except for a jolt wagon, but these boys drove ten trucks down into Tom's field and back up again. First came two young surveyors in a jeep. I found them pondering over an old government high-water gauge, trying to make its elevation tally with their own figures. They were relieved when I told them that the gauge, having fallen down, had been set up at random as a mark by which we could check the rise and fall of the river. Soon after, the drillers came with two trucks, and two tank trucks. Next day the dynamiters' four trucks shot the holes, and then the casings were pulled out by another crew—all done with the precision teamwork of a trained squad.

We have never learned whether oil was discovered there or not. Probably not, and the shores remain quiet and unspoiled. They may have fallen into an even deeper oblivion. The road to Pine Ridge has perhaps been washed out, the field abandoned, the fruit of the fig tree harvested only by the birds. Perhaps time has been a blank since we wrote our brief chapter in the annals of Bisland Bayou. The next will be—who knows and when?

11

Making ready to leave Bisland Bayou was a simple matter compared with our involved departures from Brent, Payne Hollow, and the Cumberland: all summer we had kept our shore base in hand, ready to move away if that station should become untenable in low water; harvesting the garden did not take long—we were thankful that it lasted over the summer; there was no round of farewells to make, since our circle of friends had grown no larger in the nine months we had lived there.

However, we lingered until late in the fall, through weeks of serene weather. Perhaps we did not like to leave the garden as long as it was producing okra, field peas, collards, and a few tomatoes. There was an abundance of fish, too, most of them caught in our net. Some were big spike-nose and alligator gars. The real reason for our delay, I think, was the fact that this would be our last stretch of drifting on the

Mississippi. From Natchez to the Gulf was little more than half the distance we had drifted down the Mississippi in the previous winter.

Our remaining at Bisland Bayou through the autumn gave us a chance to lay in a large store of pecans. Excursions after nuts took us up and down the river, across it and back into the hills, to trees we had seen in earlier walks. Picking up the nuts wearied our backs, but it was easier than harvesting walnuts which must be hulled and dried. Pecans are ready to use, and require less storage space than the thick-shelled walnuts. We did find a few walnuts which were added to the considerable remainder of the Cumberland River crop.

When the garden harvest was in we found a larger amount of winter stores on hand than we had expected. The peanut crop was even larger than last year's. After the false peanuts had been picked out there was a good bushel to store behind the fireplace. The sweet potatoes produced well, too. Some were large, weighing up to two and a half pounds. There were also some slender ones grown from cuttings made of the earlier planted vines.

When the weather became cool a fish smoker was set up, and a quantity of smoked catfish, goo, buffalo, gar and sturgeon was pre-pared. This was an important addition to our winter supplies.

Plenty of storage space in the hold was available since there were no white potatoes to stow away. The slender crop was used up before summer was over. Our hatches were all filled, however, for in addition to our new stores, a large supply of canned vegetables and fruits re-mained from previous years.

On November first there had been a light frost, and on the twenty-second came a hard freeze. Nothing remained in the garden now but collards and a few parsnips which could be carried along. The deck load had been put aboard long since. New sweep handles were made of willow saplings, light and strong, with a good spring to them. It was December sixth when we cast off. During our long layover we had forgotten how glorious it is to be adrift. The familiar shores were newly seen, and, released from land, we again became part of the river.

Our first day's run was but a short one, to a well-known shantyboat harbor above Natchez called Jones's Hole. It was a good-sized cove, probably hollowed out and kept open by the circling waters of an eddy, at the lower end of the cut, opposite a downstream entrance to the old bendway of the river. The shores were sandy, and to the rear, behind a fringe of willows, rose sandy cliffs which had a heavy growth of pines on top. This place was handy to town—or so we considered it, after being so far out all summer—merely a half-mile row down the shore, and a walk through the willows to a road which led past the sawmill to the hilltop. The transition from river to town along this route was gradual. A colony of fishermen and timber drifters lived in the little houses under the hill. They all had boats at the landing, open scows, mostly, with inboard engines. The best-looking to our eyes was a fine old skiff which belonged to a Negro boy they called Snookums. He had rigged up a covering to protect himself from rain and sun, made of scraps of canvas and curved willow withes, resembling somewhat a covered wagon. The bank was littered with fish boxes, nets, shrimp boxes and other gear. The same sort of stuff was in the yards of the houses—a new boat under construction, abandoned hulls and old engines, net-tarring vats, and oars standing about. The sawmill was a river concern, owning a small tug and getting its logs by raft and barge. Then as we climbed the hill, the river lay below us, and we could see far upstream.

On our way to and from Natchez we often called on Mr. and Mrs. Smith, Alfred's parents. They had moved to town this fall, taking Junior with them that he might go to school—his first year. It was hard for these old people to give up the river and live even this near town, but it seemed the only solution to the problem, since Alfred wanted to keep his upriver fishing grounds. The education of their children has influenced the course of many a shantyboater's life. We liked the Smiths' new home, a little old cottage with a stone chimney on the outside, in a grove of pecan trees. The old man worked at building nets for the winter fishing, and Mrs. Smith kept her cow—not hers exactly, but one from the herd of the landowner at Coles Creek, who had allowed the Smiths to catch one of the cattle which ran loose in the woods. In return for this and other favors, Alfred watched over the owner's riverbank property and rescued cattle mired in the mud.

We made quite a long stay of it in Jones's Hole. I took advantage of the opportunity to haul the johnboat out on the sandbar, make some minor repairs, and paint it. We overhauled all gear, and re-stowed everything. To know that all was shipshape, sound, and ready gave us new confidence.

In one particular we were not as well supplied as usual. On the Ohio River it had been easy to pick up all the corn we could carry with us. Now, since comparatively little is grown on the lower Mississippi, we had to buy it from the feed store. As for wheat, this could not even be purchased. As another source of whole grain we began using hen scratch, a mixed feed for chickens, composed of cracked corn, wheat, sorghum seeds, kafir corn, and maize. This I ground into an acceptable flour.

Our sailing was postponed for various reasons until the very end of the year. Christmas was celebrated in due style. We feasted on a roast goose which Tom had brought down to us as a parting gift. Our Christmas tree was a little pine from the sandy bluff.

At last all was ready. In the early morning we towed out of our harbor, broke through the eddy, and drifted off. As the sun rose we were slipping past Natchez, almost an unknown place, for now we looked through the eyes of travelers.

Below the bridge was the railroad transfer where we had a good look at the steamer *James Y. Lockwood,* whose whistle we had often heard during the summer. A stern-wheel boat and smaller than the *Pelican* at Helena, the *Lockwood* did not carry the freight cars on board, but towed a separate track barge. Instead of the locomotive crossing the river, as it did on the *Pelican,* there was one on each side to handle the cars. The *Pelican* and the *James Y. Lockwood* were the only railroad ferryboats we saw.

As we rounded the bend at Natchez Island, all familiar landmarks were lost to sight except the blue line of the distant bluff. We could see its end, far up the curving river. "Right there is our bayou," we said; but soon it, too, had vanished.

The day was perfect for drifting, windless and sunny. The boat required little guidance, although we did have one hard pull at Ellis Cliffs to clear a barge which was loading logs. Farther down came

Glasscock Cut-off, nearly four miles long, the last of the man-made cut-offs we would go through. At its lower end, on the left bank, we pulled into a side channel, called by the sinister name of Washout, and moored the boat. It was early enough to enjoy an hour or two on the sunny shore. Across the Washout was a dense cypress swamp. Some fishermen's boats went by, and smoke rose from a shantyboat moored behind the willows across the cut-off in the old river.

We were up at the first paling of night, and cast off at daylight, with the promise of a fair morning. A long swing took us around Dead Man's Bend with only curving river in sight each way; then a sharp turn around Jackson Point, which was a low sandbar. Down the long reach to the southeast I rode on the roof where the higher elevation afforded a wider view over water and land. Through the quiet, sunny air came the sound of birds on shore, bluebird, phoebe, Carolina wren, and the spring note of a chickadee.

We had dinner while drifting around Palmetto Bend. At the point below, the current shot over against the right bank, making a series of whirls through which we drifted fast. Ahead was a long reach down to Fort Adams, the bluffs at the end showing like far-off mountains. We pulled across to the left bank, looking for Buffalo Bayou, but could not make it out on the ragged shore flatly lit by the afternoon sun.

The opening appeared before us suddenly, we pulled in behind the upper point which was clear and grassy. A fisherman's boat had berthed there before us; his nets and tarring drum still remained on shore.

Buffalo Bayou, or Buffalo River, a name which it is wide enough to claim, is a favorite harbor and fishing ground, one often mentioned to us by river people. No houseboats were to be seen there now, however, for they had all been moved upstream for the winter. It was possible to go up Buffalo River, and into Old River Lake. They are connected by a short canal which is said to have been dug in Civil War times. One can pass from Old River Lake into the Homochitto River, then go through the Washout, where we had stopped the night before, and enter the Mississippi River at a point twenty-eight miles above the mouth of the Buffalo.

We had planned to lay over a few days here, and were more pleased than not when the weather became windy and unsettled. There was much to see on the narrow bayou. Fishermen passed, and one boat stopped to raise a net over which we had nearly moored our boat. We watched the drifters putting out into the river and towing in logs. There were some chores to be done—Anna cut my hair, and I re-arranged the deck load, making everything rat proof. A rodent who had come aboard at Jones's Hole had gotten into the pecans and was bouncing them on the roof at night. We have never had more than one rat aboard at a time, but several have taken up quarters on the roof or between decks. They are wary of poison and traps, and hard to dis-lodge. As a last resort I moved everything out of its section and drove the rat overboard. Mice are frequent stowaways, but they are easy to trap.

The Smiths had operated their fish-buying boat as far down as the Buffalo, and had told us about the town of Fort Adams there. When we visited it, after rowing up the backwater and walking across the fields, we found the same storekeeper they had mentioned. He was a keen-minded and intelligent man from whom we learned much about the place. He showed us the former course of the river, and where steamboats used to land. On the top of the bluff he pointed out the site of old Fort Adams, only a trace of which remained. We could not learn when or why it had been built. The town lay at the foot of the bluff, a cluster of gray houses and roofs dwarfed by immense trees. It is often flooded, but in former years a rise high enough to reach the town was a rare occurrence. That this fact is true is proven by the number of river settlements, some of them once thriving cities, which have been abandoned because of the increasing frequency of floods. Several reasons are given, all of which put the blame on some form of man's interference with the natural course of the river.

We were pleased to see Fort Adams, having been in few Mississippi River towns of its small size. In fact, there are not many villages close to the river.

Our trip across the fields and backwaters had showed us how high the river was after its slow rise of the past six weeks. The land to which our boat was tied was merely a higher ridge along the river, and that would soon go under. To be near dry ground, and to become acquainted with the bluff, we dropped downstream a mile to Clark Creek. Here the bluff rose directly from the river. It was not the scenery one would expect along the Lower Mississippi. The winding steep-sided creek might have been in the hills of southern Indiana.

If we were to select one place on the Mississippi to go back to, it might be Clark Creek. The bluffs and ravines there were not the impenetrable jungle around Bisland Bayou. It was open among the big trees, and there were grassy slopes. The contrast of river shore and bluff increased the interest of each. From the top of the ridge one could look out over miles of flat country which, for the most part, had the appearance of virgin forest. Seen from above, the irregularity of the shoreline was striking. In the woods we found cedars and pines, and large holly trees with red berries.

The narrow valley was a winter haven for birds—winter birds and others associated by us only with summer. One rather drab bird, of which there were large flocks about, was the myrtle warbler in winter plumage, easy to identify after locating the bright yellow spot on its rump.

There were few people to be seen. A Negro cabin stood near the creek. The man who lived there tended the Fort Adams light, which shone above us at night like an unmoving golden star. Farther off, an old fellow lived alone in a hovel near the riverbank. His seemed a wretched existence, but when he visited us one evening, rousing the dogs by his sudden appearance in the darkness, we found that he had his interests and was not insensitive. Once as we walked through the woods a half-breed cowboy rode by on a white horse, leading on the cattle by dropping something, perhaps salt, and blowing on a horn made of an actual cow's horn. The tone of this primitive instrument was at once clear and ringing, mellow and sweet.

The weather became so mild that we could eat dinner on deck—if it wasn't raining. The frequent showers allowed us to collect enough rain water for a grand washing of clothes. We were lucky to have a fair afternoon for drying them.

That very night a heavy rainstorm occurred. I looked out and could see, in the diffused light of the full moon, the current and drift moving down the creek. It was raining hard and by the time I had dressed in rain clothes the current was so swift that it was impossible to cross the creek and loose the stern line tied there. I cast the line off at the boat which swung around close to the shore. Luckily we were on the inside of a curve and there was quiet water along the bank. By this time the creek was running out violently and "haystacks," or sharp steep waves, were rising in the fastest current. It would have been impossible to move the boat out into the river because the mouth of the creek was packed full of driftwood. We were relieved when the rain stopped shortly and the current of the creek slackened. This was the closest we ever came to a runout. We could judge from this experience how dangerous it would be if a boat were caught in a bad spot.

The weather continued warm with a gusty south wind and frequent showers. One afternoon, when it seemed to be clearing, we decided to chance it to the Mud Ditch, which the Clark Creek light tender had told us was a good harbor. Though only seven miles downstream it was an uneasy run. Storms rose about us and wind seemed likely to blow from any quarter. Mist formed on the water, a slow rain began to fall. I tried to see our boat as it might look to an observer on shore—floating on the wide, drift-carrying river, in the mist and rain, passing desolate shores and caving banks, under a dark, thundering sky.

The threatening calm continued while we crossed over to the right bank. The mist increased as darkness began to fall. We held close to

327

shore, looking for the Mud Ditch. The current picked up, the boat shot past a point, a side channel opened, and we pulled into the center of a large eddy. The Mud Ditch was larger than we expected. Between us and the upper shore the backlash of the eddy flowed out to meet the main current In the johnboat I carried a line through swift water to a tree, and we pulled the boat into a growth of small willows close to a low bank. It was a flat, dreary place and we were not cheered by the sound of rushing water which came from the mist-shrouded river.

The next day was even thicker weather. We could see nothing but fog and bare trees and the point of land past which floating logs and trees went by on the fastest current we had ever seen, to disappear in the mist downstream. The roar of water was incessant. The river was rising, too, and we wondered how long we would have a shore to tie to, even a muddy, tangled one, and what the current would be like when it came over the bank. Meanwhile we studied our maps carefully and found a queer situation. This is the most western point on the Lower Mississippi. Downstream it trends to the southeast. Formerly, before it made a cut-off here, the river swung even farther to the west, and the Mud Ditch or Lower Old River, as it is properly called, was then part of its main channel. On the western point of that old bend, the Atchafalaya, pronounced Chaff'-a-lye, takes off to the south. The Mississippi sends part of its water to the Gulf by that route—through the Mud Ditch and down the Atchafalaya. The higher the Mississippi, the more water is diverted at this point.

Also, on that old western bend, the Red River, coming in from the west, once flowed into the Mississippi. Nowadays the waters of the Red go down the Atchafalaya and never reach the Mississippi unless the Red is running out strongly when the Mississippi is very low.

If we had understood all this we would have passed by the Mud Ditch and sought a harbor farther down. It was no place for a drifter. In order to go on down the Mississippi we would now have to cross the current of water which turned off to the right and went into the Mud Ditch, bound for the Atchafalaya. I made an exploratory trip down through the rough water with the johnboat. The noise of water which we had been hearing was caused by the current striking the point of a large triangle of dead water, almost like a point of land, which separated it into two streams. It looked like we might be able to reach this still water before the current bore us into the Mud Ditch, and then row or cordelle into the main river. It was worth trying. If we could not make it we would be carried into the Mud Ditch and would have to be towed back into the Mississippi.

Had we not been determined to make this first voyage down the main river, we would have followed the easier course and descended the Atchafalaya to the Gulf. The route had its attractions, but it did not appeal to us in a flood when the land it traversed was a vast swampy lake.

In our restless sleep that night we tried to cross time after time the rough water and contrary current which lay ahead of us. Early in the morning—without breakfast, so anxious were we to get it over with—we made ready for the real attempt. It was dark and still. A sudden rain delayed us while we donned rain clothes. Then, pulling hard with the backlash in order to hit the main current with as much weight as possible, we crashed into the whirls at the edge. The fast water threw the johnboat out of position, but the momentum of the heavier shanty-boat carried it through into the current. By the time we got lined up again the boats had nearly reached the triangle of still water. Sighting on a point of land above, we saw ourselves being carried away from the main river into the Ditch. We were able, however, to pull the boat out of the current before it carried us too far. The boat glided into the farthest corner of the dead water. Here we tied up to a tree, for a breathing spell and congratulations.

It was not long before we were drifting free on the Mississippi, past new shores. On the bulletin board at Red River Landing a stage of 36½ R was posted. The gauge read thirty-seven feet and a man in oilskins was approaching along the shore at that very moment, probably to correct the figure. We called to him, asking how much more water was expected. He said, "Eight feet," adding, "unless there is more coming after this."

Farther on was the landing of the Angola ferry. The ferry consisted of a steel flat towed by a stout launch whose hull was built for rough water. The town of Angola on the east bank is the first one on that side which is in Louisiana. That state would be on both shores for the rest of the way. Thus, only at the end of the Mississippi and at the beginning of the Ohio in Pennsylvania is the river within the borders of a state.

The current swung us to mid-river, and at last it was possible to relax and have breakfast. A fisherman's boat pulled alongside. By way of explanation, he said he thought I was Luther Gillison. I wasn't much complimented, but could give him the latest news of Lute, whom we had met at Natchez. The man invited us to lay over near his boat, which we soon passed, a deep-hulled craft beached out in some trees. There was washing out on the line, and the womenfolk waved from the porch.

Across the end of this reach lay another ridge, called Tunica Bluff. By the time we came up to it, our boat was drifting close to the steep shore. It looked much like the Fort Adams bluff—open, pastured woods, deep ravines, and steep clay banks. Though it was still morning, and we had no idea of stopping here, the place was so attractive that we suddenly decided to make a landing. Reaching shore just at the point where the bluff bears away from the river, we hauled the boat into a deep, narrow inlet. It was an idyllic place. The grassy banks, about as high as our roof, were shorn by grazing cattle. A stump was in such a handy spot for tying lines to that it might have been placed there for that purpose. On a narrow shelf of land above was the site of an old house, marked by scattered bricks under a chinaberry tree. Two or three gray fig trees were protected from the cattle by a paling fence. Behind rose the steep slope, tree-covered, yet open, like pictures of the classic groves and vales.

This cheerful, snug harbor brought out by its contrast the strain we had been under at the Mud Ditch. That was like a dream now— the fog and rain, the roar of water, and the bleak shores. Here we rambled about through the high woods to the abandoned railroad whose caving trestle we had seen at the upper end of the bluff. Downstream from us a low field of increasing width lay along the river, bordered with the never-failing hedge of willow. Back toward the bluff were some cabins, and walking down that way we came to a small village inhabited entirely by Negroes. As we passed by on this fine Saturday afternoon, they smiled and greeted us from the yards

and doorways, the children staring open-mouthed. In their gardens we saw peas already climbing the sticks, and small ventilated mounds of earth where sweet potatoes were stored. Tom had called these mounds, as near as we could make out, "pomps." At one end of the town stood an old plantation house, just the kind we were hoping, thus far in vain, to see along the river. In the yard were the first palmettos. The Deep South had been reached.

When we drifted away from this place, the gables and tops of the tall columns of the plantation house could be seen against the bluff. Farther downstream, near the old settlement of Pointe Coupée the tops of similar old buildings rose above the levee. On that day, after the usual joys and vicissitudes of drifting, Bayou Sara was reached. It was growing dark, and we were glad to have the opening marked for us by the entrance of a ferryboat into what looked like an unbroken willow shore. We tied up there and were preparing to cordelle in, for the outer shore was under water, when the ferry launch returned. It was operated by two boys. They looked after a lighted lantern hanging in a tree to mark the bayou entrance, but I think they came out to see if we wanted to go up the stream. We were thankful for their tow, it being a quarter of a mile to a dry shore. We tied up under two live oak trees.

The shores of Bayou Sara were almost a wilderness. Yet it was the site of a thriving city in the days of the flatboat and steamboat. One of the earliest railroads in the south had been built to haul cotton to the steamboats at Bayou Sara. When the old packets disappeared from the river the town declined. Being on low ground it was constantly ravished by the increasing floods of later years, and at last abandoned. We found there only a few cottages of fishermen, placed on logs so that they would float in high water.

St. Francisville, on the bluffs a mile back from the river, has had a different history. It was founded by the Franciscans who crossed the river from Pointe Coupée to bury their dead in high ground. Nowadays it is a prospering town on a main highway in the rolling Feliciana country where sweet potatoes are raised. St. Francisville is another river town which has a claim on Audubon, who lived on a plantation several miles back from the river for a considerable time.

We lay in Bayou Sara for a week to allow mail to catch up with us. Our trips to the post office did not take us as far as the highway; so to us St. Francisville is a town of old houses on side streets, with green lawns, flowers, and flowering trees. All were in their spring growth, the season being much advanced this mild winter. There is an old brick church with a graveyard before it in which are rows of immense live oaks. It was like part of the nether world, on a dark misty day, with a ghostly light filtering through the gray moss overhead.

Day after day was foggy. Sometimes it was only a dull half-light from daybreak to the early nightfall. The river was rising fast. To reach town we had to row down the flooded road to the railroad embankment. The fishermen's houses on their log foundations came afloat and looked like houseboats of a new design. Planks were laid on the ends of the supporting logs to make a platform on each side. Gear, plunder and firewood were piled there, and the dog ran back and forth. A bateau was tied to the front porch, and backdoor visiting was done by boat.

Our shore went under next. We moved to higher ground at the ferry landing. The ferry ceased to operate when the road was cut off, and went into the flooded Tunica Swamp to rescue marooned cattle. Later,

when the water should be deep enough to allow the boat to reach the railroad embankment it would resume its crossings.

Before the ferryboat returned, the rising water had forced us to move again. We were not ready to leave St. Francisville, having still to wait for mail. Instead of taking the shantyboat back toward the town we preferred to drop down the river a mile to a place where we had seen a high bank and a line of trees which would indicate a creek. The mouth of Bayou Sara had become choked with driftwood, but by crossing the backwater in a field, it looked like we might reach the road, also flooded, which led out to the low-water landing of the ferry, and follow that to the open river. It was hard going through the field where we got tangled up in grapevines and dewberry vines, ran aground, and had to weave among the small trees. By the time we reached the open roadway, a wind had risen, and we tied up there for the day.

Prodigious swarms of ants were everywhere. The flat land had been flooded all at once: the ants could only climb onto the trees and bushes, where they hung like swarms of bees. During the night they found their way across a vine bridge to the boat, and thousands must have come aboard what appeared to them an ark of salvation.

The following morning was another foggy one, but since the tree-tops showed above the fog, I thought we could make it down along the

333

shore to our new harbor. Once offshore, the tree line was lost sight of. After an anxious few minutes, we rowed in close enough to get our bearings. This put us in a long eddy which carried the boat back to the starting point. We lay there among the driftwood until the fog dispersed, and then drifted down to the shore we had seen from above.

After a close look at it, we began to wish we were back in Bayou Sara. The bank was only two or three feet above water. Away from the river, it sloped down to a broad lake of backwater which extended into a swamp. There was a small creek, but trees and drift blocked its entrance. We must be content with a shallow cove in which at times the driftwood spun about in a near maelstrom. Then for a short period it would be calm, but always, unceasingly, a few rods out from our boat the Mississippi rolled by at top speed.

The foggy weather continued. If it was only a morning fog, the rest of the day was windy. We lay there for six days, watching from our ringside seat the flooded Mississippi in action. One night a severe thunderstorm swept down the river, causing some rough water. We were often shaken up by boat waves, too, from the downbound boats. Those going upstream followed the mile-distant shore across the river. The tug *California* nosed in, the morning after the storm, asking if we had seen any runaway willow mats. As we had not, they must have passed at night. A floating willow mat, big as a log raft, could not have passed by unnoticed. They are used in revetment work.

These were not all days of stress, however. The boat was made secure by using a long, driftwood tree for a boom—one end tied to the bank, the other sparred off from the boat. This protected it from the driftwood in the eddy. We enjoyed many good hours within, when it was thick weather outside. On the fair, windy afternoons we looked about on the strip of shore. Not far off was a farm cabin, evidently occupied only during the summer; now it was cut off by miles of backwater. We got fresh clear water from its rain barrel. In the nearby garden were some mustard greens and turnips, most welcome to us now since our only green stuff was a box of fennel and collards on the roof. There were some rows of cabbages, too, winter cabbage, just in its prime. We helped ourselves to a head or two, and pondered much over the rest.

It was being covered by the rising water; if not soon harvested, it would be ruined.

Before it got too deep, I waded through the backwater to the long railroad fill, a section of the abandoned road, where ties and rails had been removed. Farther inland was another railroad, on which a short freight train passed now and then. There is much comfort from a train whistle in flooded country. It is a reassuring sound, reminding one amid the mud and briars that all is not formless and left to chance. On this walk the dogs started up an unfortunate rabbit who had no way to run except down the causeway. It was overtaken by Sambo when it tried to escape by swimming. Swamp rabbits are larger than cottontails, and very good to eat.

As the river rose, our deck became higher than the narrow strip of grassy shore. We could look across it to the backwater and watch a large flock of gulls which often settled there. On the river one day a line of pelicans sailed by, flapping and soaring in unison, nearly touching the water in their level flight.

The only human visitors we had there were three Negroes, in an outboard boat, with whom I had some talk when they stopped to service the navigation light.

We made the final trip to St. Francisville by rowing up through the backwater. At last came a morning when we could slip away between the fog and wind. Just before leaving, I harvested a bushel of cabbages, wading through the rows in hip boots, cutting the nearly drowned heads under water.

Down a long straight reach the wind was ahead, and it was easy going. Then we went through Fancy Point Chute, and were on a different course, with a cross wind. The waiting dinner was disregarded while we both rowed to stay in the channel, thrilled all the while by magnificent views of the river. Fancy Point Towhead, a dark mass of forest, stood offshore behind us. Ahead the river broke sharply to the right, around Point Menoir, in the face of a line of low bluff where trees, clay banks and grassy slopes made a rich pattern of color. On our left, to leeward, was Thompson Creek, an open aisle through the willows, its banks under water.

This bluff was different from those already passed. Here the river

335

seemed uncertain whether to turn left or right. It did turn to the right in a decided manner, but to the left was a wide bay of water into which part of the current flowed, swinging in a wide circle to come out into the main stream again just below the mouth of Thompson Creek. It was a good mile from this point across the eddy to the bluff, even farther from the depth of the bay to Point Menoir. The wide orbit of this reverse current was outlined by a stream of driftwood which made the long circuit under the bluff and along the close growth of willows where the low shore was under water. In the center was a dead sea of logs and mats of floating stuff.

We did our best to stay in the current and round the bend. A grove of pines on the bluff came down to the water at one point. If we could keep these dark pines on our left, we would make it. The break between the current and the still water in the center of the bay was not a straight or fixed line, but was as shifting as a thread of rising smoke. We thought we were still in the current, but the pines were on our right. Rowing was hampered by the thick drift. We knew it would be useless to try to pull back into the main current, or to go back up to the head of the backlash and try again, the wind being as it was. We let the boat sail across the bay to the willows where we crashed through into a small opening. There we tied up, and had dinner at last.

It was three-quarters of a mile to the bluff, which was the nearest land. That afternoon I went over there with the dogs. It was an easy trip in the johnboat—simply row out and drift with the current. The return along shore was easy, too, for I took advantage of the current of the eddy. If we could only handle the houseboat as easily as the johnboat! Yet that would take much of the sport out of drifting. At the bluff I landed at the grove of pines, a strange shore to find on the Lower Mississippi. The earth and air were suddenly not of the river, and the wind through the needles was a sound from far off. Over the vast flatness of the river, our little boat looked like a white bit of driftwood which had lodged in the willows. There was an old road on top of the bluff, a magnificent avenue whose tall arching trees were hung with moss and mistletoe. It led to a plantation house, Mount Pleasant, which, so the lady who lived there told me, had faced the river since

1790. She said that Civil War cannon had stood on the bluff, but were now fallen into the river.

The fog and wind kept us in our willow harbor for another day. Riding at anchor so far offshore made our craft seem less house and more boat, even though it was not really anchored but tied to trees. In the morning I rowed with the dogs up to Thompson Creek to investigate what had appeared to be a log raft when we passed the day before. It was not a log raft, but some willow mats, possibly the runaways for which the tug *California* had been searching. It could well be that they had been caught in the slackwater bay, just as we were. The mats were large enough to give the dogs and me a chance to stretch our legs. The construction was rough but very strong, the logs and poles held together with rope, wire cables, and spiked timbers. I picked up some loose ends of cordage out of which to make some new doormats.

That afternoon all of us made the circuit of the bay. Landing at the pine grove, we went north instead of to Mount Pleasant. Across the level fields, past some Negro cabins, was a road which led to a Civil War cemetery, a monument to Fort Hudson.

In the thick fog of the following morning we rowed our fleet around the trees into Thompson Creek, ready to make a break into the river when the fog thinned. This time, with no adverse wind, we kept out of the slack water, and rounded the point. It was with some regret that we looked back at the pine-topped bluff, for there remained but one more bit of high land along the river—at Baton Rouge. Near the city it could not be as fine as this in its natural setting.

It was good drifting that day. The wind was gentle and from a favorable quarter. We must row for only a few short spells at the peak of the bends and along Duvall's Eddy—just enough to make us feel that we were mastering the river and not being carried along as chance directed. We did not, however, go down the inside channel of Profit Island as we had figured. There seemed to be no current in that direction, and we knew better than to force our way into a place where there was not a good flow of water. Drifting was swift in the main channel; the six miles around the island were soon covered. At its lower end we could look back through the narrow, enticing chute. Suddenly in the other direction, across Devil's Swamp, loomed the

337

Baton Rouge bridge, and still farther off, a high tower in the city. These were soon lost sight of behind trees, but for the rest of the way down the winding river, the location of the city was marked by its smoky ceiling.

The final bend, a sharp one less than a right angle, around Free Nigger Point, was at the entrance to the city. We were hoping to land on the left bank where it was still country, but on that side the driftwood was collected into a motionless island, as if hung up on a sandbar in the river. We knew that this could not be, in high water; therefore the drift must lie in the dead center of an eddy. To clear it required a long swing out from shore, but we were able to make the land farther down, just short of the point where the current would have swept us around the bend. Later we talked with the local light tender who had seen our approach. He said, "I didn't think you would make it."

We worked the boat in among the trees. It was not a good harbor, because shallow water kept us away from the bank. I ferried the dogs in and, climbing the bank later, found them chasing around the well-kept campus of Southern University, a state college for Negroes.

The dogs make the most of whatever comes along. There is no doubt they greatly enjoy this drifting life. If the long days afloat hold some inconveniences and restrictions for them, there is the eager landing at the end, with ever new fields to explore. What tales they could tell!

I found a good place for the boat a quarter of a mile downstream at the river landing of a box factory which, these days, stood in rusty idleness. This short move was a tricky one in the sharp, treacherous current along the bend and required as much care and skill as a day's drifting in the open river. The bridge was in full view from this station, and farther down the river were the docks and buildings of Baton Rouge. The shore was almost open country. This was the last high ground we could find along the river; yet it was not high enough to be called a bluff, compared with those we had passed.

This place suited us very well—not quite in the city, not too far out. There was one house above the landing, where Mr. Ricks dwelt, a retired refinery worker. He was very obliging, supplied us with drinking water, and took quite an interest in us. Our only other acquaintance

338

was the light tender. He used a rowboat to reach his lights which were but a few on the bend. By planning a circuit up through the eddy and down in the current, he had little hard rowing to do.

It was exciting to be near a city again, to hear its strange low voice, varied and unceasing, to see its lights in the sky, to watch traffic on the nearby bridge, the long trains crossing, the hurrying cars and trucks.

Most of all, our interest lay in the river. Though two hundred and thirty miles from the Gulf, ocean ships ascend the Mississippi River to Baton Rouge. We were anxious to see what kind, and how many. Just below the bridge, perhaps a third of a mile away from us, was a huge dock, powdered with reddish-brown dust, where, Mr. Ricks told us, aluminum ore from South America was unloaded. One night soon after our arrival a great clanking of machinery began at the dock, and after the morning mist had cleared away, there was a large, deep-laden freighter being unloaded. It was a definite harbinger of ocean and salt water. Farther down the river were the docks of a great refinery, and tankers could be seen swinging in there. More freighters landed at the city wharves. What kind of waves would the ships make? we wondered.

We lay there the first half of February, waiting to learn what the river was going to do. It was still rising, and reports of floods came from the upper tributaries. During our stay several excursions were made to Baton Rouge. Here was a city at the height of its growth, not looking back on the past as a golden age. We went to the top of the skyscraper which someone was inspired to erect as a capitol building. Miles of flat country lay below us, the wide river, its yellow waters creeping back toward the city. Upriver we could make out the course

339

of our last day's run—the bends, Profit Island, the bluffs and pines of Mt. Pleasant. It was like a glimpse of the past.

We were at Baton Rouge long enough to make a transient's card at the public library worth while. Old books were put aside while we read the new ones. To our delight, *The Cruise of the Beagle* was available, and we finished reading Darwin's account of his voyage. A book read aloud lasts a long time. We had begun this one at Natchez.

By mid-February the river was apparently at the crest of its rise, about forty-one feet on the Baton Rouge gauge, which was ten feet above bankfull, eight feet below the highest reading. We made ready to leave.

The Mississippi from Baton Rouge to New Orleans, about a hundred and thirty-five miles, had been described to us as uninteresting and monotonous, running between levees built close to the river, having no islands or bluffs, no tributary streams. We did not allow such reports to make us prejudiced, however, certain that every section of the river would have its peculiar charm and interest. Its character would change, no doubt. In Audubon's account, their flatboat ran all night below Baton Rouge, testifying to the river's depth, even course, and freedom from obstructions.

Before we started, indeed ever since we had arrived at the box factory landing, we had speculated on our chances of passing the ore dock safely. It extended well out from shore, and the current would soon have us down there. It looked like we could make it if not handicapped by wind.

We cast off in the sunrise quiet. Rowing hard, we cleared the dock, though with little to spare. It would have been another story if we had attempted it when a ship was there. Three tankers were at the refinery dock—one leaving, another loading, a third just landing. They loomed up hugely in the smoky air. We rowed for the right bank, and were helped across by a set in the current. The steam ferry *Louisiana* slacked its speed to let us pass. Two ferryboats were running in the morning rush, a long line of cars waiting on the Port Allen landing. Farther along we had to row away from shore to clear a barge fleet, but soon we were drifting easily in midstream, the city fading out behind us.

Had this been a highway, a warning sign would have read "S curve ahead." In the next twenty miles, the river swings east, then west, then back east again. A light northerly wind carried us close to shore on the east-west reaches. We had something of a scare on the first one. This point was not protected by a levee, and the water had found a way across it. It was like what we imagined a crevasse would be, and to make it worse, for us, it was running through trees. We were carried close in, though rowing our hardest, and were thankful to leave the roaring water behind.

The outside of the first loop of the double bend is the location of Manchac Landing. Here was once another outlet of the Mississippi to the Gulf, southeastward through Manchac Bayou. We had read that the English made an early settlement at this point and planned to use Manchac Bayou as a route to the Gulf, thus by-passing the Spanish bottleneck at New Orleans. All we could see there was a high levee.

The next turn is Plaquemine Bend. Here a bayou called Plaquemine Bayou takes off to the west. Through it the early navigators reached Grand Lake and the Atchafalaya River. This route is still open, having been made into a barge canal, a short cut to the Intracoastal Waterway and points west. When Plaquemine had been mentioned to us by rivermen coming up from the south, it sounded as far off as the Rio Grande, but here we were, and still going.

Aided by the wind, we crowded the point on the inside of the hairpin bend. Across the river the town of Plaquemine seemed to float on the water. In its midst was the canal lock, almost level with the river. We had little time to look, however, for a tow was nosing around the bend. To keep out of its way, we got into slack water off the point. A shantyboat was moored there, and a flat with a tent on it. We wondered if this boat belonged to the friend of Henry and Lou Story. They had told us that he had moved to Plaquemine after leaving Memphis. The mere mention of Plaquemine had stirred up Lou's desire to go down the river. A motorboat crossing ahead of us asked if we needed help—he probably thought we did—and advised caution on the bend below.

At last we were out of all this, and drifting fast toward the east on the final segment of the S curve. The wind carried us in to the right

bank. Instead of calling all hands and clawing off, I caught onto a tree at the first opening and swung the boat in. That was enough drifting, enough river for one day. It was only midafternoon, but we had made thirty-two miles.

The boat lay that night in a quiet lagoon, the levee on one side, riverward a series of low, slim islands, the broken remains of an older levee. These were like a reef, protecting the lagoon within from current and waves. Our landing on shore was the grassy slope of the levee. It was a drifter's dream of a perfect harbor. We looked for similar places, and nearly always found them, on the rest of the way down the river.

This final section of our voyage was of a carefree, holiday nature all through, full of novelty and pleasant surprise. There was the animation of a flooded river flowing through a land bursting into spring. The river had lost some of its fierceness. Swift as ever, it was not so wide, its shores were more even, with few sandbars and eddies. The boat was allowed to drift close in. Sailing along near the levee top, we watched with much enjoyment the upper stratum of the landscape—a fairer view than one has at ground level where much is distracting and inharmonious. There passed by us steeples and roofs, the occasional upper stories of buildings, bare pecan trees against the sky, the rounded masses of live oaks, usually the indication of an old plantation house whose roof and columns might be seen through the trees. The tall stacks of factories at frequent intervals puzzled us. Later we learned that these were sugar houses, where raw sugar is made during the cane harvest. In spring and summer they are idle. At one point on the river is a great sugar refinery to which raw sugar is brought from many sugar houses.

Sugar cane is the crop of the lower river. Little rice is grown nowadays, but we did see a few siphons of large iron pipe which carried water over the levee to rice fields.

When we landed and climbed the levee it was strange to look down on a land lower than the river. The fields sloped inland toward the swamp which paralleled the river. Thus the river flows along a ridge. Since this is the only high ground, the roads, towns, and houses are all strung along close to the levee. This makes the country seem thickly settled in contrast to the wilderness shores upstream, where swamps and forests border the river, and the levee is far back.

The country seems older, too, which it is, the settlements having worked upriver from New Orleans. There are many French people, also German, though the few German settlers in the midst of many French gradually became French themselves, even their names. One name we noticed in many variations of spelling, Schexnayder, or Schexnuidre was a Frenchman's attempt to pronounce and spell Jack Schneider.

This fascinating, untroubled journey toward or through the river's delta—we do not know where the delta begins—was at variance with the reports of others. Perhaps they found this section of the river of little interest because they did not make their voyages on high water when you can see over the levees, and when there are no muddy banks; nor did they go down in the spring; nor did they drift.

Drifting down the Mississippi, however, could never be without some hazard and excitement. On the second day out of Baton Rouge, just after we had remarked about the easy time we were having, and that the next bend, around Philadelphia Point, should not give any trouble, I heard rough water ahead and began rowing off shore. Then all hands were called, but we went into it after all. Though not large, it was a bad place, with fast, deep whirls. The boat drifted up through the reverse current, close to a levee where a thrifty beachcomber had piled up some good wreckage to dry. He was looking at us all the while, like a spider near its web, with an idea, perhaps, that we might be his next prey. He was to be disappointed this time, for we broke out into the main stream and succeeded in clearing the eddy.

Close ahead was the bend at Eighty-one Mile Point, eighty-one miles from New Orleans, probably a steamboat landmark. As it was a sharp one, we approached with caution, holding close to the point. The head of a long tow appeared, and then the towboat, the *Kokoda,* which whistled twice when she saw us. We hugged the shore, or rather, the trees standing in water. When the boat passed, close by, a young fellow on the bridge shouted that another tow was following them. So we ran some lines out to a sycamore, swinging back and forth in the swift water to wait for the second boat. It was the *Harry Truman* with its curious tow of boxlike cargo barges. Meanwhile Anna had gotten dinner ready, so we ate it while tied up there. A small boat passed down, and just when we were ready to cast off, a loaded tanker appeared around the upstream bend. This was the first ship to pass us in the river, though we had seen one go by our harbor the night before, when its unusual sound woke us. This one made a few big swells, but they were not at all bad. The passage of ships, upstream loaded, down empty, as a rule, became a familiar sight, though always thrilling. Their waves caused no trouble when drifting, but it would be impossible to hold a boat in position against the bank with those heavy swells rolling in.

At last we got away from the point, crossed to the other shore for a landing at Donaldsonville. Another tanker appeared, coming upstream along that shore. We ducked into the first opening, found ourselves again in the slack water behind an old levee, and landed the boat at one of the scattered islands. Here the reef was so long that the inner water along the levee was like a canal.

The new levee, perhaps a hundred yards distant from our boat, was a gay sight, the grass so green, people promenading, looking at the river, dipping for shad with long-handled nets, children playing, cows grazing. Only the treetops beyond the levee could be seen, it being the edge of town where no tall buildings stood. It was a surprise to look over the levee and see so many small houses grouped there, as if they had not enough interest in the river to take a peek over the levee at it. This was the attitude of the inhabitants, too. We asked one old man how it felt to live behind a levee in high water. He answered, "We never pay no mind to it."

Donaldsonville should have been called Lafourche, standing, as it

344

does, at the fork where Bayou Lafourche begins. The bayou there is closed off from the Mississippi River by a fill and levee. Farther down, however, and on to the Gulf, which it enters near Grand Isle, it is an important waterway, busy with tugs, fishing boats, and shipyards.

We walked a little way along its course, but found only a dry ditch. Of more interest was the countryside, the yards and gardens. There were trees, bushes, and flowers new to us, some palm and orange trees. The people were gardeners, planting even the old levee. Peas were in bloom, early potatoes up, and even beans—in February.

The town was an off-to-the-side place, neat and homelike. It had a quaint, almost foreign air. Along the streets were galleries over the sidewalks, lacy ironwork, some beautiful old buildings, some bizarre ones, and many French names. We were so pleased with it all that we wished this could be the final port of our voyage. It was all we expected to find in a town near the river's end. New Orleans, but two drifting days away, filled us with apprehension.

For good or bad, however, we must go on to New Orleans, port of all drifting flatboats from the upper rivers. After four sunny days at Donaldsonville we shoved out into the river again, drifted past the town and the busy ferry, *George Prince*. We wondered if this was the former Natchez ferry which had been operated by Captain George Prince. After a few miles, a wind rose and gave us trouble. While rowing off a lee shore below Point Houmas, we noticed a large craft coming upstream. We wished she would not crowd over so close to us, but her course was unaltered. It was the large Coast Guard Cutter, *Salvia*. When abreast, she stopped her engines, and while the officers watched us with binoculars, as we bobbed about on the choppy water, a voice boomed over their loudspeaker, "Ahoy, houseboat! Are you all right?" I piped an affirmative in return, and the *Salvia* proceeded on her way, neither party quite sure I meant what I had said.

We were driven to the bank a little farther down, against the open levee. No protection here from the reef of an old levee, but the current was easy, and there were submerged trees to tie the boat to. The point below was called College Point on our map, but a boy who paddled out to our boat in his little bateau said the town of Convent was across the levee. We had seen its tall steeple. The boy was Donald Saunier, of high school age. He was so taken with our shantyboat that he was on board most of the time we lay there.

This day was Mardi Gras. It is observed all through the country. Stores are closed, workers and school children are given a holiday. This is the reason Donald Saunier had so much time to spend with us. We all took a walk in the afternoon to the seminary on College Point. It is marked Jefferson College on our map. Two or three of its old buildings have stood by the river for many years.

Later in the afternoon Donald Saunier returned with two of his pals, whose French names interested us—Noël Plaisance and Anicet Melançon. They persuaded Donald's sister and her friend, Adrienne, to come aboard; it was a lively party. Donald came to say goodbye to us next morning at breakfast, and the others watched us from the levee as they waited for the school bus.

It was showery in the morning, and we did not get away until early afternoon. Just before our casting off, the freighter *Pioneer Reef* passed down, and in the other direction, the *Tenaru River,* the towboat seen on the Ohio at Smithland. The passage around College Point was easy, though we had expected trouble. The trouble came later, as the river gave us the final drubbing of this voyage. It became windy again. We struggled to keep out of the trees which for a long way stood thickly in an unbroken line. Behind them was quiet water along the levee, but no opening to it appeared. We had to give it up. Mooring to the trees in a small dip in the shoreline, to be out of the way of upbound boats which were passing close in, we went into the cabin and began to read. If the wind should lay before dark, we would go on; if not, we would spend the night there, and two or three days besides, it might be, tossing about against the willows. It was cozy inside with a blaze in the fireplace, the shutters on both sides having been closed to protect the glass from branches. Because of our reading, and the noise of river and wind, we did not hear the approach of an outboard engine, but were roused by footsteps and voices on our deck. A man and a boy in oilskins, Shorty Deslattes, he introduced himself, and his son. They sat with us by the fire for a while, wondering, no doubt, how we happened to be there. Perhaps they had thought our boat was another drifter's prize.

The wind did lessen before evening, and we were able to make it down along the trees which still blocked the shore. It was a cheerless prospect on a rough evening. The river curved into Grandview Reach, and the set of the current was toward the other side. It looked promising over there, but by the time we could reach it, against the wind, we would be carried far downstream, where the open levee showed like a low dike along a sea. Suddenly an opening appeared on the near shore. We began rowing for it, and would have gained it, had not the wind suddenly shifted so that it blew straight from the direction we were trying to go. We could understand how the ancients personified the winds, considering them willful and god-directed.

We now turned about and rowed as hard for the other shore, far across. With the wind behind us, it was a quick crossing. We landed on the open revetment. A short distance upstream was an offset in the levee. We cordelled the boat up around the angle, and found a sheltered harbor. Daylight faded as we tied up the boat between trees. Nearby were some captive logs belonging to a soft-voiced Negro who spoke to us through the darkness from shore.

This place was Vacherie. Just where Vacherie began and ended and had its center, we could not determine. There was front Vacherie along the river, back Vacherie on the railroad, and houses strung along the levee road for miles. We saw much of it as we lay there two windy days. It was fine to walk along the levee and look over the sunny fields and the unpainted houses of weatherbeaten gray, so artless, so perfectly designed.

On the next day's run, the Bonnet Carré Spillway was passed. This had been on our minds from the time we had heard, at Baton Rouge, that its gates were being opened. The purpose of the spillway is to

divert the floodwaters of the Mississippi into Lake Pontchartrain, which at this point is close to the river, and thus lower the crest of the flood at New Orleans. We had visions of a tremendous suction into the open spillway, and for a long distance above kept close to the right bank, with a line ready to run out to a tree.

The situation was not bad, however. From the far side of the river, we felt no draw in the current. A small government boat was stationed off the upper end of the spillway. Seeing us drifting down, this boat crossed over to our side of the river to make sure we would stay close to the bank. The upper end of the spillway was screened from the river by trees, through which we could not have drifted if we had tried. The lower end was open, and the water pouring in between the open gates made a great noise.

By then our attention was on an empty tanker coming up. Another was loading at a refinery dock on the bend. We rounded a second bend, and made a landing on the right bank, below the town of Luling.

Another day's run would have taken us to New Orleans. Why not, we said, drift clear to the city and tie up at the foot of Canal Street? The shantyboater has an instinctive feeling for keeping out of the way, however. We decided to find a good harbor still in the country, but as close to the city as possible, and make a sneak entrance on a bus. Not many miles of country river remained. I unlimbered the bicycle one day and rode from Luling down along the levee to see what I could find. I rode all the way to the Mississippi River bridge, then decided to cross the bridge, ride up on the other side, and recross to Luling on the ferry.

From the high bridge, high enough to let the ships pass under at flood, I saw far off to the south, across woods and river bends, the city of New Orleans.

When I reached the ferry landing across from our boat, I was dismayed to find that the ferryboat had broken down in the afternoon and would run no more that day. The prospect of a thirty-mile bicycle ride back to the boat via the bridge was not attractive. Fortunately a Luling truck was in the same fix. It was a small dump truck. I loaded the bicycle into the body, climbed in with it, and had a quick but not easy ride back to the boat.

As a result of this exploration we dropped down the river a few miles, still on the right bank, to a good harbor behind an old levee off the little village of Ama. We were still ten miles above the bridge, twenty from downtown New Orleans, but it was the last country harbor. Downstream the shores belonged to the city.

We lay here all through March and into April. The warm southwind weather brought gardening to mind, but this spring we must be content with wild poke, and a few carrots, spinach, and cabbages from the truck farms about. Dewberries ripened before we left. An occasional 'possum caught by the dogs, and good fishing gave us plenty of food.

One day a voice called from the levee, "Got any fish?" The Negroes gladly took all our surplus, and took advantage of this unexpected windfall by organizing an American Legion fish fry. The only other contact on shore was at the combined store, post office, and bus station. The nearness of the City was felt; these were not country folk.

The river was unchanged, however. We did not like to think of leaving it. One day a familiar-looking motorboat passed upriver, towing a new ferry flat. Looking closely we saw it was the *Red Cross,* the ferryboat at St. Francisville. The boys recognized us, came out on deck and waved. We almost wished we were going back up the river with them. This idea, in fact, had been considered, but the cost and trouble of having the boat towed upstream were too much.

It was most pleasant, though, on our long island where the mockingbirds and thrashers sang together. The disturbing factor was the steady fall of the river. Where would we go when the water drained off the batture?

349

We made several bus trips to New Orleans, found the city as interesting as it was expected to be. Sight-seers in our own fashion, we saw the usual attractions, and others, along the waterfront in particular, which are not listed in the guide books—Noah's Ark Baptist Church, for instance, outside the levee and surrounded by the flood.

On each trip to the city we roamed through the Vieux Carré. Once we found a prize in a courtyard bookshop. It was a large, ornate book, illustrated with excellent wood engravings, Volume II of *Les Voyageuses du xix Siècle*. Anna read with particular delight about these other ladies who had made unusual voyages into remote regions of the world.

Learning of an exhibition of paintings to be held at the Delgado Museum, we entered two or three pictures, hastily framed with a sawed-up cedar fence post from some forgotten driftpile. A painting of Henrico Bar and an Ohio River woodblock were in the show, and these represented the cargo we brought to New Orleans from the upper rivers.

Yet we were unwilling to consider New Orleans as the final destination of our voyage; nor were we ready to give up our shantyboat life. We could drift on past New Orleans—ninety-odd miles of river remained. Yet we figured it was no place for a drifting shantyboat—no land, no harbors in low water, and many ships passing. We gave up the idea of going to the river's end with some reluctance, for we would like to see its entrance into the ocean.

There was another out—westward into the bayou country of Louisiana, by way of the Intracoastal Waterway. I made a bicycle trip to the Harvey Lock across from New Orleans, where the Waterway begins, and another long excursion to Bayou Barataria, which is part of the Intracoastal. My enthusiasm was fired by this strange new region where the land is almost water, and water is everywhere. We determined to leave the river and follow a new adventure in the land of the Cajun, where the towns face the waterways, and every house has a slip for boats.

Reluctant to leave our last river harbor, we moved the boat into a narrow ditch which separated two islands of the old levee, the deepest water to be found. The steadily falling water routed us out even from

this, and on April seventh, 1950, we put forth into the open river. After a long layover in a sheltered port we always feel somewhat edgy about setting ourselves adrift again. To this feeling was now added an uneasiness about our passage through the New Orleans harbor, where there would be many ships, tugs, and towboats to meet, ferries to avoid, and a shore lined with docks and barges. Once in mid-river, our confidence returned. The high bridge was easy, though we had looked down from the bus on the water swirling past the piers with misgiving. Farther down, the current off Nine Mile Point threw us over to the left bank along the crowded docks of the U.S. Engineers. The only mishap of the day occurred when the tug *Independent*, crossing in front of a tow of barges, ran past us at full speed and sent a wave or two over our deck and into the cabin through the open door.

We rowed close to the right bank looking for the Harvey Lock. I knew it was just below a ferry; so at the first ferry landing we pulled in under the stern of a tanker, and working fast in the swift current, made a neat check on the ferry dock. I looked about. "Where is the canal?" I asked a Negro fishing from the pier. "What canal?" he said. It was the wrong ferry.

At the next one we repeated the performance. When the boat swung in behind the pier, there was the lock. A tug went into it with two oil barges. The lockman signaled us in, and held the gates open while we rowed slowly through.

Then the gates were closed on the river. As we were being lowered to sea level, and the gates behind us loomed higher, we regretted for a moment our abrupt and unceremonious departure from the river. How much more fitting to be carried out into salt water like the river's driftwood! Yet the driftwood left the river never to return. It would at last sink into the sea or be stranded on some far beach. Like the driftwood our boat would leave its bones in that marshy land. We ourselves would be more like the river's water, which though it leave the river and mingles with the ocean, is at last by a devious course brought back again to its starting place.

CPSIA information can be obtained at www.ICGtesting.com
Printed in the USA
BVOW08s2124180614

356689BV00004B/6/P